Evangelical from the Beginning

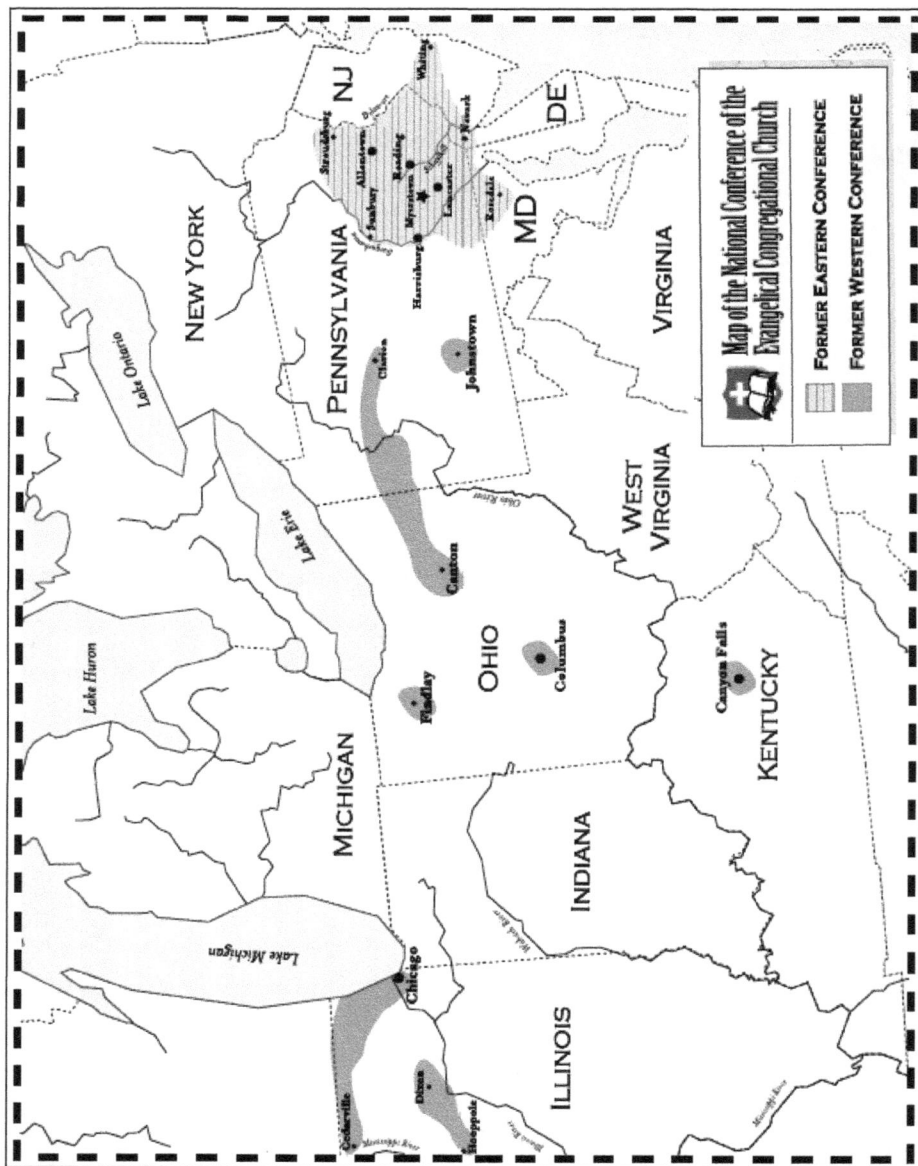

Map of the National Conference of the Evangelical Congregational Church

FORMER EASTERN CONFERENCE
FORMER WESTERN CONFERENCE

Evangelical From the Beginning

A History of the Evangelical Congregational Church and its Predecessors— The Evangelical Association And the United Evangelical Church

By a Committee of the Historical Society of the Evangelical Congregational Church—Terry M. Heisey, Robert G. Hower, Leon O. Hynson, John E. Moyer

Terry M. Heisey, Editor

Foreword by Charles Yrigoyen

Afterword by Bishop Michael W. Sigman

EMETH PRESS
www.emethpress.com

Library of Congress Cataloging-in-Publication

Heisey, Terry M., 1951-Evangelical Congregational Church. Historical Society
    Evangelical from the beginning : a history of the Evangelical Congregational
Church and its predecessors--the Evangelical Association and the United
Evangelical Church / by a committee of the Historical Society of the Evangelical
Congregational Church--Terry M. Heisey ... [et al.] ; Terry M. Heisey, editor ;
foreword by Charles Yrigoyen ; afterword by Michael W. Sigman.
    p.   cm.
Includes bibliographical references and index.
ISBN: 978-0-9776555-4-0 (alk. paper)
1. Evangelical Congregational Church--History
    BX7545.E8 E93 2006   2006931915

For further information, contact:
        Historical Society of the Evangelical Congregational Church
        100 W. Park Ave.
        Myerstown, PA 17067

Contents

Endnote Abbreviations

AdCoun	Minutes of the Administrative Council of the Evangelical Congregational Church
Albright	Raymond W. Albright, *A History of the Evangelical Church* (Harrisburg, PA: Evangelical Press, 1942)
EADisc	*The Creed, Ritual and Discipline of the Evangelical Association*
EAEPAConfJ	East Pennsylvania Conference Journal of the Evangelical Association
EAGenConfJ	General Conference Journal of the Evangelical Association
ECDisc	*The Creed, Ritual and Discipline of the Evangelical Congregational Church*
ECEConfJ	Eastern Conference Journal of the Evangelical Congregational Church
ECEPAConfJ	East Pennsylvania Conference Journal of the Evangelical Congregational Church
ECGenConfJ	General Conference Journal of the Evangelical Congregational Church
ECNConfJ	National Conference Journal of the Evangelical Congregational Church
ECWConfJ	Western Conference Journal of the Evangelical Congregational Church
EM	*Evangelical Messenger* (periodical of the Evangelical Association)
EV	*The Evangelical* (periodical of the United Evangelical Church)
UE	*The United Evangelical* (periodical of the Evangelical Congregational Church)
UEDisc	*The Creed, Ritual and Discipline of the United Evangelical Church*
UEEPAConfJ	East Pennsylvania Conference Journal of the United Evangelical Church
UEGenConfJ	General Conference Journal of the United Evangelical Church

Foreword

Someone has said that people with amnesia don't know who they are because they can't remember the past. Unfortunately, individuals are not alone in suffering from amnesia. Churches also face an identity crisis because they have forgotten their history.

What is the Evangelical Congregational Church? Where did it begin and how has it developed? What challenges has it faced and what has it accomplished? What is its mission and what are its ministries? What clues can its history contribute to understanding its identity and work in the 21st century? These are questions with which we grapple as we help the church remember who it is.

This book provides the most complete and comprehensive history of the Evangelical Congregational Church ever published. It supersedes Robert S. Wilson's 1963 volume (revised in 1976) and is the superb work of a corps of historians and church leaders who know, understand, and love the Evangelical Congregational heritage. They are aware of the importance of the church's history to inform, inspire, nurture, and equip it to fulfill God's calling in this generation and those that follow.

Effectively employing primary and secondary sources, the authors begin their narration of EC history by describing its Wesleyan roots and its predecessor denominations – the Evangelical Association and the United Evangelical Church. Each of the chapters that follow discusses how the church organized for evangelism, worship, education, missions (home and overseas), itinerant ministry, benevolent work, and much more. While appropriate attention is paid to the denomination's gifted leadership in its bishops and denominational executives, the central and essential roles of pastors and laypeople are emphasized.

This volume offers the Evangelical Congregational Church a magnificent view of its history at a critical time in its life when its evangelistic and servant ministry is as much needed as ever. Others who share the

Wesleyan tradition and who are interested in the ministry of the Christian church will also gratefully find this an illuminating and fascinating story.

Charles Yrigoyen, Jr.,
General Secretary, Emeritus
General Commission on Archives and History
The United Methodist Church

Preface

The responsibility of the Church historian is...very great; he must portray the progress of...conflict [between good and evil] and the developments involved in the course of the militant Church life correctly, impartially and as completely as possible, for the history of an ecclesiastical communion is to her a great and sacred treasure. By it she may learn to understand her calling from the historical standpoint, she may also discover her faults in the past and amend them in the future, and thus her history will have a molding and determining influence upon her denominational character in the future. Hence, the worst and most harmful of falsifiers would be those, who falsify a Church history.

But who comprehends and appreciates the labor and patience required to discover all the sources and scattered fragments of such a history and arrange them, both logically and chronologically, in such a manner that the whole shall constitute an appreciable and comprehensible presentation which will enable the reader to enter into it, and view it not only in its outward but also its inward course?[1]

Thus wrote Bishop Reuben Yeakel in the Preface to his *History of the Evangelical Association* in 1894, and thus could the present authors write with equal conviction in 2006. We share both Yeakel's belief in the importance of our efforts and his lament at the difficulty of trying to fulfill our mission. The present work was first proposed at the October 27, 1986, meeting of the Board of Trustees of the Historical Society of the Evangelical Congregational Church, and the Board first appointed Robert Hower, Terry Heisey, and Michael Sigman as an editorial committee on April 6, 1987, to complete a new history of the E. C. Church by 1992!

The writing has taken a bit longer than we originally thought, but this is not unusual for Evangelical histories, the line of which goes back to the very beginning of the denomination. Early Evangelicals placed great importance on history; every member was expected to give a testimony, to tell and re-tell his or her own salvation history. Already in 1810, before the Evangelical Association was fully formed, the third regular conference of the followers of Jacob Albright instructed George Miller, one of Albright's associates, to write a biography of their fallen founder, and the first Evangelical historical book, *Kurze Beschreibung der würkenden Gnade Gottes bey dem Jakob Albrecht* (26 pp.), was published in 1811. The 1843 General Conference commissioned the first history of the Evangelical Association from Rev. John Dreisbach, another associate of Albright, but four years later he had only finished fifteen pages and asked to be relieved of the task. The 1847 General Conference assigned the book to Rev. Adam Ettinger, but he left the church. The group designated by the 1851 General Conference was decimated by sickness and death. Finally, W. W. Orwig (later Bishop) succeeded in completing his *Geschichte der Evangelischen Gemeinschaft* (456 pp.) in 1856.[2] The quest for a revision and updating of Orwig's book started when the 1875 General Conference appointed Bishop Dubs to the task, but twelve years later he had not been able to get to it, so the Board of Publication appointed Yeakel to write his *Geschichte*, which appeared in two volumes in 1890 and 1895. Of help to Yeakel was *Landmarks of the Evangelical Association*, a compilation of conference records by S. C. Breyfogel (later Bishop) published in 1888. Both Orwig's and Yeakel's histories were translated into English.

The "Minority" party of the Evangelical Association was expelled from the church in 1895 and forced to take a new name, but it claimed a history going back to Albright. In fact, the new United Evangelical Church claimed to be the true spiritual, if not legal, descendant of Jacob Albright. Ammon Stapleton provided this church with its history in *Annals of the Evangelical Association of North America and History of the United Evangelical Church* (1898), *Flashlights of Evangelical History* (1908), and *A Wonderful Story of Old Time Evangelical Evangelism* (1917).

The Evangelical Church, formed by the re-merger of the Evangelical Association and most of the United Evangelical Church in 1922, commissioned Raymond W. Albright to write a history of this denomination in 1934; *A History of the Evangelical Church* (501 pp.) was published eight years later. Four years after that, the Evangelical Church merged with the Church of the United Brethren in Christ (New Constitution), and Evangelical history merged into the history of the Evangelical United Brethren Church (1946) and later the United Methodist Church (1968). *The History of the Evangelical United Brethren Church* by J. Bruce Behney and Paul H. Eller (1979) provides an updated picture of the EUB Church and its predecessor denominations.

Meanwhile, another ecclesiastical descendant of Jacob Albright was born in 1928, when the segment of the United Evangelical Church that did not merge into the Evangelical Church in 1922 took the name Evangelical Congregational Church. The story of this church was told by Robert S. Wilson in his *Brief History of the Evangelical Congregational Church* (1963; 59 pp.) and the revised *History of the Evangelical Congregational Church* (1976; 77 pp.).

The current work expands Wilson's works to include the Wesleyan/Methodist background of the Evangelical Association and later developments in the Evangelical Congregational Church up to the reorganization of the church under the "Basis of Union" in 2002. All of the books noted above have been consulted in the writing of the present volume; all contain valuable additional information that could not be included here. The authors based most of their work on primary sources, however, to give a better flavor of how it felt to be an Evangelical over the two hundred years since Jacob Albright first gathered his little bands of converts. We have tried to give views from the pews as well as the facts of denominational events and leaders.

The book is designed to be read "vertically" as well as "horizontally." That is, each chapter presents a many-faceted view of an historical period but is divided into sections that can stand on their own so that one could read a history of Evangelical preaching, for example, from 1816-2002 by reading the "Preaching" sections of each chapter in succession.

Responsibility for the content of this may be divided as follows: Chapter 1 (beginnings through 1816)—Robert Hower and Terry Heisey; Chapter 2 (1816-1894)—Terry Heisey; Chapter 3 (1894-1922)—Terry Heisey; Chapter 4 (1922-1950)—Robert Hower, Leon Hynson, Terry Heisey; Chapter 5 (1950-1973)—John Moyer; Chapter 6 (1973-2002)—Robert Hower, John Moyer, and Terry Heisey. Other contributors included James Schwenk, Robert Schaeffer, and Timothy Christman. In combining and revising each submission by the authors the editor endeavored to preserve as much of the author's style as possible while attempting to blend the segments into a seamless whole.

Robert Hower chaired the book committee throughout its long history. Harold P. Scanlin also served on the committee and did much to bring the book to publication. The authors gratefully acknowledge the support of the Board of Trustees of the Historical Society of the Evangelical Congregational Church and contributions from the estate of

Rev. Foster Cardwell toward the financial underwriting of the project. Ralph Owens and Maureen Logan provided valuable assistance with illustrations. The Committee also wishes to acknowledge the assistance of Dorothy Heisey, Julie Miller, and Norma Aston in research and writing and several papers written by students in EC history classes at Evangelical School of Theology.

Notes

1. Reuben Yeakel, *History of the Evangelical Association*, Vol. I (Cleveland, OH: Thomas & Mattill, 1894), [1].

2. W. W. Orwig, *History of the Evangelical Association* (Cleveland, OH: Charles Hammer, 1858), 6-7.

Acknowledgements

Front cover photo, courtesy of Albright College, Reading PA. Used by permission.

Illustrations on pages 45, 79, 84, 87, 99 [Hartzler], copyright © General Commission on Archives and History, United Methodist Church, Madison NJ. Used by permission.

Illustrations on pages 115 and 230, Evangelical School of Theology Archives, Myerstown PA. Used by permission.

All other illustrations are the property of the Historical Society of the Evangelical Congregational Church.

For further information, contact:
    Historical Society of the Evangelical Congregational Church
    100 W. Park Ave.
    Myerstown, PA   17067

1

Evangelical Foundations—To 1816

The story of the Evangelical Congregational Church begins in the pages of the New Testament. Its message of redemption through the death and resurrection of Jesus Christ—the *Evangel*—remains our message today. Our founder, Jacob Albright, proclaiming this *Evangel* as he rode through the forests and farms of Pennsylvania two centuries ago, was following in the footsteps of a long line of evangelicals. Faithful saints of God gave their lives to spread the *Evangel* through the Roman Empire and then throughout Europe, keep it alive through the Dark Ages, and bring it to America. Again and again God raised up reformers and revival, and each new reform left its mark on the faith.

Pietism

Martin Luther hoped to reform the Roman Catholic Church of his day, but when he died in 1546 he had succeeded in reforming only a part of the church in northern and central Europe. Eventually, the theology of the Lutheran church was codified in *The Book of Concord* (1580), but the fire of reform had cooled. A century after the initial stirrings of the reform, one Lutheran pastor, Johann Arndt, was deeply troubled by the moral laxity and hard-heartedness of his congregation. Concerned for true faith exemplified in godly living, he called for repentance, self-denial, regeneration, and "the right and true service of God" in his book *True Christianity* (1605).

His views were rejected by most of the self-satisfied clergy of his day, but one pastor, Jacob Spener of Frankfort, took his preaching to heart. In an effort to produce godly living in his congregation he assembled a group of believers in his home for Bible study, prayer, and discussion of his Sunday sermon. Opponents claimed that he was trying to divide the congregation into "spiritual" and "not-so-spiritual" groups and in ridicule called his beliefs "Pietism," but Spener was undaunted by his critics. In his book *Pia Desideria* (Pious Desires, 1675) he called for what amounted to a second reformation in Germany. Spener believed that reform must begin with the clergy, each pastor combining a personal knowledge of salvation with a life of devotion and service, but reform had to include lay people as well as clergy. Luther's doctrine of the priesthood of all believers could not be forgotten. Spener argued for a Lutheran Church faithful to its creedal stand, yet dynamic in matters of the Spirit—a church with the emphasis on personal faith in Christ, not mere assent to a creed.

The movement begun by Spener spread to the University of Halle. There, under the leadership of his disciple Augustus Francke thousands of German youth were trained as ministers and missionaries, and a strict ethical system was observed. The Lutheran Church and the German and Dutch Reformed Churches were established in America by Pietists. Among those influenced through study at Halle was a rich nobleman and lawyer, Nicholas Count Zinzendorf, whose patronage of the Moravian Church spread Pietism through Germany and to America.

The influence of Pietism remains today in evangelicalism's emphasis on congregational singing, missions, small-group Bible study, devotional literature, individual "new birth" and "regeneration," preaching by clergy whose works correspond to their words, toleration of others' faiths without compromise of one's own convictions, and lay involvement in the local and world-wide church. Yet, even as German, Dutch, and Swiss Pietists were bringing these ideas to America, the movement was dying in Europe. Soon, its force had been spent in America as well.[1] Revival was needed again, this time in the form developed in the English revivals of John and Charles Wesley.

The Methodist Church

The Wesleys and the Founding of the Church

John and Charles Wesley, sons of an Anglican priest, both became priests in the Church of England, but they were not typical Anglican clergy of the period. Their mother, Susanna, who was descended from English Puritans, schooled them in personal piety. While sailing to Georgia as missionaries in 1735 the Wesleys encountered Moravian Pietists and under their influence became convinced of the necessity of personal conversion and salvation by faith alone. Charles had a conversion experience on Pentecost Sunday, May 21, 1738, and the following Wednesday (May 24) while hearing a reading of Luther's preface to the Epistle to the Romans in Aldersgate John felt his "heart strangely warmed." They immediately began to preach the Good News with an enthusiasm that offended the religious leaders of the day. Forbidden to preach from pulpits, they took the Evangel to the fields, and people came to hear them. Traveling the length and breadth of the British Isles, the Wesleys and their followers, soon called Methodists, spawned a revival that rescued England from moral ruin. The Methodist message and organization quickly spread to British America, and Methodism found an ideal home there.[2]

Church Organization

Bishops and Presiding Elders

The Christian church inherited from New Testament times three types of ordained ministry: bishops, presbyters (elders or priests), and deacons. By the time of the English Reformation, the office of deacon had become merely a temporary stepping-stone to the priesthood, priests could be ordained only by bishops, and bishops were political appointees often pre-occupied with non-spiritual issues. John Wesley accepted the basic structure existing in the Church of England but was convinced by evidence from the Bible and the ancient church that he as an ordained elder should have the right to ordain other clergymen. Since British jurisdiction no longer extended to the newly independent American states, Wesley felt at liberty to establish a new precedent for Methodists there by ordaining Richard Whatcoat and Thomas Vasey elders and Thomas Coke as superintendent for America on September 2, 1784. They were to work with Francis Asbury, whom Wesley had sent in 1771. Asbury declined to accept the office of Superintendent merely on the basis of Wesley's appointment, so he and Coke called a conference of American Methodist preachers (the Christmas Conference of 1784), at which they were unanimously elected as superintendents of the new American church. The Methodist Episcopal Church was an Episcopal church, that is one headed by bishops, and Coke and Asbury soon adopted the title of "bishop" as leaders of the church.[3]

Twelve men were ordained as elders (presbyters) at the Christmas Conference, and they traveled circuits of Methodist meeting places, preaching and giving leadership to local preachers. As more elders were ordained, some were put in supervisory positions. The first General

Conference (1792) provided official status for these men as "Presiding Elders" and stipulated that they be chosen, stationed, and changed by the bishops, provided that no elder should preside in the same district more than four years successively. They were to act in place of the bishops in the bishops' absence to enforce the bishops' authority. At this very first conference James O'Kelly led a democratic faction that sought to curtail the powers of the bishops and give the Annual Conferences power to elect their own Presiding Elders, but he was defeated, and his group seceded from the church. In 1808 Bishop McKendree began the practice of meeting with Presiding Elders to station ministers. Efforts, never successful, continued through the 1810s and 1820s to make the church more democratic through lay representation at Annual Conferences and election of Presiding Elders by the conference.[4]

General and Annual Conferences

John Wesley called the first Methodist conference of clergymen and lay preachers to meet with him in June 1744.[5] He continued to call conferences annually to discuss issues of belief and practice, maintain discipline, and assign ministers to fields of service. Thomas Rankin called the first American Methodist conference in 1773 six weeks after his arrival in Philadelphia as Wesley's emissary to the American colonies, and Methodist preachers continued to meet annually from that time. The Methodist Episcopal Church was formally organized at the Christmas Conference of 1784, which adopted a Discipline patterned after the so-called Large Minutes of early conferences compiled and edited by Wesley in 1753.[6] The phenomenal growth of the church soon made annual meetings of all the clergy impractical, so Bishop Asbury began to meet the preachers in various "district" conferences. In 1792 he called what is reckoned the first General Conference, which resolved to meet as a whole body every four years. The second General Conference (1796) gave structure to the various regional conferences by fixing boundaries for six Annual Conferences. By 1804 the Annual Conference had assumed its distinctive features as the self-contained ecclesiastical unit in which the preachers held their membership, in which appointments were made, and in which the work of the denomination had its regional organization. The 1808 General Conference determined that henceforth it would be made up of delegates elected by the Annual Conferences and future General Conferences were forbidden to change the Articles of Religion or the General Rules, do away with the episcopacy or the general itinerant superintendency, or abolish the right of trial and appeal.[7]

Quarterly Conference

Even before the arrival of Wesley's official emissaries in the 1770s, Methodist lay preachers in Maryland and Virginia were holding regular meetings four times per year, and the first American Methodist Discipline (1784) assumes quarterly meetings of all the ordained and lay leaders on a circuit. From the beginning the Presiding Elder presided at the Quarterly Conferences of each church (circuit or station) in his district, providing a powerful link between the denomination and the local congregation.[8] The ordained minister appointed to the circuit was a member of the Quarterly Conference by virtue of his membership in the Annual Conference. He appointed all other members of the Quarterly Conference, including local preachers, exhorters, class leaders, and stewards. Local preachers were men unable or unwilling to travel like the circuit riding "itinerant" ministers but who were useful in giving instruction and leadership to individual societies. Exhorters were originally persons recognized by Wesley as credible witnesses to their conversion and faith, but they later served as preachers and pastoral assistants. Both local preachers and exhorters were licensed annually by the quarterly conference. Class leaders were in charge of small groups within the society. Stewards were the financial officers of the circuit, charged with collecting, guarding, and distributing society funds.[9]

Denominational Publishing

John Wesley made good use of the printing press to spread his gospel message and defend his views against critics. As soon as the Methodist Episcopal Church was organized it began publishing conference minutes, sermons, and Wesley works. The Methodist Book Concern traces its official history to the appointment of John Dickens and Philip Cox as Book Stewards in 1789. Dickens and his successors in Philadelphia and then New York produced a long list of English and American Wesleyan titles of practical theology. *The Methodist Magazine* began publication in 1818 and was followed shortly by *The Youth's Instructor and Guardian* (1823) and *Christian Advocate* (1826). Within two years the *Advocate* had the largest circulation of any publication in the United States.[10]

Church Life

Pastoral Ministry

Wesley initially appointed assistants to preach in various locations on an informal basis, but in 1746 he divided Great Britain into circuits and began appointing itinerant [i.e. traveling] preachers on a yearly basis.[11] Wesley's representatives in America continued this practice, and once the Methodist Episcopal Church was established in 1784 itinerancy became one of its cornerstones. American congregations and ministers might protest the undemocratic nature of a system that allowed them no voice in pastoral assignments, but Bishop Asbury worked tirelessly to insure that bishops had the power to marshal the forces of the church wherever they were most needed. The system was a spectacular success in converting a young country on the move. Most of the early circuit-riding preachers were single men who devoted their lives to the church and went where they were assigned. Although a preacher might rarely be assigned to the same place for two or three years in a row, Wesley's absolute limit of three years remained in place.[12]

Prayer Meetings and Class Meetings

Wesley preached to great masses of people in the fields, and Methodist circuit riders who followed in his steps continued to reach out to the unconverted through services that consisted largely of preaching. Those who joined Methodist societies, however, enjoyed a rich and varied life of worship together. On Sunday mornings Methodists were directed by Wesley to worship in their local Anglican church if allowed to, but the rest of the week was filled with lengthy meetings of other kinds, including possibly prayer meetings, Love Feasts, watch night services, covenant services, band meetings, and class meetings.[13]

Methodism began in the Thursday evening prayer meetings of Wesley's Holy Club at Oxford University, and the midweek prayer service, in which every member present was expected to take part, remained a vital component of the Methodist experience from that day forward.[14] The Love Feast was a feature of Pietism that Wesley adopted from the Moravians and incorporated into Methodism in 1737. This devotional service of singing, sharing of bread and cup, and giving of alms to the poor retained an important role in the early American church.[15] Watch night services grew from the Saturday night prayer meetings newly converted colliers in Kingswood, England, organized to replace their usual revelry in the alehouses. Wesley supported them and adopted watch nights for his society in London in 1742 to be held monthly or quarterly as a time of preaching, singing, praying, and praising. The first watch night services in America were held in 1770, the one in Philadelphia on Dec. 31 being the first New Year's Eve Watch-night Service.[16] The

Covenant Service was devised by Wesley beginning in 1755 for affirmation or re-affirmation of commitment to God.[17]

Bands were small (2-4 believers) groups of like persons (single men, single women, married men, married women), who met to hold one another accountable for sinful conduct through searching and very personal examination. Wesley adopted this Moravian concept for use among Methodists in 1738.[18] Classes began when the Methodist society in Bristol divided into groups of 10-12 on February 15, 1742, under class leaders, who were initially responsible for meeting a quota of funds needed to pay off building debt. Wesley soon made the class leaders responsible for inquiring into the moral conduct of the class members, and classes began meeting weekly to settle quarrels, receive advice and reproof from their leaders, and pray together, as well as gathering funds for the poor and outreach. Methodists were required to participate in a class, but attendance by non-members was strictly limited. This class structure proved ideal for the American frontier, where Methodist societies were at first little bigger than classes and class leaders could provide vital leadership between the visits of the circuit-riding minister.[19]

Sunday Services

All of these types of meetings were designed for believers, usually small groups of members. Regular Sunday worship services were thrown open for large numbers of potential believers. Wesley, of course, remained a priest of the Church of England all his life and believed that "there is no Liturgy in the world...which breathes more of solid, Scriptural, rational piety than the Common Prayer of the Church of England."[20] Accordingly, he sent an edited version of the Anglican liturgy to America in 1784 as *The Sunday Service of the Methodists in North America, with Other Occasional Services*. The Christmas Conference adopted *The Sunday Service*, but it was totally out of keeping with the informal, indeed anti-formal, American church, whose preachers thought they could pray better with their eyes shut than with their eyes buried in a prayer book, and it was little used.[21] The First General Conference of 1792 settled for giving only general directions for worship:

> 1. Let the morning service consist of singing and prayer, the reading of a chapter out of the Old Testament and another out of the New Testament, and preaching. 2. Let the afternoon service consist of singing, prayer, the reading of one chapter out of the Bible and preaching. 3. Let the evening service consist of singing, prayer and preaching. 4. But on the days of administering the Lord's Supper, the two chapters in the

morning service may be omitted. 5. Let the Society be met, whenever possible, on the Sabbath Day.[22]

Sacraments

The only parts of *The Sunday Service* to survive in American Methodism were the forms for Holy Communion, Infant and Adult Baptism, Matrimony, Burial of the Dead, and Ordination, which were included in the *Discipline.* Wesley made few changes in the "Order for the Administration of the Lord's Supper" when he adapted it from the 1662 English *Book of Common Prayer.* Indeed, the text of the Methodist rite is closer to the original than that used in the Episcopal Church today. Wesley, like Luther and Calvin before him, believed in and practiced frequent (weekly, even daily) Communion as a normative feature of Christian worship, but the custom in English churches of his time was quarterly Communion, and this custom was inherited by American Methodism. Holy Communion came to be associated with Quarterly Conference meetings, since these were the only times many frontier societies saw an elder authorized to celebrate Communion.[23] Wesley also upheld the Anglican understanding of baptism as incorporation into the Christian church, but he deleted explicit references to baptismal regeneration from the Anglican form for baptism he sent to the American Methodist church in 1784. American Methodists, who placed such great emphasis on being born again through conversion, deleted further passages referring to rebirth through baptism. For Wesley there was no contradiction between baptism as an operative means of grace and a subsequent need for conversion, but the nuances of Methodist baptismal doctrine made it a continuing source of controversy in the contentious denominational climate of America.[24]

Music

One thing Wesley and all Methodists of all shades agreed on, however, was the importance of singing in worship. Indeed, Methodism was largely responsible for the acceptance of hymns in English and American churches after two centuries in which congregational singing was limited to metrical psalmody.[25] John Wesley compiled the first American hymnbook, *A Collection of Psalms and Hymns*, published in Charleston SC in 1737. After this he and his brother Charles produced a steady stream of hymns and collections. John's main contribution to hymnody was translation of Pietist Moravian hymns from German into English, but Charles was a gifted and prolific hymn writer responsible for over 5000 hymns. Wesley published the first Methodist hymnal with both texts and tunes in 1761. Wesley hymnbooks were reprinted in America and formed the basis for the strong and heart-felt singing for which the Methodists were noted.[26]

Church Buildings

John Wesley built the first Methodist preaching-house in Bristol, England, in 1739 and owned all the earliest properties himself, but he wanted to find a way to keep them set apart for Methodist preaching after his death. He, therefore, drew up Deeds of Trust, vesting ownership of chapels in local trustees, who were responsible for ensuring not only that the properties were kept in repair but also that only men of sound Methodist doctrine preached there. Fellow evangelist George Whitefield pointed out to Wesley, however, that "[i]f the trustees are to name the preachers, they may exclude even you from preaching in the house you have built," so the deeds were amended in 1746 to ensure access to John, his brother Charles, and others they might appoint. The 1763 Conference adopted a Model Deed for Methodist properties that reserved them for use of preachers appointed by the conference, and this was the form used for the earliest Methodist properties in America.[27]

The Second General Conference of the Methodist Episcopal Church (1796) adopted a "Deed of Settlement" for church properties that stipulated that the lands and buildings were to be held by local trustees

> for the use of the members of the Methodist Episcopal Church.... according to the rules and discipline which from time to time may be agreed upon and adopted by the ministers and preachers of the said Church, at their General Conferences... and in further trust and confidence that they shall at all times, for ever hereafter, permit such ministers and preachers, belonging to the said Church, as shall from time to time be duly authorized by the General Conferences and yearly conferences...and none other to preach and expound God's holy word therein.[28]

The Discipline of the Evangelical Association later copied this deed word for word.

Methodist Beliefs

The doctrinal standard of American Methodism was established in 1784, when the Christmas Conference adopted the twenty-four Articles of Religion sent by John Wesley with his *Sunday Service* plus an additional Article dealing with civil government in the new republic. The Articles were Wesley's abridgement of the Thirty-nine Articles of the Church of

England.

A distinctive of Wesleyan theology was belief in what is variously called "holiness," "entire sanctification," and "Christian perfection." Wesley believed that conversion, or justification, should be followed for all Christians by a deeper work of God's grace that removes original sin, turns the heart completely to God, and enables the believer to avoid any intentional violation of God's commandments of which the person is aware. Christian perfection is gradual in the sense that the Holy Spirit may in some people take time to prepare the heart as a dwelling place for God and also instantaneous in the moment that the sanctifying work is actually consummated. Once in this "sinless" state the Christian is subject to mistakes and failures but has no willful intent to sin.[29]

North American Pluralism

Methodism found fertile soil for growth in the new United States of America, where it became a vital antidote to the irreligion of the early federal period. Clergy had come with Columbus to America in 1492 and with the first English settlers to Jamestown in 1607. Each group of immigrants brought its own varieties of Christianity to Britain's American colonies. In the religious melting pot of America tolerance for the beliefs of others became a necessity, but with it came uncertainty about one's own beliefs. Religious feeling ebbed. Then God sent revival to New England in the work of Jonathan Edwards in 1740, and the "Great Awakening" was spread up and down the east coast by the evangelistic crusades of George Whitefield (English), Theodore Freylinghausen (Dutch), and Gilbert Tennent (Scottish).

Soon, however, political tensions began to overshadow religious concerns. The Revolutionary War not only dealt severe blows to English churches like the Anglican (Episcopal) and Methodist churches and destroyed much church property, but it also had the effect of severing ties with all mother churches in Europe and turning people loose into a new world dominated by secular thinking. Among the Germans, few Lutherans, immigrant or American-born, could claim any personal experience of religion, Brethren Pietistic principles had lapsed, and Mennonites and Moravians had fallen on spiritual hard times. By 1780 only three-fifths of the populace attended church regularly, and not all of these belonged to any church. Only 2,731 church buildings were open in all of the United States! The Bill of Rights guaranteed freedom for Christians to practice their religion and evangelize the newly opened

West, but did they have the will and power to do it?[30]

Once again, God sent a revival, the Second Great Awakening (1790–1825). Strong biblical preaching and the Methodists' new methods of evangelism and organization revitalized American Christianity. In a small corner of Pennsylvania God reached a man named Jacob Albright.

Jacob Albright

Jacob Albright

A Pietist Lineage—but Lost

Jacob Albright was born on May 1, 1759, in Rushcombmanor Township, Berks Co., PA. His grandparents, Johannes and Anna Albrecht, had come to America by way of England in 1732 to escape the destruction of the wars that constantly ravaged southwestern Germany. This Pietistic Lutheran couple entered the port of Philadelphia with five children, including a sixteen-year-old son named Jacob. Jacob later married (Anna) Elizabeth Troke and fathered nine children, including another Jacob in 1759.

After young Jacob's birth, the family moved to Fox Hill, in Douglass Township in Philadelphia (now Montgomery) County. Jacob assisted his father on the farm and learned to make brick and roof tile. Baptismal and church confirmation records for the family are not complete, but records retained by the New Hanover Lutheran Church in Pottstown PA suggest that the Albright family received religious instruction there. In his late teens Albright served in the Pennsylvania militia as a drummer during the Revolutionary War. After the War he married Catharine Cope in 1785 and moved thirty-five miles southwest to Hinkletown, near Ephrata PA. In addition to farming the rich acreage he had purchased, Jacob followed his trade by manufacturing brick and roof tile. He attended the nearby Bergstrasse Lutheran Church, and his reputation as a businessman earned him the title "the honest tiler."[31] Yet, Albright was not happy. After his conversion he wrote: "I traveled with frivolous and trifling disregard, the path of life…I lived as though the span of my sinful life was unending and committed many a sin for which God had promised severe punishment."[32]

Albright may have been exposed to the ideas of experiential religion in his youth. Some historical accounts indicate that his training in the New Hanover Church may have been directed by Rev. Henry W. Muhlenberg. Muhlenberg, who had been sent to America by Halle Pietists, gave Bible-centered sermons and urged personal salvation and strict piety. He also met strong opposition from more traditional Lutherans who saw no need for any special stress on conversion and right living.[33] At Hinkletown Albright found Muhlenberg's message echoed by an itinerant evangelist, Anton Houtz. A soul hunger was aroused in Albright when three of his children died from influenza in 1790. As Houtz preached the funeral sermon, Albright, in his words, "began finally to get an insight into my sinful state and almost seized upon a resolution to improve myself, yet this resolution remained only a plan and never came to realization, because my flesh forcibly opposed it."[34]

Salvation and Sanctification

A deep conviction welled up in Albright's soul as he returned to his fields and brick kiln after the funeral. In desperation he cried out for mercy and salvation:

> I not only realized my great sinfulness but the knowledge of sin was followed by keen sorrow....I fell upon my knees, and tears of bitterness flowed down my cheeks, and a lengthy and fervent prayer ascended to the throne of God for grace and the remission of sins.[35]

Albright joined his neighbor, Adam Riegel, later a United Brethren lay minister, in long conversations about the meaning of the Bible. Their fervent prayers gave Albright inner peace. "One joyful experience followed another." Together the two friends attended the Methodist class meeting led by Isaac Davies. Albright thrived in the informal atmosphere of the class meeting, where testimonies of personal encounters with God in prayer and daily life mingled with confessions of sins. The methods Wesley had pioneered in England had touched a Pennsylvania German named Jacob Albright. While the Methodist brethren prayed in English, Albright raised his voice in the German dialect. Earnestly, he sought personal holiness, devotion, and a strict disciplined manner before the Lord. His prayer life outside the class meeting brought him further joy each day. This joy led Albright to go beyond justification in Christ (salvation) to seek sanctification.

Albright furthered his study of English in order to read more about the doctrines and practices of the class meeting in the Methodist *Discipline.* In 1796 he joined the class meeting and was granted an exhorter's license to speak in public. A new Jacob Albright was emerging like wheat from buried grain: a man of prayer, a student of the Word, zealous to speak, not eloquently, but lovingly about his Jesus. Yet, God was still not finished with him.[36]

Suffering, Submitting, Serving

Again, the Holy Spirit drove Albright to his knees, this time burdened for the souls of his lost German-speaking brethren. As he struggled with this calling, he experienced unparalleled weakness of body and distress of mind. Human fears assailed him: he had a farm and a business to run; there was no organized body of believers to provide moral or financial support; intense opposition from other Christians and the ungodly could result in physical harm. Finally, it became plain to him that God's call to evangelize could not be rejected. He went forth with joy.

In October 1796 he began traveling to nearby counties where his "erring brothers" lived. Assembling the necessary materials in advance allowed his family to carry on the tile business and farm in his absence. Planning his trips brought him home for planting and harvest. Because God had "raised him up," love for humanity cast out fear of failure. He was even prepared to venture into Maryland and western Virginia, following German settlers moving westward. Closer to home, however, Albright met opposition in Schaefferstown, Dauphin (now Lebanon) Co., PA. Opponents tried to shout down his message of salvation. He was wounded by rock throwing and only rescued when a local citizen gave him refuge in his home. Yet, he continued on, to Pottstown and then further east to Quakertown in Bucks County. He preached in barns and homes and in fields, wherever he gained a listening heart. Here and there, one by one, converts were made, including George Miller, who became one of Albright's young assistants. At meetings like one near Quakertown on Pentecost in 1797 his converts committed themselves to prayer for their German brethren.[37]

Sometime in 1798 Albright determined to form the handful of believers into class meetings like those that had nurtured his own soul. The first classes were organized in Berks, Bucks, and Northampton Counties in accordance with the Methodist *Discipline*. Thus began *Die Albrechts Leute* (The Albright's People). By 1800 there were three organized classes under class leaders with a total membership of twenty. It was not until 1803 that class membership grew to forty, "most of them blessed (converted) souls." However, several hundred additional believers in the territory visited by Albright were unorganized, although they had responded to his preaching, and hundreds more from German Reformed, Lutheran, and Schwenckfelder churches attended the "big meetings," which lasted from noon Saturday through Sunday. Albright was assisted at these meetings by John Walter (age 20) and Abraham Liesser. As early as 1800 the work had spread west across the Susquehanna River and met with great success. Pioneer United Brethren evangelists had already advanced as far as Union and Centre counties, and Albright co-operated with the United Brethren, including Bishop Newcomer.[38]

Victories Before the Final Shout

The need for closer administration of the far-flung work led to a conference on November 5, 1803, in Berks County at the home of Abraham Liesser. Here the group declared itself a Methodist society and designated Albright a "genuine evangelical preacher." This ordination performed by his brethren might have come more logically at the hands

Abraham Liesser home, Barto, PA.
Site of one of the early classes in Berks Co.

of the Methodist Episcopal Church, from whom he had received his exhorter's license, but the Methodists under Bishop Asbury were not willing to authorize preaching in the German language. Albright, confident in his calling, returned to his work with new enthusiasm and determination. There are indications that he began to administer the sacraments of Infant Baptism and Holy Communion.[39]

A second business meeting was conducted at Kleinfeltersville in May 1806. Here, the office of "local preacher" was created as directed by the Methodist Episcopal *Discipline*, salary and other financial matters were discussed, and provision was made for an Annual Conference. That same year a wearying Albright, with the help of John Walter and George Miller, held a Covenant Meeting at the home of Martin Dreisbach near New Berlin, Union Co., PA. They divided the work into two circuits separated by the Susquehanna River. Germans continued to move west in search of better land, and Albright's preachers moved with them. Within a decade, the area west of the Susquehanna had become the center of the work; new leadership came from that area and new institutions soon appeared on its soil.

The first regular Annual Conference of the "So-called Albright's People" was held in November 1807 at the home of Samuel Becker in Kleinfeltersville. Here, the group chose a name, "The Newly-formed

Methodist Conference." Total membership was 220, with five preachers, three local preachers, and twenty class leaders. The Conference adopted twenty of the twenty-five "Articles of Religion" of the Methodist Episcopal Church and commissioned Albright to write a new *Discipline*. It established an episcopal form of church government and elected Albright its first bishop.

Albright's final general meeting was held in Berks County PA in April 1808. Here he made pastoral assignments, and then, though he was too weak from advancing consumption (tuberculosis) to speak, he attended a revival service held in a barn north of Harrisburg PA. After the service he started home to die there but got no farther than George Becker's home in Kleinfeltersville. Like the prophet of old whose friends provided a place of lodging (2 Kings 4:8-11), this latter-day Elisha knew a bed and Christian fellowship would be waiting for him there. He departed this earth soon after his arrival, surrounded by friends and believers. His wife, living some fifteen miles south, was not present when he died on May 18, 1808. The funeral and burial took place at the Becker farm, the spot marked today by the Albright Chapel.

There is always human sadness when one of God's chosen falls; our Lord's disciples knew tragedy. Yet, there is always tomorrow for those who remain. The Newly-formed Methodist Conference, the young Evangelicals, wiped away their tears and returned to their tasks. Like their leader, Jacob Albright, they would stay in the saddle to the very end and homeward turn for an early death, burnt-out but victorious.[40]

The Young Evangelicals

Albright's early death robbed The Albright's People of his experienced leadership but did not kill the new church. Three young co-laborers, John Walter (1781-1811), John Dreisbach (1789-1871), and George Miller (1774-1816), pooled their resources to give the Evangelical preachers and members continued leadership. Although their combined age at the time of Albright's death was little more than 80 and they were short on experience, these servants of God prevailed against insurmountable odds. Although no Annual Conference was held in 1808, evangelization continued, classes grew, and membership slowly increased.[41]

Pennsylvania Germans were continuing to spread out into new lands in New York and Ohio, and the Evangelical preachers followed the frontier people into the wilderness. Their "aggressive Christianity," emphasizing the warm heart over cold doctrine, was enormously successful there.

Even in the settled areas of the East the broadened outlook on life prevailing in the wake of the Revolutionary War brought greater toleration for new religious views and practices. In particular, free men wanted to hear Wesleyan doctrines of free will and free grace. Methodists, United Brethren, and the young Evangelicals capitalized on the door this new mindset opened for them. Young men of relentless energy and new vision, although often unlettered and unsophisticated, built a new America. "Common people became powerful actors on the religious scene," and a score of new denominations and American versions of Old World denominations developed new Scriptural interpretations and democratic church organizations.[42] Their achievements had been predicted by Jacob Albright, who said in 1808 "men will appear among you who will be able to accomplish that which I shall not be able to do. It is the work of God, and it is in His hands, He will also provide for it."[43]

John Walter—Preacher and Poet

John Walter was the son of Peter Walter, one of Albright's class leaders. He was converted in his parent's home near Quakertown PA after one of Albright's sermons in the 1790s. In 1801 young John went to live with Albright, learning his trade and carrying on his tiling business when Albright was away preaching. Soon, Walter found himself traveling along with Albright serving as an exhorter, and in 1802 he began to preach—quite an accomplishment for a self-educated man. The 1803 Conference Minutes simply state that John Walter "had grown in grace." Ordination as a deacon followed in 1806.[44]

In 1808 Walter married Christina Becker, whose family farm at Kleinfeltersville PA was at the center of early denominational activities. He possessed a deep love for his wife and family that is reflected in several letters he wrote while traveling the Old Circuit preaching:

> My dear wife, pray earnestly for me and the cause of God. May God be your husband and comforter! I have entrusted you to him in my absence, and I believe that he will provide for you and protect you and me...My soul pours itself out daily for you in prayer. At the throne of grace you can daily meet me...So much from your loving husband, John Walter.[45]

Such sentiments are worthy of Christians of every age.

When Walter was assigned to the New Circuit (Northumberland County, PA) in 1809, he had already been ordained an elder; his traveling cohort was John Dreisbach. He was a dynamic preacher; his fiery messages "thundered" across the countryside. He was also a talented

poet; in 1810, at the direction of the 1809 Annual Conference, he published the first Evangelical hymnal, *Eine Kleine Sammlung alter und neuer
Geistreicher Lieder (A Brief Collection of Old and New Spiritual Songs)*, which
contained fifty-six of his own hymns. The most popular of these was
"Kommt, Brüder, Kommt." Here is the first of its ten stanzas:

> Kommt, Brüder, kommt, wir eilen fort
> Nach der Neu-Jerusalem!
> Vermerkt ihr nicht die golden Pfort',
>   Die dorten vor euch glimmt?
> Come, brothers, come, we journey on
> To the new Jerusalem!
> E'en now we see that golden gate
>   All sparkling like a gem.
>   —translation by K. R. Maurer

> [Through the years a refrain was added to this verse:
>   I want to go, I want to go, I want to go there too,
>   I want to go, where Jesus is, I want to go there too].

Illness ended Walter's travels on the preaching circuit in 1813. He died
from tuberculosis in 1818 and was buried on the cemetery plot on the
family farm. Over a century later, a farmer plowing his field unearthed
the casket, and it was reburied with a suitable marker in Ono, Lebanon
Co., PA.[46]

John Dreisbach—Preacher, Poet, and Administrator

Of the triumvirate of young Evangelical leaders, John Dreisbach
stands out as the logical successor to Albright. At seventeen he was in
the saddle traveling with him; at twenty-five he was elected first
Presiding Elder by the 1814 Annual Conference to provide leadership,
since no bishop had been elected after Albright's death. Unfortunately,
his overwhelming responsibilities quickly undermined his health, and,
though he lived to a ripe old age of eighty-two, he was soon forced to
retire from the preaching circuit.

Like John Walter, Dreisbach was converted as a teenager under the
preaching of Albright in his family's home. His training in both German
and English combined with that religious experience to make him a
leader in the young church. At the first conference in November 1807
he is listed as a preacher-on-trial; he assisted Walter in the New Circuit.
Soon, he was granted a preacher's license, one of the first granted; sur-
viving today, this license contains the only signature we have of Albright.

Auf Bevollmächtigung der Neuformirten Methodisten Conferenz, die ein gutes Zeugniß gegeben, dem *Johannes Dreisbach* und willens ist ihn aufzunehmen als *Prediger* - - - - in unsere Gemeinschaft; so gebe ich, der Unterschriebene, ihm die Erlaubniß das Amt nach unserer Ordnung zu bedienen, und auch dazu verordnet ist zum *Prediger auf gut Gewissensprob,* so er sich gebührend nach Gottes Wort verhalten thut.

Den *14ten Dezember* - - 180*7*   *Jacob Albrecht*

Note the signature of our founder, Jacob Albright,
on Dreisbach's 1807 license

Two years later he was granted elder's orders. He and Albright traveled together in the winter of 1807/8, and affectionate notices of his mentor, "the Bishop," dot his journal.

After Albright's death, Dreisbach was called to serve as Conference secretary (1809-13), and it was at this time that he conducted the first "merger negotiations" with the Methodist Episcopal Church. On August 2, 1810, Dreisbach came upon Bishop Asbury when Asbury was preaching in Halifax, Dauphin Co., PA, and the two rode together to Harrisburg. Asbury invited Dreisbach to become a Methodist minister and offered to pay his salary while he improved his English. Dreisbach was attracted to the offer, yet he could not deny Albright's vision of ministry to the Germans in America. He offered to bring the ministries of the Albright's People into the Methodist Episcopal Church as separate German circuits, districts, and conferences, but this Asbury declined. Asbury was convinced that the German language had no future in America. It was not until a generation later, long after Asbury's death, that German circuits, districts, and conferences began to grow in the Methodist Episcopal Church. Asbury and Dreisbach parted as friends and Christian brothers, each to his separate ministry.

Dreisbach prepared a *Catechism* for use among the children of the young church, but the exertions of constant work and travel began to take their toll. In 1812, when Walter and Miller were also showing the strain of the responsibilities placed on them, Dreisbach suffered a breakdown. "A great weakness…which affected the mind" rendered him incapacitated, but the Lord delivered him for a further decade of service. He was elected as leader of the church, with the title of Presiding Elder, by the 1814 Annual Conference. He visited Philadelphia twice in 1815 to preach and buy equipment for the church's new printing press and bookbindery in New Berlin PA. He traveled to Canada via Seneca County in New York to establish Evangelical missions. He helped to improve the church's *Discipline* and compile a new hymnal, for which he wrote several hymns. He chaired the first General Conference in 1816, where the name *"Evangelische Gemeinschaft"* (Evangelical Association) was adopted. All the while he made regular visits to campmeetings, watch-night meetings, and "big meetings" all across Pennsylvania, and he preached, powerfully urging salvation and sanctification on all who would listen.[47] Excerpts from one week of his *Tagebuch* (Daybook) in 1815 give a taste of the earliest days:

> May 17. At candle light I preached at brother Roller's from Matt. 16:26 and gave exhortation in English. I felt grace and it was effective, the members being encouraged and sinners moved to weeping.

> May 18. I met Brother Buchman at John Kleinfelter's at the mill. I preached again from my old text which I used last evening and often once after another, preached from it and each time with good results. On this evening I preached the judgment, with the curses and damnation, more so than usual, and felt good. Brother Buchman exhorted and while doing so the mother of Mrs. Kleinfelter was deeply convicted and fell on her knees in her soul agony. And there was such a cry for mercy that Buchman was compelled to stop speaking and go to prayer. She found comfort and we had a happy time in shouting and praising the Lord.

> May 19. Brother Buchman preached by candlelight…and I exhorted. A young man was under conviction in soul anguish for mercy and he found comfort and peace.

> May 20. I preached at our big meeting at Jacob Kleinfelter's…having no noticeable effect nor victory. In the evening Brother Buchman preached…and two souls were converted.

> May 21. At 10:10 AM I preached…It was a blessed wonderful time of shouting and praising God.

> May 22. In the evening I preached at Michael Reidinger's…The members were particularly blest, and the sinners were deeply convicted.

> May 23. I preached at Philip Ziegler's…One backslidden soul was in trouble and agony, praying earnestly for pardon….One wicked man tried

to pull away and drag out the poor seeking soul in trouble, but we would not permit it....And as I asked the members to pray for her, there was unusual crying and lamentation in prayer and tears for her. But she did not break through. O God, have mercy.[48]

In 1821 his health failed again, and he was forced to retire from the active ministry. His final years were spent in Ohio, and his gravesite can be visited at Circleville. The Evangelical Association, which he fondly called "Old Zion," prospered under his leadership.

George Miller—Author, Teacher, and Theologian

The oldest leader (aged 34) of the "So-called Albrights People" at the founder's death was George Miller. Raised in a Lutheran congregation, Miller had as a youth a very acute sense of God, but a contempt for "really wicked" Christians turned him away from the church. "Free-thinkers" enticed him with atheistic beliefs. Success as a millwright whetted his appetite for wealth and power. Godlessness marked his maturing years— and then he heard Jacob Albright preach! The impact of the message almost hurled him to the floor, but he would not submit to the Holy Spirit and struggled with God. Finally, an internal yieldedness led to conversion and a gnawing call to the ministry in 1805. Through his ordeal Miller became a man of prayer and learned the meaning of the sweet word "grace," the grace of God.

Acceptance as a preacher-on-trial (probationer) meant an assignment to the New Circuit in 1806. "I commenced the work," he wrote, "with prayer and fasting, relying on the help of God." One hundred souls were saved within an eight-month period in the Buffalo Valley in Union County PA. His success inspired Albright and Walter, who met for prayer with him in the Covenant Meeting later that year, to continue the work of the young church. Miller was ordained in 1807, and at the General Meeting of 1808 where Albright made his last pastoral assignments Miller was called to the New Circuit with Dreisbach. When Albright "joined the heavenly church" this oldest of the young Evangelicals seemed a "worthy successor," but the Lord of the Church had other plans; by the end of the same year a heart attack had ended Miller's time in the saddle. He had traveled the preaching circuits only four years.[49]

Miller continued to serve the Association from his home in Albany Township, Berks Co. PA, despite bodily weakness, lack of writing skill, and the attacks of the Adversary. He finished Albright's task of compiling a *Discipline*, including a church constitution and Articles of Faith, using a new German translation of the Methodist *Discipline* by Ignatius Römer. When the second Annual Conference met in his home in 1809 Miller was strong enough to preside. With his new rules in effect old confusions and misunderstandings faded, and conference sessions became "antechambers of heaven."[50] The *Discipline* gave the Association legitimacy, and the new order and stability attracted new members. A second edition of the *Discipline*, edited by Dreisbach and Henry Niebel and published in October 1817, was also the work of Miller, even though he died before its completion. This version was almost twice the size of the first edition.

Miller also wrote the first biography of Albright (1811), his own autobiography (1815), and a little book *Kurze und deutliche Lehren zum Wahren und Thätigen Christenthum* (1814), published in English as *Practical Christianity* (J. Q. A. Weller, translator, 1871), the only book of "theology," besides the *Discipline* and the *Catechism*, written by an early follower of Albright. In this work, subtitled "Short and Plain Doctrines setting forth True Godliness," Miller combines pietistic and evangelistic teachings into a call for commitment to the changed life possible in Christianity. An appeal to the heart (not emotions) of the reader, Christian and non-Christian, for wakefulnes, watchfulness, and prayer is followed by guidelines for righteous living. Salvation must lead to sanctification; grace will provide as the Christian fully surrenders all of self to God in earnest prayer. Different chapters deal with the spirituality of ministers, husbands and wives, parents and guardians, children, youth, and servants. A closing chapter commends works of love and mercy for all believers, ending with the words of seventeenth-century Puritan writer Joseph Alleine, whose influence is evident throughout the book:

> Be not only good Christians while upon your knees, but let your whole life and conduct be uniform holiness…Herein consists the excellency of the religion of Jesus Christ.[51]

The depth of Miller's own Christian walk is evident in *Practical Christianity*, and it was a powerful influence for good on generations of Evangelicals.

Conclusion

By 1816, when they held their first General Conference, the Albright's People had grown from a single man's burden for lost souls to a denomination of 1400 members in five states with its own *Discipline*, hymnal (*Das Geistliche Saitenspiel*), *Catechism*, and Book Commission. The first biography of Albright had been written (by George Miller). Missionaries were being sent to the western frontier, and new circuits were constantly being added. Enthusiasm was high; signs of God's favor were all around.

Notes

1. Dale Brown, *Understanding Pietism*, rev. ed. (Nappanee, IN: Evangel Pub. House, 1996.

2. Barrie Tabraham, *The Making of Methodism* (London: Epworth Press, 1995), 7, 23-30, 42-45.

3. *The History of American Methodism* (New York: Abingdon Press, 1964), v.1, 197-208.

4. John Kent, "Superintendent," in The Encyclopedia of World Methodism (Nashville: United Methodist Publishing House, 1974).

5. Steven Tomkins, *John Wesley: A Biography* (Grand Rapids, MI: Eerdmans, 2003), 115.

6. *The Large Minutes*, which every British Methodist minster had to sign as a symbol of loyalty to Wesley, was in turn based on a pamphlet referred to as the "Disciplinary Minutes" (in contrast to a doctrinal pamphlet) published by Wesley in 1749.

7. *The History of American Methodism*, v.1, 120-130, 226, 422-480.

8. Jame W. May, "Methodism in the United States—The Methodist Episcopal Church, 1784-1939," in *The Encyclopedia of World Methodism*

9. William Warren Sweet, *The Methodists*, Religion on the American Frontier, 1783-1840, v. 4 (Chicago: University of Chicago Press, 1946). Wesley had his Aldersgate experience in May 1738. In November 1738 the first societies were organized. In 1739 Wesley purchased the Foundery in London for the use of Methodists there. Some soon suggested that members subscribe for the expenses of maintaining the building, and Wesley appointed stewards to keep account of the money.

10. *The History of American Methodism*, v. 1, 278-287, 571-582; James Pilkington, "The Methodist Publishing House," in *The Encyclopedia of World Methodism*.

11. The Methodist Church in Britain still operates in this manner, with several (often four) ordained ministers serving a like number of congregations so that each preaches at the same place about once a month. This gives some prominence to local lay preachers who are part of each congregation.

12. Nolan B. Harmon and John Kent, "Itinerancy," in *The Encyclopedia of World Methodism*; Frank Baker, "Stationing of Preachers, in *The Encyclopedia of World Methodism*.

13. *The History of American Methodism*, v.1, 307-317.

14. Nolan B. Harmon, "Prayer Meetings," in *The Encyclopedia of World Methodism*.

15. Emory S. Bucke, "Love Feast," in *The Encyclopedia of World Methodism*.

16. Frederick E. Maser, "Watch-Night," in *The Encyclopedia of World Methodism*.

17. Nolan B. Harmon, "Covenant Service," in *The Encyclopedia of World Methodism*.

18. Nolan B. Harmon, "Bands," in *The Encyclopedia of World Methodism*.

19. Elmer T. Clark, "Class Meetings," in *The Encyclopedia of World Methodism*.

20. *John Wesley's Sunday Service of the Methodists in North America* ([Nashville]: United Methodist Publishing House, 1984).

21. Nolan B. Harmon, "Sunday Service," in *The Encyclopedia of World Methodism*.

22. *Doctrines and Discipline of the Methodist Episcopal Church ... 1792*, 40f. Quoted in Edwin E. Voigt, "Worship in American Methodism," in *Encyclopedia of World Methodism*.

23. Nolan B. Harmon, "The Lord's Supper—The Rite in American Methodism," in *Encyclopedia of World Methodism*.

24. John Lawson and W. F. Dunkle, Jr., "Baptism" in *Encyclopedia of World Methodism*.

25. John Calvin and his English followers, the Puritans, forbade singing in churches of texts of human manufacture. They allowed only the inspired texts of the Psalms set in rhyming metrical poetic versions to fit certain Psalm tunes. It took Isaac Watts to see something incongruous about Christians singing texts that never mention Christ.

26. Halford E. Luccock, Paul Hutchinson, and Robert Goodloe, *The Story of Methodism* (New York: Abingdon, 1949), 105–117; Carlton Young and Frank Baker, "Hymnody," in *Encyclopedia of World Methodism*.

27. E. Benson Perkins and Costen J. Harrell, "Deeds, Trust," in *Encyclopedia of World Methodism*. Wesley felt very strongly on this point. "[W]henever the trustees exert their power placing and displacing preachers, [he wrote in 1783] then, 1. Itinerant preaching is no more. When the trustees in any place have found and fixed a preacher they like, the rotation of preachers is at an end—at least till they are tired of their favourite preacher, and so turn him out. 2. While he stays, is not the bridle in his mouth? How dares he speak the full and the whole truth, since whenever he displeases the trustees he is liable to lose his bread?...3. But suppose any beside the Conference (who as long as they subsist will be the most impartial judges) name the preachers, should it be thirty or forty men, or the whole society?...4.The power of the trustees is greater than that of any nobleman; yea, or of the king himself. Where he is patron, he can put in a preacher, but he cannot pull him out.

28. *Journals of the General Conference of the Methodist Episcopal Church* (New York: Carlton & Phillips, 1855), v.1, 12–14.

29. Kenneth Kinghorn, "Christian Perfection," in *Encyclopedia of World Methodism*.

30 Sydney Ahlstrom, *A Religious History of the American People* (New Haven:

Yale University Press, 1973), 365f.

31. Albright, 21–31.

32. George Miller, *Kurze Beschreibung der würkenden Gnade Gottes bey dem Jakob Albrecht* (Reading: Ritter, 1811), translated as "Jacob Albright: The First Biography of the Founder of the Evangelical Association" by George E. Epp in 1959 upon the request of The Historical Society of the Evangelical United Brethren Church.

33. T. G. Tappert, "The Influence of Pietism in Colonial American Lutheranism," in *Continental Pietism and Early American Christianity* (Grand Rapids: Eerdmans, 1976), 17; John G. McEllhenney and Charles Yrigoyen, Jr., *200 Years of United Methodism: An Illustrated History* (Madison, NJ: Drew University, 1984), 13.

34. Miller, 2.

35. Albright, 34.

36. Ibid., 35–38, 58.

37. Ibid., 58, 60; J. Bruce Behney and Paul H. Eller, *The History of the Evangelical United Brethren Church* (Nashville: Abingdon, 1979), 73.

38. Albright, 31, 61; Behney and Eller, 73–75.

39. Albright, 67–74.

40. Ibid., 80–91.

41. Ibid., 92–93.

42. Nathan Hatch, *The Democratization of American Religion* (New Haven: Yale University Press, 1989), 222.

43. Reuben Yeakel, *History of the Evangelical Association* (Cleveland: Thomas & Mattill, 1894), v.1, 93.

44. Albright, 62–64.

45. Ibid., 64.

46. Behney and Eller, 73–75; "Farmer's Plow Unearths Famed Preacher's Grave," *Harrisburg Sunday Patriot News,* April 22, 1955, 2..

47. Ibid., 85–91; Reuben Yeakel, *Jacob Albright and his Co-laborers* (Cleveland: Publishing House of the Evangelical Association, 1883), 277–321.

48. John Dreisbach, *Day Book of Reverend John Dresibach, April 23, 1814–May 30, 1815*; trans. J. G. Eller., typescript carbon copy in E. C. Archives, Evangelical School of Theology, Myerstown, PA.

49. Yeakel, *Jacob Albright and his Co-laborers,* 173–248; Behney and Eller, 76–79.

50. Albright, 94–95.

51. George Miller, *Practical Christianity* (Cleveland: Evangelical Association, [1871]; Nashville: Parthenon Press, 1996), 157.

2

Spreading the Evangel:
The Evangelical Association
(1816–1894)

Overview

The earliest years of the Evangelical Association were years of undeniable accomplishment and progress. However, the Association soon began to pay the price of over-rapid expansion. Early missions sent to the western New York frontier could not be sustained. The Publishing House failed in the recession that followed the War of 1812. Men and women converted in the white heat of emotion slid back into their old way of life; of the 4000 members received into the church in its first quarter-century less than half (1854) remained on the rolls in 1823. Preachers sent to the field without adequate preparation made serious mistakes and had to be removed from office or broke under the physical demands of constant travel in summer heat and winter cold through roadless forests and mountain passes, the spiritual demands of rigorous scrutiny by colleagues and slander and persecution by enemies, and the financial burden of inadequate salaries. Between 1815 and 1828 fifty-seven itinerant preachers were received on trial, but the total number of preachers increased by only seven (15 to 22). Finally, the Association suffered its first major disruption when John Hamilton attempted to lead the English-speaking preachers out of the church in 1830, and the General Conference reacted by voting to receive only men who could preach in German, thus stifling denominational growth for a decade.

Still, the Albright People survived and in the next two decades (1830–1850) grew from a small Pennsylvania German sect of 3850 members and 34 active preachers to a respected American denomination with 21,179 members and 195 itinerant preachers in five Annual Conferences (East Pennsylvania, West Pennsylvania, Ohio, Illinois, and New York). English-language societies in western Maryland and Virginia

dwindled after 1830, but preachers followed the Germans to new terri-
tories in the Midwest. The first Evangelical church in Illinois was built as
early as 1839. Even before this a
congregation was started in
Michigan, and Evangelical preachers went from there into Indiana.
Wisconsin (Milwaukee) was
reached in 1840 and soon after
Iowa. Back East, the Association
spread to Allentown PA in 1831
(first church built 1838),
Baltimore in 1840 (first church
1841), and Reading PA in 1828
(first church 1845). The
Publishing House was re-estab-
lished permanently (1836),
German- and English-language
periodicals were started in 1836
and 1848, Sunday-schools began
in 1832, the first missionary society was organized in 1839, and
many churches were built. The
1839 General Conference elected
John Seybert (1839–1860) as the
first Bishop since Albright, and the
next General Conference added
Joseph Long (1843–1869) to the
ranks of the episcopacy.

Bishop John Seybert, 1839–1860.
This portrait with Seybert's signa-
ture hangs in Trinity EC church,
Manheim, PA

The golden anniversary of Albright's first classes (1850) was celebrated by the Association as a year of Jubilee. Evangelicals erected the
Albright Memorial Church next to their founder's grave near
Kleinfeltersville PA, sent their first missionaries overseas (to Germany),
and began initial attempts at starting both a church-related college and
a mission to the heathen. During the next quarter-century the church
organized fourteen more Annual Conferences (Pittsburgh and Indiana
in 1852, Wisconsin in 1856, Iowa in 1860, Canada, Michigan, and
Kansas in 1864, Germany in 1865, Minnesota in 1868, and Atlantic, Erie
(both German-language conferences), Des Moines (English-language),
Pacific, and Southern Indiana in 1875). Five men were elected Bishop:
W. W. Orwig (1859–1863), J. J. Esher (1863–1901), Reuben Yeakel

(1871–1879), Rudolph Dubs (1875–1902), and Thomas Bowman (1875–1915). Membership rose from 21,175 (with 380 ministers) to 95,253 (836 ministers). The Publishing House moved from New Berlin PA to modern quarters in Cleveland. New magazines were launched: *Der Christliche Kinderfreund* for children (1855), *Der Evangelische Botschafter* (1864 in Germany), *The Living Epistle* and *Das Evangelische Magazin* (both holiness papers, 1869), and *Das Evangelische Kinderfreund* (1870 in Germany). The first history of the denomination, Bishop Orwig's *Geschichte der Evangelischen Gemeinschaft,* appeared in 1857 (English translation 1858). The Board of Publication and the Board of Missions were established in 1859 to transact the business of the church between General Conference sessions. The first Episcopal Message was delivered to General Conference in 1863. A mission to Japan was authorized in 1875.

Bishop Thomas Bowman, 1875–1916

The last quarter of the century brought even greater progress and prosperity. From 1875 to 1891 membership, reflecting increases in the national population and the number of immigrants from Germany, exploded from 54,981 to 150,234. The number of ministers increased by 391 to 1227. Six new Annual Conferences were created: Switzerland (1879), Nebraska (1879), Platte River (1881), California and Oregon from Pacific (1884), Dakota (1884), and Texas (1887). Books on holiness, the Bible, denominational and church history, doctrinal and pastoral theology, missions, prophecy, and psychology in German and English poured from the Evangelical presses. Church homes and colleges were founded. Women's and young people's organizations added their strength to the church. At the same time, personal rivalries and differences over language, the holiness movement, and democracy in the church were driving the conservative, mid-western German "Majority" and the more progressive, Pennsylvania-oriented English-speaking "Minority" apart.

Denominational Activities

Publishing

The new Evangelical Publishing House established in 1816 was an immediate success. The first denominational hymnal, *Das Geistliche Saitenspiel* (1816), and the second edition of the *Discipline* (1817) sold briskly. Unfortunately, these early successes led the publishers to print an expensive German New Testament with marginal references in 1819, just when the post-War of 1812 recession and a flood of cheap imported Bibles from Germany were cutting into their market. They were unable to recover their costs, and the 1820 Annual Conference ordered the printing equipment sold. George Miller, an employee at the printing house, leased the equipment and served as unofficial church printer until 1836. Then, inspired by the success of the Methodist *Christian Advocate* (1826) and the United Brethren *Religious Telescope* (1834), the Evangelicals began their own church paper, *Der Christliche Botschafter*, and started a new Publishing House to print it. The *Botschafter* was the first German religious paper in the world.[1] Its twin goals were the defense of the fundamental truths of the Bible and the preservation of the German language. Adam Ettinger edited it from the first issue (January 1836) until the 1836 General Conference elected W. W. Orwig editor. At first a monthly selling for 75 cents a year (in advance), it became a semi-monthly in 1839 (subscription $1.00) and a weekly in 1861. Circulation rose from 700 (1836) to 3000 in 1845, 5500 in 1854, 11,000 in 1862, and 20,000 in 1875.[2]

Meanwhile, the 1843 General Conference authorized the publication of an English-language church paper as soon as 800 subscribers could be secured, and this condition was finally met in 1848. *The Evangelical Messenger* began publication as a semi-monthly of four large pages (subscription $1.00/year in advance) under *Botschafter* editor Nicholas Gehr. Circulation rose to 2350 in 1854, 6625 in 1863, 9620 in 1874, and 12,000 in 1889.[3]

The Evangelical Publishing House was always a profitable business, paying annual dividends to the Annual Conferences for support of needy ministers. It moved with the church headquarters to larger, more modern facilities in Cleveland in 1854 and came under the supervision of a Board of Publication in 1859. Each succeeding decade brought greater production and sales.[4]

Church Homes

The informal *Briefschaftsteuer* (collection to aid needy Evangelicals) of the early years was replaced by the Charitable Society, incorporated in 1835 to allow acceptance of bequests, as well as donations, for the support of retired ministers and ministers' widows and orphans.[5] During the 1850s, however, rising prosperity made many Evangelicals sensitive to the needs of others outside the church, particularly orphans. Conservatives argued that the care of orphans was too costly for the church, whose job was evangelism, and should be left to the government, but the cries of children orphaned by the Civil War could not be ignored, and the 1863 General Conference, while not establishing an orphanage, recommended that Annual Conferences start homes for orphans and, if possible, widows. A call by the Ohio Conference in the *Christliche Botschafter* for 100 acres of land on which to found an orphanage was answered, and the Ebenezer Orphan Home opened in 1866 near Tifflin OH with eight children. Moved to larger quarters at Flat Rock OH, it was accepted by the 1867 General Conference as a charitable work of the denomination.[6]

The Ebenezer Home was never expanded to provide for widows. Yet, there were those who believed that aged saints deserved better than the county poor house. Sallie Mack of the Dauphin Street Church in Philadelphia worked in support of this cause, and on April 19, 1888, forty women from Evangelical churches in that city organized the German Home Society. The first Evangelical home for the aged opened on June 6, 1888, in a rented house in Philadelphia. Within months the Home was able to move to larger, more rural quarters and in 1893 added an adjoining residence for men.[7]

Missions and Church Extension

The early Evangelical Association did not *have* a missionary society; it *was* "in fact, nothing else but a missionary society, and all its ministers were missionaries."[8] Early conferences sent out up to one-third of their members to form new circuits in new counties and states, and as Evangelicals moved west, circuit-riding preachers followed. Sometimes, laypeople formed classes and asked the nearest Annual Conference for a preacher. Sometimes, preachers tracked down Evangelicals who had moved out of the church's territory. Sometimes, preachers rode from cabin to cabin making appointments to preach on their next time around the circuit, and the people called their neighbors together for this opportunity to hear a preacher. Evangelical preachers even turned frontier funerals, which they were asked to conduct in the absence of other clergy, into evangelistic services.[9]

Still, there was no organized collection of funds for missions, and missionary sermons were unknown. Then, Bishop Seybert acquired several volumes of a Swiss missionary magazine (*Basler Missions Magazin*) with some books he purchased and passed them along to the editor of the *Botschafter*, W.W. Orwig. Soon, missionary editorials began to appear in the church paper, and under Orwig's leadership the 1838 Eastern Conference organized the German Missionary Society of North America. The next year, the General Conference ratified a constitution for the Missionary Society of the Evangelical Association of North America, set dues at $2.00, and elected Bishop Seybert president.[10] Four missionaries were sent out immediately, two to Evangelicals settled in Ontario, one to western New York state, and one to German immigrants in New York City. When, a year later, two of these fields were already strong enough to form circuits, new mission fields were opened in Baltimore and the Milwaukee frontier. Spurred by missionary reports and pleas in the *Botschafter*, missionary auxiliaries formed, including the first (albeit short-lived) Woman's Missionary Society (Nov. 11, 1839) at the church of Missionary Society President Jacob Vogelbach in Philadelphia.[11]

All early mission work was conducted in German, so it was only natural that the first overseas mission should be to Germany. The revolutions that rocked Europe in 1848 and the pleas of an Evangelical layman who had returned to the Fatherland in 1845 to preach to his countrymen prompted the 1850 East Pennsylvania Conference to propose to the other Annual Conferences that a German Mission Board, with one delegate from each conference plus the Bishops, be formed to honor the fiftieth anniversary of the denomination. All the conferences appointed delegates at their 1850 sessions, and the Board immediately sent two ministers (John Link and John Marquardt) to Germany. Only Link was able to go, but he was joined a year later by John Nikolai. The mission prospered despite opposition in Germany from the state churches and at home from Evangelicals opposed to sending missionaries to a "Christian" nation. A church was built at Plochingen in 1859, a church paper (*Der Evangelische Botschafter*) started in 1863, Germany Conference organized in 1865, missions sent out to Switzerland and Alsace (France) in 1865 and 1868, a printing press set up in 1872, the church's first theological seminary founded in 1877, and the first

Evangelical Deaconess Society established in 1886.[12]

Still, many Evangelicals pressed for a mission to heathen peoples, while others feared the cost of such a venture. The first meeting of the Board of Missions (organized in 1860) considered a mission to the newly explored lands of central Africa. The next meeting decided on India, but the Civil War took its toll on both funds and enthusiasm, and in 1863 the Board sent three ministers to California and Oregon rather than overseas.[13] Missions supporters continued to collect funds, however, and $25,650 was available when the Board (1874) and the General Conference (1875) approved a mission to Japan. On October 18, 1876, Dr. and Mrs. Frederick Krecker from Lebanon PA, a Pennsylvania teacher named Rachel Hudson, and Rev. Adolph Halmhuber from Germany set sail for Tokyo and Osaka. Differences over the conduct of this mission would lead directly to the division of the Association in 1891–1894, and the missionaries were plagued with misfortune.[14] Yet, the Japan mission survived, and the enthusiasm it generated in the denomination also led directly to the formation of Woman's Missionary Societies as auxiliaries of the denominational Missionary Society. The first of these auxiliaries formed on October 27, 1880, at Lindsay OH and South Chicago IL. Soon, the church papers were full of both Japan and the women's initiatives.[15]

Meanwhile, church planting in the United States continued as well. The Board of Missions sent approved home missions to California and Oregon in 1864, Texas in 1879, and Colorado in 1882.[16] The East Pennsylvania Conference sent missionary pastors to Evangelicals who had moved to Florida, and by 1887 small congregations had grown up in Orlando, Bronson, and Fairmount.[17] Within established conferences the earlier custom of authorizing people to travel from church to church soliciting funds for new mission congregations gave way to more concrete aid from conference church building associations. In order to build up funds for church planting the East Pennsylvania Conference resolved in 1888 that one-half of all money obtained by authorized collectors outside of their own congregations should go to the receiving church as a gift and one-half as a loan from the Church Extension Society, repayable within 15 years for use in building other churches.[18] The Illinois Conference established a Church Extension Society in 1893 to aid congregations deprived of their buildings by the 1891–94 division of the Association in erecting new churches.[19]

Urban Church Planting

John Dreisbach had preached in Philadelphia as early as 1815, but organized urban church planting dates from 1833, when Jacob Schnerr, pastor of the church in Lebanon PA, was sent to organize a church in Philadelphia. This became the Association's first "station" (non-circuit appointment) in 1835. From beginnings in a school house the society grew to a membership of 72 by the end of 1835 and 124 a year later. It began one of the denomination's first Sunday Schools in 1836, dedicated a two-story building on October 1, 1837, and organized the first Evangelical women's missionary society in 1838. Soon, Emmanuel Evangelical established missions of its own in German neighborhoods throughout the city: South Philadelphia (1850), which started a mission in Camden NJ in 1855; Dauphin Street (1857); and North Philadelphia (1858).[20]

Meanwhile, the newly formed Missionary Society sent one of its first four missionaries to New York City in 1839. Progress was slow for several years, but in 1841 a church building was erected with the assistance of other Evangelical congregations. From here missionaries went out to Newark in 1857 and Jersey City in 1867.[21]

Central Pennsylvania Conference sent Jacob Boas to Baltimore in 1841. Discontent in the large United Brethren church there brought the Evangelicals many members, 215 by the end of the first year. Having outgrown its first building, the new congregation immediately began work on the largest and most expensive church in the denomination. Evangelical preaching began in Pittsburgh in 1843, and Evangelical churches grew with newer cities like Cleveland, Chicago, Buffalo, and Indianapolis.[22]

A generation later, Civil War patriotism inspired Central Pennsylvania Conference to start a mission in the nation's capital (1864; first building 1867).[23] The War also showed the Association's leadership the vital importance of cities as the hubs of the new transportation and communication networks binding the country. Influence, they realized, always "flows from city to country, not the other way." The Association, they believed, lacked national influence because it had always avoided cities like the plague, but it could be successful in the cities if it tried.[24] Yet, most Evangelicals feared the cities, teaming with poverty-stricken aliens and controlled by the hated liquor industry, as the "chief perils of the Republic." Though the churches of the German-language Atlantic Conference prospered for half a century by following the movement of

German neighborhoods through the great eastern cities, the Association never caught the vision of its leaders.[25]

Higher Education

The nineteenth century was the age of the denominational college in America. Once the Evangelical Association had a church paper and publishing house (1836), progressives began to campaign for a church college. Evangelicals from both Mennonite and Lutheran/Reformed backgrounds feared that an educated ministry would be proud and lacking in spirituality, and they opposed the move. The 1843 General Conference even amended the *Discipline* to prohibit theological schools ("preacher factories") but did appoint a committee to prepare a course of study for junior preachers and candidates for the ministry. The first reading list included German translations of standard Methodist works by Wesley, Watson, and Fletcher; a German grammar; an introduction to the Bible; books on world, Bible, and church history; the works of Josephus; the *Discipline*; and the Bible. The first examinations were given three years later. A proposal by John Dreisbach to the 1847 General Conference for a college of general sciences was first given to the entire church membership for a vote and then dropped due to strenuous opposition from this minority.[26]

Annual Conferences, meanwhile, took educational matters into their own hands. Pittsburgh Conference established Albright Seminary at Berlin, Somerset County PA, in 1852, then closed it in 1855 to join with Ohio Conference in support of Greensburg (OH) Seminary, which was in turn forced to close in 1865, despite the heroic efforts of Bishop Long to see it through the turmoil of the Civil War. Central Pennsylvania and East Pennsylvania Conferences opened Union Seminary at New Berlin PA in January 1856. This school, though closed from 1863 to 1865, did survive the War and was incorporated as Central Pennsylvania College in 1887 before merging with Albright College in Myerstown PA in 1902. Illinois Conference, with Wisconsin, Indiana, and Iowa Conferences, accepted an offer of land to establish a school at Plainfield IL in 1862. Plainfield College became Northwestern College in 1864 and moved to Naperville IL in 1870.[27]

Still, the lack of *theological* education was keenly felt by many Evangelical preachers. Ohio Conference began annual District Meetings in 1857 to provide a forum for ministers to discuss theological issues. The 1859 General Conference ordered a revision and expansion of the course of study for ministerial candidates. However, it was concern for missions that finally persuaded the 1867 General Conference to lift the ban on theological schools. At home, the simple Evangelical testimony was not effective with the humanistic, actively atheistic Germans now landing on American shores. Abroad, missionary candidates had to be qualified as never before. Several western conferences joined to form the Union Biblical Institute at Naperville in 1873. Here, two- and three-year courses in biblical and theological subjects were available for ministerial students.[28] Germany and Switzerland Conferences established the *Predigerseminar* at Reutigen in 1877.[29] In addition, the course of study was expanded to four years with written examinations administered each year before Annual Conference sessions. Required books ranged from Methodist theologies of Foster, Wakefield, Pope, and Peck to apologetics, political science, physical science, homiletics, history, and philosophy.

In the 1880s East Pennsylvania Conference founded its own college, Schuylkill Seminary (1881), at Reading, and Oregon Conference established Lafayette Seminary (1889). Schuylkill Seminary moved to land near Fredericksburg PA donated by Col. John Lick in 1886, but like all the Evangelical colleges it struggled for existence in the face of inadequate financial support, denominational indifference, low enrollment, and frequent staff turnover.[30]

Ecumenical Relations

The Evangelical Association was always aware of its close relationship to other Methodist churches. The very first General Conference (1816) was called primarily to consider a proposal for merger with the Church of the United Brethren in Christ (the other "German Methodist" church) developed by UB Bishop Newcomer and EA Presiding Elder Dreisbach in the years since an earlier joint conference in 1813. The merger attempt failed amid disagreement over the itinerant system and the authority of the church *Discipline*, but cooperation, if not actual union, with other Methodist bodies continued.[31] The 1818 Annual Conference ordered Evangelical preachers not to take members away from Methodist churches.[32] The second Evangelical church building was built jointly with the Methodists in Shrewsbury PA.[33] The 1843 General Conference responded positively to a proposal from the 1840 Methodist Episcopal General Conference for joint work among German Americans, a joint German hymnal, joint publication of Wesley's works, and a public recognition of friendship.[34] The United Brethren, Wesleyan Methodist Connection, Evangelical Association, and Free Presbyterian Church all agreed in 1855 to co-operate in selling each other's books and Sunday School papers, supplying and exchanging pulpits, and building union churches.[35]

William Nast, who had begun German-language preaching in the Methodist Episcopal Church, addressed the 1859 Evangelical General Conference and came to the 1867 Conference with a plan of union that would transfer all German Methodist churches to Evangelical conferences and all English Evangelical churches to Methodist conferences within one denomination. Supporters of the plan, including Bishop Dubs, saw the promise of participation in established colleges and missions, while opponents, like *Evangelical Messenger* Editor Clewell (who later joined the Methodist Episcopal Church), feared loss of identity. General Conference compromised with a resolution stressing "unity of spirit," but merger advocates remained active until the next General Conference, fearing defection by opponents of merger, finally rejected the proposal.[36] From that time, however, the Methodist Episcopal and Evangelical General Conferences regularly exchanged delegates. The Association was invited in 1879 to a proposed Ecumenical Methodist Conference in London, though by the time the Conference was actually held in 1891 the choice of delegates had become a battleground in the civil war within the Association, and no delegates were sent.[37]

Delegates were also exchanged between Evangelical and United Brethren General Conferences from 1877–1879. The division of the Church of the United Brethren in Christ in 1889 aroused great interest in its sister denomination also wracked with strife. The Evangelical "Minority" felt a great affinity for the United Brethren Majority (New Constitution) and compared the "dignified, Christian, gentlemanly" treatment of the Old Constitution Minority with the harsh treatment accorded them by the Evangelical "Majority."[38]

Church Life

Language

Albright inspired his followers with his vision for bringing the Gospel to the "poor, neglected" Germans in America. Twenty years after his death, however, many of these Germans' children were speaking English. Evangelical preachers began to preach in English, particularly in Maryland, Virginia, and central Pennsylvania, and men who could not speak German were even accepted as ministers. This was too much for conservatives, who feared "that the English language might prevail" in the church. The 1830 General Conference voted to accept no more English preachers, and present itinerants were ordered to "in general confine their labors to the German portion of the population." John Hamilton, the leader of the English-speaking ministers, did not succeed in leading them into a separate "Old Albright Church," but by 1831 most of them had left the church, and the English work was soon extinct.[39]

Some Evangelicals felt no loss. Seybert wrote in connection with his drive to establish German Sunday Schools that:

> The English speaking people were already amply provided for in this particular, by other churches. The Germans are in special need. Our church should work among them, and for their benefit. If the Evangelical Association does not help the Germans in the United States, nobody else will.[40]

Other leaders, however, soon came to regret this impediment to growth, not only on the frontier, but also among their own children. After the Methodists began German preaching in 1838, the 1843 General Conference of the Association voted to allow English preaching, separate English conferences, an English church paper, and an enlarged English hymnal, even while it reaffirmed that "the Evangelical Association was called of God to take care of the Germans of this country."[41]

Over the next generation, English became the principal language in many eastern congregations; the English service added to the afternoon or evening schedule became the main Sunday morning service. On the local level, the transition, though not always smooth, was accomplished without major disruption. On the denominational level, the language question pitted German-born immigrants against Americans of German ancestry and divided the church.[42] German Evangelicals began to fear the "inevitable and natural tendency" of English to supplant their native tongue and demanded separate German Annual Conferences. Iowa, Atlantic, and Erie Conferences were formed for them in 1875.[43] At the same time, English-speaking Evangelicals feared the "hostile army" of atheists, communists, criminals, and drunkards invading American shores from Europe.[44]

Throughout the nineteenth century the Evangelical Association was primarily a German-speaking church in an English-speaking land. Even in the 1890s, about two-thirds of the membership spoke German in preference to English.[45]

The Pastorate

Evangelical Congregational pastors are still formally called "itinerant" (traveling), but in the early years of the church, itinerant preachers were truly on the move. One experienced preacher and one beginner would be assigned to a circuit consisting of dozens of preaching places scattered over several counties, or even an entire state. When preachers outnumbered circuits, pairs were sent out to start new circuits. Together, these preachers rode by day, reading or praying, over rough roads or trails and preached almost every evening for less-than-subsistence wages. Naturally, few men lasted long enough in the itinerancy to gain much experience, and this was "doubtless one of the main causes why the Society for so many years made such slow progress."[46] Some of these early preachers worked themselves into an early grave, some "located" (took other jobs to support their families) either temporarily or permanently, some left the denomination for another with more adequate salaries.[47] Those who remained in the itinerancy certainly did not lack zeal and dedication, but many admittedly were not the best preachers. Moreover, many "pastoral" duties, such as teaching, visiting, counseling, and administration, were of necessity done by lay class leaders and local (located) preachers.[48]

By the 1830s some classes had grown into congregations and were building churches. Philadelphia became the first "station" (non-circuit) appointment in 1835. Other early stations were Buffalo NY and Pottsville-Minersville PA. In 1839 there were thirty-six circuits and two stations.[49] Since 1812, Annual Conferences had been urging congregations to build parsonages. Now, some were actually built, and itinerant ministers began to take their families with them to their assigned churches. Many circuits, however, lacked parsonages even twenty years later, forcing preachers in need of lodging to rent "cold miserable huts" that no one else would take at exorbitant rates or forcing congregations to accept year after year a limited selection of preachers with homes in their vicinity.[50]

This settling down of the itinerancy was also reflected in longer terms of service. The early circuit riders had met each year at Conference to exchange circuits. Soon, preachers were allowed to retain the same circuit for two years. After the Civil War many ministers argued that this limit was too short: a new face might draw the curious into church, but a pastor had no time to disciple and confirm converts in the faith. The 1871 General Conference, therefore, following the lead of the

Methodists, raised the limit on pastorates to three years.[51]

The typical Evangelical preacher of 1820 was, like his country and his membership, young, rough, plain, emotional, and full of spirit. The typical Evangelical pastor of 1890 was older with a wife and children, some polish and pretense to education, and a certain community status. Housing was still a problem in some places, however, and salaries had not risen as fast or as far as expectations of what a pastor should be and do.[52] Commitment to the call of Christ remained essential for Evangelical pastors.

Sunday Services

Evangelical worship grew from the kernel of evangelistic preaching. Early circuit riders preached at houses, barns, schools, markets, courthouses, and even frontier funerals to anyone who would listen. Converts banded together into classes, which elected leaders and met as often as they could, but the visits of the itinerant preachers (maybe one weekday in two months) were always special events. Joyfully, Evangelicals would gather, sometimes behind locked doors. Hated by family and neighbors, attacked by respectable church people and drunken rowdies alike, they grew close, and their joy in the Lord and in each other found expression in raucous chorus singing, heart-rending prayers, shouting, and jumping. Sermons were simple, blunt, and emotional. The best preachers preached until the unsaved begged for God's mercy and the saved "got happy." Lay exhorters followed ninety-minute sermons with stirring calls for repentance, and then the people lifted up their voices in prayer and song. Sinners (including some of those sent to "rescue" family or friends from the *Straweler* ["dancer"] fanatics and some of those hired to break up the meeting) felt the sword of the Lord and fell to the ground as if struck dead screaming for mercy, only to leap up shouting and praising God.[53]

Of course, not every service reached these emotional heights. The Association always had with the pious and devoted members "some very troublesome, selfish, proud, and disobedient ones," and the sermons, while strong on passion, were often weak on substance. Furthermore, no movement can maintain its emotional fervor forever. When opposition faded and the little Evangelical meetinghouse took its place alongside the other churches in town, when the preacher's visits settled into a predictable pattern and the benches began to fill with young people who knew no other type of worship, those electrifying words became commonplace, and the same old prayers, choruses, and testimonies of the same old people became in many places empty form themselves.

Some Evangelicals took to dozing off in their pews, which in turn increased the call by the wealthier, better-educated, city-bred sort for more reverent deportment in the House of God. *Evangelical Messenger* editorials complained of smoking (by both men and women), tobacco chewing, and laughing in churches and compared Evangelical worship services to taverns and auctions. Primitive emotionalism and spontaneity, the old "Evangelical shout," came in for criticism.[54] Bishop Orwig in the first Episcopal Address (1863) complained that:

> [T]he devotion and solemnity of the worshipers is seriously disturbed by the custom prevalent in many places, of allowing almost any one who desires to do so, to select the hymn, verse, tune and all, and thus, according to his own notion, conduct this important branch of public service... Would it not be infinitely better that the preacher himself select the hymns to be sung after the first prayer, as well as at the close of the services? and the singing of senseless or absurd choruses, to irreverent tunes, we are sorry to say, is still prevailing in many places, to an extent that seriously disturbs the solemnity of the worship.[55]

"As society advances," explained the *Evangelical Messenger*, "decorum chastens our exhibition of emotion and the cultivation of the intellect, and the refinement of taste, while they deepen our better feelings, soften their expression."[56]

Conservatives tried to stem the tide, but the fine city churches built after the Civil War soon boasted pipe organs and choirs and even allowed "mixed seating" (men and women together) and standing (rather than kneeling) for prayer (too many gowns were ruined by puddles of "tobacco juice").[57] Amid complaints from some that "stiff formality" had "eaten the life out of too many [Evangelical] churches already," emotionalism was further de-emphasized.[58] "Shouting and praising God is perfectly right and proper," wrote Rev. J.H. Keeler, "when constrained to do so by the Spirit and love of God, as is frequently the case. But to make a great ado about a little animal excitement, with very little or no love of God in the heart is abominable and ridiculous, and should not be tolerated."[59] Church headquarters began publishing orders of worship ("Sunday-School liturgies" to opponents of the faction in power).[60]

By the end of this period Evangelical worship had assumed the form it would retain through much of the twentieth century. In general, the order of service followed the pattern of Morning Prayer with Sermon inherited by the Methodists from the Church of England: invocation,

hymn(s), scripture, hymn, prayer, offering, anthem, sermon, hymn, bene-
diction, and doxology. Organs and choirs were almost universally accepted. Sermons were more likely to be twenty minutes than an hour. The
altar service was in decline; penitents raised their hand for prayers rather
than falling on their knees begging for mercy.[61] The old Evangelical
"shout" was decidedly out of fashion, and

> when a good, old brother or sister occasionally gets shouting full—I say
> occasionally, for it rarely happens—and explodes with a loud "HALLELU-
> JAH," and a solid "AMEN" tacked on to it, why, the people begin to crane
> their necks and whisper all manner of fore-bodings, for they surely can't
> conclude otherwise in their refined brains but that the old man or
> woman are getting off their base.[62]

The Association had grown up and become respectable.

Preaching

Early Evangelical preaching was unlike anything Pennsylvania
Germans had ever heard in the established churches. In content, it was
thoroughly biblical; in style, it was blunt, earnest, and animated.
Scripture verses ("prooftexts") were taken uncritically and out-of-context
to bolster the preacher's call for holiness and repentance. Earthy illustrations drawn from common life would often trigger spirited rebuttals
from the congregation. Delivered dozens of times at different stops on
the circuit, Evangelical sermons were, if not exactly polished, at least
"well-digested." Most were about two hours in length. At their best, when
a preacher "got to shouting" and Bible truth poured from his lips in a
flood, saints and sinners alike felt the mighty power of God.[63] Hear
Bishop Seybert speak in this short excerpt from a sermon on Job:

> My text is the book of Job, and from this I will preach without a
> sketch, praying that the eternal God may add His blessing, power and
> life! Much has already been spoken and written about Job, but right here
> in the first chapter I find something about him that no one has yet clear-
> ly brought out—namely that Job was, at the same time, both very rich and
> very pious! Is not that a rare case? [Pause] I guess he was entirely sanc-
> tified. Wonder whether there is another Job to be found now-a-days in
> the church? I doubt whether there is one in the Evangelical Association.
> We have people who are as pious as Job was, but they are not so rich.
> Great God, how important it is that our rich professors of religion should
> be entirely redeemed and purified from all vanity, pride, avarice, and
> worldly-mindedness! O that the generation of Jobs might
> increase!…[Satan spotted Job on an inspection of humanity and accused

him before God.] The devil does pass up through the land and has a great deal of business...He must help the ladies before the glass to make their fool-fashions set right, and must see to it that the men chase after the world with the necessary earnestness...Especially where there are spiritual meetings, where sinners are resurrected into life eternal, and where the children of God leap for joy and praise their Redeemer, there he begins to rage like a steam boiler, and his anger is wreaked on some pious Job.

....Oh my brethren and sisters! whatever you do, press deeply into God. Watch and pray, submit yourselves wholly unto the Lord, and trust him in the greatest adversities.[64]

Not everyone could preach like Seybert, however, and many of these improvised sermons were deadly boring. With the passing years, the novelty of Evangelical preaching wore off, congregations became better-educated and less-isolated, and shrinking circuits meant less "digestion time" for each new sermon.[65] At its worst by mid-century the old style had clearly ceased to be effective:

The minister hunts for his hymn and text for fifteen minutes, prays 25, and takes up 5 more in apologizing for a "bad cold," and not having time to prepare himself, &c, &c, and after all this rigmarole, begins to talk about the "context," and in order to make it plain, reads and explains nearly the whole chapter; and in doing so, tells a great many strange and wonderful things which nearly everybody knows...just as though it had to be so. And then, after dividing the subject, starts out for a regular two hours preaching, during which time he is sure to talk about Adam and Eve, Abraham and Jacob, Noah and the flood, the Hebrew children and Daniel, faith and repentance, justification and sanctification, &c....All this done in a go-a-head, sing-song, tautologous manner.[66]

Evangelical preachers began turning to published sermon outlines.[67] They also had a new model in the shorter (30–40 minutes), better organized, and more polished sermons of Rev. Solomon Neitz, the popular Presiding Elder in the East Pennsylvania Conference whose fame as a preacher had spread far beyond his own denomination.[68] Critics accused him of unseemly levity, conformity to the styles of the world, fatal neglect of the central truths of the faith,[69] but young preachers were drawn to his style of preaching and his deeper, more critical study of a wider range of Bible texts.[70] They considered his preaching every bit as spiritual, if less overtly emotional, as the best of the circuit riders. "Man is not so much interested in how to feel happy," said one supporter, "as in how to lead a holy life. The minister is appointed to be an instructor to the people, not a magician or exorcist."[71] By the end of the period, many Evangelical preachers had adopted a more learned style that would remain popular for several generations.[72] Hear a few excerpts from a sermon by Rev. Samuel L. Wiest (1844–1924), son-in-law of Bishop Orwig, Corresponding Secretary (1880–1884) and Treasurer (1884–1888) of the denominational Missionary Society, and later Publisher of the United Evangelical Publishing House (1889–1911) on Romans 1:1–7:

> The church at Rome was a gentile church although there must have been converted Jews in the church. It is probable its beginning dates back to Pentecost...The letter was written from Corinth in the house of Gaius, who was his host. Tertius was his amenuensis. The date was about 56 A.D. Dr. Dummelow says: "It is the greatest of Paul's writing in importance, as in length, the most characteristic and comprehensive, the letter best suited to form an introduction to his teaching and an epitome of his thought." It has been called "the gospel according to Paul," "the profoundest book in existence," "the cathedral of church faith," "the chief part of the New Testament and the perfect gospel."

The evangelical message was the same, but the style of the message had changed with the rising educational and cultural levels of both preachers and hearers.

The Sacraments

Baptism

The tensions inherent in the Wesleyan understanding of baptism remained, for the most part beneath the surface, throughout the century. On the one hand, the *Discipline* emphasized baptism, infant and adult, as "not merely a token of Christian profession...but...also a sign of internal ablution, renovation and new birth." Evangelicals likened infant baptism to circumcision as a sign identifying children with, even incorporating children into, a covenant community. The 1829 Western and Eastern Conferences unanimously voted to forbid preachers from re-baptizing after conversion anyone already baptized as an infant. On the other hand, Evangelical spirituality was grounded in the conversion experience, the conscious and dramatic turning from sin to new life, often by persons baptized many years before. The 1839 General Conference forbade preachers to advocate re-baptism, but approved re-baptism of members requesting it, "who cannot otherwise satisfy their consciences."[73]

After mid-century second-generation Evangelicals, who could not testify to dramatic conversions from lives of gross sin, argued for less emphasis on conversion experiences and increased concern for the children as members of the covenant community. A proposal to the 1859 General Conference to count baptized children as members of the church was only narrowly defeated by conservatives under Bishop Seybert (dramatically converted in 1810), who feared that "such a step...would...lay the foundation for a heap of dead bones among us." Later, discussion of baptism dwindled after progressives, like *Evangelical Messenger* Editor Clewell, ran afoul of the leadership on the subject of holiness and were silenced or driven from the church.[74]

Holy Communion

The first Evangelicals held Holy Communion in very high esteem. For them, as for Wesley, it was "not merely a token of love and union...but rather...a representation of our redemption by the suffering and death of Christ; insomuch, that such as rightly, and worthily, and faithfully receive the same, partake of the body and blood of Christ by faith."[75] In the early years the Friday before each quarterly "big meeting" was a time of prayer and fasting in preparation for Communion. The Quarterly Conference examined each member on Saturday morning to determine worthiness for the Sacrament, and the Saturday afternoon sermon stressed the seriousness of Christian commitment. Sunday morning the Lord's Supper was celebrated with joy and solemnity using words taken by Wesley from the Anglican *Book of Common Prayer*. Early campmeetings also culminated in Holy Communion. Men in their Sunday clothes and women in white dresses gathered on Friday morning for this impressive farewell service.[76]

As with so many Evangelical customs, however, the special interest and solemnity attached to Holy Communion declined through the course of the century. The Lord's Supper continued to be observed four times each year but without examination or fasting. Toward the end of the period strong temperance agitation led gradually to the substitution of unfermented grape juice for sacramental wine.[77]

Music

Music has always been a vital part of Evangelical worship. By 1818 the small sect had both an official hymnal containing mostly German Lutheran chorales, *Das Geistliche Saitenspiel* (The Spiritual Lyre; 1816; 436 pp.), and a collection of Evangelical spirituals, *Die Geistliche Viole* (The Spiritual Viol; 1818; 192 hymns).

In actual practice, church hymns, like those in the *Saitenspiel* were "lined out," since few people owned hymnals. The preacher or lay precentor (*Vorsinger*) would sing hymns one line at a time with the congregation repeating as best they could follow or remember, or the preacher would read a line of text and the precentor pick a likely tune and lead the congregation in singing each phrase after it was read. Lined hymns, of course, lost much of their energy and message as worshipers mumbled misunderstood or forgotten words and stumbled through unfamiliar tunes or simply sang whatever tune each knew best. Spiritual choruses, on the other hand, though theologically lean were easily learned and emotionally charged. They could be sung by themselves, attached to almost any hymn, or even sung one line at a time between phrases of any hymn. As early Evangelicals gathered around the altar after the sermon, they bellowed their choruses with the thunder of many waters. The *Viole* grew through thirteen editions in 37 years and remained a source of inspiration for generations. The final early Evangelical songbook, *Eine Sammlung Neuer Geistlicher Lieder* (A Collection of New Spiritual Songs; 1821) compiled by Presiding Elder John Dreisbach (1789–1871) and Daniel Bertolet (1781–1867), was the first book to record the choruses Evangelicals used with hymn verses, written evidence of worship practice. In all these early books hymns of testimony and pilgrimage vastly outnumber hymns of worship and social responsibility.[78]

The first English-language hymnal, *A Collection of Hymns, Selected from Various Authors, for the Use of the Evangelical Association,* was published in 1838. Its 333 hymn texts were standard hymns by Charles Wesley (over 1/3 of the total), Isaac Watts, and other Englishmen, not translations of German hymns. Almost immediately, work began on a larger hymnal, and the *Evangelical Hymn Book* (1857) more than doubled in size to 716 hymns (still English Methodist standards). Yet, since churches did not provide hymnals for the pews and members did not buy their own, most congregations sang only a very few hymns week after week, sometimes more than once in the same service. Elisha Albright Hoffman (1839–1929), writer of over 2000 hymns, reported that by mid-century English-speaking Evangelicals knew a total of nine hymns,[79] and Bishop Bowman (1836–1923) said the church of his youth could sing but three hymns: "When I Can Read My Title Clear," "Jesus My All to Heaven is Gone," and "A Charge to Keep I Have."[80] Even chorus singing settled in many places into dull, lifeless routine. According to one Evangelical writing in 1856,

> The old tunes which have been sung fifty years ago, some of which never expressed any musical sense, are still drummed over and over. To some hymns

a genius has composed a chorus between every line, and that often a non-sensical one, which must then be repeated time and again to the disgust and pain of the well-cultivated ear.[81]

Denominational leaders tried to remedy the situation with a still-larger hymnal, *The New Evangelical Hymn-Book* (1262 hymns), in 1868. In the prosperous years after the Civil War, however, many church members took matters into their own hands, donating reed organs for their daughters and sons to play in Sunday School, and later church, and organizing "mixed" choirs.[82] Conservatives feared that choirs would kill congregational song, and General Conference amended the *Discipline* to express its disapproval of confining singing in public to choirs.[83] In fact, Evangelicals found a new voice in the Gospel Hymn movement that grew from the Sunday School songs of William Bradbury. W. W. Orwig had prepared the first Evangelical Sunday School songbook (*Evangelisches Liederbüchlein für Sontags-Schulen*) in 1840. By 1866 this book had grown from 48 to 239 pages, and between 1871 and 1892 the Evangelical Association published thirteen German and English Sunday School hymnals (totaling over 2000 pages). These books, reflecting the needs of Sunday School organists, were the first to include music as well as texts. New church hymnals (*Das Evangelisches Gesangbuch*, 1877, and the *Evangelical Hymn and Tune Book*, 1882) also contained music. Almost one-half of the hymns in this English hymnal were new to Evangelicals, and the selection, with its "careful expulsion of everything flippant or undevotional,"[84] reflected the growing sophistication of urban Evangelical worship. By 1894 organs (reed and pipe), choirs, and vocal soloists were almost universally accepted, and orchestras and men's, youth, and junior choirs were becoming more common. At the same time, nostalgia for the old choruses and the old enthusiasm was also on the rise.[85]

Church Buildings

The first Evangelical church building at church headquarters in New Berlin PA was dedicated on March 2, 1817, by the Presiding Elder, John Dreisbach. It was modeled after the Lutheran and Reformed churches the people knew, with a high pulpit, rounded in front, on one side, a center aisle, wood-stove in the middle, and no altar railing. Later, a steeple and bell were added and the log exterior covered with weatherboards and painted white. The 1817 Annual Conference was held there, and from that time Conference sessions were held in church buildings, usually the newest one available. The Association's second church was built in collaboration with the Methodists in Strassburg (now Shrewsbury), York County PA, shortly before the 1823 Annual Conference held there. The great 1824 revival in Orwigsburg, Schuylkill County PA, resulted in the third church in 1826.[86]

Church building accelerated in the 1830s. Now as a general rule, congregations established or strengthened by revival would build permanent homes. Most of these churches were larger (30'x45') and higher than the first Evangelical churches, with a lower pulpit, altar railing, and two aisles. Many of these buildings followed

Communion Cup
from the New Berlin Church

the plan advocated by Bishop Seybert: two aisles with an additional par-

Worcester Church. Built in 1845, the Worcester site in Montgomery Co. has double front doors. It served as a station on the Underground Railroad.

tition through the center to separate the men (left) from the women (right), two stoves halfway back, pulpit front and center, slightly raised, "amen corners" on either side of the pulpit, and two doors at the front of the church. However, two-story brick churches, with rooms on the ground floor for prayer meetings and, later, Sunday School classes, were also making their appearance in towns and cities. Church leaders encouraged societies to build adequate churches in convenient locations, avoiding both exaggerated economy and prideful indulgence.[87]

After the Civil War, national prosperity encouraged a new round of church building. Even one-room country churches acquired carpet (at least in the chancel) or matting in the aisles, sofas in the pulpit alcove, and frescoed walls or paneling. Many buildings, including the one that replaced the first church at New Berlin in 1874, had smaller rooms that could be opened into the auditorium. Through the 1880s new churches became ever more elaborate. City, and some village, churches boasted thick carpet, damask pew cushions, pipe organs, walnut pulpit furniture, and stained glass windows. Church leaders thought wealthy Evangelicals living in fine homes should be building the finest possible churches.[88]

Class Meeting

Like the Methodist Episcopal Church the Evangelical Association long retained the form of Wesley's class meeting, but by mid-century little of its power. By 1889 only memories remained of the genuine, old Evangelical Class Meeting, that "foretaste of heaven for the true people of God," where every member had to give adequate testimony of personal holiness in response to the Leader's questioning.[89] Apparently, such meetings were not widespread after the first generation of Evangelicals. Their children and grandchildren, who had grown up in the church and could not give account of dramatic conversion experiences, had less taste for testimony and were less willing to subject themselves to cross-examination. No longer persecuted by established churches, they lost their holier-than-thou sectarian mentality and became more tolerant of others' failures. Church leaders looked back at the early years of slow growth and concluded that many Evangelicals expelled for minor lapses should have been won back with love and patience.[90] In the larger churches (with resident pastors) classes became too big to be supervised as before, while the need for a Class Leader to substitute for the itinerant preacher when he was away riding his circuit was eliminated.[91] Class Leaders in most places did little more than lead weekly Prayer

Meeting with assistance from Exhorters, whose early function had been to close the preachers' sermons with pleas for repentance.[92]

The 1847 General Conference found it necessary to require every class leader to meet the class at least once every four weeks.[93] It was estimated in 1853 that only one in twenty classes actually met this requirement,[94] but the requirement remained in the Discipline, and the need remained for small mutual-support groups in the church. Some Evangelical leaders in the 1890s saw Christian Endeavor as filling the vacuum created by the decline of the Class Meeting.[95]

Prayer Meeting

In the early years classes met every week under their elected Class Leaders, not only for testimony meetings, but also for prayer meetings. Surely, these first prayer meetings were times of joy and spiritual renewal, but as with class meetings decline set in when spontaneity degenerated into "stereotyped formalism." By 1849 critics were calling them "cold as ice and tedious as winter."[96]

> The one that opens the meeting, takes up to 10 or 15 minutes to hunt a chapter and a hymn, whilst he should be opening the meeting, and then, perhaps a long chapter is read, followed by a long, lifeless exhortation, and then a prayer of from 5 to 10 minutes, and that cold and powerless…Someone commences to pray, mentioning every thing he can think of…and so on till another 5 or 10 minutes are taken up, and then followed by a long lifeless hymn. At this rate it is a wonder to me, if some of the congregation are not almost or quite asleep by this time…A few more such prayers (for it would be useless to expect any thing lively then) and the meeting will close.[97]

Class leaders complained as the century wore on that many brothers and sisters were not willing to pray aloud, while members complained about "Brother Forty-Years Ago," whose prayer had not varied one week in at least that long.[98] By 1869 some congregations had less than half of their members in prayer meeting; twenty years later it was said that nearly one-half of the denomination's members never attended and hardly more than 20% attended regularly.[99] Yet, the Association remained committed to Prayer Meeting. Bishop Dubs called it "an indispensable necessity," despite slow hymns, over-long, ill-prepared exhortations, drawn-out meetings, and the old routine "litanies" repeated week after week by the same few pray-ers. His vision of small home Bible study classes attractive even to little children remains viable today.[100]

Church Year

Most of the early Evangelicals acquired a rudimentary knowledge of the Church Year in the Lutheran and Reformed homes of their youth. They continued to observe Easter, Christmas, New Year's Day, and even Advent, Ascension Day, and Pentecost, though as times of solemn worship rather than wild celebrations like their neighbors. (The Missionary Society of the Evangelical Association, for example, was born on Christmas Day 1838 during a protracted meeting.)[101] By mid-century the Evangelical church year was divided into two seasons: Campmeeting in the summer and Protracted (Revival) Meeting in the winter, but after the Civil War gift- and candy-covered Christmas trees, Christmas programs, and even Santa Claus in Sunday School (and later in church) reintroduced celebration of Christian holy days in a new form.[102] Church leaders and the large city churches took the lead in special observances of Holy Week, Good Friday, Easter, and Harvest Home, although not everyone was comfortable with these "Catholic" innovations.[103] In the 1880s Children's Day was imported from the Methodist Church and required of all churches by the 1883 General Conference. This was a holiday made to capture the Victorian heart, and soon elaborate programs of recitations and music were being staged amid flowers and singing birds. The Missionary Society, which benefited from the Children's Day offering, gave the new holiday its full support, and by the end of the century it had joined Christmas, Campmeeting, and Revival at the center of the Evangelical year.[104]

Campmeetings

The first campmeetings erupted on the Kentucky frontier in 1800, when Presbyterian sacramental meetings attracted such crowds and generated such enthusiasm that tents were pitched for an extended series of meetings. The Methodists quickly spread the practice; by 1808 they were holding 400–500 campmeetings a year, including several in southeastern Pennsylvania that attracted the Albright People.[105] The 1810 (third) Annual Conference resolved to hold two Evangelical campmeetings, the first German campmeetings in America, one on May 30 on land of Michael Maize near New Berlin PA and one in October on George Miller's farm in Berks County PA. In 1814, when Dreisbach was elected first Presiding Elder, the organization of campmeetings was listed among his duties, and the 1000-member denomination held four that year, six the next.[106] These early meetings, being a novelty, attracted hundreds and thousands of the curious, many of whom screamed for mercy as the preachers described the torments of hell and the faithful sang and danced.[107]

Campmeetings continued to arouse both enthusiasm and opposition in the 1820s, but over time they became established as a summer institution. Year after year Evangelicals would pack their white linen tents and travel to the hallowed groves. Wooden tabernacles were built, and then boarding halls to free the sisters from the hours of cooking the bountiful feasts typical of the early years.[108] The first campmeetings lasted from Wednesday evening to Monday morning with preaching at 10:00, 2:00, and dusk every day.[109] Soon, Monday-Friday campmeetings became standard, because many Evangelicals objected to travel on the Sabbath and congregations came to expect their preachers to be home every Sunday. By the 1850s campmeetings had entered a period of "decadence." Hucksters of peanuts, melons, sweets, drinks, and tobacco, as well as local horse-drawn cab companies, paid bonuses for permission to cash in on the traffic, and courting and gossip flourished.[110] Critics complained that church buildings had rendered campmeetings obsolete, that congregations suffered from the eight-week absence of preachers touring the campmeetings in their district, and that the abundance of good campmeeting preaching made congregations dissatisfied with their own pastors.[111]

Campmeeting revival was sparked by the first (Vineland NJ, 1867) and second (Manheim PA, 1868) National Campmeetings for the Promotion of Holiness organized by Methodist evangelist John Inskip. The Manheim campmeeting attracted thousands of Evangelicals and had an immediate and profound effect on both the content and the form of the Evangelical campmeeting. Conversion and sanctification were vigorously preached, and specialized Prayer and Praise meetings, leaders' meetings, preachers' meetings, missions meetings, and children's meetings were added to preaching services in an new ten-day (two weekend) schedule packed full from 5:00 AM to 10 PM.[112] A dozen campmeetings were held in the East Pennsylvania Conference, and Sunday services attracted thousands (6000 at Seven Points Campmeeting near Herndon PA in 1871; 12,000 at Manheim (PA) Campmeeting in 1877), despite admission fees at some places. Concession stands were closed on Sundays and resisting hucksters arrested.[113] As Jacob Hartzler noted in 1876:

> We may never again see such scenes of violent physical demonstrations and intense overwhelming excitements of spiritual exercises as our

fathers witnessed. In our settled and evangelized sections of country [campmeetings] can no longer serve the purpose of an aggressive pioneer agency. The pioneer work is done...But the spiritual labors and beneficial results of properly conducted modern camp-meetings are as effective and abundant now as ever before. It is true there is a great deal of frivolity, fashionable display, pleasure-seeking and self-indulgence at many of our camp-meetings. It is likewise true that many of our people fail to enter into the spirit and work of the occasion with the ardor and zeal necessary to success. But the same was true of the early camp-meetings. What is now excess of vanity and folly was then excess of coarse, bold, and often brutal opposition to the work of the Lord.[114]

In the 1880s cottages began to replace tents in the campmeetings, beginning at Perkasie Park near Philadelphia. Conservative critics from the Midwest complained that the summer-resort "Delilah" would shear the rude camp- meeting "Samson" of his strength. The expenses of individuals in buying a lot, building a cottage, and furnishing it and of the new campmeeting associations in buying, clearing, and laying out a camp ground, furnishing water works and other necessaries, and building tabernacles, auditoriums, pavilions, hotels, and "other paraphernalia," wrote *Evangelical Messenger* Editor Spreng in 1890, were beyond the reach of the poor and so threatened to make the Evangelical campmeeting a "high-toned, aristocratic affair." "Camp-grounds were battle-fields once; now they are parade-grounds—occasions to display to a gawking world, the 'talent' of the church."[115] Yet, at scores of rural campmeetings, East and West, the simple tent, the hearty shout of praise, the forceful preaching, and the old farewell circle continued to define campmeeting for thousands of Evangelicals.[116] Even at Perkasie Park "though the general home-life, is promoted, as...not...seen elsewhere at an Evangelical Camp-meeting," there was no evidence that it had "'become a high-toned, aristocratic affair,' and judging from the deeply spiritual services and old-fashioned manifestations of life and fervor" the Presiding Elder in charge saw "no immediate danger in that direction."[117] As the century drew to a close, the Evangelical campmeeting was still very much alive and well. In 1893 fifteen campmeetings attracting well over 100,000 people were held by the East Pennsylvania Conference alone.

Revivals

From the beginning Evangelical members and ministers gathered for occasional "big meetings." Often held in conjunction with watch night services, these meetings lasted from Saturday afternoon to Sunday evening and included Holy Communion. As the church spread out and Annual Conference sessions became more regular these general meetings were confined to individual circuits and with a business meeting added after the first worship service became Quarterly Conferences under the direction of Presiding Elders.[118]

Around 1836 several big meetings in the West were prolonged ("protracted") for those still struggling through to conversion at the end of the scheduled services. Circuits had become small enough and ministers numerous enough to permit concentration of effort in one place, and the new church paper, *Der Christliche Botschafter*, was quick to publicize the successes of these meetings. Soon, revival season (November-May) had joined Campmeeting season in the Evangelical church year.[119] *Evangelical Messenger* Editor Clewell wrote in 1862 that:

> Protracted meetings have become an institution among us. No surer does Winter come, than protracted meetings are expected to follow as certainly as Thanksgiving dinners, Christmas festivities, and sleigh rides. They are part and parcel, almost, of our social Christian life of that season, and many congregations would think it a serious omission of duty were their ministers not to hold one or more of them.[120]

As the novelty of this new method wore off, however, the fervor became more forced, and many members came to rely on them for their annual dose of spiritual enthusiasm, content the rest of the year with "spiritual drought."[121] Still, the pattern, once set, proved both durable and useful. Revival meetings remained an Evangelical institution.

Sunday School

Robert Raikes is usually credited with the founding of the first Sunday School in Gloucester, England, in 1780. Within five years the idea had spread to America, and the first International Sunday School Association was organized in Philadelphia in 1791, but the movement did not gain momentum until after the War of 1812. The American Sunday-School Union, reorganized in 1824, aggressively promoted the movement and published vast quantities of literature for Sunday School libraries (over 200 books by 1830). Rev. Jacob Schnerr (1806–1849), the young Evangelical pastor at Lebanon PA, saw the potential of this new idea and helped organize the first Sunday School for Evangelical children in 1832. Sunday School enthusiasts at the 1835 General Conference won agreement of conservatives to a resolution calling on all Evangelical congregations to form German Sabbath Schools, and Schools were organized immediately at the New Berlin PA headquarters church and at Schnerr's new location, Philadelphia. Quickly, Rev. Henry Bucks spread the movement through Ohio, and Rev. Joseph Harlacher carried it to the New York churches. By 1838 Sunday Schools had even reached the frontier at Des Plaines IL.[122] The new church paper, *Der Christliche Botschafter*, promoted the movement, and successive General Conferences lent their support, but for a time many Evangelicals were suspicious of the new Schools and many others were indifferent. Few books (and even fewer good books) were available in church libraries, facilities were often poor, teachers were often ignorant and ill-prepared, and instruction often consisted of nothing more than rote memorization of the catechism or the Bible.[123]

In 1856, however, the Evangelical Association began publishing a children's Sunday School magazine, *Der Christliche Kinderfreund* (The Christian Children's Friend). Three years later, the Sunday-School and Tract Union of the Evangelical Association began operation and published over one million pages of tracts and three million pages of Sunday School literature in its first year. *The Sunday-School Messenger* containing English-language lessons began in 1864. Teachers got additional help when *The Living Epistle*, originally the denomination's holiness magazine, was divided in 1873 into equal sections on holiness, The Family Circle, and Sunday School lesson notes, explanations, and illustrations. At about the same time, the Board of Publication adopted the International Sunday School Lesson plan, approved by the International Sunday School Convention of 1872, for all Evangelical lesson materials.[124] At district Sunday School institutes teachers were regularly inspired to both prepare their lessons and take an active interest in the lives of their scholars. New church buildings, particularly in cities, contained bright Sunday School rooms with carpet, pictures, child-size furniture, and organs, and Sunday Schools finally began offering classes for adults, as well as children.[125] The 1875 General Conference alone started three new publications (*The Evangelical Sunday-School Teacher* for teachers, *My Lesson* for little children, and *The Evangelical Lesson Leaf* for adults) and a new weekly edition, in addition to the monthly and semi-monthly editions, of *The Sunday-School Messenger*.[126]

By the 1890s there were still small rural churches with floundering, ill-equipped Schools for children only. Most Evangelical Sunday Schools, however, had reached a form recognizable even a century later: classes with materials suitable for all ages, often taught in rooms branching off from a large room used for opening devotions. The Sunday School had become an essential part of the Evangelical church, replacing circuit riders, campmeetings, and revival services as the main "recruiting office" of the church. In fact, after 1875 Evangelical Sunday Schools had more members than the Evangelical church and, indeed, had taken over the church's social and spiritual functions for many Evangelicals.[127]

School of Methods

Concern for Sunday School teaching also spawned the School of Methods program, which in turn gave rise to Evangelical church camping programs. The 1879 and 1883 General Conferences had given their approval to normal (teacher training) classes organized by pastors and had ordered the preparation of a course of study for prospective Sunday School teachers. Ten volumes, largely by P.N. Raidabaugh, were published in 1884–1885 covering teaching methods, church history, and the geography, chronology, archaeology, history, theology, and science of the Bible.[128] In 1888 three pastors from the East Pennsylvania Conference organized an Evangelical Normal Assembly for teacher training to be held each year before campmeeting at Perkasie Park, near Quakertown PA. The first class (four men, including three ministers, and three women), graduated one year later. Soon, these assemblies at Perkasie, as well as Lynwood Park on Lake Erie in Ohio, focused on the religious education and inspiration of young people.[129] The first Bible Conference, held at Perkasie Park July 17–20, 1893, was an expansion of Normal Assembly training.[130]

Women in the Church

Though they did not ride the circuits, women played a prominent role in the early years of the Evangelical Association. Wives, as well as husbands, provided food and shelter for the early preachers; daughters, as well as sons, were driven from home by unbelieving parents or led their families to the Lord. When congregations formed, women, as well as men, were expected to pray at prayer meetings, revivals, and Sunday services. "If it is the duty of females to pray to God for the pardon of their sins publicly in the Church," wrote an Evangelical preacher in 1852, "it is also their duty to pray in public afterward."[131] Rev. Jacob Vogelbach, who had been the secretary of the very first missionary society, took the lead in organizing the first Woman's Missionary Society with over sixty members in Philadelphia on November 11, 1839, just months after the denominational Missionary Society was organized. This society disappeared after Vogelbach left the denomination,[132] but women found a permanent place in the Sunday School as teachers, organists, and superintendents.

Throughout the century old-timers fought the confinement of women to the Victorian gilded pedestal.

> Look at those starched up, aristocratic churches in which females are not allowed to open their lips in prayer, or testimony, but sit in silence! What the result? cold formality, spiritual starvation, spiritual death! And is it not manifestly evident that in those worshiping assemblies where the sisters are not only allowed to speak for God, but requested to take part in religious exercises, that a more lively, healthful, spiritual interest is enkindled?...This closing the lips of Christian women in the Church of God is a great evil.[133]

In the next generation, progressive church leaders supported the women's rights movement and urged women to use their talents for the church.

> To hold them under restraint and disability by official restrictions, as if they were unworthy of confidence, or incapable of wise and prudent action [wrote *Evangelical Messenger* editor H.B. Hartzler] is neither complimentary to them, nor to their brothers, nor can it be promotive of the great interests that demand all the strength of woman's brain and heart, as well as man's. The work is too great and the urgency of perishing souls too awful to waste time and energy in holding back those who would rush to the rescue.[134]

Evangelical Messenger Editor T. T. Clewell and Rev. D.B. Byers argued persuasively after the Civil War for the licensing of women as ministers in the Evangelical Association as was done by the Primitive Methodists and the Church of the United Brethren in Christ.[135] Though this was not permitted, women were made eligible for election as Sunday School superintendents in 1871 and as stewards in 1879. Evangelicals in Germany organized the church's first Deaconess Society in 1886 to provide women an opportunity for full-time service to the church as nurses, teachers, and pastoral assistants.[136]

All of the Association's schools and colleges were co-educational from the beginning, and female faculty and staff were essential for their operation. The Ebenezer Orphan's Home also depended on female staff. Ladies Aid Societies made essential contributions to the operation and support of local churches. Yet, it was in missions that Evangelical women found their greatest role. The first group of missionaries sent to Japan in 1875 included both women and men (Frederick and Elizabeth Krecker, Rachel Hudson, and Adolf Halmhuber), and soon women of the church were demanding a more active part in their support. The Board of Missions, controlled by Bishop Esher and the conservatives, refused the first request for approval of a Woman's Missionary Society in 1878, but a revised petition supported by the editors of the church papers was approved (provided men as well as women were eligible for membership) in 1880, and the first local societies were organized immediately. The Board approved a constitution for the new Society in 1884, and the Woman's Missionary Society of the Evangelical Association held its first convention on October 13, 1884. Beginning with the January 1, 1885, issue *The Evangelical Messenger* included regular monthly articles by the Corresponding Secretary of the Society and program suggestions for local society meetings. The next year, the WMS started its own paper, *The Missionary Messenger,* which was adopted as an official church paper in 1887. That same year, the Society appointed its first Superintendent of Mission Bands for children and assumed full support for missionaries in Washington Territory and Japan. The first Conference Branch Missionary Society was organized in Platte River Conference on March 15, 1890. By this time the number of local societies had grown from 10 (1884) to 124 (1889) with a membership of 7959.[137] Under the presidency of Mrs. H. B. Hartzler the WMS gained additional stature in the East as the only denominational organization to side with the Minority in the disputes that led to division in 1894.

By the 1890s women constituted a majority of many Evangelical congregations, taught most Evangelical Sunday School classes, and formed in many places the chief support of the Evangelical prayer meeting.[138]

Youth

The leaders of the Evangelical Association always showed special concern for the education and nurture of the children of the church and as the century advanced a growing awareness of their special needs. One of the first books printed by the church was a small catechism translated into German by John Dreisbach, himself only nineteen years old. The fourth Annual Conference (1811) instructed ministers to form catechetical classes on each circuit. Sunday Schools were provided with a junior catechism in 1839 and children's lesson literature beginning in 1856.[139] Teenagers, though, who worked like adults during the week, were expected to act like adults on Sundays. At first they did; services in the primitive church were lively, and young people were quickly put in positions of leadership after their conversion experiences.

As the century progressed, however, the church leadership on all levels aged, worship became more dignified and sermons more refined, campmeetings settled into more of a social routine, and prayer meetings fossilized.[140] At the same time, increasing wealth and urbanization were transforming American adolescence into a period of prolonged schooling and freedom from adult toil and responsibility with fewer outlets for youthful energy. When in 1880 Rev. C.F. Hansing organized the first Evangelical *Jugend-Bund* (Youth League) in Dayton OH, the idea quickly spread to other Evangelical churches in the Midwest. Here, teenagers could assist the church in visitation and evangelism while gaining experience in leading discussions and running an organization.[141]

Meanwhile, Francis Clark, responding to the same social changes, had formed the first Young People's Society of Christian Endeavor (CE) in his Congregational church in Williston ME on February 2, 1881. In CE young people met for weekly prayer meetings and monthly testimony and reconsecration meetings and set out to serve the church and the world. Clark's movement soon spread to other places and denomina-

Christian Endeavor window,
St. Luke's EC Church, Shillington, PA

tions, including the Evangelical Association.[142] Bishop Esher and his allies in the Majority party organized a denominational Young People's Alliance in January 1891,[143] but his opponents, who controlled several Annual Conferences in Pennsylvania and the Plains States, organized an Evangelical league of Christian Endeavor, the Keystone League (named for its central role in the arch of Evangelical institutions and for the Keystone State, Pennsylvania).[144] The very first General Conference of the Minority group appointed a K.L.C.E. General Managing Board on October 9, 1891, which acted immediately to organize CE societies throughout Minority Annual Conferences.[145]

Beliefs

Theology

Early Evangelicalism was less a religion of the head than a religion of the heart. The conversion experience, instantaneous and life-transforming, was central. Its emotional imprint provided assurance of salvation. Its power gave victory over sin and guaranteed a life of good works. Its joy overflowed into a lifetime of praise and evangelism. On many doctrinal issues, like baptism, the church did not take a stand. Beside the *Discipline* and the *Catechism*, George Miller's small book, *Practical Christianity*, represented their theology. Accounts of the exemplary lives and conversion experiences of Albright and other early Evangelicals were far more popular. After the Civil War, some Evangelicals awoke to the new intellectual threats posed by German rationalism and atheism, liberal theology, and science (i.e., evolution), and the 1875 General Conference even offered a $1000.00 prize for a "systematic theology" defining Evangelical doctrine for both friends and foes, but the prize went unclaimed. The Evangelical Normal Series for Sunday School teachers contained many shades of belief.

Still, no church can rely entirely on individual experience; experiences must be weighed and judged. Early Evangelicals recognized three criteria for evaluation: 1. Scripture—every word of the Bible, literally inspired by God; 2. Common Sense—reason in its simplest form; and 3.Good Works—the visible fruits of the changed life, including industry, frugality, simplicity, piety, strict Sabbath observance, and, later, abstinence from alcohol and tobacco. Indeed, the Bible and the Articles of Faith (fixed permanently in 1839) were prized as a clear, distinct, comprehensible, and indisputable standard that was to be met and defended, but not debated. For four decades after John Hamilton was expelled for heresy in 1831 Evangelical preachers were prohibited from publishing any work not approved by their Annual Conference. Bishops kept close watch on the ministerial ranks and moved decisively to squelch any deviation from the core beliefs of the faith. Again and again, they acted to enforce belief in the Wesleyan doctrine of sanctification, or Christian perfection.

Christian Perfection

Even Wesley had difficulty translating the experience of sanctification into a strict doctrine. German (Lutheran) theology knew nothing of a second, advanced stage of Christian life beyond the reach of sin, and Evangelicals who had not had the experience often refused to believe it was possible. The great Holiness crusades of Charles Finney and Phoebe Palmer in the 1830s, 1840s, and 1850s kept the attention of all the Wesleyan churches focused on the subject, and the exaggerated claims ("boasting") of Evangelicals still aglow from their "second blessing" experiences did not endear them to their unsanctified brothers and sisters in the church. Moreover, there was "much indefiniteness and misconception" among clergy as to time and manner of sanctification, the possibility of sin after sanctification, the necessity of the Second Blessing for salvation, and the exact relation of conversion to sanctification.[146]

In fact, it took half a century for the official Wesleyan doctrine, backed by the *Discipline* and all the authority the leadership could muster, to finally conquer the German heritage of the church. As early as 1833, Rev. James Bruer was forced from the church for deviation on the doctrine of holiness. Rev. Nicholas Gehr, editor of both German and English church papers, followed in 1849. Rev. T.G. Clewell, Editor of *The Evangelical Messenger* from 1859 to 1870, met a similar fate. Presiding Elder D. B. Byers of Illinois Conference was forced to recant and agree to the public burning of one of his articles. Rev. Solomon Neitz, the popular Presiding Elder from East Pennsylvania Conference, was too powerful to oust, but various attempts by the Bishops to do this consumed the bulk of three General Conferences (1859, 1863, and 1867), ended the episcopal career of Neitz's chief opponent W.W. Orwig, and permanently alienated the Pennsylvania conferences from the denominational leadership.

The 1867 General Conference adopted a definitive Declaration on Sanctification, and the Second National Holiness Campmeeting held in the Evangelical heartland at Manheim PA won many Evangelical pastors to the holiness movement. A group of ministers and laymen began an

Evangelical holiness journal, *The Living Epistle,* in 1869, and Bishop Esher started a German holiness magazine, *Das Evangelische Magazin,* soon afterward, but soon the two regular church papers, *The Evangelical Messenger* and *Der Christliche Botschafter* were themselves holiness journals. The victory was complete; although up to one-half of the pastors in the Association never advocated the Holiness Movement, they were careful not to criticize it. Soon, even the Bishops tired of its excesses (special holiness meetings led by traveling evangelists, continued disparagement of the "merely converted"). *The Living Epistle* was divided into equal sections on Holiness, family, and Sunday School in 1875, and *Das Evangelische Magazin* was made a Sunday School magazine in 1877. Many Evangelicals were influenced by D.L. Moody's evangelistic crusades to a new emphasis on conversion. Evangelicals had always been legalistic; the chief evidence of the sanctification experience was a strictly controlled lifestyle. Now, as thought of the experience faded, holiness became for many Evangelicals synonymous with moral conduct.

Christian Conduct

Evangelicals were expected to live their faith. The Sabbath was especially to be kept as a holy day of rest and worship. Even the early camp-meetings were closed on Sundays. As the century progressed, church leaders urged members to resist employers' demands and enticements to work on Sundays and frowned on Sunday railroad travel and Sunday newspapers because they forced others to work on the Sabbath. Sunday picnics, amusements, and even visiting met with similar disapproval.[147]

In fact, all amusements were suspect, for Evangelicals were to derive their joy from Christ. First and second generation Evangelicals did, indeed, "get happy" in church, jumping and shouting "Hallelujah!" but even after worship became more dignified extra "church sociables" were condemned as silly and unspiritual. "The church was not commissioned to amuse but to convert." Dancing, card playing, circuses, roller skating, and the theater were, of course, considered great evils.[148]

Early Evangelicals also lived their faith by dressing plainly. Clothing was seen as a token of the fallen state, a "sort of Cain's mark," and fashionable display was both boasting and conformity to the world.[149] In the words of the 1817 *Discipline:*

> Though we are persuaded that dress can save none, be it ever so plain, if it be not clothed with the garment of salvation, and covered with the robe of righteousness, through Christ; yet, it is undesirable, that sumptuous attire is unbecoming of true Christians, and, that each of our

RULES

OF

ST. JOHN'S CHURCH,

OF THE

EVANGELICAL ASSOCIATION,

AT BETHLEHEM, PENN.

RULE 1. All persons desiring to worship with us are requested not to stand in FRONT of the Church, in the Vestibule, nor on the Stairways, but to enter and quietly take their seats.

RULE 2. A conversation during service is POSITIVELY Forbidden.

RULE 3. Persons will not be allowed to Pass in and Out during service, except in case of necessity.

RULE 4. The filthy practice of SPITTING Tobacco Juice upon the Floor or Carpets, whereby clothes may be stained, is Positively Prohibited.

RULE 5. All persons Violating any of these Rules, will be dealt with according to LAW.

By order of the

BOARD OF TRUSTEES.

Printed Rules of Conduct, published ca. 1875

fellow-members may be appraised thereof, be it known, that none shall be permitted to wear the following articles: (1) ear and finger-rings; (2) curls and the powdering of hair; unbecoming ruffles and scallops, or bunches of ribbons on any piece of clothing, and the such like.[150]

The next Conference forbade preachers to wear gloves in summer or use silver bridle-bits or stirrups, and "in no case...adorn their person with large watch-keys."[151] Bishop Seybert was a particular foe of fashion, that "ornament of harlots," and his black suits were noticeably plain, even shabby.[152] Only after his death was the list of prohibited adornments removed from the *Discipline*. Yet, even at the end of the century, the pastoral vestment was still the black suit, and some Evangelical women still wore simple dark dresses and plain bonnets to church.[153]

In addition, the church expected Evangelicals to care for their bodies as the temples of the Lord, and here concern increased through the century. The first Evangelical Disciplines prohibited "intemperance and uncleanness of every kind, especially drunkenness and unnecessary use of strong drink." The 1839 General Conference extended this prohibition to include the making, preparing, selling, and use of all spirituous or intoxicating liquor, except as medicine. Later, Evangelicals were in the forefront of the temperance movement, working to drive "Demon Rum" from county, state, and nation, as well as the church. By the end of the century, Prohibition had become one of the Association's major concerns; every Conference session ended with resolutions for greater vigilance in the crusade against anti-temperance interests and politicians.[154]

With respect to tobacco, the Association, growing as it did among the rich tobacco fields of southeastern Pennsylvania, was less decisive. The East Pennsylvania Conference (1838) prohibited its ministers from growing or selling it, but the General Conference did not follow suit. In the Midwest tobacco was barred from campmeeting grounds, and Bishop Seybert insisted upon asking candidates for the ministry about their use of tobacco,[155] but Evangelicals from the 1850s left vivid descriptions of blackened spittoons hidden under pulpits and after-church gatherings of men and women smoking and chewing around the church stove.[156] The 1867 General Conference resolved that

we regard the daily habitual use of tobacco, as smoking, chewing and snuffing, highly improper, conflicting with good manners and Christian purity,...by which health is injured, religious services are often hindered, and much money, enormous sums, spent unnecessarily.[157]

In the closing years of the century, "the weed" was generally regarded as a great evil, even by those members (and ministers) who used it, but in 1889 as many as 30,000 of the Evangelicals were users.[158] Morphine and cocaine addiction was, of course, not as widespread a problem, but the presence of ads for drug addiction "cures" in the church papers gives one indication that drug use was present in the church.

Secret Societies

Evangelical sentiment always opposed secret alliances with unbelievers that were immune from the Class Leader's scrutiny and that might conflict with loyalty to Christ and His church. Yet, the church was never willing to risk disruption to take a firm stand on the issue. In 1847 every Annual Conference resolved to forbid Evangelicals from joining oath-bound societies (e.g., Free Masonry), but a vocal minority was able to block the move at General Conference.[159] Again in 1866, inclusion of Masonic rites at the laying of a church cornerstone at Tamaqua, PA, set off a storm of protest from every corner of the denomination, but church leaders avoided a showdown. [160] Finally, in the 1890s the heated debate over Secret Societies in the Church of the United Brethren in Christ renewed discussion of the matter in the Association. Though never officially condemned, membership in secret societies was generally suspect in the Evangelical Association.[161]

Slavery and Race Relations

The first Evangelicals were, like Blacks, despised by their neighbors, and in more than one town the humble hovel of an African American freedman was the only building opened to Evangelical circuit riders. Evangelical preaching in Allentown PA began in such a house, as did the great Orwigsburg revival of 1823 that set the church on a decade of expansion. Blacks and German- and English-speaking whites mingled freely at the early campmeetings, and the Association received Blacks into its fellowship in the early years. The 1816 *Discipline* contained a prohibition against the buying and selling of men and women that became a full section on slavery in 1839.[162] During the 1850s, the Association, no longer having churches in slave territory, was free to denounce slavery, and it gave the Union cause its full support in the Civil War. After the War, the 1867 General Conference authorized missions among freed slaves in the South, but this was never successful, and the Association lost contact with people of color.[163]

Church Organization (Polity)

Between 1800 and 1850, the highly structured, centralized organization of the Methodist Episcopal Church was a source both of its greatest success and its greatest trials. Methodism became the dominant religion of each new frontier because its Bishops had the authority and flexibility to mobilize the church's resources in response to each new opportunity. By 1850 one of every three American Christians (over 1,250,000 people) was a Methodist. At the same time, Methodist authorities constantly faced rebellion by factions demanding greater freedom in the church (Republican Methodist Church, 1792; Methodist Protestant Church, 1830; Wesleyan Methodist Church, 1840; Methodist Episcopal Church, South, 1844).

No one knows what form the Evangelical Association would have taken had its founder and first Bishop, Jacob Albright, lived longer, but Evangelical preachers, forced by Albright's early death to govern themselves, were reluctant to subordinate themselves to the whole Methodist Episcopal hierarchy mandated in their *Discipline*. No new Bishop was elected for thirty-one years after Albright's death, and in this interval numerous limitations were placed on the power of the executive office. The 1830 General Conference limited Evangelical Bishops to two four-year terms (Methodist Bishops held office for life) and made stationing of preachers a joint responsibility of Bishops and Presiding Elders (Methodist preachers received their assignments from the Bishops; early Evangelical preachers, having no Bishop, were assigned to their circuits by Presiding Elders assisted by committees of their choice). When the 1839 General Conference finally elected a Bishop (John Seybert), it added a prohibition against transfer of preachers from one Annual Conference to another and stripped Bishops of their vote at Conference sessions. Bishops were not even permitted to speak at Conference unless requested to. The sentiment prevailed that "the less power in the hands of the bishop...the more safe for the society in the future."[164]

Yet, Bishops retained wide powers as presiding officers at conferences, and the two-term limit was repealed in 1847 to allow Seybert to continue as Bishop (he and Bishop Long were, in effect, Bishops for life). As the Association grew in size and wealth, organizational complexity and structure increased at all levels. On the local level, the Quarterly Conference (class leaders, exhorters, local and itinerant preachers) became less of a moral watchdog and more of an administrative cabinet, less concerned with individual conduct and more pre-occupied with finances and policy. Early circuit riders had been paid a uniform wage from the common conference treasury. Around 1850, the various Annual Conferences made individual charges (congregations or circuits) responsible for paying their preachers and directed Quarterly Conferences to elect stewards to collect the salaries, as was done in the Methodist Episcopal Church. The 1859 General Conference added a chapter on stewards to the *Discipline* and ordered Quarterly Conferences enlarged to include them. Further additions were Sunday School superintendents in 1872 and representatives from each Board of Trustees on the charge in 1880. The *Discipline* had provided for such Boards from the beginning; all church land and buildings were to be the property of the denomination (not the local congregation that built them), but local people were needed to care for properties (hold them in trust) for the General Conference. When congregations actually started building churches, and then parsonages, in the 1830s and 1840s, Boards of Trustees were elected. As church buildings grew in size, value, and importance, these Boards naturally acquired greater status. Pastors, now settled for longer terms, also overshadowed class leaders and local preachers.[165]

On the denominational level, Boards of Missions and Publication, each with a full-time executive officer, were added in 1859 to provide continuity of administration between General Conference sessions. New publications had full-time editors, who joined the growing staff at Cleveland headquarters. Bishops gained power as growing telegraph and railroad networks gave them immediate access to every corner of the denomination. Finally, in 1867 General Conference made the five general church officers and the Bishops (when not presiding) full voting members of General Conference *ex officio* (by virtue of their office) and declared itself the "supreme law court of the church" with authority to decide the legality of any Annual Conference action.[166] This sealed the fate of the Neitz faction controlling the Pennsylvania conferences, who could neither win control of the central authority nor act independently of it. Centralization of church government ("an ecclesiastical despotism unparalleled in the history of Protestant Christianity"[167]) now became an issue itself in the Evangelical civil war between Neitz and Esher. Bishops Esher and Bowman clung ever more tenaciously to their powers, trying to force obedience from those no longer willing to give it voluntarily. Their opponents embraced church democracy, demanding a limit on episcopal terms, greater local autonomy, and equal lay representation at Annual and General Conferences.

The Division of the Church

Rapid growth is almost always stressful. In the nation and the church the nineteenth century was a time of bustle and accomplishment, but the price was upheaval and sometimes fracture. By 1890 the Evangelical Association was in the midst of its own civil war.

The feud had no single cause. The "Majority," led by Bishops Esher and Bowman, was centered in the German immigrant population of the Midwest and favorably disposed to the Holiness movement and strong

| Bishop John J. Esher, 1863 – 1901 | Bishop Rudolph Dubs, 1875–1890 |

central church government. The "Minority," led by Bishop Dubs, was centered among American-born Pennsylvania Germans, who were less supportive of the Holiness movement and generally more progressive and democratic in outlook. Yet, Bishop Bowman, born in Pennsylvania, was a lukewarm advocate of Holiness, while Bishop Dubs, born in Germany, was a fervent advocate of both Holiness and democracy. Clashes of personality, belief, ambition, and culture fed upon one another until co-existence became impossible. "No one of these causes were [*sic.*] sufficiently strong to divide the church. Unfortunately, their accumulated divisive influence...led to the division in the ranks of the Evangelical Association."[168]

Conservative German-speaking and progressive Americanized English-speaking factions collided as early as 1830, with the result that the English segment was ejected from the church. Only founding father John Dreisbach's concern for unity prevented collision between East and West over Secret Societies in 1847. When W. W. Orwig, acting for

Bishops Seybert and Long, challenged the views of the East's most popular and powerful Presiding Elder, Solomon Neitz, on Christian perfection and as a result won election over him as Bishop in 1859, a chasm was opened that would become unbridgeable. Neitz's party was able to defeat Orwig's bid for re-election four years later but could not elect Neitz. After a long stalemate, Jacob Esher of Illinois secured a majority, amid charges of fraud from the Neitz party, but he made no secret of his contempt for the eastern conferences, and they made no attempt to hide their ill-will toward him. At the next General Conference, Neitz and his supporters won control of the church papers and the support of an influential Presiding Elder from Illinois, Daniel B. Byers, who had been publicly humiliated by Bishop Long for his views on sanctification.[169]

The 1875 General Conference drew the first dividing lines, when it created three separate German-speaking conferences. Eastern votes elected two new Bishops: Thomas Bowman from East Pennsylvania Conference and Rudolf Dubs, a young man from Iowa conference indebted to Neitz but with an unassailable record on the Holiness issue. Bishop Esher, meanwhile, continued to make enemies. His attempts to replace a popular professor at Northwestern College with his own son-in-law further alienated Illinois Conference. His attempt to appoint Bishop Bowman (by now an ally and relative by marriage) and Heinrich Hintze of Germany Conference as delegates to the Ecumenical Conference of Methodist Bodies in place of the representatives elected by the 1879 General Conference, Bishop Dubs and D. B. Byers, was quickly exposed by his enemies at *The Evangelical Messenger* and caused such strife that the next General Conference decided against sending any delegates. His attempts to eliminate criticism from the church papers led to increasing friction with *Messenger* editors, Jacob Hartzler (1871–1879) and his brother Henry Hartzler (1879–1887). The Bishops made a temporary truce when the 1883 General Conference refused to re-elect any of them until they settled their differences, but the factions soon came to blows over the mission to Japan.[170]

Jacob Hartzler, a member of the Central Pennsylvania Conference, had been appointed superintendent of the mission in 1880 upon the recommendation of Bishop Dubs, and Editor H. B. Hartzler printed glowing accounts of his progress in the *Messenger*. Unfortunately, a dispute developed between the superintendent and one of the missionaries, W. E. Walz. Walz appealed to the Board of Missions, and Bishop Esher went to Japan to render a decision. Not unexpectedly, the Bishop's report was highly critical of the superintendent. When the editor refused to publish what he considered lies about his brother and rallied friends of free speech to his aid, Bishop Esher's son Edward, an attorney who was married to Bishop Bowman's daughter, brought legal charges of misconduct against H. B. Hartzler at the 1887 General Conference. After two weeks of protracted debate, the Conference found him guilty on a strict party vote of 57–47. Forty-one of the 104 delegates protested that a two-thirds majority was necessary for conviction, but Bishops Esher and Bowman ruled against the protest and refused to permit its publication in the Conference Minutes. Everyone showing any hint of disloyalty to Esher and Bowman was swept from office by the Majority. In the end, eleven delegates refused to sign the Minutes and so many other delegates left early that Conference could not finish its business, so it left instructions for the Board of Publication to choose the site of the next conference. Denied a voice in the church, the Minority started its own paper, *The Evangelical,* with H. B. Hartzler as editor, and the mud-slinging began in earnest.[171]

Esherites denounced "turbulent spirits, moved in some cases by envy, in others by a spirit of revenge, in others by an unsanctified ambition" who "have together resorted to dishonest and disreputable methods to get control of the machinery of the church."[172]

> Any compromise with the party of this mischievous movement is utterly out of the question. The church has given no cause whatever to said party for its doings. The church has done not wrong. On the other hand, the disturbing movement is evil, a wrong through and through, a crime against Christ and his body. Nor is there anything in the entire movement for which the church has any use at all…God save us from compromise of any kind with that which is wrong.[173]

Minority partisans denounced the "selfish ambition of men who cannot endure the appreciation of the church for the labor of others." They did not want to divide the church, but they refused to bow down and worship the "official image" of episcopal authority."[174]

> This situation is not here because we invited it or desired it, but because we could not prevent it without a total and unconditional surrender of our individual rights as members of the church of our choice, and complete submission to the most tyrannical ecclesiastical rule ever known in the history of Protestant Christianity. These individual rights and the cherished simplicity of our representative church government are dearer to us than life itself.[175]

The final rupture came when friends of Bishop Esher brought Bishop

Dubs to trial on February 18, 1890, under conditions that the *Cleveland Leader* called "about as gross an outrage as an ecclesiastical court could be guilty of," and not surprisingly found him guilty of falsehood and failure to prove himself innocent of evil rumors about his chastity and purity. Minority ministers conducted trials of Bishops Esher and Bowman (with more concern for their constitutional rights) and found them guilty of other charges.[176] Bishop Dubs, in obedience to the provisions of the *Discipline*, refrained from exercising his office while under indictment, but the other Bishops declared their suspensions illegal. They had taken the precaution of holding earlier secret trials where their friends could rule them innocent of all charges and so preclude any subsequent real trials on the same charges. They attempted to continue in office, and deposed any minister who opposed them. When 1890 Annual Conference sessions controlled by the Minority physically barred Bishops Esher and Bowman, whom they considered suspended, from presiding, the Bishops declared the Conferences illegal. The Bishops then left with any minister who would follow to organize separate "legal" conferences. Lawsuits followed when Esherite "conferences" tried to force congregations to eject their ministers in favor of men loyal to the Bishops. The Majority rejected all attempts at mediation by the Minority, the church laity, and outside parties.[177]

The Minority claimed that since the last General Conference had not itself chosen a site for the 1891 General Conference, the oldest Annual Conference (East Pennsylvania) had a disciplinary right to do so; Minority delegates accordingly met on October 1, 1891, in Philadelphia. The Majority met on the same date in Indianapolis, the site chosen by the Board of Publication. Both claimed to be the only legal conference. The Indianapolis conference naturally sustained the conviction of Bishop Dubs; the Philadelphia conference naturally sustained the convictions of Bishops Esher and Bowman and elected C. S. Haman and W. M. Stanford in their place. A laymen's

Bishop Wesley M. Stanford, 1894–1902

convention met concurrently with Philadelphia General Conference, which passed a recommendation to the Annual Conferences for an amendment to the *Discipline* allowing equal lay and ministerial representation beginning at the next General Conference.[178]

For a time, each side was able to maintain the fiction that it was the only legal Evangelical Association, but Attorney Esher and his team of lawyers spared no effort or expense to legally deprive Minority Evangelicals of the churches, parsonages, and colleges they had built but deeded to the denomination. When the Illinois Supreme Court ruled against the Minority, the 1893 Illinois Conference, meeting in a Presbyterian church, was forced to take a new name, Illinois Conference of the Regular Evangelical Association, and begin the task of acquiring all new church properties. A restraining order forced the 1893 Oregon Conference to do the same. Finally, the 1894 session of the Illinois Conference adopted the name "United Evangelical Church" and called for a General Conference to establish a new denomination. Ohio and Des Moines Conferences followed suit. When the Pennsylvania Supreme Court ruled against the Minority on October 1, 1894, the Minority members of East Pennsylvania Conference met in Metropolitan Hall in Reading PA, constituted themselves as the East Pennsylvania Conference of the United Evangelical Church, and as the oldest Annual Conference called a General Conference for November 29, 1894, in Naperville, IL. The other Annual Conferences reconstituted themselves and answered the call.

Hundreds of congregations found themselves in a new church and homeless as Evangelical Association authorities claimed their properties under the old Trust Clause reserving them to the Evangelical Association.[179]

Notes

1. R. W. Albright, *A History of the Evangelical Church* (Harrisburg: Evangelical Press, 1942), 130-133, 203-204.

2. R. Dubs, "A History of the 'Christliche Botschafter,'" EM, October 15, 1874, 329–330.

3. [Jacob Hartzler] "Brief Sketch of the Evangelical Messenger," EM, October 15, 1874, 332; Albright, 206–207.

4. Albright, 210.

5. Albright, 195–197;

6. C. G. Koch, "The Proposed Orphan Asylum," EM, August 5, 1863, 249; Albright, 271; R. Yeakel, *History of the Evangelical Association, Vol. II , 1850–1875*

(Cleveland: Thomas & Mattill, 1895), 129–131.

7. M, "A Home for the Aged Poor of our Church, EM, September 2, 1875, 273; J. H. Shirey, "The First Home for Aged Members of the Evangelical Association," EM, July 2, 1889, 420; Edward F. Ohms, *A Grain of Mustard Seed* (s.l.: the Author, 1985), 34.

8. W. W. Orwig, *History of the Evangelical Association, Vol. I* (Cleveland: Charles Hammer, 1858), 53.

9. Orwig, 62–68; Albright, 127, 166–172; R. Yeakel, *History of the Evangelical Association, Vol. I , 1750–1850* (Cleveland: Thomas & Mattill, 1894), 136–137; Ammon Stapleton, *Flashlights on Evangelical History* (York, PA: The Author, 1908), 63–92.

10. Yeakel, Vol. I, 267–273.

11. Albright, 197–201; Orwig, 299–301.

12. Albright, 414–436.

13. Yeakel, Vol. II, 100–106; [T. G. Clewell], "Our Proposed Heathen Mission, EM, September 2, 1863, 284.

14. Albright, 436–437; Paul Eller, *History of Evangelical Missions* (Harrisburg: Evangelical Press, 1942), 203–208.

15. Albright, 320–323.

16. Eller, 78–88.

17. J. C. Hornberger, "A Visit to Florida," EM, February 15, 1887, 106–107.

18. S. C. Breyfogel, "Church Extension in the East Pennsylvania Conference," EM, November 20, 1888, 737–738.

19. W. M. Stanford, "That Church Erection Movement," EV, May 24, 1893, 161.

20. Albright, 114, 192–193; Yeakel, Vol. I, 234, 243, 255; Ohms, 3–4, 29.

21. Yeakel, Vol. I, 300–301; Orwig, 325–327; Ohms, 5–6, 28.

22. Yeakel, Vol. I, 312–314, 371, 321.

23. Ohms, 8.

24. [T. C. Clewell] "Our Working in Cities—Its Importance," EM, August 15, 1866, 260–261.

25. [S. P. Spreng] "The Church in Cities and in the Country," EM, January 18, 1889, 24.

26. Albright, 217–218; Ammon Stapelton, *Annals of the Evangelical Association of North America and History of the United Evangelical Church* (Harrisburg : Publishing House of the United Evangelical Church, 1896), 182; John Seybert, *et al.*, "Ein Plan zum Studien der jungen Prediger in der Evangelischen Gemeinschaft,"*Christliche Botschafter*, March 1, 1844, 37.

27. Yeakel, Vol. II, 218–222; Albright, 406.

28. Yeakel, Vol. II, 222.

29. Albright, 408.

30. Albright, 406–407; G. Holzappel, "Schuykill Seminary," EV, March 20, 1889, 95.

31. Albright, 121–124.

32. Orwig, 97.

33. Yeakel, Vol. I, 160.

34. Yeakel, Vol. I, 361–367.

35. "The Union!" EM, April 18, 1855, 60; "Convention," EM, June 13, 1855, 94.

36. Albright, 282–284; Reuben Yeakel, "The Mother Conference—III," EM, July 17, 1888, 4, 49–50.

37. Albright, 318.

38. Albright, 318–319; J. M. Ettinger, "The U.B. General Conference," EV, May 29, 1889, 173; W. M. Stanford, "Two Significant Decisions," EV, August 12, 1891, 253.

39. Yeakel, Vol. I, 200, 202; Albright, 221–222, 238.

40. S. P. Spreng, *The Life and Labors of John Seybert* (Cleveland: Publishing House of the Evangelical Association, 1888), 151.

41. Yeakel, Vol. I, 361–366; Orwig, 366–367.

42. John Seybert, "Progress of the English Language in the Evangelical Association," EM, May 12, 1852, 76–77; [T. Clewell] "Our English Work," EM, March 19, 1862, 92

43. Terry Heisey, "Immigration as a Factor in the Division of the Evangelical Association," *Methodist History* 19 (October 1980) 50.

44. "A Great Danger," EM, May 9, 1878, 4.

45. Heisey, 50.

46. Albright, 106–108; Orwig, 59–60, 75.

47. W. W. Orwig, "A Call to Preach the Gospel," EM, February 25, 1855, 26.

48. Orwig, *History*, 136.

49. S. C. Breyfogel, *Landmarks of the Evangelical Association* (Reading, PA: Eagle Book Print, 1888), 81–95; Orwig, 266–267.

50. Orwig, 62, 130; [T. G. Clewell] "Four Years instead of Two," EM, May 16, 1866, 156.

51. [T. G. Clewell] "A Problem to be Solved," EM, April 11, 1866, 116; Breyfogel, 240.

52. J. M. Ettinger, "Are Our Preachers Adequately Paid?" EM, January 26, 1888, 37; February 2, 1888, 45.

53. Albright, 76–79; Yeakel, Vol. I, 321–323, 395, 449–451.

54. And So Say I, "Sleeping at Church—How to Prevent It," EM, January 24, 1855, 11; Z. Hornberger, "Deportment at Church," EM, December 4, 1861, 209; [T. Clewell] "Decorum in God's House," EM, November 6, 1861, 180; [T. Clewell] "Shouting and Jumping in Worship," EM, February 21, 1861, 26.

55. W. W. Orwig, "Episcopal Message to the General Conference of the Evangelical Association," EM, November 21, 1863, 340.

56. Clewell, "Shouting and Jumping in Worship," 26.

57. J. W. Loose, "Exclusive Choir Singing?—Which, and How?" EM, February 22, 1887, 114; Charles Nauman, "Kneeling in Churches," EM, June 3, 1875, 169.

58. B. J. Smoyer, "Sunday-School Liturgies," EM, August 23, 1877, 265.

59. J. H. Keeler, "Erroneous Views in the Church and How to Counteract their Influence," EM, October 10, 1878, 1.

60. Smoyer, 265.

61. W. H. Bucks, "Unbecoming Practices in the House of God," EM, March 19, 1889, 177–178; [S. P. Spreng] "Decline of the Altar Service," EM, December 10, 1889, 792.

62. Mark Wells, "Hallelujah," EM, March 19, 1890, 89.

63. Ammon Stapleton, "Old Time Evangelical Preaching," EM, October 3, 1894, 313; Yeakel, Vol. I, 132, 137.

64. Spreng, *Seybert*, 389.

65. D. B. Byers, "Preaching Years Ago," EM, April 25, 1878, 1.

66. And so say I, 11.

67. W. W. Orwig, "Episcopal Message to the General Conference of the Evangelical Association," EM, October 21, 1863, 340.

68. Observer, "Long Preaching, Long Praying, Long Confessing," EM, February 19, 1874, 57; Ralph Kendall Schwab, *The History of the Doctrine of Christian Perfection in the Evangelical Association* (Menasha, WI: George Banta, 1922), 45.

69. Yeakel, Vol. II, 14–15.

70. Stapleton, *Annals*, 548.

71. Byers, "Preaching Years Ago," 1.

72. [S. P. Spreng] "The Preaching of the Times in our Church," EM, July 16, 1889, 956.

73. Stapleton, *Annals*, 238, 258–9.

74. J.N. "The Relation of Baptized Children to the Visible Church," EM, Sept. 16, 1858, 145; [T.C. Clewell], "The Care and Conversion of our Children, EM, Sept. 16, 1858, 148; Spreng, *Seybert*, 354f.

75. "Articles of Faith, XVI. Of the Lord's Supper," EADisc, 1852, 15

76. Yeakel, *History*, Vol. I, 449–450.

77. See W.H. Bucks, "A Needed Reform," EM, March 29, 1887, 193–194; I.A. Smith, "Sacramental Wine," EM, September 27, 1887, 309.

78. Don Yoder, *Pennsylvania Spirituals* (Lancaster, Pa.: Pennsylvania Folklore Society, 1961), 126–130, 140–151, 396; Musicus, "Thoughts on Singing," EM, August 8, 1849, 58; Upsilon, "On Singing," EM, July 22, 1848, 54; J. Hartzler, "Music in Church and Home," EM, December 20, 1877, 404.

79. Elisha A. Hoffman, "Choirs," EM, January 28, 1869, 25.

80. Quoted in Albright, 400.

81. An Amateur, "Music," EM, October 29, 1856, 171.

82. "Instumental Music in the Church," EM, September 18, 1883, 300.

83. Hoffman, "Choirs," 25.

84. "Guerilla on the New Hymn & Tune Book," EM, May 2, 1882, 137.

85. See for example, A. B. Saylor, "Sacred Music—Its Character," EM, December 10, 1890, 393; J. W. Loose, "Exclusive Choir Singing?" 114; Yoder, 153–155.

86. Yeakel, Vol. I, 143–144, 160, 167.

87. Yeakel, Vol. I, 336–337, 394; Albright, 250–251; W. L. Reber, "Thoughts on Building Churches," EM, January 8, 1852.

88. See for example R. Dubs, "Dedication at Harrisburg," EM, February 15, 1887, 105; [S. P, Spreng] "Question Drawer," EM, March 26, 1889, 200.

89. [S. P. Spreng] "Class-Meetings," EM, August 6, 1889, 504.

90. Yeakel, Vol. I, 210.

91. One of the B.'s, "A few questions—Will some one please answer them?" EM, March 26, 1874, 97.

92. J. Lerch, "Recommendations: Assistant Class-Leaders and Exhorters," EM, January 30, 1879, 2.

93. Yeakel, Vol. I, 388–389.

94. U. Eberhart, "Class-Meetings," EM, March 16, 1853, 42–43.

95. W. M. Stanford, "The Christian Endeavor Movement," EV, July 15, 1891, 220.

96. "The Prayer Meeting," EM, March 22, 1849, 21.

97. An Exhorter, "Long Prayers Kill Devotion," EM, May 8, 1850, 34.

98. "Do You Pray in Public?" EM, May 11, 1871, 148; One of Them, "The Class-Leader's Difficulties," EM, October 11, 1887, 641; Observer, "Prayer-Meetings after Revivals," EM, April 3, 1879, 1.

99. J. F. Worick, "Neglecting the Prayer Meeting," EM, August 26, 1869, 265; [S. P. Spreng] "Still More Landmarks," EM, September 2, 1890, 553.

100. Rudolf Dubs, "About Prayer-Meetings," EM, January 15, 1889, 33.

101. "Christmas," EM, December 23, 1850; Orwig, *History*, p. 230.

102. W. Haupt, "Hyndman Circuit, Pittsburgh Conference," EM, February 9, 1888, 59; "Christmas Exercises—What Shall They Be?" EM, December 18, 1883, p. 402; the December 17, 1890, issue of the EM included a Christmas exercise by Ammon Stapleton entitled "Children's Call to Santa Claus."

103. [T.C. Clewell] "Is Good Friday a Catholic Institution?" EM, April 29, 1869, 132; [S.P. Spreng] "Question Drawer," EM, April 10, 1888, 233.

104. W. Yost, "Children's Day: It's History and Results," EM, June 9, 1891, 353.

105. [Yoder, 41–42]

106. Yeakel, *History*, Vol. I, 106–7, 119–27

107. A.P. Dutcher, "An Old Time Camp-Meeting," EM, May 15, 1883, 153.

108. Yoder, 56–77; "Campmeetings," EM, July 8, 1857, 108–109.

109. R. Yeakel, "Report of an Evangelical Camp-Meeting, held in the year 1815," EM, July 23, 1874, 236.

110. Yeakel, *History*, Vol. II, 134; Yoder, 70–75; J. S. Shimer, "Camp-Meetings," EM, August 1, 1866, 241; Marih, "Camp-Meeting Sabbath-Breaking," EM, October 21, 1869, 329.

111. Aquila, "Camp-Meetings," EM, January 8, 1852, 2–3; J. Kanagy, "Camp-Meetings," EM, April 27, 1853, 66–67;

112. Yeakel, *History*, Vol.II, 170–172

113. S. W. Raker, "Seven Point Camp-Meeting, Mahatongo Circuit, East Pennaylvania Conference," EM, September 21, 1871, 802; Reporter, "Manheim Camp-Meeting," EM, September 6, 1877, 286; B. J. Smoyer, "East Mahanoy Junction Camp-Meeting," EM, September 13, 1877, 294.

114. J. Hartzler, "Camp-Meetings," EM, July 27, 1876, 236.

115. [S. P. Spreng] "The Modern Summer-Resort Camp-Meeting," EM, July 22, 1890, 456.

116. [W.M. Stanford] "At the Camps," EM, September 10, 1890, 292.

117. J. H. Shirey, "Perkasie Park Camp-Meeting," EM, August 19, 1890, 517.

118. Yeakel, *History*, Vol. I, 127,214.

119. Orwig, *History*, 191, 195–196.

120. [T.C. Clewell] "Protracted Meetings," EM, December 24, 1862, 412.

121. Yeakel, *History*, Vol. I, 244–245.

122. Albright, 190–195;

123. Franklin Hartzler, "Sabbath School," EM, June 13, 1861, 90.

124. J. Young, "Our Sunday School Literature," EM, October 15, 1874, 330.

125. F. Krecker, "How Can We Make our Sunday-Schools More Pleasant and Attractive," EM, July 17, 1873, 225; E. Swengel, "Church Members and the Sunday School," EM, December 14, 1886, 785.

126. Elisha A. Hoffman, "Our Sunday-School Literature," EM, December 23, 1875, 401.

127. J. W. Walton, "The Church and its Sunday School," EM, December 7, 1886, 769–770; E. M. Allen, "How to Keep the Older Scholars in Sunday-School," EV, January 14, 1891, 9.

128. Albright, 307–311.

129. D. A. Medlar, "Perkasie Park Evangelical Normal Assembly," EM, August 14, 1888; J. H. Shirey, "Perkasie Camp-Meeting," EM, August 20, 1889, 539; N. Shupp, "The Linwood Park Correspondence Normal Course, EM, September 10, 1889, 578; "Normal Assembly Day at Perkasie Park," EV, July 1, 1891, 201.

130. J. Berg Esenwein, "That Bible Conference," EV, July 12, 1893, 221.

131. J. Kanagy, "Should Females Pray in Public?" EM, August 18, 1852, 132.

132. Albright, 320.

133. N, "Female Testimony," EM, August 6, 1862, 251.

134. "What of Our Women?" EV, March 8, 1888, 88. Hartzler was outspoken in his support of women's rights. In a subsequent article ("Women Helpers," EV, May 30, 1888) he stated that women were coming to the fore. "In many churches this mighty force is unemployed because high and mighty sons of Adam stand loftily over 'weaker vessels.' Let the fossils take notice that their time is coming!"

135. [Clewell], "Female preachers," EM, May 27, 1869, 164; D. B. Byers, "The Nineteenth Century and the Women Are Upon Us," EM, March 21, 1872, 89.

136. Albright, 430.

137. Albright, 321–323.

138. Emma F. Divan, "Woman's Sphere in the Church," EV, October 14,

1891, 322–323.

139. Albright, 215–216.

140. W. H. Fouke, "A Keystone League," EV, July 8, 1891, 210; W. M. Stanford, "The Christian Endeavor Movement," EV, July 15, 1891, 220.

141. Albright, 324.

142. U. F. Swengel, "Y.P.S.C.E.," EV, January 23, 1889, 27.

143. "Constitution of the Young People's Alliance of the Evangelical Association," EM, January 20, 1891, 41.

144. "An Address," EV, November 11, 1891, 357.

145. Albright, 325.

146. Yeakel, Vol. II, 63–64; [T. Clewell], "Christian Perfection, Holiness, Sanctification, &c," EM, August 15, 1866, 260; J. Dick, "Thoughts on Sanctification," EM, November 24, 1852, 187.

147. Albright, 313–314; "The Sunday Newspaper," EM, February 23, 1886, 121; J. W. Walton, "Sunday Railroading," EM, March 9, 1886, 145.

148. [H. B. Hartzler] "Amusements," EM, August 14, 1883, 201; Albright, 314; "The Snare of Card Playing," EM, August 11, 1891, 502.

149. Yeakel, Vol. II, 55–57.

150. EADisc, 1817, 30.

151. Breyfogel, *Landmarks*, 34.

152. Yeakel, Vol. II, 55–56.

153. C.C., "Style, Dress, Ornament, and God's Law," EM, October 12,1871, 321; Albright, 235–236.

154. Albright, 232, 314–315.

155. Albright, 233–235.

156. [T.T. Clewell] "Decorum in God's House," EM, November 6, 1861, 180.

157. General Conference Journal, 1867, 65.

158. S. W. Patterson, "Tobacco," EM, April 15, 1891, 113; [S.P. Spreng] "Our Mission Work," EM, October 15, 1889, 664.

159. Albright, 188–190.

160. [T. G. Clewell] "Free-Masonry, Secret Societies, etc." EM, May 9, 1866, 152.

161. [S. Spreng] "Two on Secret Societies," EM, July 9, 1889, 440.

162. Albright, 231; Orwig, 118; Yoder, 24.

163. Albright, 299–300.

164. Stapleton, *Annals*, 165–167, 300.

165. Albright, 186–188; Stapleton, 285, 295, 296, 326;

166. Stapleton, 325–326, 361–363.

167. "East Pennsylvania Conference," EV, March 11, 1891, 74–75.

168. Albright, Raymond, "Chapter IX – The Division of the Church," unpublished chapter of his *History*, 1.

169. Yeakel, Vol. I, 200; Albright, 189–190, 267; Heisey, 47; Albright, "Chapter IX," 3.

170. Albright, 281; Albright, "Chapter IX," 4–8

171. Albright, "Chapter IX, 9–12; Stapleton, *Annals*, 562–567.

172. Thomas Bowman, "What Will the Harvest Be?" EM, November 6, 1888, 705–706.

173. J. J. Esher, "To the Ministers and Members of the Evangelical Association," EM, December 18, 1888, 804.

174. Josiah Henderson, "From Josiah Henderson," EV, October 30, 1889, 347; A Life-long Evangelical, "The Majority Plan," EV, August 7, 1889, 253.

175. Rudolph Dubs, C. S. Haman, and W. M. Stanford, "Address of the Bishops," EV, January 6, 1892, 4–5.

176. Heisey, 44; S. P. Spreng, "The Cleveland Leader and our Church," EM, March 4, 1890, 136.

177. Albright, "Chapter IX," 13; Stapleton, 568–572.

178. Stapleton, 570–571, 585.

179. Stapleton, 592–604; Albright, 330–333.

3

Evangelicals Divided:
The United Evangelical Church
(1894–1922)

Overview

Men in office resorted to the most unjustifiable abuse, the most high-handed usurpation of powers, in open and flagrant violation of the discipline. A General Conference, under the control of these men, declared all these violations of the discipline to be lawful and enacted laws which practically made the bishops autocrats in the church, and the undisputed interpreters of the law. The civil courts, refusing to consider the moral and equitable phases of the question involved, upon technical grounds decided against us. [We were left with the choice of applying for readmission into a church we no longer recognized as our own, disbanding, or continuing on our own.] Our convictions of duty as well as our love for, and loyalty to the fundamental principles and simple polity of the church as originally contributed, commanded us to go right on, and we did.[1]

Thus was a new church born. Years later, Bishop Dubs recalled his part in naming the church. At the 1894 session of the East Pennsylvania Conference he suggested the name United Evangelical Church, if a new name should be required, and his suggestion was quietly adopted almost unanimously. He then went to the sessions of the Central Pennsylvania and Pittsburgh Conferences with the same suggestion and the same result. Finally, he met Illinois Conference on April 4, 1894, and informed them that a court injunction was coming against the "Regular Evangelical Association," the name the Conference had chosen. He told them of the actions of the Pennsylvania conferences, and the Illinois Conference quietly followed suit. The next day, as he continued in his recollection,

> We were informed that Lawyer Esher [Bishop Esher's son] with the sheriff and others had come to enforce an injunction. The sheriff met me in the hall of the church, saying very politely, that he had a paper to read to me. He read the injunction of the court against the Illinois Conference of the Regular Evangelical Association forbidding that body to do any business, &c. I replied that he had come to the wrong place and to the wrong people, there was no such a Religious body here. He inquired: What are you? We answered: *The United Evangelical Church.* "Since when?" asked the sheriff. Answer: "Since yesterday morning." The sheriff thought that that was a smart move and placed his papers in his pocket and in company with Lawyer Esher, who looked queer indeed, left for Chicago. In this manner we got our present beautiful church name.[2]

The first General Conference of the United Evangelical Church meeting November 29-December 13, 1894, in Naperville IL claimed a membership of 61,120 with 415 itinerant ministers. The Conference perpetuated many of the institutions of the Evangelical Association and the decisions of the 1891 Philadelphia General Conference, but in many ways it had to create a new denomination in one two-week session. The Conference had to decide on a structure for the church that would embody the democratic principles it valued so highly while maintaining denominational cohesion. It had to approve new Articles of Faith. It had to make provisions for new German and English hymnals, a new catechism, and other publications. Missionary supporters were clamoring for a new foreign mission field, since the Japan mission was closed to them. Fortunately, leadership was already in place; Bishops Dubs and Stanford were re-elected to the episcopate. The Evangelical Publishing House in Harrisburg PA and the church newspaper, *The Evangelical,* were well-established and needed only official sanction. The Conference succeeded in compiling and adopting a new *Discipline* for submission to the Annual Conferences.

Yet, the fact remained that no congregation had clear legal title to any place of worship or parsonage for its minister because all properties were held in the name of the Evangelical Association and these people were now United Evangelicals. Defense Bureaus were organized by Annual Conferences to help congregations with legal costs; Church Extension Societies struggled to provide loans to congregations building new churches and parsonages. In some areas, like central and western Pennsylvania, where UE support was unanimous and churches were often small, the Evangelical Association eventually decided to sell properties back to the UE congregations who were worshiping in them and allow the areas to slip from the Association fold. In other areas, where small remnants of congregations remained loyal to the Association, the EA fought back by giving these groups financial support and properties in an attempt to build congregations to rival the UE congregations they had lost. United Evangelical congregations in eastern Pennsylvania, then at the height of its industrial-age prosperity, could afford to respond by building new churches, bigger and better than their old ones, to overshadow any rival Association buildings. In the Midwest, however, building even simple churches placed a huge financial burden on small congregations, and many would later question the wisdom of maintaining two struggling Evangelical churches in the same small town.

The early years were years of rebuilding and re-organization under the continuing leadership of Bishops Dubs and Stanford. Several hundred churches were built, and a mission to China was begun in 1900. In 1902, however, the Bishops were ineligible for re-election, because the new church had placed a two-term limit on its leaders to prevent the accumulation of power they saw in the EA. The 1902 Conference, therefore, elected the Editor of *The Evangelical,* Henry Burns Hartzler, and an influential Presiding Elder in the East Pennsylvania Conference, William

| Bishop H. B. Hartzler, 1902–1910 | Bishop William F. Heil, 1902–1910, 1918– 1926 |

F. Heil, as Bishops. Both men had taken leading roles in the formation of the church. Dubs was elected Editor of *Die Evangelische Zeitschrift,* and Stanford was elected as new Editor of *The Evangelical.*[3]

During the tenure of Hartzler and Heil (1902-1910) the church continued to flourish. In 1910 one Presiding Elder made particular note of improved systems of finance, payment of church debts, increased salaries of ministers, larger benevolent contributions, awakened interest in missionary enterprise, more efficient Sunday School grading and organizations, and better prayer-meeting attendance.[4]

The next Bishops (1910-1918) were U. F. Swengel, formerly a Presiding Elder in the Central Pennsylvania Conference and Chairman of the Managing Board of the Sunday School, and W. H. Fouke, former Editor of the Sunday School and Keystone League of Christian Endeavor literature. They began their tenure with a renewed interest in young people and ended with the Great War. In October 1917 the Board of Missions adopted a resolution recommending that the Bishops appoint a committee of five to see how the Church could co-operate with the War Work Commission of the Federal Council of Churches. The War Service Commission (W. F. Heil, president; H. F. Schlegel, executive secretary; A. E. Gobble, treasurer; A. A. Winter; and J. Q. A. Curry) compiled a roster of all men and women from United Evangelical homes, churches, and schools serving in the armed services so that they could send them personal letters, New Testaments, and subscriptions to *The Evangelical.* Letters of sympathy were sent to families of the killed and wounded. The Commission also facilitated acceptance of UE ministers as military chaplains and provided support for them. After the War the Commission was renamed the National Service Commission.[5] In their last Episcopal Message Bishops Schwengel and Fouke noted all the activities of their years in office and called for greater emphasis in two areas, spiritual life and the development of lay talent, while rejoicing in the imminent triumph of Prohibition.[6]

The 1918 General Conference promised to be one of unusual importance. A movement toward re-uniting the United Evangelical Church with the Evangelical Association had been gathering strength for some time but was also beginning to ignite opposition in certain quarters of the church, particularly eastern Pennsylvania, and some leaders were hoping for a thorough discussion of this matter at the General Conference. A fund-raising drive was being proposed. Term limits would require the election of a new slate of leaders. Unfortunately, the scheduled date of conference fell in the middle of the great influenza pan-

✠ The Evangelical ✠

VOL. 31.   HARRISBURG, PA., OCTOBER 16, 1918.   No 42

An Urgent Emergency Call!

Prevalent Influenza

necessitated the closing of many of our churches in the East. This, unfortunately, occurred on the regularly appointed time for the observance of Foreign Mission Day.

We Must Not Allow

this unfortunate circumstance to prevent the observance of this occasion at the earliest possible date.

The $25,000 Call for China

represents a present need of our China Mission to meet the expenses of the current year.

Pastors and People

Let every one of us do our full duty. Doing this will insure success.

"Give, and it shall be given unto you."

The Evangelical, October 16, 1918 issue

demic of 1918. On the second day of Conference in York PA local authorities declared the gathering a health threat, put the delegates under quarantine, and ordered the delegates to disperse. Negotiations with state officials gave the delegates twelve more hours for one all-night session, but only the "absolutely necessary business could be transacted. Time for proper deliberation was out of the question."[7] William F. Heil from East Pennsylvania Conference was elected Bishop after eight years out of the episcopal office, and Mathew T. Maze, Treasurer of Western Union College in LeMars IA and former Presiding Elder in the Nebraska Conference, was newly elected. The merger negotiations were reviewed quickly and ordered to be continued. A Committee on Episcopal Activities was appointed to enlist the new Bishops in the fund-raising campaign. Then, Conference adjourned, having authorized many things it did not have time to thoroughly evaluate, and the church surged ahead as separate initiatives took on lives of their own. Various segments of the church prepared impatiently for re-merger with the Evangelical Association, while others worked strenuously to build up the UE Church so that it could better stand on its own. The focus of all their efforts was the Forward Campaign, a prototype of later fund-raising campaigns in the Evangelical Congregational Church.

World War I had helped to sweep away many old limitations throughout American society, and its victorious conclusion released a flood of energy, enthusiasm, and economic expansion. As Rev. E. Crumbling of Central Pennsylvania Conference stated in an address to the UE Ministerium of Harrisburg on The Forward Campaign,

> We have long been taught not to despise the day of small things, and the admonition is still good; but we are living now in the day of big things, in the day of great enterprises and great accomplishments. We used to think in this country, in terms of hundreds and thousands. Now we think in terms of millions and billions. ...This nation was ready to mobilize its last man and its last dollar to win the war, and make the world safe for democracy. The Church of Jesus Christ can do no less than to mobilize its last member and its last dollar, to win the world for Christ....The great need of the world; the urgent call for an advance into unoccupied territories of the world and the readiness of the people to undertake great things in connection with the world war, and put them across, have prompted the Church, in all its denominational branches, to plan great forward movements.[8]

The Committee on Episcopal Activities appointed by the General Conference met two weeks after Conference (October 22, 1918) and elected H. Franklin Schlegel as President and E. S. Woodring as Secretary. The original goal of the fund-raising campaign was $200,000 for college endowments, but a superannuation campaign of $200,000 for the support of retired ministers was soon given priority. Then, during the 1919 East Pennsylvania Conference a layman proposed a total campaign goal of one million dollars over four years. Central Pennsylvania Conference concurred with this plan provided that the campaign include spiritual, as well as monetary, goals. The Committee met again on May 21, 1919, and approved a campaign called "Our Forward Campaign" to "deepen the spiritual life of the church [and] to effect a more enthusiastic fellowship of its members and a more efficient coordination of the activities of the church, to be followed by a canvass for a fund of at least one million dollars." The Bishops, as campaign directors, were ordered to have two sets of cards printed for use in the campaign: a Covenant Card containing spiritual objectives (Bible study, personal devotion, prayer meeting attendance, family worship, and stewardship) and a Pledge Card. The fund total was apportioned among the Annual Conferences, East Pennsylvania being responsible for $300,000 and Central Pennsylvania for $230,000. Contributions would be allocated among the general activities of the church: church extension fund— $100,000; educational endowments—$400,000; missions—$200,000; superannuation fund—$200,000; and United Evangelical Home endowment—$100,000.[9] The Campaign was thoroughly organized with campaign directors at the conference, district, and congregational levels and constant appeals in *The Evangelical*. Within a week after the opening of the canvass, three-fourths of the financial goal had been pledged, and contributions began to accumulate. Progress in the spiritual objectives was more difficult to gauge, although some parts of the church reported increased evangelistic efforts and retreat centers for meditation and prayer.[10] When the Campaign ended at the 1922 General Conference, a total of $411,990 had been received.[11]

The forward look of Our Forward Campaign also marked the end of an era. As negotiations that would end in the re-merger of the United Evangelical Church with the Evangelical Association in 1922 proceeded, the church lost the leaders who had brought it into being and nurtured it through its brief life. Bishop Dubs died on March 31, 1915, Bishop Haman on January 14, 1916, Bishop Hartzler on September 3, 1920, Bishop Swengel on March 8, 1921, Bishop Fouke on February 6, 1923, and Bishop Stanford on April 8, 1923. A new generation with a new perspective would lead the church into new paths.

The United Evangelical Church did not always accomplish its goals, and its bitter division from the Evangelical Association robbed both groups of the "spiritual and material aggressiveness and success which they together had enjoyed before 1891,"[12] but in general its brief life was one of accomplishment. In the early years the enormous task of rebuilding was completed with amazing success. Over its twenty-eight-year history the United Evangelical Church more than maintained the four to five per cent growth rate of the earlier Evangelical Association.

Date	Membership	Added	Lost	Net Gain	PercentGain	Conversions
1895	50,240					
1898	59,190	30,933	21,983	8,950	18 %	26,683
1902	63,390	35,034	30,834	4,200	7 %	27,279
1906	69,046	40,248	34,592	5,656	8.9 %	32,622
1910	73,551	38,184	33,679	4,505	6.6 %	33,173
1914	79,292	38,095	32,354	5,741	7.8 %	34,693
1918	89,271	45,074	35,095	9,979	12.6 %	46,188
1922	92,001	33,992	31,256	2,736	3.6 %	29,984

From 1895 to 1922 membership increased by 41,761 or 83 %. By comparison, the Evangelical Association increased from 110,095 to 167,416 during the same period, or 52 %. Between the national religious censuses of 1906 and 1916 the United Evangelical Church increased by 28.5 %. This compares with: Evangelical Association—15.1 %, United Brethren in Christ—27 %, Methodist Episcopal—24.5 %, Presbyterian Church in the U.S.A.—36.6 %, and Roman Catholics—10.6 %. Overall, Christian denominations lost 0.3 % during that period when the population of the United States rose by 19 %.[13] In addition, property values in the United Evangelical Church increased from $1,946,299 in 1895 to $9,515,328 in 1922, an increase of 389 %.

Yet, denominational leaders were troubled by the large losses that always nearly negated large gains in members and converts. "We do good work in getting the people, but fail in keeping them."[14] Bishops Hartzler and Heil in their 1906 Episcopal Message complained that "in some instances the [membership] records seem to have been purged a little too severely in order to avoid large apportionments for the various benevolent collections,"[15] but most of the losses resulted from members moving to areas not served by a United Evangelical Church. "Could all our scattered people be sought out and served, our membership would be much larger than it is, and we would grow much faster as a church."[16] The resources of the church simply could not be stretched to reach all the growing sections of the country. This realization fed the desire to be part of a larger organization that could reach every state.

Denominational Activities

Publishing

United Evangelical publishing predates the organization of the denomination and was, in fact, a vital ingredient in its formation. Six weeks after the 1887 General Conference purged "Minority" opinion from *The Evangelical Messenger* the ousted editor, H. B. Hartzler, and his allies launched a rival publication, *The Evangelical* (first issue dated November 14, 1887), which bound the scattered adherents of the Minority together, gave them an identity, and presented their case to others. The first "Publishing House" was an unheated second-floor room at Fourth and Market Streets in Harrisburg PA, but the business grew rapidly. The Publishing House moved to a large building at Second and Locust Streets in Harrisburg in the spring of 1893, but substantial additions were necessary in 1895 and again in 1897.[17]

The first General Conference of the United Evangelical Church (1894) brought *The Evangelical* and the *Evangelische Zeitschrift* (its German counterpart produced in Chicago by Bishop Dubs and his son C. N. Dubs) officially under the control of a denominational Board of Publication. It also ordered publication of German and English almanacs (later renamed Yearbooks).[18] By 1896 the church was publishing nine English and three German periodicals for all ages (including *The Evangelical, Evangelische Zeitschrift, Missionary Tidings, Sunday School Evangelical, Missionary Evangelical, Bright Jewels, Jugend Freund, Our Little Folks, and Bible Teacher*), and German and English Sunday School quarterlies and lesson leaves for adults and youth with an aggregate circulation of almost 110,000.[19]

Under publishers Rev. S. L. Wiest (1888-1910) and J. J. Nungesser (1910-1922) the Publishing House prospered. *The Evangelical* under editors H. B. Hartzler (1895-1902, 1918-1920) and W. M. Stanford (1902-1918) doubled its circulation and doubled it again, rising to 13,834. The *K.L.C.E. Journal* (of the UE Christian Endeavor) was taken over by the Publishing House in 1898. Printing and bindery work for various book publishers and nearby Pennsylvania state government offices brought in additional revenue but eventually overtaxed the old buildings. The

Board of Publication appointed a committee in 1912 to build a completely new publishing plant. A site in Harrisburg was purchased in 1916, and though wartime inflation and material and labor shortages hampered construction the new Publishing House, a large and modern industrial facility, opened on October 1, 1918. It became the headquarters of the denomination, accommodating the printing plant and bookstore, the offices of the general church officers and the Woman's Missionary Society, and the church archives in the Historical Society Room.[20]

The importance of the Publishing House cannot be over-estimated. As the Bishops stated in their 1902 Address,

> Every considerable organization among men, whether of a secular or religious character, finds it absolutely necessary to publish some sort of an organ at regular intervals....But for this it would be doomed to failure ....We might almost as well disorganize our church, disband our forces, and advise every man to strike out for himself, as to close down our presses, and stop all public intercommunication. In such a case we would necessarily disintegrate as a body.[21]

The United Evangelical Publishing House served the communication needs of the denomination well and provided extra income as well.

Church Home

After the division of the Evangelical Association, the Ebenezer Orphanage and the Evangelical Home for the Aged in Philadelphia were, of course, off-limits to the people of the United Evangelical Church. Little was done to replace them for over a decade, though the Central Pennsylvania Conference continued to receive its "orphanage home collections." In 1907 a minister of the Central Pennsylvania Conference, P.C. Weidenmeyer, added to these accumulated funds a bequest made many years before by his father for the same purpose, and the Conference appointed a committee to organize an Orphans' Fund Society to prepare for such an institution within the bounds of the Conference. The 1910 Central Pennsylvania Conference formed an Orphans' and Old Folks Home Society, and with some prodding from Rev. Ammon Stapleton events now began to move more quickly. Money accumulated, the United Evangelical Home was incorporated (January 1912), and committees investigated several sites, including the old Union Seminary (Central Pennsylvania College) campus in New Berlin and Central Oak Heights Campmeeting. The Home Society decided at its March 9, 1914, meeting that an offering should be received for the Home throughout the Central Pennsylvania Conference each year on Mother's Day. One year later, the Society voted to buy the 189-acre Slifer farm overlooking Lewisburg PA and the Susquehanna River. On February 3, 1916, the first superintendent and matron, Rev. and Mrs. A. A. Winter of Oregon Conference, were elected, and the first two guests (Mr. and Mrs. J. W. Loyer) arrived on May 31, 1916. The United Evangelical Church Home was dedicated on August 4, 1916 by Bishop U. F. Swengel.[22]

Guests at Lewisburg were not charged a fixed fee. Persons with wealth and/or income were expected to give at least a good portion, if not all, of it to the Home, but those without means were also welcome. Admission was not limited to members of the United Evangelical Church, but they were given preference. At first, the Home was little different from other farms in its neighborhood. Facilities were sparse. Guests helped with canning, cleaning, and other chores as they were able.[23] Yet, the Home was poised for rapid growth. Already in 1916 two Woman's Auxiliaries (Central Pennsylvania and East Pennsylvania) were raising money for furnishings at the Home. Each auxiliary was entitled to representation on the Home's Board of Trustees, and women had part in the dedication. In the Home's first year East Pennsylvania, Pittsburgh, and Ohio Conferences voted it their endorsements and joined the Central Pennsylvania Conference in its administration. In his second Annual Report Superintendent Winter wrote that

> The United Evangelical Home has already passed the experimental stage. In spite of limited means at the beginning, needed equipment, furnishing and remodeling of buildings, the difficult labor situation and the many readjustments, it by the grace of God has won its way gradually and continuously until it is now one of the recognized institutions of the community and of the Church....Our visions and dreams of other days have become realities.[24]

Support flowed to the Home from all directions. Electricity came to the Home in 1917 when a large heating and power plant was completed. The first Anniversary Day, including a bazaar and lunch by the Woman's Auxiliaries, was a huge success.[25] The second Anniversary Day saw ground broken for a fifty-room dormitory (complete with elevator and private baths), which was dedicated at the third Anniversary Day. The first individual cottage was built in 1919. Roads were laid and farm buildings improved. On Thanksgiving Day 1919 ground was broken for the airy, modern orphanage that was part of the original plan.[26] This home for eighty children was dedicated on the fifth Anniversary Day

(August 5, 1921), when its first superintendent and matron were elected and ground was broken for a home/community hospital. By 1922 the Old Folks Home was at full capacity and planning further expansion, and forty-four children were filling the Orphanage with life. All in all, the church home at Lewisburg witnessed an impressive string of accomplishments in six short years.[27]

Home Missions and Church Extension

Whether it was labeled home missions, church extension, or church planting, expansion was the goal and policy of the United Evangelical Church. Three of the seven original Annual Conferences (Des Moines, Platte River, Oregon) were mission conferences, sustained by funds from the other four conferences. Even within these four conferences, many congregations were at one time or another missions, supported at least partially by the conference. While establishment of foreign missions was deferred for lack of sufficient funds during the early years of the church, the Corresponding Secretary of the Board of Missions, B. J. Smoyer, worked vigorously in 1893-94 raising the necessary funds for home missions, that is churches in the vast expanses within the bounds of the western conferences. [28] Despite his success, the 1894 General Conference was forced to eliminate his position, and fund raising on a more limited scale shifted to direct appeals in the church papers for help with individual church projects.

Central Pennsylvania Conference organized the first church extension society in 1893 to raise money to lend to congregations in need of help in rebuilding after the loss of their properties to the Evangelical Association.[29] East Pennsylvania Conference organized its church extension society on March 6, 1895. Early recipients of loans were congregations at Harrisburg, Annville, and Cressona.[30] At the prompting of the Bishops the next (1898) General Conference organized a denominational Church Extension Society, which over the next four years raised $1600 for five churches.[31] Still, in 1902 there were 159 organized congregations without church buildings and many more places in the cities and in the rural Northwest without a UE mission. Bishops Dubs and Stanford in their 1902 Episcopal Address stressed two principal reasons why church extension should receive special attention:

> First. Because only as this is done can the money appropriated for Home Missions be properly utilized. A church building is an immediate necessity upon new missions, especially in the cities. Missions are mostly too weak to build without help.

Second. If we expect to grow as a church we must extend our borders and take better care of our scattered membership. The statistics
show that more than one-half as many members move away as we
receive. Besides the care of members already received, it is our duty as
an evangelizing force to extend our borders to the utmost of our ability.

This meant making the work of church extension "systematic, effective, and permanent."[32] The 1902 General Conference established a
Board of Church Extension (consisting of three ministers, three laymen,
the Bishops, and a corresponding secretary) and directed all preachers
to "push" church extension. All Annual Conferences were requested to
establish church extension societies and forward one-third of their revenue to the Board's general fund.[33]

The Board's General Secretary, B. H. Niebel, promoted church extension heavily in *The Evangelical*, and while the money trickled in the
church leaders set about organizing for their task. The United States was
a country on the move, from farm to city and from East to West, and
the coming of the automobile only increased this mobility.[34] Between
1894 and 1922 the United Evangelical Church recorded 214,940 conversions and 209,889 accessions but lost 105,362 members who "moved
away."[35] The 1904 Annual Conference sessions passed resolutions
aimed at keeping track of members who had moved out of United
Evangelical territory so that churches could be started where a UE nucleus increased the chances of success, and Bishops Hartzler and Heil
repeatedly urged the closest co-ordination between the home missions
and church extension programs.[36] "Unproductive missions," that is
churches, often in rural areas, that had long been dependent on denominational assistance and had little prospect for growth, were closed. New
churches would be located only in territory that offered a good opportunity for success.[37]

In practice, although every Annual Conference had its share of mission churches, denominational church planting efforts particularly targeted the Northwest A special denominational Church Extension Day
(Dec. 2, 1917) raised almost $4000 for the Board of Church Extension,
and though no loans were made by the Board for church building during World War I, home missions and church extension remained a priority throughout the life of the United Evangelical Church.[38] A mission
among the Appalachian poor in Bell Country KY was established in
1921.[39]

In all, the Board raised $120,000, and the Annual Conference church
extension societies raised almost as much to provide interest-free loans

for United Evangelical building projects. In any given year between one-fourth and one-third of all United Evangelical congregations were "missions" (non-self-supporting congregations receiving Conference funds). From 1904 to 1918 home mission congregations (36% of the church membership) accounted for 49,770 conversions and 50,131 other added members (43% of total conversions). The United Evangelical church took outreach seriously.

Foreign Missions

The United Evangelical Church took foreign, as well as home, missions seriously. "Scarcely anywhere in church history will you find a record to surpass the missionary zeal of the United Evangelical Church in home and foreign lands."[40] From its beginning the UE Church had a Missionary Society with officers drawn from the highest echelons of clergy and laity. The first General Conference (1894) established a General Board of Home and Foreign Missions, and the second General Conference (1898) unanimously charged the Board to start a foreign mission.[41] Church leaders promoted the 1910 World Missionary Conference and sent ten delegates to the 1910 Men's National Missionary Congress,[42] but foreign missions in the United Evangelical church was also very much a result of the prayer and work of UE women.

The Woman's Missionary Society (WMS) of the EA had given valuable support to the Minority cause before 1894, and it remained a vital part of the new denomination. The Society had branches in every Annual Conference and over 400 local church auxiliaries. It also supervised the work of the Young People's Missionary Society, Mission Bands for children, and the Home and Cradle Roll Missions Departments for homebound people and infants. Each local congregation was encouraged to develop a full complement of societies to support the cause of missions. The WMS published two magazines: *Missionary Tidings* geared to adults and youth; and *The Missionary Gem*, a twelve-page publication for children. Annual missionary conventions also helped to educate the church about the importance of missions.[43] The WMS supported home missions, but the women were eager to resume foreign missions, like the Evangelical Association mission to Japan in which they had been so actively involved.

The Board of Missions acted quickly in response to the mandate of the 1898 General Conference. It chose missionaries and a mission field, the Hunan Province of China, "then one of the most religiously neglected and also exclusively native areas of China." Rev. C. Newton Dubs, son of Bishop Dubs, was appointed superintendent on January 19, 1900.[44] Dubs, with his wife and son Homer, departed for China on November 20, 1900. After a year of language study in China, they arrived a thousand miles inland at Changsha, the capital of Hunan Province, on Nov. 21, 1901. About this time Rev. and Mrs. Charles A. Fussle, Jr., and their infant son left Le Mars IA for Changsha as the United Evangelicals' second missionary family.[45]

The missionaries opened a chapel on June 15, 1902, and Dubs and a Chinese evangelist conducted daily vesper services, family devotions, and Sunday services "for those who know a little doctrine," but the Chinese people were hostile to the foreigners.[46] They believed rumors that missionaries removed eyes and other organs from Chinese corpses for medicinal purposes. Dubs wrote that "oft-times it seems as if we were living on the side of a volcano that would pour forth its hot streams of lava at any moment."[47] It took the saintly death and dignified funeral of a Chinese convert to open the eyes of the Chinese to the power of the gospel.

After long months of toil the missionaries baptized their first converts in 1903. A church was organized, and the first communion service was celebrated as more Chinese people accepted Christ and lives were transformed.[48] By 1907 there were four mission stations with a total membership of fifty: Chansha 18; Siangtan 21; Chucheo 3; and Liling 8. Nine missionaries witnessed twenty-five baptisms in that year alone, and the General Board allocated funds to build a summer residence for missionaries, the Elizabeth Krecker Memorial Home.[49] By 1920 the Hunan mission had grown to thirty-six foreign missionaries, seventy-five native workers, thirty preaching stations, 678 members, and 1846 Sunday School scholars. Eight day schools for boys and six for girls were scattered throughout the province, the Albright Preparatory School (for boys) was opened in Liling, and a Girls' Boarding School stood in Changsha. Two hospitals and a dispensary met physical needs.[50]

Across the world United Evangelical missionaries were also active in Nigeria. Rev. and Mrs. C. W. Guinter of the Central Pennsylvania Conference went to the Wukari region in 1906 under the joint auspices of the UE General Board of Home and Foreign Missions and the Sudan United Mission. Guinther worked on translating the Bible in local languages.[51] Both Chinese and Nigerian missions were continued by the Evangelical Church after 1922.

Funds for foreign missions came primarily from the WMS and its associated societies, the Keystone League of Christian Endeavor which adopted several building projects in China, and offerings collected each year on Foreign Mission Day, the first Sunday in October. The mission board set financial goals for Foreign Mission Day and supplied extensive program ideas. Yet, funds never met the needs on the fields. In 1911 the church spent 38 cents per member on foreign missions, but as the Foreign Mission Day Program for the year stated, "We could easily average five times that much did we not spend so much money uselessly!"[52]

Higher Education

Higher education was a high priority for the United Evangelical Church. As the Bishops stated in their 1898 Episcopal Address:

> We must furnish to our youth the opportunity for education under the guidance and influence of Christian teachers, and it is further necessary that this be done in institutions of learning which are under the supervision of men of our faith. Without church institutions of learning, we cannot expect to hold our young people, and it is questionable whether, as a church, we can extend and preserve the work to which we are called. The intellectual culture of those young men who are divinely called to the ministry, and become applicants for work, make such institutions a necessity....If God has called us as a church into existence, of which we entertain no doubt, then it is also His will that we should establish the institutions necessary to our continued existence. With our call as a church all this is implied.[53]

All four of the Evangelical Association's colleges were within Minority Annual Conferences, and their faculties and student bodies heavily favored the Minority. The Majority was only too happy to be rid of the two smaller schools, Central Pennsylvania College and Lafayette Seminary, which were struggling under loads of debt. These were sold for nominal fees to trustees elected by United Evangelical Annual Conferences after the 1894 court decisions awarded all Evangelical Association property to the Majority. The other two properties, which had valuable assets, were guarded jealously, and Northwestern College and Schuylkill Seminary were reorganized as Evangelical Association schools.[54]

Central Pennsylvania College in New Berlin PA traced its history back to Union Seminary, established in 1861, but its life as a United Evangelical institution was short. Both enrollment and finances were never more than marginal. The graduating class of 1897 numbered only nine. By the winter of 1898 its president, Dr. A. E. Gobble, was sounding an alarm, and the Bishops added their warning that "if sufficient funds for an endowment cannot be secured, then the school will finally have to be closed."[55] An 1895 Pennsylvania law required colleges to have assets of at least $100,000, and Central Pennsylvania College fell far short of this.[56] Discussion turned to consolidation of Central Pennsylvania College with another UE college, Albright College, possibly in Harrisburg.[57] The schools finally merged in 1902, with the combined college located "temporarily" on the Albright campus in Myerstown PA.[58]

Lafayette Seminary had been established in Lafayette OR by the Oregon Conference of the Evangelical Association in 1889. For eleven years the institution struggled. Its peak enrollment was sixty in 1898, but its graduating classes were very small, totaling four in 1897 and six in 1899. By 1900 a decision to relocate or close had to be made, and relocation was chosen. When Lacreole Academy in Dallas OR was offered for sale, the trustees of Lafayette Seminary purchased the Academy and merged the schools as Dallas College, a school offering both preparatory and college courses.[59] Yet, even now the small Oregon Conference could not meet the state's requirement of a $200,000 endowment. In 1914 Dallas College was forced to close its doors.[60] Bishop Fouke called the closing a "temporary suspension" and wrote of "resuming [the] work."[61] It re-emerged as the Oregon Bible Training School in Corvallis OR in October 1916, but in the midst of World War I it never had a chance of success.[62] Moving once again, this time to Portland, it continued in name and spirit until the end of the United Evangelical period.[63]

The third United Evangelical college, Albright College, was actually the old Schuylkill Seminary under a new name. Through the years of division and litigation trustees elected by the East Pennsylvania Conference continued to operate the Seminary at its Fredericksburg PA campus, but rival trustees elected by the Esherites did not relinquish their claim to the property. When the Pennsylvania Supreme Court ruled against the Minority in November 1894, the United Evangelical trustees peacefully turned control over to the Evangelical Association trustees and agreed to vacate the campus over Christmas vacation. The principal, faculty, students, custodial staff, and (despite the vigilance of Esherite guards) many of the furnishings of the Seminary withdrew to the former campus of Palatinate College in Myerstown PA. Here they reorganized as the Albright Collegiate Institute and purchased the four-acre campus from the Reformed Church for $10,000. The Institute became Albright College on September 6, 1898, when the East Pennsylvania Conference and the state approved its change to four-year college status. In 1902 Albright College was strengthened when it absorbed the Central Pennsylvania College.[64]

An early advertisement for Albright College in *The Evangelical* (June 23, 1897) boasted twelve competent instructors and a low tuition and board cost of $4.25 per week. "Unusual prosperity" marked its early years. By 1898 enrollment was already 141, an increase of thirty over the year before, the art department had outgrown its facilities, and an additional music teacher was needed. Courses were offered in education, shorthand, and bookkeeping. The cost was a mere $51.00 per semester.[65] Tuition and board increased to $225.00 in 1913 and $400.00 in 1921.

Albright College, Myerstown, PA, circa 1928

As Albright College's enrollment grew, so did its property value. During the 1897 summer break, hot and cold water and baths were installed in the dormitory areas of Old Main. The next year saw the addition of new offices, a reading room, and a recitation room. Six years later, thirty "men, friends and Albrightians" formed a syndicate to buy the former Behney mansion across the street from the College. After renting from the syndicate for one year, the College bought the building for use as a women's dormitory, renaming it Mohn Hall in 1908 after benefactor Jeremiah G. Mohn. The same syndicate purchased another building adjoining the campus (called South Hall, later renamed Isaiah Bower Science Hall) and rented it to the College.[66]

The Central Pennsylvania Conference agreed to the merger of its college with Albright in 1902 with the understanding that Myerstown was to be a temporary location for the college, but the first attempt of the Harrisburg Board of Trade to lure Albright College to Pennsylvania's capital city failed when the East Pennsylvania, Central Pennsylvania, and Pittsburgh Conferences that supported the College voted in 1902 to keep it in Myerstown.[67] The Harrisburg Board of Trade tried again in 1904, attempting to raise $50,000 to attract the college to relocate.[68] The Board of Trade of Berwick PA also issued an invitation to Albright College the same year.[69] The powerful East Pennsylvania Conference unanimously endorsed the Myerstown location at its 1905 session, however, and started a $100,000 capital fund drive to solidify this decision.[70] An athletic field, gymnasium (1907), science hall, recitation hall (now the International Office of the EC Church) (1913), and chapel/dining hall (1921) enlarged the Myerstown facilities. Albright College prospered and grew into the denomination's strongest educational institution.[71]

A fourth college was founded by the Illinois, Des Moines, Platte River, and Kansas Conferences. Incorporated as Western Union College on April 10, 1900, it was based in a private "normal" (i.e., teacher training) school building that was purchased by the conferences in Le Mars IA. Western Union College offered eight courses of study: Theological, Collegiate, Normal Preparatory, German, Commercial, Musical, and Art. Theology courses were taught in both English and German. All students were required to attend daily devotional services and Sunday services. In the absence of dormitories, students lived in private homes.[72] By 1905 this college had an enrollment of 215 and an endowment of $50,000 and had graduated seventy-two men and women.[73]

There were attempts to establish a fifth school in Freeport IL. Little is known of this effort except that an endowment of $100,000 was required by the state, and the Illinois Conference apparently could not raise this amount.[74]

In addition to college-level studies, many people in the United Evangelical Church felt the need for theological education. The 1898 and 1902 General Conferences authorized all United Evangelical colleges to develop theological departments, but this proved to be an added expense that the church could not afford.[75] In the absence of a denominational theological seminary, the Illinois Training School for Christian Workers was approved for United Evangelical students.[76] In 1910 Albright College proposed the establishment of a Theological Department, but the plan was deferred by the East Pennsylvania Conference until the College could increase its endowment to $200,000. Instead, the three Pennsylvania conferences endorsed the Bible Teacher Training School in New York City for the training of ministers and missionaries.[77] This School offered scholarships to Albright College students, and by 1916 it had trained nearly one-half of the missionaries of the United Evangelical Church.[78] The mid-western conferences sent many ministerial candidates to Moody Bible Institute in Chicago for training. As the United Evangelical period was drawing to a close, Western Union College finalized plans to open a Theological Seminary.[79]

"Worthy theological students" were assisted by Educational Aid Societies in the Annual Conferences. Funds were also used to "aid Bible institute work in our colleges." The 1914 General Conference created a denominational Board of Education to diffuse information on, investigate the needs of, and provide aid to the United Evangelical Colleges, but it met rarely and its activities were limited.[80]

Ecumenical Relations

Early twentieth-century Americans were very aware of the economies of scale. Laborers, businesses, nations, and churches all united in the pursuit of common goals.

> The spirit of co-operation has inspired a number of efforts to bring about interdenominational relations whereby "overlapping" in church work might be avoided and the whole realm of Protestant Christendom might be united in the movements for moral reform....We are persuaded that the manifold denominations in the Church of Christ do not fully express the spirit of Christianity, and that they will disappear in its ultimate triumph, and that every unselfish movement to bring about interdenominational unity is in harmony with correct Christian teaching.[81]

The United Evangelical Church maintained fraternal relations and exchanged conference delegates with other Wesleyan denominations like the United Brethren in Christ and the Methodist Episcopal Church. The United Brethren even proposed organic union with the United Evangelicals after hearing a stirring message from Bishop Dubs at their

1897 General Conference.[82] The Church also agreed to participate in the Third (1901) and Fourth (1911) Ecumenical Methodist Conferences, but the elected delegates were not able to attend because no provision had been made to pay their travel expenses.[83]

Local churches and Annual Conferences worked with community ministerial associations and churches of other denominations. Union evangelistic services, union campmeetings, and joint holiday services were common. UE churches continued to participate in ecumenical Week of Prayer services. Special services like church dedications often featured local clergy from other denominations.[84]

The United Evangelical Church was also a founding member of the Federal Council of Churches of Christ in America. U. F. Swengel headed the UE delegation to the 1905 Inter-church Conference on Federation, at which the Federal Council was organized. Bishops Hartzler and Heil, former Bishops Stanford, Dubs, Fouke, and Swengel, and B. H. Niebel represented the United Evangelicals at the first meeting of the Federal Council in Philadelphia December 2-8, 1908.[85] UE leaders became active members of the Council's committees. The Council made many positive initiatives, including the first Vacation Bible School,[86] and the United Evangelical Church benefited from involvement with major denominations on a national level. The Church also endorsed Interchurch World Movement in 1920.[87]

Of course, there was always some ambivalence about ecumenism, and some United Evangelicals were more open to church federation and union than others. Editor Stanford reviewed the pros and cons of membership in the Federal Council of Churches and concluded that:

> To have other denominations to come in and help us hold our revival meetings, for instance, would have to be a compromise of methods....Such procedure would also result in superficial work, and would be very likely to generate dissatisfaction and dissensions. The great point is to keep our own house well, and then be neighborly.[88]

The 1914 General Conference reaffirmed continued membership in the Federal Council *because* it had no authority to "draw up a common creed or form of government or of worship, or in any way to limit the full autonomy of the Christian bodies adhering to it."[89] W. M. Stanford made it very clear to the fourth quadrennial meeting of the Council that as far as the United Evangelical Church was concerned the Council's "chief function is that of a clearing house for the churches' activities in the field of social and civic reforms." Other UE observers worried that more was made at the meeting of the social gospel than of the "blood of Christ, and the necessity of a conviction for sin wrought by the Holy Spirit."[90]

Charitable Society and Support of Retired Clergy

All of the funds accumulated by the Charitable Society of the Evangelical Association for the support of aged, "worn-out," and needy preachers and the widows and orphans of deceased ministers were retained by the Majority, which continued as the Evangelical Association. Ministers who sided with the Minority that became the United Evangelical Church lost their old-age pensions as well as their parsonages. The first General Conference of the United Evangelical Church appointed a committee of ministers and laymen to organize a new Charitable Society. This committee met in Reading PA on February 1, 1895, to elect officers and adopt a constitution. The committee determined that no money would be paid out to beneficiaries until the Society's assets reached $10,000, and despite repeated financial appeals by the Bishops this level was not reached until 1907. Even then disagreement over the basis of distribution delayed the first disbursement until 1911, when a total of $1025.77 was paid out to the nine Annual Conferences that had contributed to the Society.[91] By 1921 the Charitable Society's assets totaled only $33,154.85, and disbursements over the nine Conferences in that year came to only a little over $3,000.[92]

Of course, other attempts were made to raise funds for retired and incapacitated ministers of the United Evangelical Church. Annual Conferences formed Superannuated Funds, which often had greater incomes than the general fund.[93] The East Pennsylvania Conference took the lead here, organizing a Preachers' Aid Society in 1910 and assessing its ministerial members one per cent of cash salary for the support of superannuated (retired) and disabled ministers and ministers' widows and orphans.[94] Two decades into the church's history the United Evangelical Publishing House was finally in a position to begin paying dividends to the Annual Conferences (about $1000/year) for the support of superannuated ministers.[95] Yet, the need remained. "One of the trying things for a minister," wrote the Bishops in 1918, "is the forward look to the days of enforced superannuation without a reasonable prospect for anything for him and his family to depend on."

At its October 1917 meeting the Board of Missions, prompted by an appeal from two laymen, appointed a committee to present the idea of a Ministers' Benefit Association to General Conference,[96] but this body, while endorsing the concept, referred the matter to the Commission on Church Federation and Church Union, where inclusion of United Evangelical ministers in the much-better-funded Superannuation Fund of the Evangelical Association helped persuade many UE ministers to support the merger of 1922.[97]

Historical Interests

The United Evangelical Church may not have been the legal heir of Jacob Albright's church, but its founders considered themselves the true heirs of his spiritual legacy. In their struggle with the Esherites they looked to the Evangelical pioneers for inspiration and justification, and this emphasis on history continued in the new denomination. Under the prodding and leadership of Rev. Ammon Stapleton (1850-1916) the Evangelical heritage was preserved and celebrated. Stapleton recorded the memories of the last survivors of the pioneer generation and combined them with written records to produce three invaluable denominational histories: *Annals of the Evangelical Association of North America and History of the United Evangelical Church*[98] (665 p.); *Flashlights on Evangelical History*[99] (193 p.); and *A Wonderful Story of Old Time Evangelical Evangelism, Being a Simple Account of the Life and Time of the Rev. Jacob Albright, Founder of the Evangelical Association*[100] (143 p.), written at the request of the 1906 General Conference. As Centennial Committee Secretary, Stapleton helped to organize the celebration of the centennial of the organization of the Evangelical Association and promoted history with articles in *The Evangelical.*[101] Prompted by a request from the Kleinfeltersville PA congregation to the 1906 General Conference,[102] the Committee arranged centennial services to be held on September 25-26, 1907, at the Albright Chapel in Kleinfeltersville,[103] and the renewed interest in history resulted in the organization of a permanent Historical Society.

Stapleton and U. F. Swengel had made attempts to form such a society at church headquarters as early as 1893. With planning for the 1907 centennial moving to a climax they succeeded in organizing a United Evangelical Historical Society under the auspices of the Central Pennsylvania Conference in 1907.[104] This Society in turn initiated plans for the next Evangelical centennial celebration at its March 11, 1913, meeting.[105] The 1914 General Conference authorized it to make plans in cooperation with the Evangelical Association for the 1916 centennial of the first Evangelical General Conference,[106] and the Centennial Celebration was held September 26-27, 1916, at four nearby sites:

Dreisbach's Church, Buffalo Valley PA, commemorating the first General Conference; Lewisburg PA commemorating the beginning of Evangelical work in New York and Canada; the Eyer barn at Winfield PA commemorating beginning of Evangelical publishing and the first missionaries; and New Berlin PA commemorating the first church building and publishing house. Over two thousand sons and daughters of Albright joined the Bishops and other leaders of the United Evangelical Church and the Evangelical Association in what future Bishop M. T. Maze called "the greatest event in the history of the two branches of the Evangelical Church in recent years."[107]

The Historical Society continued its activities after the Centennial. In 1918 it moved its collection of books, periodicals, deeds, relics, and artifacts to an exhibit room in the new church center and publishing house in Harrisburg.[108] In 1921 it began placing historical markers at significant sites, including the site of the first Evangelical church in New Berlin PA, which the Society owned.[109]

Church Life

Language

Broadly speaking, the division of the Evangelical Association in 1891/94 could be seen as a split between a German-speaking, German-born faction centered in the Midwest and an English-speaking, American-born faction centered in Pennsylvania. With the exception of Illinois Conference, where Bishop Esher had made powerful enemies, the Annual Conferences of the Evangelical Association that united to form the United Evangelical Church were precisely those Conferences that had English-speaking majorities. All those Conferences that remained loyal to Bishop Esher were, like him, German-speaking and German-born.[110] In 1887 most of the Conferences that would still be Evangelical Association conferences in 1897 were 80 to over 90 % German-speaking, while the Conferences that would form the United Evangelical Church (except for Illinois, which was three-fourths German) were only 20 (Ohio, Platte River, Central Pennsylvania, Pittsburgh, Des Moines) to 30 % (East Pennsylvania) German-speaking.[111]

In the 1890s some United Evangelical churches had both English and German services every Sunday, but the transition from German to English in the United Evangelical Church was rapid, even in Illinois and the Northwest, where UE missions had met with some success among German immigrants.[112] The church in St. Paul MN, for example, conducted all of its services in German in the first years of the twentieth century, but the pastor could not induce the Germans who attended on Sunday mornings to return Sunday evenings. At the urging of the young people he began preaching in English at the evening services. Soon many English-speaking persons had been drawn to the church. The congregation's Quarterly Conference decided that if the Germans didn't show more interest all the preaching would be in English, and by 1907 German language preaching had ended at that church.[113] Disgruntled German-speaking United Evangelicals undoubtedly made their way to an Evangelical Association church nearby in many western towns, even as young people in German Evangelical Association congregations sometimes found their way to neighboring United Evangelical churches.

By 1910 only about five per cent of the UE membership was German-speaking, and only a few exclusively German preachers could be used in the itinerancy. Anti-German prejudice engendered by the First World War completed the language conversion. By the end of the War all United Evangelical publications were in English. The Evangelical Association, in contrast, was still printing over ten per cent of its Sunday School quarterlies and lesson leaves in German in 1922, and the circulation of *Der Christliche Botschafter* was still half as large as that of *The Evangelical Messenger*.[114]

The Pastorate

The Pastor's Job

A pastorate in the United Evangelical Church was not a forty-hour-a-week job. Only men dedicated to Christ would work studying, writing, teaching, preaching, and visiting the sick, the well, and the lost, for long hours for meager pay. Rev. J. Q. A. Curry reported that in four years at Franklin PA he preached 879 sermons, led 150 mid-week meetings, conducted 50 funerals, and married 62 couples.[115] His successor, A. J. Beal, in one year (1898/99) preached 251 sermons, made 721 pastoral and sick visits, conducted 27 funerals, tied 26 nuptial knots, and reported 297 souls converted.[116] Pastors' wives also had to be consecrated Christians, content with their lot, neat in appearance, intelligent with common sense, and devoted to the church.[117] Yet, with great labor often came great rewards when genuine love grew between congregations and their pastors. Lay people often shared their substance with the preacher's family. At holidays and the beginning of each conference year surprise parties and gifts of money, food, or clothing greeted pastors and their families. Visiting church leaders had words of commendation for the "success" of the "well-loved" or "highly esteemed" pastor.[118]

The United Evangelical Church was blessed at its birth with a strong nucleus of dedicated pastors, "a body of noble men whose piety, ability, devotion and zeal commend them to the confidence, esteem and love of the people whom they so faithfully serve."[119] One problem the United Evangelical Church had was finding enough of these "noble men" to fill all of its pulpits.[120] In the tumult of division and reorganization "every available man was pressed into service, and sometimes the urgent demand for men brought volunteers into service who were very inadequately prepared for the work,"[121] yet replacing these "men of an mediocre quality" proved to be difficult.[122] Minimal qualifications for clergy were rising. It was "no longer possible," wrote the Bishops in 1910, "save for men of unusual ability, or under exceptional conditions, for men to enter the ministry with less than the equivalent of a high school training," yet in a dynamic economy educated men had many lucrative employment opportunities.[123]

Even when, against all odds, the United Evangelical Church succeeded in raising "more men for the ministry than any church in America, in proportion to church membership," it lost many of these ministers to other denominations.[124] Despite the large number of men added to the ministerial rolls, the net gain in ministers between 1902 and 1910 was only thirty-five.[125] Church leaders repeatedly warned ministers than they would not fare any better in other denominations,[126] but the twin lures of better salary and a "settled pastorate" significantly reduced the ranks of United Evangelical ministers for much of its history.

Salaries

Of course, Evangelical preachers had rarely had more than subsistence salaries,[127] but the increasing cost of preparing for the ministry exacerbated the problem. If an educated man "does not receive a larger compensation for his services than many congregations are in the habit of paying," argued the Bishops in 1898, "he must either devote himself to a different calling, or go to some denomination where his services are better remunerated; as with these meager stipends he will hardly be able to pay the debts incurred in his education," much less support a family.[128] In 1898 the average salary of United Evangelical ministers was $487, less than "most of the better artisans and clerks in our stores."[129] In 1902 average salary, including housing, was only $537, still less than many mechanics and clerks.[130] In later years the efforts of the Presiding Elders kept salaries on a steady rise ($588 in 1906, $828 in 1914, $1452 in 1922), and church leaders, possibly in order not to fuel dissatisfaction within the ranks, tended to emphasize the progress made. Yet, C. H. Stauffacher lamented to a Cedar Rapids (IA) District Ministers meeting as late as 1912 that a United Evangelical minister had to be a saint, a scholar, a well-dressed socialite, and a businessman on less than the wages received by a hod-carrier or a street sweeper,[131] and gains in United Evangelical ministerial salaries did not kept pace with the American national average of ministers' salaries (dropping from 88% of the national average in 1906 to 81% in 1916). The greatest increase in pastoral support was made during and after World War I, when inflation and prosperity tripled many laborers' wages.[132]

Appointment and Tenure

Even more than inadequate salaries, vocal critics objected to the itin-erant system, which they saw as constantly uprooting families from com-fortable positions to new uncertainties. This system, in which ministers were assigned to congregations every year at Annual Conference by a committee consisting of the Conference President (ordinarily a Bishop) and the Conference's Presiding Elders, was an inheritance of the old cir-cuit-riding days in the Evangelical Association and the early Methodist Church. The United Evangelical *Discipline* proclaimed that "The itineran-cy shall never be abolished." Since each congregation had control of its own property, the itinerant system was in the eyes of the Bishops the principal remaining "bond of harmony" that kept the church together, yet dissatisfaction with the system ran deep, and congregations constant-ly tried to circumvent it.[133]

The First General Conference of the United Evangelical Church (1894) continued a long-term trend toward longer stops for the itinerant (traveling) preachers, raising the maximum time limit for a pastor at a congregation to four consecutive years, but this did not appease oppo-nents of the itinerant system.[134] Critics argued that four years was not sufficient for a minister to get to know his people and their circum-stances and that churches were hurt when they lost ministers they loved and were given a minister not to their liking. Besides, constant moving was laborious and expensive.[135] Defenders of the system maintained that it was scriptural and efficient, good for the pastor, the people, the denomination, the country, and the world. Settled pastorates, they claimed, in many instances had become stagnant pools. The average minister exhausts his fund of sermon material in a few years, but station-ing brings excitement and freshness, a sense of new approaches and new beginnings.[136] "In four years a minister can tell a congregation about all he knows."[137] Church leadership, in particular, opposed longer pastorates. "While the entire removal of the time limit would not be equivalent to abolishing the itinerancy, seeing that each preacher is always appointed for only one year, and may be changed at the end of every year," the Bishops wrote in 1902, "we are of the opinion that it will be far better for the perpetuation of the system among us if this limitation is not removed or disturbed."[138] Yet, circumvention of the system was so widespread that Bishop Dubs was finally persuaded that the *Discipline* should be changed to allow legal extensions with the approval of the local Quarterly Conference and the Annual Conference.[139] His proposal was soundly rejected by both 1910 and 1914 General Conferences. An amendment to raise the term limit for all ministers to five years approved by the 1910 General Conference failed to receive the necessary votes in the Annual Conferences, but a similar amendment approved unanimously by the 1914 General Conference was approved by the Annual Conferences.[140] In the United Evangelical Church the itinerant system enjoyed widespread support, but it was also in many cases strained "almost to its utmost tension, and at some places to the breaking point" by unofficial direct negotiations between pastors and congregations who thought they knew better than the stationing committees who should go where.[141] The system survived but not without controversy.

Sunday Services

United Evangelical worship was an amalgam of diverse influences: the revivalist tent, the old-fashioned campmeeting, the etiquette book, the schoolroom, and the Gothic cathedral. Morning worship in city churches might be as stately and majestic as in any mainline Protestant church. Yet, these same city churches also held fire-and-brimstone revivals and old-fashioned prayer meetings. Country churches tended, of course, to be more folksy and informal, plainer with fewer expensive trappings like pipe organs and pew cushions, but the same concerns for both order and fervor, propriety and spontaneity were evident. Congregational bulletins were popular early in the period, but as some became so substantial as to rival *The Evangelical*, they were discouraged and disappeared, only reappearing again in the 1920s.[142]

Revivalism affected every Protestant denomination in nineteenth-century America. Especially was this true in churches like the United Evangelical Church, and especially was this true of worship. The United

Evangelical Church inherited from the Evangelical Association the idea that worship was for inducing conversion and an approach to worship that was emotional, subjective, and individualistic.[143] Old-timers might complain that the AMENS weren't as loud as those they remembered hearing years ago,[144] and HALLELUJAHS might come in for "adverse criticism" from polished urbanites,[145] but the leaders of the United Evangelical Church rejoiced that "the shout has not been banished or suppressed from our public meetings,"[146] and old-fashioned AMENS were still common even in Eastern city churches.[147] Sophisticates might mutter against the old Evangelical altar service, but it was in no danger of disappearing.[148] Bishops might discern a "drift" in the larger church toward the dry, mechanical prayer and cold sermon,[149] but they were assured "that formality in worship is not now one of our threatening dangers."[150]

Preaching

The revivalistic approach to worship tended to focus on the pulpit and pulpit personalities. Sermons were calls to conversion and holiness with a "prooftext" verse often used as a pretext for the message the preacher wanted to give. Pulpits were centered on large platforms that provided room for the preacher to move, plead, and kneel. Choirs and organs were often placed so as to provide an impressive and worshipful backdrop to the preacher. The emphasis was on hearing the word in "auditoriums" often patterned after theaters with sloping aisles fanning out from the platform. The danger was that congregations would become passive audiences for those who read, prayed, preached, and sang to them.[151]

Early Evangelical preaching had been blunt and earnest, very plain and practical, unlearned, highly emotional, and spontaneous. United Evangelical ministers one hundred years later preached "more polished, scholarly and symmetrical sermons," and, as Ammon Stapleton asked, "Why should they not?"

> A large number of our ministers have the advantage of a superior education, and hence are enabled to use better language than the old time itinerant. Many have theological training, and are familiar with the principles of homiletics, and are better equipped, mentally at least, to produce a better sermon from a scholastic point of view. There is also, we believe, a better delivery of the sermon than in the early days.[152]

The early itinerants could, Stapleton said, have preached most United Evangelical ministers "under the bench" because after long years of lonely travel with only their well-worn Bibles in their sacks the itinerants had the Scriptures "at tongues' end," but United Evangelical preachers were no less effective in winning souls because changed times demanded changed preaching.[153] United Evangelical sermons were praised as "uplifting and heart melting" or "philosophic, thought-provoking and inspiring." Of J. H. Shirey's sermon at the 1910 General Conference it was written that "with beauty of diction, and simplicity of arrangement, and strength of thought the speaker led his auditors along in soulful pleasure."[154]

Sermons were also shorter than those of the early days.

> There has been an increasing tendency in the past few years to shorten the sermon in church services. The conventional hour for beginning has been changed from half past ten to about a quarter to eleven, and a half an hour is usually taken up with opening exercises – responses, singing by the choir, reading of announcements, and more singing until twenty minutes is about all there is for the sermon. ...Whatever may have been the case once, long sermons are not popular unless they are the work of a man of pre-eminent ability.[155]

Sacraments

Observance of the sacraments did not change dramatically during the three decades of the United Evangelical Church. Communion services were scheduled four times per year, still with a connection in some places to the Presiding Elder's visit and Quarterly Conference but also with regard to the festivals of the church year (particularly Easter) and other special days.[156] Grape juice gradually replaced wine and individual cups the common cup.[157] Both infants and adults continued to be baptized, infant baptisms accounting for about two-thirds of the total throughout the period.[158]

Music

The leaders of the UE church continued the Evangelical stress on the "two great objects" of church music: singing with the spirit and with the understanding also. United Evangelical singing was to be animated and spiritual; in prayer and testimony meetings music "should be mostly spontaneous and informal." Contemporary gospel songs held a prominent place in United Evangelical services, and there was room for choruses and even the old camp-meeting spirituals, but for worship services, Holy Communion, and other ceremonies and rituals, things were done "as orderly and impressively as possible." Traditional hymns, which were more edifying to the mind, were not neglected.[159] Instrumental music, whether organ, piano, band, or orchestra music, was no longer controversial. United Evangelical churches were among those that benefited from industrialist Andrew Carnegie's grants for the purchase of pipe organs.[160]

Choirs, though they were wrong to "monopolize the song service too much," also had a place in United Evangelical worship as leaders of congregational song and providers of special music. Bishop Stanford wrote, "Now we most certainly believe, if a choir be composed of truly Christian, and consecrated, spirits, who can sing 'with the spirit and with the understanding also', that God can most effectively use such an instrumentality to the edification of his people, and to his glory."[161] "Of all the positions of honor and trust in a congregation, it must be conceded that the work of the choir is one of the most exacting and the most trying. Moreover, in many congregations, it is also the most thankless."[162]

One innovation that rapidly became the norm in United Evangelical churches was the arm-waving song leader. Bliss, Sankey, and other earlier revivalist song leaders led crusade singing seated at a reed organ, but around the turn of the twentieth century Charles M. Alexander introduced a new model of song leading and a new instrument of choice in worship, the piano. The florid, improvisatory style of his pianist, Robert Harkness, was soon imitated in revival meetings, and then church services, around the world.[163]

As to what the United Evangelicals sang, the mixture of divergent influences that characterized all their worship is also evident in their repertoire. The first General Conference of the United Evangelical Church (1894) appointed committees to prepare German and English hymnals. The German committee (R. Dubs, J. Schneider, C. A. Fuesele, S. Busse, W. F. Schmalle, G. Barth, T. Suhr, and C. Newton Dubs) took a collection of contemporary gospel songs translated by Carl Kohland and E. C. Margaret (*Die Kleine Palme;* 159 texts with music) and added 164 more traditional hymn texts grouped under 73 tunes plus 54 choruses to form the *Evangelisches Gesangbuch: Die Kleine Palme mit Anhang* (1896).[164] The English committee (H. B. Hartzler, W. M. Stanford, J. D. Woodring, U. F. Swengel, and Prof. Otis L. Jacobs, music editor) produced the *Hymnal of the Evangelical Church,* published in 1897. This book included 631 "of the choicest old standard hymns and tunes of the church universal" for the "regular public worship of the church," seven Anglican chants for liturgical use, and eighty-four gospel songs and choruses, old and new, "for the various special and social meetings and protracted revival services" of the church.[165] Later printings bore the title

Hymnal of the United Evangelical Church and included six pages of texts of choruses and Pennsylvania German spirituals translated into English.

Church Buildings

Evangelical Association church deeds limited the use of their buildings to preachers of the Association. When the courts ruled that Minority ministers were not members of the Association, they could no longer preach in the buildings used by Minority congregations. If the congregations accepted United Evangelical pastors, they had to vacate their old Evangelical Association buildings.[166] Some UE congregations were able to buy back their old buildings from the Evangelical Association, but many were forced to or chose to build anew, preferably a grand new building overshadowing the old Association church across the street. In the words of Ammon Stapleton, after the Division

> [e]difices sprang up everywhere as if by magic, from four to six dedications on a Sunday was no unusual occurrence [in 1895], and church projects and dedications formed the chief topic in church periodicals. ...
> In all there were purchased about two hundred, and newly built about one hundred and fifty churches during this year.[167]

By the spring of 1898 there were 684 UE churches valued at $1,727,643 and 152 parsonages valued at $164,196. As the Bishops stated in their Episcopal Message that year:

> Whoever is familiar with the terrible losses in church property which we sustained, must say that this is a quite extraordinary showing, and a striking proof of the willingness to sacrifice, and of the self-denial of our people. We know of no cases where congregations made greater sacrifices, and in so short a time for the re-erection of their churches, than were made by those in church-fellowship with us.[168]

Few churches were as opulent as the new First Church in Reading PA, with its cushioned pews, velvet carpet, and electric chandeliers, but even frame country churches had stained glass windows, oak furniture, a furnace, gas/electric lights, and even pipe organs.[169] Churches in towns and cities often had Sunday School rooms and an infant room separated by sliding partitions on the first floor with the main auditorium on the floor above. Country churches were more likely to be in one floor.

United Evangelicals shared in the prosperity of early twentieth-century America and continued to erect and improve church buildings throughout the church's short history.

Dates	1898	1902	1906	1910	1914	1918	1922
Church Buildings	684	820	885	907	924	900	882
Parsonage	152	240	332	365	399	406	457
Total Value of Property ($1000s)	1946	2749	3593	4610	5478	6449	9515

While the number of church buildings declined after 1914 as small rural churches were closed, parsonage construction continued until over one-half of the churches had parsonages, and property value continued to increase.[170]

Prayer Meetings and Class Meetings

As the Bishops repeatedly noted in their Episcopal Messages to General Conference, classes, class-meetings, and class leaders had by the early years of the twentieth century ceased to function as John Wesley originally intended.

> [I]n many instances, and even including some of our larger societies, we are pained to find an almost lamentable lack of class organization, and a corresponding lack of attendance at the regular weekly prayer meeting. In a few instances we find societies with a membership ranging from 100 to even 250 or more, where there is but one class, one class-leader, and consequently but one prayer-meeting a week, and even that one rather poorly attended.[171]
>
> The tendency to supersede the smaller by one or two larger classes, contravenes the original purpose of class organization. In the early days of Methodism the enrollment of more than twenty-five in one class was discouraged. A larger number made it difficult if not impossible for the leader to give the members proper attention and to accord them appropriate opportunity for participation in the class service. How many leaders now carry out the original purpose of their office?[172]
>
> The present tendency is to enlarge the classes and to substitute for the individual class prayer-meeting, a union service, the result of which is often a lessened sense of responsibility on the part of the members, the non-enforcement of class obligations and diminished interest in the class service. ... It is impossible to know accurately the average attendance at prayer-meetings, but it is not above twenty-five per cent of the entire membership.[173]

Class leaders had long since become simply prayer-meeting leaders. Their role in shepherding the flock[174] had devolved onto the pastor and adult Sunday School teachers and class officers. Bishops, Presiding

Elders, and Annual Conferences might express their alarm at the decline in prayer- and class-meeting attendance, but as Bishop Stanford noted in an *Evangelical* editorial "the meeting itself must draw." "Cut out your long chapters, and your long dry speeches, and your new songs that nobody knows," he said "and introduce more fervor, faith, spirit and spontaneity in your meetings, and the prayer-meeting problem will be solved."[175]

Unfortunately, the "prayer-meeting problem" was not solved in the United Evangelical Church. The 1914 Sunday School and Keystone League of Christian Endeavor convention discussed ways to deal with the "vacant front seat" problem, as well as over-long prayers and speakers, tardy meetings, and backseat gigglers, but prayer meetings were no more enticing at the end of the United Evangelical period than they were in Stanford's day[176] and average attendance still hovered around twenty-five per cent of church membership.[177]

Church Year

For the early Albright People every visit by a circuit-riding preacher was a special day. As church life became more settled and routine, campmeetings and revivals became special times of religious fervor. Sunday School teachers introduced other special days and observance of civil holidays to maintain the interest of their pupils. Cooperation and competition with more established denominations spurred a rediscovery of the traditional Christian holy days. By the early years of the twentieth century the United Evangelical church calendar was an eclectic mixture of ancient and modern, sacred and civic observances.

The new year began in many United Evangelical churches with a watchnight service, which might last from 8 PM to midnight on New Year's Eve and include prayers, worship, and testimonies. In Albright's time the watchnight service was held along with Quarterly Conference as preparation for Holy Communion. Later, watchnight was associated with revival meetings, and some United Evangelical churches still maintained this connection by beginning their revivals on Jan. 1.[178] The first full week of January had been chosen by the World Evangelical Alliance at its 1846 meeting as Universal Week of Prayer, and this week was observed widely in the United Evangelical Church, as in other Protestant denominations.[179]

Most United Evangelicals "made little of the Lenten season as such," believing that Christians should be pious all the time, not just for forty days,[180] but Easter developed during the United Evangelical period as an occasion for special services, musicals, cantatas, and recitations. Reading

(PA) First Church conducted its first Easter dawn service in 1903. Holy Communion, baptisms, and reception of new members were also linked with the Easter celebration. Church leaders lent their encouragement throughout the United Evangelical period to observance of Passion Week, including Palm Sunday and Good Friday, as well as Ascension Day and Pentecost.[181] The denominational Self-Denial Week for the support of missions sometimes coincided with Passion Week (1895, 1912 1914), but not being tied to Lent it sometimes fell after Easter (1902, 1903), even as late as the week before Pentecost (1894).

Mother's Day was started by Anna Jarvis of Andrews Methodist Church of Grafton WV in 1908 and rapidly reached the United Evangelical Church. Even before Congress made it an official holiday in 1914 reports of Sunday School Mothers Day programs and elaborate floral decorations marked the pages of *The Evangelical*. Memorial Day, like Independence Day and Labor Day, also migrated from the civic calendar to United Evangelical Sunday Schools and church services.

June brought Children's Day. The Children's Day offering was a major source of funds for missions, so denominational leaders did all they could to foster its celebration. Preparations began weeks in advance. When the great day arrived, overflow crowds came to see elaborate decorations (including floral crosses and fern fountains) and hear children's plays, recitations, and musicales.

After this, the focus of United Evangelicals shifted to outdoor camp-meetings, Bible conferences, missions conferences, and Schools of Methods, but Labor Day brought a new Sunday School year and the Rally Day season.

> Rally Days [wrote H. B. Hartzler in 1914] have become one of the fixed institutions of our Church activities. Most, if not all, the congregations include rallies of various kinds in their reassembling of scattered forces of the church and Sunday school.[182]

Rally Day was generally an all-day event: morning, afternoon, and evening. It was sometimes combined with Holy Communion, or Harvest Home, or even Old People's Day. Churches were decorated with banners and flags. Other fall observances were Harvest Home (when churches decorated with the fruits of the field and orchard), Foreign Day (the first Sunday in October designated for a special offering for foreign missions), Thanksgiving, and the missionary thankoffering service.

The calendar year came to a close with Christmas celebrations, in which the Christmas tree and Santa Claus often overshadowed the manger. Gift giving, children's programs, special entertainments, and gaudy decorations brought winter cheer. Offerings were received for the poor, and the pastor received special gifts, maybe a pumpkin pie or a mustache cup.[183]

World War I did much to wring the worst excesses of Victorian sentimentality from United Evangelical holiday observances. By the end of the United Evangelical period Evangelicals were rediscovering the ancient Christian holy days and seasons.

> Christmas, and Palm Sunday, and Good Friday, and Easter, and Ascension Day, and Whitsuntide, in many of our churches, are being celebrated in such a way as to set out their meaning more clearly to the worshipper. Our conviction [wrote *Evangelical* Editor A. E. Hangen in 1922] is that we have not made as much of these days in all of our churches as their importance justifies. At once some one reminds us that in such observance a tendency to formalism can easily present itself. Granted! But there is a three-fold answer: First, a prayer-meeting, a revival meeting, in which we thoroughly believe, can be formal, and often is. The fact is, that there is just as much opportunity for formalism in any of these as in the observance of any of the festal days of the year … Second, the events these days commemorate have too vital a relation with our actual salvation to be totally disregarded … Third, such services do not have to be formal and ought not to be.[184]

Campmeetings

Good singing, good preaching, good wells, and good access to railroads—these were four key ingredients to a good campmeeting, and during the United Evangelical era good campmeetings continued to flourish. Each summer saw some two dozen camp meetings scattered across United Evangelical territory. Five thousand people heard the Gospel on Sunday at Herndon (PA) Camp Meeting in 1894.[185] The Millway Camp Meeting near Lititz PA reported four thousand at its closing service in 1897.[186] A meeting at Pine Swamp PA drew one thousand on a Sunday evening, and Catasauqua (PA) Camp Meeting attracted ten thousand to the grounds on a Sunday in 1900.[187] The first campmeeting in Iowa was a seven-day event that drew 1200-1500 people each evening and resulted in twenty conversions.[188]

Campmeetings conducted by individual congregations might be less structured, but district gatherings were tightly scheduled. At Barrington (IL) Camp Meeting, for example, the day began with an early morning prayer service, followed by a 9 AM "quiet hour." Preaching services

(German and English) were conducted at 10:45 AM, 2:45 PM, and 8:00 PM. Children attended a 10 AM Bible school and 1:30 PM children's hour. Missions received considerable attention, with a daily 1:30 PM missionary conference. At 7 PM a workers' meeting was held for the camp meeting's spiritual leaders.[189]

Portable tents and temporary clapboard preaching stands were still the norm on campmeeting grounds from Pennsylvania to Oregon, but the trend through the years of the United Evangelical Church was toward permanent groves purchased, developed, and maintained by Campmeeting Associations of stockholders for the use of the church. Herndon camp grove was purchased in 1901. Within a year a frame tabernacle and a boarding house had been erected, and by 1910 thirty-one cottages graced the mountainside.[190] The United Evangelical Waldheim Association purchased Waldheim Park near Allentown PA in 1904. Tabernacle, wells, and dining hall were built immediately, and by 1915 thirty-three cottages had risen on its lots. Waldheim, with its "romantic paths through thick forests [and] miniature lake nestling on the hill" just a short trolley ride from the city, quickly became the site of a Chautauqua assembly and numerous Sunday School picnics.[191]

Interest in campmeetings remained high throughout the United Evangelical years, but the high tide of spiritual enthusiasm sensed at the beginning of the period became a more settled "religious fervor" as the church and country matured.[192] As H. B. Hartzler wrote in *The Evangelical*:

> The old time camp meeting is dead....The old time camp meeting was adapted to the conditions of the former days. It served its high purpose well. Changed conditions wrought inevitable readjustment and adaptation. So it must needs be. But...[u]nder some name, in some form, the camp-meeting spirit must be embodied.[193]

Revivals and Evangelistic Services

> It should never be forgotten that we are essentially an evangelistic church, and if the day should ever come when we cease to be such, then there would be no longer any reason for us to exist as a church.[194]

Winning souls was the church's driving force, and the revival meeting was still an important means of evangelism. The church papers regularly reported revival triumphs and exhorted congregations to greater effort with articles like "How to Reach Non-Church Goers," "Concern for the Salvation of Others," and "The Church and Evangelism."[195]

Churches usually held revivals in winter, although summer meetings were not unknown,[196] and the meetings were still usually "protracted," lasting four weeks or more. A revival in Franklin PA began on January 2, 1898, and lasted until the end of April. Between "300 and 325 were happily converted to God, at least two thirds being men and…hundreds were turned away" for lack of room.[197] Preachers often announced conversion goals at the beginning of the revival series, and the goals were usually met. The Conemaugh PA mission envisioned one hundred converts from its 1897 revival.[198]

Among these converts were undoubtedly some children, for United Evangelicals believed that conversion was for children as well as adults. It would be an

> injustice to children to rob them of their birthright, as in adult skepticism of their capacity to know God. Jesus did not say that a child must become a man in order to know God, but that a man must become a child. God comes to childhood first.[199]

Evangelism was taken to the Sunday School in the Decision Day service set apart to call children, young people, and adults to Christ.[200]

Several Annual Conferences appointed conference evangelists whose job was leading revival series; the blind preacher W. P. Rhoda was Evangelist of the Central Pennsylvania and East Pennsylvania Conferences.[201] Churches brought in evangelistic teams, like the Ackley Brothers, Rev. G. Kilmer Ackley of Ohio Conference and his brother Alfred, the famous gospel hymn writer and singer.[202] UE churches also participated in union evangelistic efforts like the Billy Sunday campaigns. Nevertheless, church leaders believed that local pastors knew their congregations best and encouraged them to conduct their own meetings using the tried and true methods that had worked so well in the past.

> Some revivals are held in connection with elaborate church fairs and bazaars. There is an overestimation of human agencies and underestimation of the Divine, ignoring the great essentials of faith and prayer. Attempts to make meetings sensational rather than spiritual. The church must first be Spirit-baptized. There is promiscuous employment of evangelists, some of whom are too concerned with popularity and reputation and the subletting of congregational singing to a choir or paid singers. There is the limiting of God's time of quickening his people to revival "season." No program or service should be stereotyped as not to admit the Holy Spirit to the order or form.[203]

As Bishops Hartzler and Heil proclaimed in their Episcopal Message to the 1910 General Conference, evangelism was the work to which the United Evangelical Church was specially called. The denomination truly believed that "soul-saving and soul-nurture" were the "chief duty of the Church,"[204] and the United Evangelical Church grew because it emphasized evangelism.

Catechetical Instruction

The United Evangelical *Discipline*, like its Evangelical Association predecessor, enjoined upon all pastors the duty of conducting catechetical classes for the instruction of new Christians. A German catechism (*Christliche Katechismus der Vereinigten Evangelischen Kirche*) by Jacob Kaechle was accepted by the Board of Publication at its May 22, 1895, meeting and published (Harrisburg: United Evangelical Publishing House, 1895. 133 p.).[205] An English catechism prepared by Ammon Stapleton failed to win approval, so the 1898 General Conference appointed a committee (H. B. Hartzler, C. Newton Dubs, Jacob Hartzler, and J. D. Woodring) to prepare an English-language catechism usable with both adults and children. The appointment of C. Newton Dubs as missionary to China caused further delay, but his place was taken by his father, Bishop Rudolf Dubs. Finally, in 1901 the catechism (*Catechism of Christian Doctrine as Taught in the United Evangelical Church*. 106 p.) was finished, approved, and published.[206]

Now the task was getting pastors to use these resources. "If our young people are to be loyal to our doctrines," exhorted the 1906 General Conference, "they must know them, and there is no better way of indoctrinating them, than by catechetical instruction."[207] A simplified *Catechism for Children* was prepared by Jacob Hartzler in 1907 at the request of this Conference (58 p.),[208] and the 1910 General Conference instructed Presiding Elders to make regular inquiries about catechetical instruction and pastors to keep a statistical record of classes and catechumens taught.[209] A catechetical department was added to the *K.L.C.E. Journal* under Junior Superintendent J. G. Walz.[210] Despite the lack of a truly child-oriented catechism, catechetical instruction increased in the closing years of the United Evangelical Church (from 26 classes and 678 catechumens in 1914 to 158 classes and 2624 catechumens in 1922), though it was still the exception rather than the rule.

Sunday Schools

In our Church as now organized there is no department of Christian work that is more important, or that has larger possibilities, or higher incentives, than the Sunday School, or better said, the Bible School of the Church. Encouraging progress has been made in this indispensable department both in organization and methods, in providing improved facilities for better service, and in intelligent preparation for more thorough work....To-day the Sunday School is thoroughly organized and provides a place for every person within the reach of its influence, teaching is reduced to an orderly system, and a measure of preparation is required for those who teach.[211]

While other churches, like the Northern and Southern Methodists, reported fewer Sunday School scholars than church members, the United Evangelical Church consistently reported significantly more.

Sunday Schools provided instruction for people of all ages, from the

YEAR	1898	1902	1906	1910	1914	1918	1922
Church Members	59,190	63,390	69,046	73,551	79,292	89,271	92,001
S. S. Scholars	85,253	94,730	104,934	113,682	122,709	126,055	128,643

Cradle Roll for infants, through Beginners, Primary, Junior, Intermediate, and Senior Departments and men's and women's adult classes, to the Home Department for the aged, the sick, and those obliged to work Sundays. Uniform International Lessons and graded lesson materials for all ages were published by the denomination.[212] Fall Rally Days and Decision Days were a common feature of Sunday School life, and Spring Rally Days were introduced.[213] The 1894 General Conference provided for local Sunday School Boards, consisting of the pastor and officers and teachers of the School.[214]

Larger United Evangelical churches had long included adult Sunday School classes, but the Men's and Women's Bible Class movement, which started in the 1890s and organized between 1903 and 1909, spread quickly through UE churches and left a lasting impression. Organized classes with officers and regular class meetings grew to immense size (149 average attendance in the Men's Bible Class of First Church in Reading PA in 1910 out of a total Sunday School attendance of 754).[215] By 1914 495 Men's and Women's Classes with 13,061 members were organized under constitutions registered with the International Sunday School Association.[216]

UE Sunday Schools placed great emphasis on teacher training. There were almost two hundred training classes throughout the church by 1914, when the textbook *Evangelical Teacher Training* by W. E. Peffley was published.[217] Intensive teacher education was a primary purpose of the summer Normal Assembly or School of Methods begun in the last years before the church division. The Central Pennsylvania Conference School of Methods at Central Oak Heights camp grove, for example, provided a four-year course of study for older youth and adults, as well learning activities for children.[218] A three-day Bible Conference developed from Normal Assembly at Perkasie Park PA in 1893. Audio-visuals came early on; the second Bible Conference featured a stereopticon lecture on the Holy Land.[219] By 1906 Bible Conferences were common throughout the denomination.[220] District and Annual Conference Christian Endeavor and Sunday School Conventions also provided educational opportunities.

Women and Men in the Church

All the pastors and most of lay officials of the United Evangelical Church were men, but the church provided many opportunities for women who desired to serve Christ in the church and supported their efforts. UE churches employed women as evangelists, at least in the early years, and as deaconesses, or pastoral assistants. Sister A. C. Davis, a member of the UE Church in Anita IA and Sister E. Fowler of Allison IA were popular revival preachers in that state.[221] Emma Divan preached the word with power at services at Dixon IL in 1897 and made it so plain that some who had been listening to the preached word for years said that they had never heard it so thoroughly explained.[222] Grace Wiest conducted weeks of revival services at Bridgeville PA in 1899, and Sarah Snyder preached at a revival at York PA in 1910.[223] The Deaconess ministry was established at the instigation of the Woman's Missionary Society. The Central Pennsylvania Conference appointed a Deaconess Board in 1907, and the first two United Evangelical deaconesses, Georgiana Hoke and Grace Hershman, began work in churches within the Conference. *The Evangelical* gave the ministry constant support, and by 1912 there were five deaconesses, three at the Deaconess House in Baltimore, one at the Church Union in Carlisle PA, and one assisting a pastor in Williamsport PA.[224] Deaconesses ministered to church and the community. In 1918, for example, Hoke, Hershman, and Bessie Ihrie in Baltimore made 9,207 visits, distributed 11,430 pieces of literature, conducted 168 meetings, carried 445 bouquets to sick and shut-ins, gave 387 articles of clothing to the needy, donated food to 435 hungry souls, visited 152 new homes, obtained 75 new Sunday School scholars, and taught sewing classes.[225] The 1914 General Conference considered making the Deaconess ministry a denominational organization, but the delegates, while very solicitous that no action be taken which would in any degree grieve or discourage the women, decided to keep the ministry an Annual Conference and local church initiative.[226]

Women played particularly prominent roles in the educational activities of the church. All of the denomination's colleges were co-educational, and many of the instructors were women, particularly in the arts. Church leaders like Bishop Swengel maintained that women needed higher education not only to be good wives and mothers but to succeed in the business world:

> Are there not the same reasons for the education of women as there are for the education of men? Why should a human being, a man's equal, exist in enforced helplessness in business and educational life simply because she is a woman? The mere statement of such a question in a Christian land is a refutation of it.[227]

The Illinois Training School for Christian Workers was founded by a group of women of the Illinois Branch of the Woman's Missionary Society to provide education in United Evangelical history, doctrine, and polity for women and men enrolled in Moody Bible Institute and other Chicago area training schools. Its superintendents were women with standing (sometimes as salaried Conference Trainers) in the Illinois Conference.[228] The School of Methods of the Central Pennsylvania Conference was founded and led by a woman, Emma D. Messinger.[229] In local Sunday Schools most teachers were women, and they taught men as well as women and children. C. Elizabeth Snyder, for example, was teacher of the Kutztown (PA) Men's Bible Class (fifty members), and Jennie Noot taught the fifty-five members of the Men's Baraca Class of Nescopek PA.[230]

Women were also prominent in the missionary activities of the church. The Woman's Missionary Society under Elizabeth Krecker was the only denominational organization of the Evangelical Association that was controlled by the Minority and came over with leadership intact into the United Evangelical Church. As such it assumed added importance in the new denomination. Mrs. Krecker addressed the first General Conference (1894), which voted to give the Society representation on the Board of Missions and local societies representation on local Quarterly Conferences.[231] In 1897 the Woman's Board of Missions had its first meeting and immediately launched its campaign for a United Evangelical mission overseas. The cautious men on the Board of

Missions were often reluctant to go along with the women's plans, but the two Boards worked together with mutual respect and confidence until the Board finally approved the mission to China. The WMS quickly raised the necessary funds and continued to provide essential financial support throughout the years of its existence. One means of support was Spend-a-Day calendars introduced in 1917 to raise salaries for single lady missionaries. The Society also edited and published two magazines, *Missionary Tidings* for adults and *Missionary Gem* (first called *Illustrated Leaflet*) for children, and maintained a library of books on missions.[232]

Many women were active in local churches. Some women served as stewards and class and prayer meeting leaders. Many more served as church musicians. Ladies Aid Societies spearheaded major projects in many congregations. Representatives of local Woman's Missionary Societies participated in the Quarterly Conferences that were still the official governing bodies of local churches. Pastor's wives, in particular, were expected to teach Sunday School, sing in the choir, lead WMS and Christian Endeavor meetings, visit the sick, and promote temperance, while also entertaining church members and guests and raising exemplary children.[233] They were considered full partners in ministry and on dying were memorialized at Annual Conference just as pastors were. Bishops Dubs, Hartzler, Fouke, and Swengel encouraged women to participate fully in ministry, and their wives were important church leaders in their own right. Fouke reminded the women of Adams Street Church in Chicago in 1896 that they belonged to a church "which was among the first to recognize and encourage the work of woman, and one which has taken the most advanced ground."[234]

Not all United Evangelical men were equally supportive of women in positions of leadership. Ammon Stapleton lamented that

> [t]he service of women, as a divinely ordained agency, co-ordinate with that of man, has never to our knowledge been recognized in our church .... To man, who has usurped all the prerogatives of the Church, and relegated women to subordination and tutelage, it mattered little that she was the *mother* of all church memberships, that she constituted *three-fourths* of all worshiping assemblies.[235]

By the early years of the twentieth century women outnumbered men two to one in the pews of most churches.[236] Church leaders, fearing a complete feminization of the church, tried to present a robust image that would appeal to men. The "universal cry of the church" became: "What can we do to get men interested in religious work?"[237] Answers came in several forms: organized Men's Bible Classes in the

Sunday School, the Laymen's Missionary Movement (1906), the Men and Religion Forward Movement (1912), and various denominational brotherhoods. Men's rallies were held in local churches, and local and conference male choruses were popular. Local Men's Missionary Societies were organized.[238] In some UE Churches Men's Bible Classes organized themselves into a "Brotherhood" to collect money for worthy causes, call on the sick and needy, hold prayer meetings, and get together for social fellowship. The Brotherhood of First Church in Williamsport PA organized as the first Albright Brotherhood in 1913.[239]

Youth (Christian Endeavor)

The Keystone League of Christian Endeavor (K.L.C.E.) had played an important role in the formation of the United Evangelical Church. The K.L.C.E. Managing Board (consisting of five ministers and four laypersons) elected by the 1891 General Conference in Philadelphia met immediately to elect officers, adopt a badge, and prepare a model constitution, pledge cards, prayer-meeting topic cards, and instructions for local society organization. The editors of *The Evangelical* and *Die Evangelische Zeitschrift* opened their pages to weekly comments on Christian Endeavor meeting topics and regular feature articles. Special K.L.C.E. periodicals were established in Illinois *(Bee Hive)*, Pennsylvania *(Pathfinder)*, and Iowa *(Evangelical Review)*. District and Annual Conference K.L.C.E. conventions rallied United Evangelical youth. With an estimated 12,500 members (one-fourth of the church's entire membership) K.L.C.E. was truly the "right hand of the pastor" and the "life of the church" in many congregations. The 1894 General Conference made the president of the local K.L.C.E. society a member of the Quarterly Conference that governed each congregation and circuit.[240]

The next four years were ones of growth and "steady, sturdy, stable development" for the Keystone League. Denominational rallies were held at each International Christian Endeavor convention. The League reached every Annual Conference and almost every district. Ministers, "the strongest friends of the K.L.C.E.," recognized the value of youth work and encouraged it. The local K.L.C.E. periodicals were combined into a denominational *K.L.C.E. Journal* in January 1897. By 1898 the Keystone League of Christian Endeavor numbered 17,837 active (15,170 senior and 2,667 junior) and 4,369 associate members. "More than one third the number enrolled on our church records are written on our K.L.C.E. pledges."[241]

Then, the period of "rapid enlargement" gave way to "a period of pruning and testing." In 1902 K.L.C.E. membership was actually down from four years before. "The period of enthusiasm usually attendant upon the inauguration and early progress of any work has passed," wrote W. H. Fouke, U. F. Swengel, and J. Q. A. Curry for the Managing Board, "the novelty of the movement is over."[242] The Keystone League of Christian Endeavor, now fully organized with departments of missions, devotional life, and temperance, settled into the busyness of a mature organization: annual district and city conventions, K.L.C.E. days at camp-meetings, Bible study courses, and prayer-meetings.

In line with the Christian Endeavor motto "For Christ and the Church" the Keystone League gave concrete support to UE church extension by raising money to build a church at Dallas OR, home of the denomination's Dallas College, and to missions by paying for the erection of a church at Siangtan, China.

The church leadership, in turn, continued their support of K.L.C.E.

Members and Inquirers at Siangtan Gathering

The 1902 General Conference created the office of K.L.C.E. General Secretary, though in electing W. H. Fouke, who was also Secretary of the K.L.C.E. Managing Board and editor of the denomination's English

Sunday School literature and the *K.L.C.E. Journal,* to the office "without salary" it failed to provide a full-time director of youth work. The same General Conference (1910) that elected as Bishops long-time K.L.C.E. Managing Board President U. F. Swengel and Secretary W. H. Fouke placed the church's Sunday School work under the K.L.C.E. Board and finally elected a salaried General Secretary for Youth (Sunday School and K.L.C.E.), Rev. Daniel A. Poling, Secretary of the Ohio Christian Endeavor Union.[243] Poling resigned as General Secretary in 1912 and as editor of the *K.L.C.E. Journal* in 1913, but under the leadership of Rev. W. E. Peffley enthusiasm engendered by the "Increase and Betterment Campaign" of 1911-1912 climaxed in the highly successful First General Convention of the United Evangelical Sunday School and K.L.C.E. held in Chicago, Sept. 25-30, 1914. At the next UE General Conference the name of the Board was changed to "The Sunday School and K.L.C.E. Managing Board of the United Evangelical Church" and the *K.L.C.E. Journal* became *The Evangelical Endeavorer.* Conference and district conventions also began to combine Sunday School and K.L.C.E. interests.[244] World War I and the influenza epidemic that followed it placed great strains on youth work in the closing years of the United Evangelical Church, sabotaging among other things the plans for a second General Sunday School and K.L.C.E. Convention in 1918.[245]

Still, the Keystone League of Christian Endeavor remained a vital part of the United Evangelical Church throughout its history. In this "training school," wrote Bishops Fouke and Swengel in their 1914 Episcopal Address,

> a pledged, trained and devoted body of young people [were] fitted for and inducted into active service for the Master along every line of church work....The devotional life, Bible study, missions, benevolences, the cause of temperance and reform and everything that pertains to a practical Christian service have felt the impulse of the faithful and intelligent action of this band of young people.[246]

Over 21,000 young people were converted in the K.L.C.E. and thousands were prepared for Christian service.

Beliefs

Theology

Like most Protestants the United Evangelicals claimed simple belief in the clear teachings of the Bible. As Bishops Dubs and Stanford wrote in their Episcopal Message to the 1902 General Conference:

> Our articles of faith are not encumbered by the dogmatic explanations and definitions of certain creeds. They are directly and clearly taken from the Word of God....There is remarkable unanimity among us in teaching the fundamental doctrines of Christianity, because the experience of the salvation of our God confirms and corroborates our teaching. The doctrines are verified by our experience and the glorious experience is the result of our Scriptlral [sic] doctrines.[247]

In his pamphlet "The United Evangelical Church and What It Stands For" Bishop H. B. Hartzler said that the church stood for the itinerant system, lay representation in church bodies, missions, temperance, strict discipline of members, aggressive evangelism, ecumenical cooperation, and certain beliefs:

> 1. It stands, in common with all Evangelical Protestant Churches, for the great fundamental principles of Christianity, the essentials of salvation in Jesus Christ.
> 2. It stands for experiential religion—repentance toward God by renunciation of all sin; acceptance of Jesus Christ as Saviour and Lord; realization of the witness of the Holy Spirit; a new life of obedience to the will of God, resulting in a hearty, happy, joyful, winsome religion.
> 3. It stands for the highest privileges, experiences and attainments in Christian character and life as set forth in the Scriptures—constant growth in grace and divine knowledge; abiding fellowship with God; abundant fruitfulness in Christian graces and works; perfect love, entire sanctification, victorious holiness, fullness of the Spirit, and final perseverance in the life of faith.
> 4. It stands for the glorious hope of the second coming of Christ; the resurrection and glorification of believers; the everlasting triumph of righteousness; the restitution of all things in Christ.
> 5. It stands for a Church membership either soundly converted, or earnestly seeking salvation in Christ....
> 15. It stands for the Bible, the whole Bible, the Bible in its integrity, as given by inspiration of God.[248]

In reality, the United Evangelical Church stood squarely within the Methodist understanding of biblical truth. Its Articles of Faith (retained by the Evangelical Congregational Church) were taken from a pamphlet "Doctrines of Arminian Methodism" (1887) by Milton S. Terry, a professor at Garrett Theological Seminary in Chicago.[249] Only Articles I, IV, and XXII were replaced with language from the Articles of the Evangelical Association by the 1894 General Conference, which adopted the Articles of Faith as the permanent faith of the church.

The Church used John Wesley's own words to state its stance on holiness/sanctification/perfection, adding Wesley's summary at the end of his "A Plain Account of Christian Perfection" (1st ed., 1766) to the Articles of Faith.[250] Sanctification might be instantaneous,[251] but it was ordinarily a lifelong process of growth and submission to the Holy Spirit.[252]

> A certain class of promoters of holiness call it a definite and distinct work of grace, while others contend that it is a growth of grace, the beginning acquaintance of which is experienced at the time of conversion. This latter view is the view of the Bible as well as that of our church.[253]

Holiness was the birthright and duty in one degree or another of every Christian, not a special state or blessing to be prayed down at a Pentecostal meeting.[254]

Christian Conduct and Moral Issues

Holiness was not just an article of faith for United Evangelicals; it was a way of life for the believer and a moral vision for all of society. In the early years of the church Bishops and other church leaders condemned extravagant jewelry and dress, tobacco in all forms, Sunday newspapers, dime novels, dancing, card playing, the theater, circuses, and church fairs.[255] Even bicycling for pleasure, baseball, and other "unnecessary recreation" were suspect.[256] Warnings continued to be issued throughout the United Evangelical period against the evils of the theater (and later moving pictures) and the "so-called 'innocent dance,'"[257] but the church remained focused most intently on the evils of Sabbath desecration and alcohol.

The first General Conference declared the Christian Sabbath "an institution of the gospel dispensation" and "absolutely essential to the perpetuity of the Christian religion."[258] The last General Conference declared that "No secular work or amusement or unnecessary privilege should receive attention on the Lord's Day. This is the Divine idea."[259] Annual Conferences condemned all Sunday excursions, visiting for pleasure or recreation, Sunday newspapers, businesses that required employees to work on Sundays, Sunday trains, and all work that could possibly be avoided.[260] Of course, not all United Evangelicals were as scrupulous in the observance of Sunday as others would have liked. The Bishops noted in 1922 that "the church must continue to preach and teach against all manner of Sabbath desecration; but her message will, in large measure, be ineffective so long as individual members of the church dispute her teachings by their conduct."[261]

On the subject of Prohibition United Evangelicals were united in denouncing the "greatest sin in the world," the root of all other sins, demon liquor.

> When the "whiskey devil," with his bewitching charm and lying tongue, once gets inside, he then turns every laudable purpose and noble senti-ment outside, and immediately assumes absolute control of the *whole man*. Once in possession, this deadly foe to humanity becomes the absolute monarch, and reduces his victim to nothing but an abject slave. He is *totally* and *awfully* bad, and the unrelenting enemy of all good.[262]

United Evangelicals were active in the Woman's Christian Temperance Union and the Anti-Saloon League. They spoke and preached and wrote and voted for prohibition and rejoiced when national prohibition finally became a reality.[263]

Obviously, United Evangelical concern for moral reform extended beyond the individual conduct of UE church members. The church took stands on the important moral and political issues of the day.

> We desire no union of church and state, but with this we do not admit that the State has a righf [sic] to be irreligious, or devoid of all religion. We are a *Christian* people, our morality and civilization are rooted in and derived from Christianity. It is the duty of the church to protect and pre-serve these high endowments of our people. All Christian citizens, with-out regard to party affiliations, must stand and unitedly contend for hon-esty and righteousness.[264]

The church regularly denounced "loose and unscriptural divorce laws,"[265] political corruption,[266] socialism,[267] and the "rapacity and avarice" of captains of industry as well as arbitrary work stoppage by organized labor.[268] Before and after World War I church leaders and organizations supported the cause of world peace, although during the War *The Evangelical* did its best to support the war effort, and a War Service Commission was established to attend to the spiritual needs of military personnel.[269]

Church Organization (Polity)

The United Evangelical Church was the result of a dispute over poli-ty: should the church of Jacob Albright be organized as an army of God under the command of its senior Bishop or as a democratic and volun-tary association of like-minded believers? United Evangelicals were those

who took the latter view. In their mind, the polity of the United
Evangelical Church was specifically designed to be American, democrat-
ic, and republican — "of the people, by the people, and for the people."
The *Discipline* strictly limited the powers of central authorities (Bishops,
General Conference, general church officers), reserving rights to the
Annual Conferences and individual congregations. Lay people had
equal representation with clergy at Annual and General Conferences.
Congregations controlled their properties through elected trustees, and
congregations even had the right (with certain qualifications) to leave
the denomination entirely. Stationing of ministers, however, remained
the prerogative of the Bishop and Presiding Elders at Annual
Conference. Leaders like Bishop Dubs argued that this was essential for
the health of the church, though of course the counsel and suggestions
of the local congregation would be considered and so far as possible
complied with.[270]

The highest authority on the local level was still officially the
Quarterly Conference, which included itinerant and local preachers,
class leaders and assistants, stewards, Sunday School superintendents,
presidents of Keystone League of Christian Endeavor, a representative
from each Women's Missionary Society, and a representative from each
board of trustees. All of these, except the preachers, were elected by
members of the congregation, though the Presiding Elder normally
chaired the meetings. The Quarterly Conference structure, however, was
breaking down during this period. Overworked Presiding Elders were
not attending Quarterly Conferences at all their churches, local members were absent from them, and in many congregations, noted Bishops
Dubs and Stanford in 1898, it had "become the practice, that much business which of right belongs to the quarterly conferences, is now contracted by the so-called official boards. The business thus transacted is with-
drawn from the supervision and inspection of the presiding elder ... and
... annual conferences." The 1898 General Conference passed a resolution "[t]hat we recognize the quarterly conference as the only official
body to which all the departments of church work on the station, mission or charge are directly or indirectly accountable, and that no legiti-
mate quarterly conference business can be legally transacted by so-
called official boards,"[271] but many congregations found that their business could not wait for the quarterly visit of the Presiding Elder. By the
1920s monthly meetings of the Official Board (basically the Quarterly
Conference minus the Presiding Elder) were the preferred business
model.[272] The Quarterly Conference had become "a sort of 'makeshift'

business affair."[273]

Conference apportionments also had their origin in the United Evangelical period. In the early years Annual Conferences would make pledges, usually to the UE college they supported but also sometimes to missions, and direct the Presiding Elders to determine how much of this each congregation was expected to contribute. The 1896 East Pennsylvania Conference, in great need of funds to build up Albright College, appointed a Committee on Educational Apportionments.[274] Two years later, the Conference, noting that the Presiding Elders had been unable to apportion the missionary appropriations to the respective Presiding Elder districts during this session, appointed a committee to "apportion the amount of missionary money to be raised for this conference by each charge during the ensuing conference year." The Laws of Conference were amended to provide for the appointment of a missionary apportionment committee in each district, consisting of the Presiding Elder plus two ministers and two laymen appointed by the Conference Committee on Appropriations.[275] Soon, the educational and missionary apportionments were combined.

Re-Merger and Response

Events

The United Evangelical Church was formed in the white heat of controversy; amid name-calling and lawsuits ministers and whole congregations were locked out of their own properties and thrown out of the Evangelical Association. After Bishop Esher died, however, and United Evangelicals had time to consider what they had lost in their struggle, some people, especially in the Midwest and West where Evangelical Association churches were more numerous, began to think that their departure had been too hasty and not altogether wise.

The early twentieth century was a time of church co-operation and ecumenical good feeling. Both Evangelical churches participated in the organization of the Federal Council of Churches of Christ in America in 1905. Young people from both denominations in Chicago participated in a citywide revival crusade conducted by Gypsy Smith in 1907 and concluded that if Christians of so many conflicting creeds could work together for Christ, then Evangelicals with so much in common should be able work in unity. The Chicago Union of the Young People's Alliance [EA] sent an official representative to the annual meeting of the Chicago Union of the Keystone League of Christian Endeavor [UE] with instructions to organize a joint meeting. Approximately one thousand young people from the two groups met at the Chicago YMCA on April 8, 1907, and sent a resolution urging reunion of the churches to the 1907 General Conference of the Evangelical Association. This Conference appointed a Commission on Church Union and Federation to begin negotiations with the United Evangelical Church that "the spiritual descendants of Jacob Albright will all again be united in one fold."[276] At the 1910 General Conference of the United Evangelical Church, the lay delegates to the Conference met to consider this EA proposal. They concluded that

> WHEREAS, Sentiment for union between the Evangelical Association and the United Evangelical Church have found expression in various forms during the past four years in different parts of the church:
> In Union Communion services, Banquets, Mass meetings, rallies, free exchange of pulpits, etc., and
> WHEREAS, in many places we are duplicating our work, hindering rather than helping the coming of the kingdom, in many instances both churches paying missionary money to support the pastors and thus continuing the unnecessary conflict, and
> WHEREAS, The consolidation of our various institutions, such as our colleges, home and foreign missionary enterprises and charitable institutions, could be much more effectively and economically carried on if an organized union of our two denominations could be honorably and equitably effected, and
> WHEREAS, The Evangelical Association at its General Conference assembled at Milwaukee, Wis, in October, 1907, appointed a Commission on Church Federation and Union, and have communicated to our General Conference Secretary, a copy of their resolution, empowering their Commission to meet a similar commission from our General Conference, therefore be it,
> *Resolved,* That we believe such a commission should be elected by the same methods employed in the selection of our various boards consisting of equal representation.

The 1910 General Conference had also received an invitation for union from the United Brethren Church, so the Conference appointed a Commission on Church Federation and Union to meet with "similar commissions of other churches of the same faith and doctrine, and especially the commission of the United Brethren in Christ and the Evangelical Association, to consider the matter of organic union." This Commission consisted of the Senior Bishop (Swengel) plus ten ministers and ten laymen elected by the various delegations to General Conference grouped in five districts.[277] The United Brethren proposal was later deferred in favor of prior union with the Evangelical Association.

The EA and UE Commissions met together on February 1-2, 1911, in Chicago with a "genuine spirit of fraternal feeling"[278] and appointed an Executive Committee (Bishops Breyfogel, Heinmiller, and Swengel plus former Bishop W. F. Heil) to continue negotiations. At their first meeting in Reading PA on February 28 it was decided "that the members of the executive committee from each denomination should outline the points of difference between the two denominations and prepare a plan according to which these differences may be adjusted." The differences as presented at the next meeting of the Executive Committee on January 23, 1912, were striking: the EA refused to consider any changes to its Articles of Faith, its episcopal structure, or its title to church properties, while the UE asked that nine Articles of Faith not in the Articles of the Association be added, the democratic structure of the UE Church be retained, and titles to property be drawn according to the desire of the people creating them.[279] The full commissions met again at Linwood Park OH on July 30, 1912. The EA commissioners restated their previous position, but after hearing counterproposals by the UE commissioners seemed to accept various limitations on the power of General Conference that the United Evangelicals considered essential to prevent a reoccurrence of the events of 1891. However, at the next meeting of the Executive Committee in Allentown PA on January 28, 1913, the EA Bishops denied agreeing to any changes.[280]

Between the UE General Conferences of 1910 and 1914 the commissioners met frequently but had reached an impasse. Bishop Swengel wrote to the UE commissioners that insuperable barriers "make it appear impossible to bring about a harmonious union at this time. If this be so, it seems futile to continue the work of the commissioners."[281] EA Bishop Heinmiller gave an impassioned plea for union in his address to the 1914 UE General Conference.

> I think I am in a position to know the sentiment that prevails among the tribe of Evangelicals I have the honor to represent, and I know that I express that sentiment when I say, *We want union, we pray for union,* and we are ready to continue the negotiations for union until we have either adjusted our differences or agreed to disagree....True, we do not want union *at any price,* but we are willing to pay a big price for it....[N]o Evangelical can remain indifferent to the great movement which has

been started for the purpose of bringing Evangelical forces together....*We should be careful at least not to stand in God's way.*

Yet, even Heinmiller admitted that the negotiations "struck a snag" on the issue of the relative powers of the General Conference and the Annual Conferences, the very issue that ruptured the church in 1891. Despite his plea, the 1914 UE General Conference merely ratified the United Evangelical position on the points of difference.[282] The EA commissioners regarded this as an unacceptable ultimatum and negotiations ceased for four years.

Meanwhile, sentiment for re-union continued to grow in many quarters of the church. The 1916 Centennial Celebration brought leaders and members of both denominations together in a very positive way. The stresses of World War I showed the advantages of inter-church cooperation and hastened the demise of the German language in the Evangelical Association. The commissioners appointed by the 1914 and 1915 General Conferences of the two churches finally met on September 18, 1918, and the UE commissioners were disposed to break the deadlock by accepting EA proposals. Those UE commissioners (including Heil) who had reservations made no protest because they understood that "finally the whole matter would be submitted to the constituency of the whole Church and then the people would have an opportunity to declare themselves either for or against the merger." The tentative Basis of Union was presented to the 1918 General Conference of the United Evangelical Church two weeks later in York PA. Unfortunately, an influenza epidemic closed the Conference after one all-night session, and the Conference had little time to consider the question of merger. The Conference appointed a committee to work with the EA to prepare a basis of union for a re-united church. When this was completed and approved by the joint commissions, the committee was empowered to call a special session of the General Conference to consider the agreement.[283]

The meetings of the joint commissions continued, but without Bishop Heil, who was severely injured when struck by a locomotive while crossing the tracks at the Hamilton Street Railroad Station in Allentown PA on Dec. 5, 1918, and confined during a prolonged recovery from complications of the accident.[284] The commissioners agreed to a Basis of Union that, while accepting certain UE provisions, did not explicitly include the democratic guarantees the UE church had at one time demanded. This document was approved by the 1919 General Conference of the Evangelical Association, which authorized a special uniting conference at the time of the 1922 United Evangelical General Conference. A "majority of the members and delegates of the United Evangelical Church were enthusiastically anticipating the consummation of the merger,"[285] but Bishop Maze and other church leaders knew that the church's "mother conference" and source of one-third of its resources, East Pennsylvania Conference, was restive. Congregational meetings there were already denouncing the terms of the merger when Maze and the Presiding Elders of the Conference (A. J. Brunner, A. E. Hangen, and H. F. Schlegel) issued a letter to the Conference ministers "earnestly request[ing] and urg[ing]" that Official Boards, Quarterly Conferences or congregations refrain from taking any action whatsoever on this important question" until the Joint Commission had approved the final terms of the merger. "To take any action at this time," they said, "would be to pre-judge the case without having the facts at hand." They promised that the entire matter would be submitted to the church at the right time, that is after the Basis was approved by the two Commissions on Church Union.[286]

The two Commissions met in Chicago on January 21, 1921, with Bishop Heil present but very ill.[287] The official record states that the Commissions in joint session "adopted without a dissenting vote the Basis of Union and the revised Book of Discipline, which were submitted to the annual conferences for consideration and action."[288] Bishop Heil had up until this point signed all the reports of the Commission, but he now realized that this was widely seen as an endorsement of the terms of the agreements, not, as he claimed, agreement to a process for getting the terms to the church membership for their discussion and decision. In a letter to EA Bishop Breyfogel (February 21, 1921) he lamented that he did "not know now just how to best avoid such a misrepresentation of my signature." He did not want to "give an uncertain tone" to the Episcopal Message accompanying the Basis of Union by his dissent, so he asked that the words "without a dissenting vote" be struck from the report.[289]

The merger issue was not brought before the East Pennsylvania Conference at its 1921 session but was submitted to the other Annual Conferences later that spring and summer. The East Pennsylvania Conference first considered the merger on February 27, 1922. When the motion to accede to the merger was made, Rev. E. S. Woodring moved "That this conference declines to consider the Basis of Union because it is presented to us as an amendment to the Discipline and as much is irregular and out of order." Bishop Maze, who was presiding, ruled against the motion. Rev. A. W. Cooper then appealed to the Conference to over-rule the decision of the chair. After discussion the Conference unanimously adopted a motion by a merger supporter, Rev. R. C. Deibert:

> Whereas, It is the sense of this conference that the Joint Commission was without authority when it referred the Basis of Union to the annual conferences for action before the General Conference passed on it; therefore,
> Resolved, 1. That we defer action on the proposed Basis of Union until it shall have been passed by the General Conference.
> 2. That this action shall not be construed as a position for or against the principle of union upon a satisfactory basis.[290]

The delegates elected to represent the East Pennsylvania Conference at the 1922 General Conference, except Rev. A. J. Brunner, then met and adopted the conditions under which support for the merger could be had from the East Pennsylvania Conference. They objected to the condemnations of the founders of the United Evangelical Church still extant in the records of the Evangelical Association, the abrogation of rights of congregations and Annual Conferences in the Basis of Union without the approval of those congregations and Conferences, the irregular way in which the Basis had been submitted for approval, the altering of the "unalterable" Articles of Faith of the United Evangelical Church, and the ambiguous language of the Basis concerning the rights of conferences and congregations. They maintained that their position was that of the UE General Conference of 1914; it was the church leaders who wavered and given up their principles, but not they.[291]

The General Conferences of the United Evangelical Church and the Evangelical Association were both called to order at 2:00 PM on October 5, 1922, the UE meeting at Barrington IL and the EA at Detroit. Following consideration of the usual procedural matters, the report of the Commission on Church Federation and Union was presented on Friday afternoon, October 6. E. S. Woodring immediately entered a protest on behalf of the East Pennsylvania Conference delegation, raising all of the objections they had discussed earlier in Pennsylvania plus an additional one: the merger, they contended, had not been approved by "two-thirds of the members of all the Annual Conferences," as stipulated in the *Discipline*, but only by two-thirds of the members of the Annual Conferences present and voting on it. After discussion the General Conference decided at its October 7, 1922, afternoon session to refer the protest to a Committee of Twenty composed of one minister and one lay person from each Annual Conference delegation. This was the last session of the Conference at which Bishop Heil presided.

The Committee in its report Monday evening issued its decision that two-thirds of the conference members present and voting was sufficient for approval of the merger. The East Pennsylvania Conference delegation then issued its final protest. Here it presented its six objections: I. Since the *Discipline* makes no provision for merger, the question should have been submitted to a vote by the constituency, i.e. all the members of the church; II. The Commission on Church Union was instructed by the 1918 General Conference to report back to General Conference but instead submitted a Basis of Union to the Annual Conferences for vote without any authority to make this change in procedure; III. The Basis of Union provided new Articles of Religion, essentially those of the Evangelical Association, whereas the UE *Discipline* declares that "The Articles of Faith shall never be changed"; IV. The Basis of Union takes away the Annual Conference's right to determine the legality of its own organization, a right that the *Discipline* says no Annual Conference shall be deprived of; V. The Basis of Union proposes to move every UE congregation into a new denomination, whereas the *Discipline* gives a different procedure for a congregation wishing to change denominational affiliation; VI. The Basis of Union is not really an amendment to the *Discipline* as presented by its sponsors and even if it were it did not have the approval of two-thirds of the members of all the Annual Conferences as any amendment must have to pass. The General Conference then proceeded to approve the Basis of Union by a vote of 77-0, with all East Pennsylvania Conference delegates except A. J. Brunner abstaining, and adjourned to Detroit.[292]

The UE General Conference reconvened in Detroit on October 11, 1922. The East Pennsylvania delegation had been persuaded to go there with the other delegates, but now it issued a statement that it could no longer participate in any further business. Finally, on October 13 the Conference adjourned to meet again the next morning in joint session with the General Conference of the Evangelical Association, first issuing an appeal and a warning to those opposed to the merger:

Think deeply, whether, considering the way this great proposal has come to this consummation, it is not of God. If it has not his approval, then what in his church has ever come to pass that can be so described? And if this is *his* work you may not pass by the open door to a holy compact for individual and unified affirmation and cooperation, lest haply you should be found fighting against God.[293]

The dissenting delegates from East Pennsylvania immediately organized as the General Conference of the United Evangelical Church under Bishop Heil and adjourned to meet at the call of the chairman. Meanwhile, the merged delegations joined in a time of joyful fellowship. "Never," wrote A. J. Brunner, "were Evangelical hearts more deeply moved and more joyously blended as when this host of sons and daughters of Jacob Albright united in singing."[294] Heil, on the other hand, saw it as "an orgie of jubilation which those who participated in it described as a wonderful manifestation of the Holy Spirit" but which Heil believed was "not of the Lord."[295]

Name of Conference	Votes for Union	Against	Total
Northwestern	40	0	40
Des Moines	60	1	61
Illinois	56	21	77
Ohio	45	20	65
Pittsburgh	85	3	88
Central Pennsylvania	215	13	228
Oregon	40	0	40
Kansas	11	0	11
Platte River	62	0	62
Grand Total	614	58	672

Perceptions
As can be seen in the Table above, approval of the Basis of Union was overwhelming when it was presented to the Annual Conferences. Obviously, many United Evangelical ministers were convinced that reconciliation was the practical and Christian course to take,[296] but the vote may or may not be a true picture of the opinion of the whole membership of these Conferences. It will never be known how many UE members approved the *Basis of Union,* how many wanted merger on better terms, how many were opposed to merger on any terms, and how many were "outspokenly or tacitly indifferent."[297] Bishop Heil claimed that a majority of lay people in the Ohio and Illinois conferences opposed the merger, but Presiding Elders used their authority to "coerce the quarterly conference [in each congregation] to elect as delegate [to Annual

Conference], a person who was committed to the merger."[298] Men, said Heil, were selected for each Annual Conference and given sufficient "consideration" to bring it into line with the merger; opponents were "silently assailed" by smear campaigns to "destroy the influence and wreck the repute" of these men, while "formidable political pressure was brought to bear on the delegates" to vote for merger.[299] Heil was told at the 1922 General Conference that the mergerites were planning to use a letter he had written to blackmail him into silence, so he demanded a committee of inquiry and called on all who knew aught against him to come forward, but none came.[300] By then the merger was inevitable, and he was irrelevant.

Yet, even if these charges of mergerite dirty tricks are exaggerated, it is obvious that those in favor of the merger were skilled political operatives. The UE Commission on Church Union was instructed by the 1918 General Conference to call a special session of General Conference when they arrived at an agreement with the Evangelical Association, but the Basis of Union "was not referred to the General Conference because the merger leaders did not want to have a public discussion so long as the members of the conferences had not been politically fixed in favor of the Basis." Instead, the Basis was submitted it to the Annual Conferences one-by-one as an amendment to the *Discipline*, starting not as was usual with the first Annual Conference to meet (East Pennsylvania) but with the small western Conferences, where it had support, to "create the impression that public opinion favored the Basis."[301] Public discussion of the merger was discouraged and banned from *The Evangelical* before the Basis was completed; after all, one could not argue with an agreement that did not yet exist. But after the Basis was complete the church was told it was too late to discuss the terms at length because the other side had agreed to them and negotiations were finished. "It was to be hurried through shrouded in the robes of a pious sentiment because the exposure of its gaunt features would have lost it the support of the constituency of our Church."[302]

Opponents of the merger claimed that ministers who supported it were persuaded by the "bread and butter issue," that is promises of improvements of their material and professional position in a larger church. There was, however, undoubtedly strong desire for merger in many parts of the church, and many believed that merger was the will of God.

> An exceedingly rare phenomenon in Church History is the fact that a
> goodly number of leaders of the Evangelical Church who saw the

denomination divide between 1887 and 1894 were among the leaders who brought the Evangelical Association and the United Evangelical Church together again a generation later in 1922. Scarcely had the records of the last law suits, occasioned by the division, been printed before some far-sighted and unbiased souls began to dream that this separation must eventually be corrected by a reunion.[303]

Some UE members, congregations, and even Conferences were swept up in the events of 1891-1894 without really thinking about the issues at stake; once the dust settled they wondered what damage they might have done to their ministry. Some saw the issue solely as Bishop Esher, and once he was dead (1901) they saw no reason for two Albright churches. Some sincerely believed that the cause of Christ would be better served by church union; these were "get together" days, in which the church had to unite to save the world.[304] As the East Pennsylvania Conference itself stated in 1920, "A common parentage urges upon us a spirit of unity; the great work of the kingdom demands coöperation."[305] Moreover, the western Conferences, churches, and pastors of the United Evangelical Church never had the resources they needed to minister effectively over great distances, despite the best efforts of eastern Conferences to help them. The Evangelical Association had a strong presence in many western areas, comparable to or exceeding UE membership (see below), and there was much intermingling between the churches as children of German Evangelicals sought English-language services in United Evangelical churches. According to merger leaders,

Comparison of Overlapping EA and UE Annual Conferences–1922		
Name of Conference	Membership of EA Conference	Membereship of UE Conference
Central Pennsylvania	None	27,191
East Pennsylvania	9,797	25,800
Illinois	8, 625	7,251
Iowa (EA)/DesMoines	5,953	3,878
Kansas	7,982	953
Nebraska (EA)/Platte River (UE)	3,222	3,501
Ohio	12,658	5,547
Oregon	1,918	1,580
Pittsburg	2,067	13,569

western conferences were desperate for the support a larger church would bring and felt they could not maintain an independent existence.

Wealthy laymen and their pastors in the East, on the other hand, were just as desperate to avoid losing the church buildings and democratic church structure that had sacrificed so much for in 1894. As Bishop Heil wrote to Bishop Maze on February 21,1921,

> The union movement has been the most serious problem to decide. My convictions are against a strongly centralized government....In case of union the attitude of our large congregations in the east is unsettled. Two or three possibilities face us, first a number of our best people may withdraw and reduce the strength and influence of the congregations decidedly, or second the congregations may assume an independent attitude. Knowing the struggle of 1890-95 as I do, it is evident that to the men who stand out we owe very largely our existence as a church and their position today is practically what it was then.[306]

Eastern Pennsylvania was still a wealthy industrial area, and East Pennsylvania Conference had large city churches with wealthy and socially prominent members. According to Heil, the Conference had single-handedly rescued the Central, Pittsburg, Illinois, Des Moines, Platte River, and Oregon Conferences in 1890-4 when "they were threatened with destruction by the crusade of the Association against them."[307] "Without her [East Pennsylvania] aid the United Evangelical Church would soon have occupied the grave which the Association friends had made ready."[308] The well-off and committed lay people of East Pennsylvania Conference gave 62 % of the general missionary contributions between 1895-1922 and "carried approximately one half of the general finances of the Church." The Boards of the church were drawn largely from East Pennsylvania; according to Heil, Bishop Dubs once tried to transfer the Executive Committee of the Board of Missions to Chicago but was soon back asking eastern men to take charge because the Committee could not manage without them.[309]

Of course, East Penn did not always get its way in the United Evangelical Church. Annual Conference membership consisted of ministers and one lay delegate from each congregation, and representation to General Conference was based on number of Annual Conference members. Conferences with many small churches, therefore, were allotted more General Conference delegates than Conferences with fewer but larger churches. East Pennsylvania Conference was entitled to only sixteen General Conference delegates, while "the five [western] conferences with less than half the membership of the older conference on whose bounty they subsisted, were entitled to 26 delegates."[310] In 1906 Presiding Elder A. M. Sampsel warned that this "inequitable arrangement is bound to bring trouble sooner or later," and the Schuylkill Valley (PA) U. E. Ministerial Association in his district proposed amending the *Discipline* to base General Conference representation on Annual Conference "population." The East Pennsylvania Conference approved the amendment 125-4, but Bishop Dubs denounced it in *The Evangelical,* saying the East already had too much power and the rest of the church would not be intimidated by "threats" like Sampsel's statement. Central Pennsylvania Conference, which had more members and more churches but less power than East Penn and many points of rivalry with it, rejected the amendment by unanimous vote (0-144),[311] and the amendment was assured of defeat.[312]

The events of 1922 could be predicted based on just this one episode. Going back to the crisis of 1894 in which the United Evangelical Church had its origin, the East Pennsylvania Conference placed a principled priority on lay rights and congregational autonomy that was shared by others in the church but overshadowed in other Annual Conferences. "The position of this conference was based on personal conviction of right in the controversy of 1894 and is again so based in the present agitation."[313] The ink on the *Basis of Union* was not dry before nine congregations with a combined membership of over 4,500 members and annual income of over $100,000 (more than the income of six of the Annual Conferences) took official action against the union; they simply would not be part of any union that surrendered their democratic rights.[314] Heil had written in 1891 that "those people on both sides of this controversy" for whom it was "a question of like and dislike for persons" had "not thought deeply on the subject of our trouble. It is a question of right and wrong, and while right is not altogether on one side, we are convinced there is much more right on the 'minority' side than anywhere else. It is conscience over expediency. Let us stand for CONSCIENCE."[315] The East Pennsylvania Conference did just that in 1894 and never wavered in its supreme commitment to its principles in 1922.

> The Evangelical Association, a simple Pennsylvania religious society, was led to support missionary operations among a foreign people and when an ambitious leader arose among them they were taught to forget the rock from whence they were hewn and shared in an effort to enslave their benefactors in a foreign polity. The East Pennsylvania Conference with thousands of laymen in other conferences, withstands this perversion of earlier ideals.[316]

Those unfavorable to union are, in a degree, conservators of the Church. They have neither introduced the movement now disturbing her nor are they pressing any other new movement. They are simply holding on to the Church they have learned to know and love and this position can not be condemned as either wrong nor unreasonable.[317]

Notes

1. [B. J. Smoyer] "Principles, Polity and Faith of the United Evangelical Church," UE, April 24, 1895, 129.

2. Rudolf Dubs, "East Prospect, Pa.," EV, January 22, 1913, 21.

3. Raymond Albright, *A History of the Evangelical Church* (Harrisburg: Evangelical Press, 1942), 330–335.

4. H. B. Hartzler and W. F. Heil, "The Episcopal Message," UEGenConf], 1910, 43.

5. H. Franklin Schlegel, "The National Service Commission of the United Evangelical Church," UEGenConf], 1922, 48b–49b.

6. U. F. Swengel and W. H. Fouke, "The Episcopal Message," UEGenConf], 1918, 47.

7. UEGenConf], 1918, 26.

8. E. Crumbling, "The Forward Campaign," EV, July 2, 1919, 4.

9. W. M. Stanford, "Our Church and Her Important Need in this Pivotal Hour of Her History," EV, August 27, 1919, 4–5; "Report of the Committee of Episcopal Activities and of Forward Campaign Committee," UEGenConf], 1922, 51b–52b; E. Crumbling, "The Forward Campaign," EV, July 9, 1919, 4–5.

10. [H. B. Hartzler] "Our Forward Campaign," EV, August 6, 1919, 7; W. F. Heil, "The Forward Campaign," EV, August 4, 1920, 8; "Report on the Forward Campaign," EV, March 8, 1921, 2–3.

11. "Report of the Committee of Episcopal Activities ...," 53b.

12. Albright, 345.

13. Department of Commerce, Bureau of the Census, *Religious Bodies 1916* (Washington, DC: Government Printing Office, 1919), v. 1, 30.

14. B. H. Niebel, "Our Church Statistics," EV, June 14, 1902, 388.

15. UEGenConf], 1906, 29.

16. Rudolf Dubs and Wesley M. Stanford, "The Episcopal Message," UEGenConf], 1902, 31.

17. J. H. Shirey, "An Historical Sketch: The Progressive Development of the Publishing Interests of the United Evangelical Church," EV, October 9, 1918, 9.

18. A. Stapleton, *Annals of the Evangelical Association of North America and History of the United Evangelical Church* (Harrisburg: Publishing House of the United Evangelical Church, 1900), 605; Albright, 302.

19. A. J. Brunner, "East Penna. Conf.," EV, March 10, 1897, 77; H. B. Hartzler, "The United Evangelical Church," EV, January 6, 1897, 1.

20. Shirey, 9; H. B. Hartzler, "The New Publishing House," EV, April 25, 1917,

6.

21. Dubs and Stanford, 44.

22. A. A. Winter, "Address at the Dedication of the United Evangelical Home," EV, September 13, 1916, 4–5; A. A. Winter, "Historical Sketch" in *Superintendent's Second Annual Report of United Evangelical Home of the United Evangelical Church... 1917* [Harrisburg: Publishing House of the United Evangelical Church, 1918?], 21–23.

23. A. A. Winter, *Superintendent's First Annual Report...1916*, 14–15, 20.

24. Winter, Second Annual Report, 11.

25. *Ibid.*, 17, 28.

26. A. A. Winter, *Superintendent's Third Annual Report...1918*, 19; A. A. Winter, *Superintendent's Fourth Annual Report... 1919*, 12, 14, 18.

27. A. A. Winter, Superintendent's *Sixth Annual Report...* 1921, 13, 25; A. A. Winter, Superintendent's *Seventh Annual Report...* 1922, 15.

28. W. F. Heil, "Home Missions I," EV, February 2, 1910, 76.

29. Stapleton, *Annals*, 593.

30. J. H. Shirey, "Church Extension Society," UEEPAConfJ, 1895, 77–78.

31. Stapleton, p. 625.

32. Dubs and Stanford, 38.

33. "Church Extension," UEGenConfJ, 1902, 65–66; B. H. Niebel, "Church Extension," EV, January 22, 1903, 51.

34. B. H. Niebel, "Home Mission Problems," EV, December 10, 1919, 5.

35. B. H. Niebel and Homer H. Dubs, *Evangelical Missions* (Harrisburg, PA: Home and Foreign Missionary Society of the United Evangelical Church, 1919), 146.

36. H. B. Hartzler and W. F. Heil, "Quadrennial Episcopal Message," UEGenConfJ, 1906, 40.

37. H. B. Hartzler and W. F. Heil, "Episcopal Message," UEGenConfJ, 1910, 44, 46.

38. B. H. Niebel, "Report of the Secretary of the Board of Church Extension," UEGenConfJ, 1918, 55.

39. W. F. Heil and M. T. Maze, "Episcopal Message," UEGenConfJ, 1922, 36b.

40. C. D. Huber, "The Probable Results of Church Union Bearing on Missionary Interests," EV, December 13, 1921, 9.

41. Dubs and Stanford, 48–49.

42. [W. M. Stanford,] "That World Missionary Conference," EV, April 13, 1910, 232–233; B. H. Niebel, "From the Corresponding Secretary," EV, April 20, 1910, 244.

43. Benjamin H. Niebel, "The Missionary Principles and Practice of the United Evangelical Church," in Niebel and Dubs, *Evangelical Missions*, 108–111.

44. Albright, *History*, 440.

45. Dubs and Stanford, 49.

46. C. Newton Dubs, "Chapel Opening in Changsha," EV, July 26, 1902,

481.

47. C. Newton Dubs, "Changsha, Hunan," EV, October 30, 1902, 706.

48. Homer H. Dubs, "A Venture of Faith,".in Niebel and Dubs, *Evangelical Missions*, 188, 194–195, 214.

49. W. H. Fouke, ed., *The Evangelical Almanac and Year Book 1907* (Harrisburg, PA: Publishing House of the United Evangelical Church, 1907), 39–40.

50. A. E. Hangen and W. H. Fouke, eds., *The Year Book of the United Evangelical Church 1922* (Harrisburg, PA: Publishing House of the United Evangelical Church, 1922), 42–43.

51. Albright, 441.

52. Foreign Mission Day Program, October 6, 1912, 3.

53. R. Dubs and W. M. Stanford, "Episcopal Message," UEGenConfJ, 1898, 23–24.

54. Stapleton, *Annals*, 631.

55. A. E. Gobble, "Central Penna. College," EV, February 2, 1898, 61; R. Dubs and W. M. Stanford, "An Appeal for Central Pa. College," EV, July 19, 1898, 229.

56. Eugene H. Barth, *Discovery and Promise: A History of Albright College 1856–1981* (Reading, PA: Albright College, 1989), 51.

57. H. Franklin Schlegel, "Harrisburg and the College," EV, February 1, 1902, 85.

58. J. W. Domer, "The Consolidated College," EV, April 5, 1902, 233.

59. Chas. C. Poling, "Lafayette Seminary, Hereafter Dallas College," EV, May 22, 1900, 175.

60. W. H. Fouke and U. F. Swengel, "Episcopal Message," UEGenConfJ, 1914, 42.

61. W. H. Fouke, "The Field at Large—The Oregon Conference," EV, June 9, 1915, 19.

62. W. H. Fouke and U. F. Swengel, "Episcopal Message," UEGenConfJ, 1918, 38.

63. W. F. Heil and M. T. Maze, "Episcopal Message," UEGenConfJ, 1922, 70b.

64. Barth, 85–92.

65. Advertisement, EV, April 5, 1898, 112; O. B. Server, "Albright College Notes," EV, November 15, 1898, 364.

66. B. J. Smoyer, "Commencement Exercises at Albright Collegiate Institute," EV, July 7, 1897, 213; C. A. Bowman, "Annual Educational Address," EV, March 15, 1898, 82; J. D. Woodring, "Ampler Accommodations for Albright College," EV, July 14, 1904, 441.

67. Schlegel, 85; Domer, 233.

68. "Harrisburg's Effort to Get Albright College," EV, July 14, 1904, 440.

69. Chas. A. Shaffer, "Berwick After Albright College," EV, July 21, 1904, 453.

70. "East Pa. Conference Proceedings," EV, March 1, 1905, 132.

71. Barth, 85–111.

72. W. M. Stanford, "Our Western Union College," EV, May 15, 1900, 167; "Western Union College," EV, August 7, 1900, 263.

73. E. S. Woodring, "A Visit to Western Union College," EV, July 5, 1905, 420.

74. Wm. Caton, "Proposed Institution of Learning," EV, December 15, 1897, 397.

75. R. Dubs, "Should the Law of the United Evangelical Church on Biblical and Theological Schools be Amended?" EV, September 19, 1906, 594–595.

76. "Education," UEGenConfJ, 1910, 94–95.

77. H. Franklin Schlegel, "The Training of Our Ministry," EV, May 8, 1912, 290.

78. H. Franklin Schlegel, "Another Recognition for Albright College," EV, February 23, 1916, 11.

79. Charles A. Mock, "Western Union Theological Seminary," EV, March 3, 1920, 9.

80. H. H. Thoren, "Meeting of the Board of Education," EV, June 6, 1917, 8.

81. H. B. Hartzler and W. F. Heil, "Episcopal Message," UEGenConfJ, 1910, 58.

82. M. R. Drury, "The Following Brotherly References…," EV, June 9, 1897, 177.

83. "Ecumenical Conference," UEGenConfJ, 1898, 52–53; W. H. Fouke and U. F. Swengel, "Episcopal Message," UEGenConfJ, 1914, 44.

84. see "Proceedings of the Central Pennsylvania Conference, Sixteenth Annual Session," EV, March 9, 1910, 145; W. F. Heil, "Two Weeks in the Platte River Conference," EV, January 16, 1907, 36; A. E. Gobble, "A Splendid Day in Gratz," EV, January 9, 1907, 20–21.

85. H. B. Hartzler and W. F. Heil, 58–59.

86. R. G. Boville, "The National Federation of Churches Conducts Daily Vacation Bible Schools in Philadelphia and Chicago," EV, October 2, 1907, 625.

87. W. F. Heil, "Denominational Rally in Connection with the Ministers' Conference of the Interchurch World Movement, EV, March 3, 1920, 8.

88. [W. M. Stanford], "The Great Inter-church Conference for Federation," EV, December 6, 1905, 776–777.

89. "Ways and Means Committee," UEGenConfJ, 1914, 115.

90. H. V. Summers, "At the Federal Council," EV, December 29, 1920, 12–13.

91. "Report of The Charitable Society," UEGenConfJ, 1910, 70–71.

92. "Report of Commitee of the Charitable Society," UEGenConfJ, 1922, 66b–67b.

93. "Report of the Charitable Society," UEGenConfJ, 1910, 49.

94. "Preachers' Aid Society," UEEPAConfJ, 1910, 91–93.

95. U. F. Swengel and W. H. Fouke, "Episcopal Message," UEGenConfJ, 1914, 48.

96. U. F. Swengel and W. H. Fouke, "Episcopal Message," UEGenConfJ,

1918, 42.

97. W. F. Heil and M. T. Maze, "Episcopal Message," UEGenConfJ, 1922, 44b.

98. (Harrisburg, PA: Publishing House of the United Evangelical Church, 1896).

99. A Volume of Entertaining Narratives, Anecdotes and Incidents, Illustrative of the Evangelical Work Founded by Rev. Jacob Albright in A.D. 1800, also Evangelical Daughters of Song (York, PA: The Author, 1908).

100. With the Historical Background and Antecedents; also a Biographical Supplement Embracing Brief Biographies of Albright's Colleagues and Coworkers, and his Chief Contemporary Evangelists (Harrisburg, PA: Publishing House of the United Evangelical Church, 1917).

101. See A. Stepleton, "Centennial Echoes—I–III," EV, October 2–23, 1907, 628, 659, 680.

102. "Centennial Celebration," UEGenConfJ, 1906, 62–63.

103. [W. M. Stanford], "The Celebration at Kleinfeltersville," EV, October 2, 1907, 632.

104. A. Stapleton, "The Historical Society of the United Evangelical Church," EV, October 30, 1907, 693.

105. John D. Shortress and A. D. Gramley, eds., *The Evangelical Centennial Celebration September 26–27, 1916…* (Harrisburg, PA: Historical Society of the United Evangelical Church, 1917), 5.

106. UEGenConfJ, 1914, 34.

107. A. D. Gramley, "The Evangelical Centennial Celebration, EV, October 25, 1916, 2–3; Shortress and Gramley, 161.

108. U. F. Swengel, "Opening and Dedication of the Historical Society Room," EV, October 9, 1918, 13; John D. Shortress, "Historical Data of Relics," EV, October 9, 1918, 14–15.

109. Hangen and Fouke, *Year Book of the United Evangelical Church 1922*, 54.

110. Terry M. Heisey, "Immigration as a Factor in the Division of the Evangelical Association," *Methodist History* 19 (October 1980):54.

111. "Statistics of the Official Periodicals of Our Church as Reported by the Annual Conferences," EV, June 26, 1889, 204.

112. H. B. Hartzler and W. F. Heil, "Episcopal Message," UEGenConfJ, 1910, 48.

113. W. Jonas, "St. Paul Mission, Northwestern Conf.," *The Evangelical,* January 16, 1907, 45

114. UEGenConfJ, 1922.

115. J. Q. A. Curry, "Franklin, Pa.," EV, April 7, 1907, 109.

116. A. J. Beal, "Franklin, Pa.," EV, March 28, 1909, 103.

117. An Evangelical, "An Ideal Wife for an Evangelical Preacher," EV, February 8, 1905, 82.

118. See for example C. E. Hess, "Pastor's Christmas Gift," EV, January 6, 1897, 5.

119. Hartzler and Heil, "Episcopal Message," UEGenConf], 1906, 31.

120. Dubs and Stanford, "Episcopal Message," UEGenConf], 1902, 40.

121. Hartzler and Heil, "Episcopal Message," UEGenConf], 1910, 48

122. R. Dubs, "The Decline in Ministerial Recruits," EV, January 18, 1902, 50.

123. Harztler and Heil, "Episcopal Message," UEGenConf], 1910, 48.

124. [W. M. Stanford], "Who Will Answer?" EV, February 16, 1910, 104.

125. Hartzler and Heil, "Episcopal Message," UEGenConf], 1910, 48.

126. Fouke and Swengel, "Episcopal Message," UEGenConf], 1914, 48.

127. Simeon G. Domer, "The Pastor's Salary," EV, September 11, 1895, 289.

128. Dubs and Stanford, "Episcopal Message, UEGenConf], 1898, 16.

129. *Ibid*; B. H. Niebel, "Preachers' Salaries," EV, July 26, 1898, 233.

130. Dubs and Stanford, "Episcopal Message," UEGenConf], 1902, 42.

131. C. H. Stauffacher, "The Minister's Salary," EV, October 2, 1912, 628.

132. [H. B. Hartzler] "Why Not Enough Preachers?" EV, March 3, 1920, 6–7.

133. R. Dubs and W. M. Stanford, "Episcopal Message," UEGenConf], 1898, 16–17.

134. Stapleton, *Annals*, 606.

135. D. Berkey, "Itinerancy and Lay Representation," EV, July 15, 1908, 450.

136. Benjamin Hengst, "The Itinerant Ministry," EV, April 10, 1907, 226.

137. R. Dubs, "The Young Ministers of the United Evangelical Church," EV, January 17, 1912, 34–35.

138. Dubs and Stanford, "Episcopal Message," UEGenConf], 1902, 43.

139. R. Dubs, "Shall the Pastoral Term in Special Cases Be Extended?" EV, February 25, 1914, 8; but see also H. H. Thoren, "Shall the Pastoral Term in Special Cases be Extended? EV, June 3, 1914, 8–9.

140. "Revision," UEGenConf], 1914, 112.

141. R. Dubs, "Shall the Pastoral Term in Special Cases Be Extended?" 4.

142. [W. F. Heil], "The Local Congregational Bulletin," UE, October 20, 1925, 5.

143. James F. White, *Protestant Worship and Church Architecture* (New York: Oxford University Press, 1964), 121–124.

144. H. B. Hartzler, "Amen! Amen!" EV, January 14, 1914, 3; G. W. Imboden, "The Amen Corner," EV, May 13, 1914, 16.

145. Benjamin Hengst, "Would Not Have the Hallelujahs, Amens and Glorys Abolished," EV, August 14, 1900, 270.

146. G. W. Gross, "Shamokin, Pa.," EV, February 21, 1899, 61.

147. W. M. Stanford, "Re-opening of St. Paul's, Reading, Pa.," EV, August 23, 1916, 15.

148. W. M. Stanford, "Our Evangelical Altar Service," EV, January 10, 1906, 24; "That Altar Service Again," EV, January 17, 1906, 40–41.

149. Dubs and Stanford, "Episcopal Message," UEGenConf], 1902, 33.

150. Hartzler and Heil, "Quadrennial Episcopal Message," UEGenConf], 1906, 32.

151. White, 124–127.

152. Ammon Stapleton, "Old Time Evangelical Preaching," EV, October 3, 1894, 313; October 10, 1894, 321.

153. *Ibid.*

154. "Sunday Services at the Seat of Conference," UEGenConfJ, 1910, 21.

155. [W. M. Stanford] "Short Sermons," EV, June 4, 1903, 355.

156. D. A. Medlar, "Quarterly Conference and Communion in Our Church," EV, May 30, 1894, 169; Edward Haines Kistler, "Reading, Pa., First Church, East Pa. Conf.," EV, February 13, 1907, 101; W. F. Heil and M. T. Maze, "Episcopal Message," UEGenConfJ, 1922, 38b.

157. J. H. Shirey, "Presiding Elder's Report, Reading District, East Pa. Conf.," EV, March 9, 1910, 156–157; Dubs and Stanford, "Episcopal Message," UEGenConfJ, 1902, 35.

158. "Statistics" in UEGenConfJ, 1898–1922.

159. Dubs and Stanford, "Episcopal Message," UEGenConfJ, 1902, 33–34.

160. B. F. Ludy, "The Importance of Good Music in Our Churches," EV, July 26, 1905, 466–467; Rudolf Dubs, "Organ Dedication at Carlisle, Pa.," EV, October 31, 1906, 694–695.

161. W. M. Stanford, "How About the Choir Question?" EV, March 28, 1906, 200.

162. W. M. Stanford, "That Choir Question Once More," EV, April 4, 1906, 216.

163. Mel R. Wilhoit, "Alexander the Great; or, Just Plain Charlie," *The Hymn*, 46 (April 1995): 23–24.

164. Stapleton, *Annals*, 606; United Evangelical Church, *Evangelisches Gesangbuch: Die Kleine Palme mit Anhang* (Harrisburg, PA: Publishing House of the United Evangelical Church, 1896), Vorwort.

165. United Evangelical Church, *Hymnal of the Evangelical Church* (Harrisburg, PA : Publishing House of the United Evangelical Church, 1897), [iii].

166. Terry Heisey, "Why We're Celebrating a Centennial," *E. C. Doors and Windows*, 5 (May–June 1994), 2.

167. Stapleton, *Annals*, 612.

168. Dubs and Stanford, "Bishops' Message," UEGenConfJ, 1898, 14.

169. Rudolf Dubs, "Bishop Dubs' Story of the Reading Church Dedication," EV, July 1, 1896, 213; C. W. Finkbinder, "Church Dedication at Loyalsock, Pa.," EV, January 24, 1912, 60; Arthur R. King, "Williamstown, Pa., East Pa. Conf.," EV, February 13, 1907.

170. "Statistics," in UEGenConfJ, 1898–1922

171. Dubs and Stanford, "Episcopal Message," UEGenConfJ, 1902, 34.

172. Hartzler and Heil, "Quadrennial Episcopal Message," UEGenConfJ, 1906, 32–33.

173. Hartzler and Heil, "Episcopal Message," UEGenConfJ, 1910, 50.

174. Dubs and Stanford, "Episcopal Message," UEGenConfJ, 1902, 34.

175. W. M. Stanford, "The Meeting Itself Must Draw," EV, April 12, 1905, 232.

176. W. F. Heil, "The Prayer Meeting," EV, October 1, 1919, 1.

177. A. E. Hangen, "An Open Letter on a Vital Matter to the Officials in the Local Congregations in the United Evangelical Church," EV, June 21, 1921, 1.

178. C. D. Huber, "Watch Night Service, Hazelton, Pa.," EV, January 9, 1900, 15.

179. "History of the Week of Prayer," EV, December 30, 1896, 417.

180. A. E. Hangen, "The Pre-Easter Season and Evangelism," EV, February 7, 1922, 4–5.

181. B. J. Smoyer, "Under the Shadow of the Cross," EV, April 10, 1895, 117; Rudolf Dubs, "Passion Week–Ascension–Pentecost," EV, April 30, 1903, 277.

182. H. B. Hartzler, "Did the Rally Stay?" EV, February 11, 1914, 4.

183. "Evergreen Charge, Des Moines Conf.," EV, January 23, 1907, 60.

184. Hangen, "The Pre-Easter Season ...," 4.

185. Reporter, "Herndon Campmeeting, Harrisburg District, East Penna. Conf.," EV, September 5, 1894, 285.

186. Reporter, "Lititz Camp-Meeting," EV, August 25, 1897, 269.

187. W. M. Stanford, "The Camp-meeting Campaign," EV, September 4, 1900, 294.

188. Wm. Jonas, "An Iowa Camp-meeting," EV, June 30, 1897, 205.

189. "Barrington Camp-Meeting," EV, August 3, 1910, 489.

190. Ida M. Zerby, A Brief History of The Herndon Camp Meeting (1972), 2–4.

191. *Waldheim 75th Anniversary 1904–1979* (1979); W. H. Christ, "Waldheim Camp-Meeting," EV, September 6, 1911, 573.

192. A. B. Saylor, "Waldheim Camp-Meeting," EV, August 23, 1916, 23.

193. [H. B. Saylor], "Campmeeting–Old and New," EV, July 15, 1914, 14.

194. [W. M. Stanford], "Our Winter Campaign," EV, January 26, 1910, 56.

195. See H. A. Benfer, "The Church and Evangelism I," EV, November 8, 1911, 706–707.

196. [W. M. Stanford], "Our Summer Campaign for Souls," EV, May 21, 1903, 328.

197. A. J. Beale, "Franklin, Pa.," EV, May 3, 1898, 141.

198. A. G. Musselman, "Conemaugh Mission," EV, March 3, 1897, 70.

199. "The Conversion of Children," EV, January 16, 1907, 54.

200. J. Max Longsdorf, "Decision Day in the Sunday School," EV, June 12, 1912, 371.

201. W. P. Rhoda, "Report of Church Work," EV, August 3, 1910, 485.

202. "The Ackley Brothers, Evangelists," EV, February 21, 1917, 10.

203. G. L. Maice, "Some Questionable Modern Revival Methods," EV, January 30, 1907, 67.

204. Hartzler and Heil, "Episcopal Message," UEGenConf], 1910, 42.

205. "Abstract of the Proceedings of the Board of Publication," EV, May 22,

1895, 165.

206. Jacob Hartzler, *Catechism of Christian Doctrine as Taught in the United Evangelical Church.*(Harrisburg, PA: Publishing House of the United Evangelical Church, 1901), [5–6].

207. E. B. Utt and A. J. Bird, "Family, Sunday-School and Youth," UEGenConf], 1906, 57.

208. Jacob Hartzler, *Catechism for Children* (Harrisburg, PA: Publishing House of the United Evangelical Church, 1908), 5.

209. J. P. Miller and F. C. Bowersox, "Family, Sunday School and Youth," UEGenConf], 1910, 99.

210. "K.L.C.E. Managing Board Report," UEGenConf], 1914, 69.

211. Hartzler and Heil, "Episcopal Message," UEGenConf], 1910, 54.

212. Fouke and Swengel, "Episcopal Message," UEGenConf], 1914, 51–52.

213. E. S. Woodring, "Spring Rally, First Church, Lebanon," EV, May 11, 1910, 300.

214. Stapleton, *Annals,* 606.

215. W. H. Fouke, "Second Anniversary—Ministers' Class, First Church, Reading, Pa.," EV, 36–37.

216. Fouke and Swengel, "Episcopal Message," UEGenConf], 1914, 51–52.

217. *Ibid.*

218. [H. B. Hartzler] "A Summer School of Methods," EV, August 26, 1914, 2.

219. E. H. R., "Evangelical Bible Conference, Perkasie Park, Pa.," EV, August 22, 1894, 266.

220. Hartzler and Heil, "Episcopal Message," UEGenConf], 1906, 35.

221. See Charles Pickford, "Iowa Center, Des Moines Conference, Tabernacle Service," EV, August 23, 1898, 271; J. E. Stauffacher, "DeMoines [sic] District," EV, November 13, 1900, 377; W. H. Warburton, "Manley Charge, Des Moines Conf.," EV, April 3, 1907, 221; V. Urbino, "Belle Plain Mission, Des Moines Conf.," EV, March 24, 1897, 95.

222. D. J. Klopp, "S. Dixon, Ill. Conf.," EV, March 17, 1897, 85.

223. L. O. Wiest, "Conestoga Circuit," EV, February 7, 1899; M. I. Jamison, "York, Trinity, Central Pa. Conf.," EV, February 9, 1910, 92.

224. A. Stapleton, "Deaconess Work in the UE Church," EV, December 2, 1908, 770; A. Stapleton, "Deaconess Work," in *Year Book of the United Evangelical Church for 1916,* W. M. Stanford, editor (Harrisburg, PA: Publishing House of the Unite Evangelical Church, 1916), 77–78.

225. J. W. Thompson, "United Evangelical Deaconess Work," in *Year Book of the United Evangelical Church for 1918,* 83–84.

226. "Deaconess Work," EV, October 21, 1914, 3.

227. U. F. Swengel, "The Need of College Education for Women," EV, November 30, 1895, 344.

228. B. R. Schultze, "The Illinois Training School for Christian Workers," in *The Year Book of the United Evangelical Church for 1912,* 43–44; B. R. Schultze,

"The Illinois Training School for Christian Workers," *The Year Book of the United Evangelical Church for 1913*, 48.

229. Emma D. Messinger, "Oak Heights School of Methods," *The Year Book of the United Evangelical Church for 1913*, 52.

230. R. Dubs, "A Visit to Kutztown, Pa.," EV, February 21, 1912, 124; "Men's Baraca Class of Nescopeak, Pa.," EV, February 9, 1916, 1.

231. Stapleton, *Annals,* 629, 605–606.

232. The Abiding Past: Fifty Years of the Woman's Missionary Society of the Evangelical Church, 1884–1934 (Harrisburg, PA?: Woman's Missionary Society, 1936), 131–134, 138–139, 142–143, 168.

233. See "Ministers' Wives," EV, February 26, 1896, 66.

234. W. H. Fouke, "Installation Service," EV, February 5, 1896, 42.

235. A. Stapleton, "The Deaconess Office, and Its Relation to the United Evan. Church," EV, July 17, 1907, 450.

236. J. Willis Hoover, "The Significance of the Men's Movement," EV, November 18, 1911, 706.

237. Report of the Family, Sunday School and Youth Committee, J. P. Miller, president, UEGenConfJ, 1910, 98–99.

238. B. H. Niebel, "Laymen's Great Missions Congress in Chicago, Ill.," EV, May 11, 1910, 1; C. S. Fleck, "A Men's Missionary Society," EV, May 4, 1910, 4.

239. Ammon Stapleton, "The Albright Brotherhood," EV, July 8, 1914, 4.

240. W. H. Fouke and U. F. Swengel, "Report of the Managing Board of the Keystone League of Christian Endeavor," UEGenConfJ, 1894, 62–64.

241. UEGenConfJ, 1898, 21, 93–95.

242. "Managing Board of the Keystone League of Christian Endeavor," UEGenConfJ, 1902, 82–83.

243. "Report of the Managing Board of the K.L.C.E.," UEGenConfJ, 1910, 72–75; W. H. Fouke and U. F. Swengel, "A Message from the Bishops," EV, January 25, 1911, 57.

244. "K.L.C.E. Managing Board Report," UEGenConfJ, 1914, 64–69; Elwood E. Oplinger, "East Pa. K.L.C.E. Convention," EV, October 13, 1915, 23–25.

245. J.Q.A. Curry and W. E. Peffley, "Letter from the General Managing Board," UEGenConfJ, 1918, 55–59.

246. Fouke and Swengel, "Episcopal Message," UEGenConfJ, 1914, 52.

247. Dubs and Stanford, "Episcopal Message," UEGenConfJ, 1902, 44.

248. H. B. Hartzler, *The United Evangelical Church and What It Stands For* (Harrisburg, PA: Publishing House of the United Evangelical Church [n.d.]), 2–4.

249. Robert S. Wilson, "The Origin of Our Articles of Faith," UE, July 14, 1964, 3, 7. Jacobus Arminius (1560-1609) was a professor at the University of Leyden who objected to the strict Calvinist doctrine that Christ's work of atonement is limited to only those persons predestined by God before birth for salvation (these "elect" can do nothing to resist God's grace or to lose their salva-

tion), all other people being incapable of faith and destined for hell. Wesley followed Arminius in his belief that God's grace, including prevenient grace that enables people to accept God's offer of salvation, is available to all.

250. Harold P. Scanlin. "The Origin of the Articles of Faith of the United Evangelical Church," *Methodist History* 18 (July 1980): 219–238.

251. George R. Riffert, "A Plain Account of Entire Sanctification," EV, January 31, 1912, 66.

252. C. C. Poling, "Scriptural Holiness," EV, February 18, 1914, 6–7.

253. William H. Rhoads, "Christian Holiness," EV, December 4, 1902, 787.

254. Rudolf Dubs, "Theses on Sanctification," EV, January 5, 1916, 9–10.

255. "Sabbath, Temperance, and Other Moral Reforms," UEGenConfJ, 1894, 77; "Sabbath and Moral Reform," GenConfJ, 1898, 69. However, a proposed amendment to the Discipline advising all members to abstain from the use of tobacco was defeated at the 1902 General Conference 24–55 ("Revision," 56).

256. "Sabbath and Moral Reform," 67; "Questions About Base Ball," EV, August 21, 1900, 278; A. M. Sampsel, "Those 'Questions About Baseball,'" EV, September 4, 1900, 294.

257. See Elsie Bentz, "The Theatre," EV, February 14, 1922, 9; H. Franklin Schlegel, "Some Real Facts Regarding the Moving Pictures," EV, July 14, 1917, 6–7; W. M. Stanford, "That 'Dance' Question Again," EV, August 22, 1906, 536; C. C. Mizener, "The Amusement Question," EV, August 1, 1909, 546–547.

258. "Sabbath, Temperance, and Other Moral Reforms," 76.

259. W.F. Heil and M. T. Maze, "Episcopal Message," UEGenConfJ, 1922, 42b.

260. See "East Penna. Conference," EV, March 10, 1897, 76; "East Pa. Conference Proceedings," EV, March 1, 1905, 132.

261. Heil and Maze, 42b.

262. R. Dubs and W. M. Stanford, "Episcopal Message," UEGenConfJ, 1902, 69.

263. See "What Temperance Work Have You Done?" EV, January 13, 1897, 12; "The GreatVictory," EV, February 5, 1919, 6.

264. R Dubs and W. M. Stanford, "Episcopal Message," UEGenConfJ, 1898, 25.

265. *Ibid.*

266. H. B. Hartzler and W. F. Heil, "Episcopal Message," UEGenConfJ, 1910, 60.

267. "Sabbath and Moral Reform," UEGenConfJ, 1898, 69.

268. *Ibid.*, 69–70; W. F. Heil, "The Duty of the Church Toward the Laboring Classes," EV, May 20, 1896, 161.

269. W. H. Fouke and U. F. Swengel, "Episcopal Message," UEGenConfJ, 1914, 44; A. E. Gobble, "Christianity Demands Disarmament," EV, October 25, 1921, 8–9; H. Franklin Schlegel, "Report of Commission to Bishops," EV, December 19, 1917, 10.

270. Rudolf Dubs, "The General Conference at Naperville," EV, November

7, 1894, 357.

271. UEGenConf], 1898, 18, 63.

272. See for example, Class Leader, "That Request for Larger Official Boards," EV, January 5, 1910, 3.

273. G. W. Imboden, "Presiding Elders," EV, January 22, 1919, 9.

274. UEEPAConf], 1896, 32.

275. UEEPAConf], 1898, 45–46, 21.

276. Albright, 377–378.

277. UEGenConf], 1910, 90–91.

278. Albright, 378.

279. W. F. Heil, "History of the Merger: The Commissioners in Session," UE, June 26, 1923, 5–6.

280. W. F. Heil, "History of the Merger: The Linwood Park Meeting," UE, July 3, 1923, 4–6.

281. W. F. Heil, "History of the Merger," UE, July 31, 1923, 5–6.

282. UEGenConf], 1914, 32, 80–81, 91.

283. Albright, 379–380; W. F. Heil, "History of the Merger," UE, July 31, 1923, 5–6.

284. "Bishop Heil Seriously Injured," EV, Dec. 11, 1918, 7; W. F. Heil, "History of the Merger," UE, August 7, 1923, 5..

285. Albright, 381.

286. W. F. Heil, "A History of the Merger," UE, August 14, 1923, 5–6.

287. "At the joint session at Chicago I was too ill to take part in debate and was compelled to leave session before adjournment and when I reached the home of my daughter my temperature had risen to 103." – W. F. Heil, "History of that Facsimile," [1922].

288. "Uniform Report of the Two Commissions on Church Union," UEGenConf], 1922, 14b–15b.

289. W. F. Heil, "History of that Facsimile," [1922], 6.

290. W. F. Heil, "History of the Merger: Attitude of The East Pennsylvania Conference," UE, October 30, 1923, 5–6.

291. W. F. Heil, "History of the Merger: The East Pennsylvania Conference Delegates," UE, November 13, 1923, 5–6.

292. UEGenConf], 1922, 11b–25b.

293. Ibid, 70b.

294. EAGenConf], 1922, 144.

295. W. F. Heil, "History of the Merger: The Delegation of the East Pennsylvania Conference at Detroit," UE, December 11, 1922, 6.

296. John Hoerner, "The Practicableness of Union, With Reference to the Spirit, Genius, History and Method of the Two Churches," EV, December 27, 1921, 8–9.

297. A. E. Hangen, "Shall It Now Fail?" EV, August 22, 1922, 4.

298. W. F. Heil, "History of the Merger," UE August 28, 1923, 6.

299. W. F. Heil, "History of the Merger," UE, November 20, 1923, 7.

300. Ibid.
301. W. F. Heil, "History of the Merger," UE, August 21, 1923, 6.
302. Ibid.
303. Albright, 377.
304. Circular letter from the Executive Committee of the Inter-Conference Committee of One Hundred for the Promotion of Church Union, Harrisburg PA, to ministers of the East Pennsylvania Conference, November 9, 1922, mimeograph, Archives of the Evangelical Congregational Church, Myerstown, PA.
305. "East Pennsylvania Conference Proceedings," EV, March 10, 1920, 14.
306. Heil, "History of that Facsimile," 8–9
307. Heil, "History of the Merger: The Heart of the United Evangelical Church," 6.
308. W. F. Heil, "History of the Merger: The Contribution of the East Pennsylvania Conference to the United Evangelical Church," UE, October 16, 1923, 5.
309. Ibid, 5.
310. W. F. Heil, "History of the Merger," UE, August 21,1923, 6.
311. "Recommendations to our coming General Conference," EV, January 31, 1906, 65; A. M. Sampsel, "Those 'Recommendations,'" EV, February 7, 1906, 81; R. Dubs, "Recommendation No. 4," EV, February 21, 1906, 116–117; "East Pennsylvania Conference," EV, February 28, 1906, 132; "Central Pa. Conference," EV, March 7, 1906, 149; A. M. Sampsel, "Recommendation No. 4 once more," EV, March 14, 1906, 165.
312. In the words of one western preacher, "Did you hear the shouting on the western plains as the splendid EVANGELICAL made its welcome visit this week, announcing the Central Pa. Conference vote on 'Those recommendations'?
313. W. F. Heil, "History of the Merger," UE, July 17, 1923, 6.
314. C. H. Mengel, "Will the Church Union Conserve Men and Means?" EV, December 6, 1921, 13–14.
315. W. F. Heil, "Conscience as a Factor in the Present Conflict," EV, February 18, 1891, 53.
316. "History of the Merger: The Heart of the United Evangelical Church," UE, January 22, 1924, 6.
317. Church Union Publicity League, "A Message in the Interest of Our Future" (Allentown, PA: The League, 1922)

4

Perpetuating An Ideal:
The Evangelical Congregational Church
(1922-1950)

Overview

The Crisis of 1922

The sons and daughters of Jacob Albright in eastern Pennsylvania, the land of his birth, believed that the *Basis of Union* was a betrayal of his ideals and vision. This remnant felt that they had to remain true to their democratic ideals even if it meant starting over again and building a church on their own. They did not automatically lose their churches and parsonages as they had in 1894, but their desire to continue a denomination that had voted itself out of existence (the United Evangelical Church) cast a cloud over their legal status and thus over all their activities.

With the merger vote taken despite their protests, the Presiding Elders of the East Pennsylvania Conference called for a meeting of the Conference ministerial and lay delegates for November 14, 1922, in Bethlehem PA. Several churches from western Pennsylvania, Ohio, and Illinois joined the delegates from East Pennsylvania. The assembly, now severed from the newly organized Evangelical Church, heard a full report of what had occurred at both Barrington and Detroit. After listening to the report of their delegation, the Conference unanimously endorsed the position taken by their representatives and reaffirmed the polity and doctrines embodied in the church since the time of Albright. "We are not held by law," they said, "we are maintaining an ideal." They considered the newly formed Evangelical Church a new denomination with a different polity and *Discipline* from the old United Evangelical Church.[1]

The East Pennsylvania Conference met for its first regular session after the merger on February 23, 1923, in Trinity Church, Allentown. Representatives from 136 churches (82 % of the pre-merger conference) with 18,675 members (72 % of the previous conference) from the Harrisburg, Reading, and Allentown Districts plus four churches from Ohio Conference, four churches from Illinois, and nine churches from Pittsburgh Conference assembled with Bishop Heil presiding. The work was divided into four districts under distinguished Presiding Elders: E. S. Woodring and C. H. Mengel in East Pennsylvania, Charles Unganst in Illinois, and Henry Schultz in Ohio. In September 1923 Bishop Heil met with Schultz, Rev. W. E. Seesholtz, and David Wilson, the lay delegate of the Canton OH church, in Wilson's home to organize the Ohio Conference as a mission conference. By 1924 this Conference included seven churches, and by the end of the decade it included churches in Akron, Canton, Columbus, Delightful, and Findlay OH plus Venango Charge and Johnstown PA.

Going it alone renewed memories of the bitter litigation resulting from disputes over property rights when the United Evangelical Church was born in 1894. In an attempt to avoid this situation, the Conference adopted five proposals on November 15, 1922 asking that

> the merged church recognize the right of the East Pennsylvania Conference and portions of other United Evangelical conferences to continue as the United Evangelical Church; that individual United Evangelical churches be given the opportunity to determine whether or not to enter the merger; that church properties be deeded to those who represented the majority of the members in each church; that a pro-rata share of the value of the general church properties and of the balances in the general church treasuries be given to the continuing United Evangelical Church and finally that the congregations be notified of the proposal and be given sufficient time to respond.[2]

Unfortunately, legal battles could not be completely avoided. In Greensburg OH the few members remaining in the Evangelical church after most of the congregation left to form a continuing UE church sold the church property, which they no longer needed, and delivered the proceeds to the merged denomination. When the East Pennsylvania Conference objected, the Ohio court ruled that "when the merger took place the congregations of the United Evangelical Church were absorbed into the merged church...."[3] In Highland Park IL First United Evangelical Church sought to eject a "merger" pastor from the parsonage, but here the courts favored the local church by ruling that the local deed took precedence over denominational change. Other legal battles were fought on the local level.

In the case of Albright College in Myerstown PA, East Pennsylvania congregations had given liberally to the school over the years, and the East Pennsylvania Conference claimed the right to appoint college trustees as it had in the past. The East Pennsylvania United Conference of the Evangelical Church (the few former UE congregations in eastern Pennsylvania that participated in the merger) also claimed the right to name the designated trustees. At first a Lebanon County PA judge ruled in favor of the non-merged East Pennsylvania Conference. The ruling was immediately challenged by the Evangelical Church, since this action called the merger into question. After two years, the Pennsylvania Supreme Court reversed the local decision. Its ruling in 1927 was based on the principle that the decisions of ecclesiastical courts are binding on civil courts, and it did not examine the merits of the claim of the East Pennsylvania Conference that the merger violated the Articles of Faith of the United Evangelical Church. Following these battles, the Evangelical Church moved Albright College to Reading PA in 1929, and its Myerstown campus stood vacant.[4]

The 1927 decision of the Supreme Court of Pennsylvania did, however, uphold the right of individual UE congregations to abstain from the merger and granted the church members the right to hold the deed to their church property. This meant that the East Pennsylvania Conference had a legal standing but was not allowed to use the name "United Evangelical." After a series of joint meetings in 1928 representatives of the Evangelical Church expressed a desire to settle future property issues without litigation. They invited congregations to join in the merger, but if they would not do so a "quitclaim" would be granted giving the congregations clear and uncontested title to their properties. Congregations would thus have no fear of losing their buildings. Congregational meetings were quickly convened to grant approval to secure the quitclaims. A sense of normalcy returned to local churches as trustees once again began to repair and maintain churches and parsonages. Ownership evoked the sense of a hard-won victory that took almost six years!

Denied the name "United Evangelical" by the Pennsylvania Supreme Court decision, a special General Conference of the anti-merger United Evangelicals convened in January 1928 and chose the name "United Protestant Church" from a list of eleven possibilities.[5] Before the next East Pennsylvania Conference session could act upon the proposal, it was learned that another denomination was already using that name, so a special General Conference session was convened the night before the Annual Conference met, and this Conference chose the name "Evangelical Congregational."[6] The name retains "Evangelical" from the *Evangelical* Association and United *Evangelical*, while the term "Congregational" recognizes the thirty-four-year battle to retain property rights of the individual congregations. Bishop Edwin Woodring identified these terms in his 1930 Episcopal address:

> Two important ideas, which we have always stressed as a Church are linked together in a new name. One relates to doctrine and the other to polity. In doctrine we want men to know that we are 'evangelical,' as were our 'Fathers,' maintaining the Fundamental Faith of Protestantism in its simplicity and purity…In polity we proclaim the fact, in our name, that we are not an oligarchy; that authority is not vested in a few, but that authority and power must and does come from the congregations.[7]

Thus, in a unanimous vote of the East Pennsylvania Conference, another American denomination was born, the Evangelical Congregational Church. (See picture of the charter on next page).

The Illinois courts also upheld the Chicago Kimball Ave., Chicago Highland Park, Cedarville, Dixon, Afolkey, and Hoopole churches in the ownership of their properties. In 1931 they united with the Ohio Conference to create the Western Conference under Presiding Elder Seesholtz.

The 1928 General Conference appointed a committee to amend the *Discipline* so as to assure "congregational independence and the connectional interests" of the church.[8] Local churches were permitted to instruct their lay delegates on how to vote on vital issues of property ownership that came before the Annual Conference. The Evangelical Congregational Articles of Faith, denominational government, local membership regulations, and Rules of Christian Practice reflected the "ideals" the dissidents cherished and were structured along the traditional lines of the United Evangelical *Discipline*. The array of boards, societies, agencies, federations, and committees at the Annual and General Conference levels would serve well at this point but become a burden later on.

The Bishops

Bishop Heil

William Heil (1857-1930) had served twice as Bishop in the United Evangelical Church (1902-1910 and 1918-1922), and he was re-elected in 1922. As a member of the merger committee, he had supported the

COPY *In Rev. C. H. Mengel.*

Re: : In the Court of Common Pleas
                                                            of Berks County, Pennsylvania
    Incorporation of   :
                                                            No. 252 Aug.   Term, 1928.
    THE EAST PENNSYLVANIA CON-   :
    FERENCE OF THE EVANGELICAL
    CONGREGATIONAL CHURCH   :

<u>CHARTER APPLICATION</u>

TO THE HONORABLE THE JUDGES OF SAID COURT:

    Agreeably to the provisions of the Act of General Assembly of the Commonwealth of Pennsylvania, entitled "An Act to provide for the incorporation and regulation of certain corporations" approved the 29th day of April, A.D. 1874 and the several supplements and amendments thereto, the undersigned, all of whom are citizens and residents of the State of Pennsylvania, have associated themselves together for the purposes and upon the terms and by the name hereinafter set forth, and to the end that they may be duly incorporated according to law, hereby certify:

    1. The name of the corporation shall be THE EAST PENNSYLVANIA CONFERENCE OF THE EVANGELICAL CONGREGATIONAL CHURCH.

    2. The purpose of the corporation shall be to promote, maintain and support public worship of Almighty God, in conformity with the faith, doctrine, creed, discipline and usages of The Evangelical Congregational Church, and, in such conformity, to promote, foster and supervise the ministry of God's Word, in the several churches established and located within the territorial limits of the East Pennsylvania Conference of the Evangelical Congregational Church as fixed and determined by the Discipline of The Evangelical Congregational Church, and in furtherance of such purpose to hold annual and other conferences or meetings to be

Charter issued by the Commonwealth of Pennsylvania, designating the name Evangelical Congregational Church work of the committee in order, as he later explained, "to allow a full hearing by the conferences,"[9] though he himself opposed the merger. "His desire [was] that no one would say that he influenced [the merger] one way or the other."[10] Heil explained his position as follows: "We stood for the right of the people to consider and decide...[and] we never believed the merger leaders would try to force the people without giving them the opportunity to cast their votes for or against."[11] After the merger, Bishop Heil refused to assume his place as a Bishop of the new Evangelical Church and became the leader of the dissenting minority. Some people considered him authoritarian, while others felt he was not decisive enough, but he had a pastoral heart as well as great administrative ability, and he brought the non-merging group through its most difficult formative years so as to assure its survival as the Evangelical Congregational Church. Bishop Woodring called him "a natural born leader of men."[12] Following the close of his episcopacy in 1926 Heil continued as the editor of the church weekly, *The United Evangelical*, serving in that capacity until his death in 1930.

Bishop Woodring

Heil's successor, Edwin S. Woodring (1872 -1957), was a former Presiding Elder and head of the United Evangelical delegation to the critical 1922 merger conference in Detroit, which he called "an unholy determination to force union upon an unwilling people."[13] Woodring had been licensed to preach the first year of the newly formed United Evangelical Church (1894). In 1921 he founded the School of Methods at Waldheim Park in Allentown PA, a week-long training institute for laity. Daily classes in biblical and practical topics by renowned preachers and teachers drew large numbers each summer. This work would always be close to his heart. Woodring's tenure as Presiding Elder of the Harrisburg District (1922-1925) was difficult. Harrisburg had been the headquarters of the United Evangelical Church and became one of the

Bishop Edwin S. Woodring, 1926–1935

two centers of the new Evangelical Church. The Evangelical Publishing House remained in Harrisburg, and many pastors and congregations in the local area were influenced by denominational leaders to accede to the merger. Both friends and foes of the merger exerted themselves to win the area. Woodring worked against what he termed "a bureau for propaganda purposes" organized to discredit the anti-merger cause. He labeled the period "years of reconstruction."[14]

Woodring served two terms as Bishop (1926-1935). During this time the name "Evangelical Congregational" was adopted (1928), and the legal position of the new church was established. In June 1931 a special session of the East Pennsylvania Conference meeting in Myerstown voted to accept the offer of the Evangelical Church to sell the former Albright College campus to the EC Church for $25,000. Woodring had a vision to develop the college campus into an orphanage, a theological school, and a printing house. The Conference launched a Church Center Campaign reminiscent of the UE "Our Forward Fund" campaign

EVANGELICAL CONGREGATIONAL

FIELD DAY

AT THE

CHURCH CENTER

Myerstown, Pa. Tuesday, June 27, 1933

(Daylight Saving Time)

Bishop E. S. Woodring, Chairman - - - Rev. N. N. Lower, Musical Director

PROGRAM - - 10:00 A. M. - - 2:00 P. M. - - 7:30 P. M.

MUSIC, Instrumental and Vocal - - Short Snappy Addresses
4:00 P. M., Baseball by Ministers - Eastern vs Western Districts
6:30 P. M. - 7:30 P. M. Band Concert - Myerstown Band

A Day of Fine Fellowship
A Day of Healthful Recreation
A Day of Genuine Inspiration
A Day of Joyful Acclamation

COME - BRING YOUR LUNCH - SPEND THE DAY

TENNIS - - CROQUET - - OTHER RECREATIONS

Poster announcing activities for 1933, including "Short Snappy Addresses" with pledge cards, campaign committees at the conference, regional, and local levels, and a goal to raise $35,000 during February 1932. Annual Field Days were held on the campus from 1932 to 1937 to instill denominational identification with the site. When the campaign was closed in 1934 it had received about $23,000 of the $32,000 pledged. In his farewell address (1934) Woodring urged the Church to create a training school followed by a college and seminary. "[T]raining of the heart as well as the head" was necessary to combat false teaching in the schools and "false ethics and moral standards in society."[15] Bishop Woodring presided during two General Conferences and then returned to the pastorate from 1934 to 1942, where he was hailed as "a prince of preachers."

Bishop Mengel.

The third Bishop, Charles H. Mengel (1879 - 1964), was another warrior of the 1922 crisis. One theory of history claims that "the times make the man"; that might be said of Mengel, who served during times of stress (the Great Depression and the Second World War) that required great leadership. On the other hand, Mengel had the personality and the drive to meet challenges, and he was indefatigable in his purposes. Leon O. Hynson writes:

Bishop Charles H. Mengel, 1935 –1942

> From a pastorate in Herndon to his election as Presiding Elder in 1922, and bishop in 1934, he represented a prominent voice for education and benevolence. He became the leader in 1926 for the development of the Burd and Rogers Home...As a bishop, Mengel was keenly aware of the "Moral confusion" of the time and general political and economic trends.[16]

At East Pennsylvania Conference in 1938 Mengel reviewed the progress of the church, addressing the restlessness of local churches that too quickly called for pastoral changes. In his next annual address he wrestled with the impending tragedy of World War II: "War is wholesale suicide and should receive the moral condemnation of the Church." He detested the "wild, weird diabolic efforts to institute a new social order" by the Nazi, Soviet, and Japanese and Italian governments. His vision included cooperation with like-minded Christians, and he urged the annual conference delegates to associate with "present day" movements, such as the American Bible Society, the Pennsylvania Federation of Churches, and the Federal Council of Churches, as they deemed advisable. He endorsed a plan to use buildings on the former Albright College campus in Myerstown for educational work, and he recommended a financial drive, which became the "Victory Through Loyalty to Christ" campaign with a quadrennial goal of $110,000, to accomplish the denomination's goals. [17]

In 1938, during Mengel's episcopacy, total church membership reached 24,713 with approximately 35,000 Sunday school students in 160 churches. Despite the economic depression many churches made progress in making their allotted contributions to the denomination; those delinquent in payments dropped from twenty-four in 1935 to zero by 1941. World War II took its toll on attendance, however. The 1942 statistics showed a loss in Sunday School attendance of 1,700, although the denomination as a whole showed a gain of 528 members; worship attendance figures were not compiled at this time. [18]

Mengel's work did not cease when he was succeeded as Bishop by Albert Cooper in 1942. He returned to a seven-year pastorate in Allentown PA and then became a driving force in the creation of Evangelical Congregational School of Theology. [19] When he died in 1964 he was praised in the *Allentown Morning Call*:

> He knew only one mission. This was to preach the Gospel and win more men to the Master…Bishop Mengel is one whose long record is written into the hearts of the many thousands…he served as preacher, teacher, counselor and friend. [20]

Bishop Cooper (1879–1950)

The fourth and last Bishop of this period was Albert W. Cooper. Licensed in 1900, he too was a ministerial delegate to the Barrington and Detroit conferences. Unlike Woodring and Mengel he did not participate in the denomination's Boards. His legacy was his well-placed utterances backed by strong convictions. [21] Before his election to the episcopacy in 1942 he served as the corresponding secretary of the Conference Missionary Society and after forty-three years as pastor was selected to the denomination's highest office. Cooper was a strong advocate of ecumenical co-operation. He proposed the establishment of a new category of Lay Preachers. Cooper also helped to bring the "Victory Through Loyalty to Christ" campaign to a successful conclusion. The General Conference report of 1946 showed a total of $65,359 raised in this campaign. The proposed theological seminary was to receive $10,000, and the rest was to go to the Retirement Home, the Pension Fund, the Board of Missions, and the Publishing House.[22]

The final years of the World War and the uncertainty of the postwar period engaged Cooper's attention. In

Bishop Albert W. Cooper, 1943– 1950

his 1943 Episcopal Address he wrestled with the hard issue of war: it was, he believed, caused by the rejection of God by individuals and nations. America, having "sought to relegate God into a minor place in its affairs," must accept some responsibility. Half of Cooper's message centered on this theme, while he also spoke of the need for evangelism, stewardship, and concern for service personnel.[23] In his first postwar Episcopal Address Cooper focused on alcoholism as one of the widespread problems that the social breakdowns of war had spawned. A spiritual awakening was necessary, he said, if the laws of God and social order were to be sustained. He appealed for a "crusading spirit" and the revival of Christianity especially among youth in Sunday School and Christian Endeavor.[24]

Through Depression and War

In 1938 Bishop Mengel declared that

> [t]he present outlook is much more encouraging than it was fifteen years ago, even though we face a strangely distracted world....We have found our proper place in the sisterhood of Churches ... We should also remember that our church has certain historic ideals to which we must adhere.[25]

This optimism, voiced in the midst of the Depression but using the term "ideals" from 1922, was reassuring to the church. Local church life, however, had reached a peak, and in the next decade, a downturn appeared. The effects of the worldwide Depression, and then World War II, when many people were relocated in the armed forces and defense jobs, accelerated the decline. Despite repeated evangelism efforts in the late 1930s and early 1940s to increase giving and membership, this period saw losses in prayer meeting attendance, Sunday school enrollment and attendance, and church membership. Each Conference *Journal* published pleas from administrators, committees, and General Boards for additional growth and advancement, but "fixing" the situation was hard. The aura of newness was wearing thin, and a "distracted" secular culture was beginning to take its toll on the church.

Denominational Activities

Publications

United Evangelicals opposed to the merger of 1922 were very aware of the need for a periodical to publicize their views, rally their supporters, and build a spirit of unity. The first issue of *The United Evangelical*, a weekly of sixteen pages taking its name from the old denomination, appeared on Dec. 5, 1922, two months after the merger. In subsequent issues Bishop Heil defended the United Evangelical position in a monumental series of forty articles. Other clergy and lay delegates to the merger conferences also critiqued the merger and wrote spirited defenses of the anit-merger position in its pages. Readership grew steadily through the 1920s, then declined in the Depression years.

Bishop Heil served as part-time editor from 1922 to 1926 and full-time editor from 1926 to 1930. He urged all departments of the church to use the *UE* instead of forming their own periodicals.[26] Rev. Henry Messersmith prepared and printed each issue until 1931 in a home located on North Ninth St. in Allentown PA. A four-man editorial committee succeeded Heil in 1930. Then, Rev. J. S. Heisler served as editor from 1934 to 1943, and Messersmith, the former publisher, took over in 1943. After the June 1931 purchase of the former Albright College campus, the publishing enterprise moved to South (Recitation) Hall on W. Park Ave. in Myerstown PA. This building housed the presses and the editorial offices and was named Church Center Press.[27] Conference *Journals*, Sunday School quarterlies, *Disciplines*, and hymnals rolled off its presses. For a time Ralph Houser, lay delegate from Annville PA, supervised the operation. Church Center Press also provided a book and literature service for pastors and churches. The Press derived income from the Board of Publication, sale of stock, and profit from secular print jobs.[28]

For fifty years *The United Evangelical* served as a source of information and inspiration binding Evangelical Congregational churches together and providing national religious news. Editorials stressed character in the believers and membership in the growing church. Sermons by notable EC preachers, like S. L. Wiest, expounded doctrine and biblical truths.[29] Reports of church dedications inspired readers. Newsy, personable, detailed information about church anniversaries, youth work, and EC laypeople appealed to the heart and soul of readers living in Pennsylvania, Ohio, and Illinois. Educational (Sunday School lessons), social (temperance), and missionary pages kept people informed about progress in the Conferences. In our current nonlinear world it is difficult to estimate the positive effect *The United Evangelical* had on the denomination in this period.

Church Home

The merger cost the East Pennsylvania Conference its stake in the Evangelical Home in Lewisburg PA, but in 1924 a generous businessman from Shamokin PA, Isaac C. Burd, together with his wife and his sister-in-law, Kathryn Rogers, purchased and donated a farm next to the Herndon PA Campmeeting Grove to provide a home for needy aging saints and orphans of the new denomination.[30] Guests who could not go to campmeeting could hear the services each August broadcast to the farm.[31] The one hundred-acre farm with its herd of beef and dairy cattle provided crops for food and income, and its quiet location was perfect for the elderly. The property was renovated and a dormitory added to accommodate six, and later with additions thirty, guests. Bequests from interested church members supported construction, and Mother's Day offerings from the congregations continued to provide working capital. To prevent a recurrence of the loss of the Lewisburg Home, the Burd and Rogers Home for the Aged was governed by a *self-perpetuating* Board long chaired by Rev. (later Bishop) C. H. Mengel. Although the Board reported to the Annual and General Conferences, it had no legal connection to the denomination. A by-law developed by the Board of Directors called for an ordained elder of the EC Church to serve as Superintendent of the Home with his wife as Matron. Thomas Knecht (1924-1929), Samuel A. Heisey (1929-1937), and Albert R. Kratzer (1937-1970) and their wives served in these roles.

By 1941 the Board realized that vast changes were coming in the nursing home field. Hospital care for Herndon residents was negligible. As Kratzer explained in a 1985 interview, "there was a pressing need to provide skilled nursing care and this plus the need to conform to ever increasing state regulations, i.e., wider doors, etc. meant we had to consider expanding and/or a major renovation of our premises or moving....So, preparations were made to relocate the home."[32] The former Mohn Hall (the girl's dormitory) of Albright College in Myerstown provided rooms for thirty residents. The nearby Science building was also deeded to the Board for future use. The Kratzers supervised both the Herndon and Myerstown facilities. The idea of an orphanage was put on hold because there was a greater need to care for the elderly than for orphans.[33]

Church Extension

Bishop Heil reported in 1926 that "[t]he Board of Church Extension at the beginning of the past quadrennium was very much in the condition of the man on the Jericho road, stripped of all their possessions temporarily. Therefore, we have not been able to accomplish very much aside from giving advice and suggestions."[34] The funds of the UE Board of Church Extension had become the property of the Evangelical Church, and Heil had little money to give to struggling congregations that chose not to merge into the Evangelical Church. From this inglorious beginning the Board and the two Annual Conference Church Extension Societies struggled to provide funds to build and repair EC church properties.

Even the meager funds of the 1920s dried up during the Depression of the 1930s and during World War II. After the War, however, with increased contributions the Board of Church Extension could state that it was doing its task in an acceptable manner: appropriations from the conference churches (three cents per member, later increased to ten cents) provided money for loans to churches. Other churches were repaying their loans, making additional funds available. Corresponding Secretary F. R. Cardwell joyfully reported in 1946 that a gift from the "Victory Through Loyalty to Christ" campaign netted $1,500, and the Board gladly lent money interest free for the first five years to needy congregations of both conferences.[35] In his history of Western Conference R. S. Wilson tells the thrilling story of churches established in Norwood Heights IL and Akron and Hubbard OH with church extension money.[36] In the East a new church in Reading PA, Greenmont EC, was birthed in 1948. Western Conference territories saw new works in Ohio and

Illinois. By 1951 the West had twenty-nine congregations using Church Extension monies, while in East Pennsylvania Conference nineteen more churches were added to those borrowing funds.

Missions

The United Evangelical Church had devoted much time and energy to missions. That interest carried over into the new EC denomination but had to be directed into new channels, as the Hunan Mission in China and the Red Bird Mission in Kentucky were now missions of the Evangelical Church. Rather than trying to independently open new mission fields and recruit, train, and supervise mission workers, the new EC Board of Missions decided to rely on "faith missions," in which those called to the mission field raised their support while serving under an interdenominational mission board. "Faith missions" candidates were endorsed by the EC Board of Missions and supported by local churches who worked through the Eastern and Western Branches of the Women's Home and Foreign Missionary Societies (W.H. & F. M.S.), which continued to function exactly as it had in the United Evangelical Church. Soon, youthful candidates began applying as pastors, evangelists, and medical workers to Africa Inland Mission and the Christian and Missionary Alliance; missionaries continued to serve in Hunan Province, China, under the non-denominational China Inland Mission. In place of the Red Bird Mission the EC Church embraced an African-American orphanage on Leonard Street in Atlanta GA supervised by Amy Chadwick. In the 1920s the church supported ten missionaries in China, eight in Africa, and two in South America.[37]

Among the notable missionaries in the next decades were Carl and Marie Becker, a medical doctor and his wife from Boyertown PA. These unassuming and hard-working people lived among the pygmies of the (Belgian) Congo. For his efforts Dr. Becker was cited in *Time* magazine following his evacuation during the Congolese rebellion of 1964. Another successful missionary, Mae Royer of Ephrata PA, founded a home for orphan children in Mexico in 1940; her efforts led to the establishment of EC churches in that area.[38]

On the other side of the globe a mission work had been established in Manipur State of British India under Watkin Roberts in the wake of the Welsh revival of 1910. The North East India General Mission (NEIGM) became an indigenous church featuring training schools and field evangelism in villages. Among its workers were Rev. Paul Rostad and his wife Ella, who was a member of the Kimball Ave. EC Church in

The Rostads with the Training School's Soccer Team, ca. late 1930s

Chicago IL. The EC Board of Missions began to provide some financial support for the couple, as well as for students and native workers. Gradually, leadership of the NEIGM came to be vested primarily in EC people, although donations continued to come from several denominations.[39]

The desire for an identifiably EC field of mission work remained, however. As early as 1936 both the Board of Missions and the W. H. & F. M. S. looked to the Appalachian Mountains as a possible mission field, and the General Conference of 1942 endorsed a program in Glen Eden, Lee County, KY, founded by Eliza Richards. Rev. A. M. Herman was assigned in 1946 to teach at the Canyon Falls School there, and Rev. and Mrs. R. C. Hillegass followed in 1948 to develop a congregation. This mission field was supervised directly by the EC Board of Missions.[40]

Many congregations had active programs to promote enthusiasm for missions among people of all ages. In addition to the women's society Young People's Missionary Societies, Mission Bands for children, and Cradle Roll Departments (babies enrolled for the cause of missions) that had been active in the United Evangelical Church continued to function. These groups prayed for mission work, raised funds, and studied missions and the missionaries' activities through the reading of letters from mission fields. Each issue of *The United Evangelical* contained a section on missions edited by Mrs. H. E. (Flossie) Messersmith.

C. D. Huber, a pastor and later Presiding Elder, served as first Corresponding Secretary of the Board of Missions. His extensive reports to Annual and General Conferences gleaning details from conversations with and letters from missionaries and mission church congregations kept people abreast of missionary activity. The eastern and western Branches of the W. H. & F. M. S. worked at promotion, fund raising, and recruitment. A Women's Board of Missions was created in 1934 to coordinate the activities of the Branches. Finally, in 1947 the Board of Missions was reorganized to include direct representation from both Branches, and Rev. Thomas Paul was elected first full-time Corresponding Secretary of the Board of Missions. Marian Paul assisted her husband in the office at the house in Shillington PA purchased to serve as mission headquarters and a home for EC missionaries on furlough. Women who served as Branch Presidents during this period were: Eastern Branch—Carrie Neitz (1923-1934) and Alice Schlappich (1934-1952); and Western Branch—Rebecca Shultz (1923-1927), Jennie Wilson (1927-1942), and Stella Mineely (1942-1958).[41]

"Missions" meant domestic and foreign missionaries to most people in the church, but the Annual Conference Missionary Societies also supported many EC congregations that needed aid to cover salaries and building and property repair programs.[42] In 1925, for example, the East Pennsylvania Conference reported fifty missionaries (assigned pastors) in forty-eight charges (actually eighty-four organized congregations) within the Conference, while four of the eight churches and both Presiding Elders in Ohio Conference needed mission funding.[43] Congregations desiring to join the EC Church as missions were welcomed as long as they understood that only partial funding could be obtained from the denomination. Admitted to the list of mission congregations were Allentown (PA) Boulevard (1929), Akron (OH) Cottage Grove (1929), Mansfield OH (1931), Findlay (OH) Trinity (1932), Youngstown OH (1932), Hubbard OH (1935), Leavittsburg OH (1935), Akron (OH) Tallmadge Ave. (1936), Dixon (IL) St. James (1938), Akron (OH) Trinity (1940).

Support for these missionary endeavors came through denominational "envelope offerings": home missions support from the Christmas Offering and Self-Denial collections in the spring and foreign missions support from World-wide Missions Sunday in the fall. Local church missionary societies also collected dues (still $2/year). Missions also received the largest percentage of the apportionment assessed each congregation by the Conference. After World War II financial support for missions increased; the 1950 General Conference Journal reveals a sizeable increase for 1946-1950 over the previous four-year period for both home and foreign work. The number of "mission" congregations stood at sixty-eight by 1950.[44]

Higher Education

When the United Evangelical Church merged with the Evangelical Association, its colleges, Western Union College in Iowa and Albright College in Myerstown PA, became schools of the Evangelical Church. The East Pennsylvania Conference fought valiantly in the courts to retain its heavy investment in Albright College, but in 1927 the Pennsylvania Supreme Court ruled that the Conference was not entitled to appoint college trustees as it had in the past. The Evangelical Church moved the College to Reading in 1929, however, and had no use for the old fourteen-acre campus. As a gesture of goodwill the Evangelical Church offered to sell the campus to the EC Church for $25,000. Although the church had no money for this purpose, many members of the East Pennsylvania Conference, including Dr. Levi C. Hunt, President of the College from 1915 to 1923, urged acceptance of this offer. A conference committee report highlighted possibilities for the land's use, including publishing facilities, an orphanage, and an institution of higher education. Bishop Woodring's Episcopal Address of 1934 endorsed "starting a Religious Training School on a small scale...so that our dream of a College and Theological Seminary will be realized."[45]

The Church Center Campaign yielded enough money to purchase the campus, and in the 1930s the annual Bible Conferences and Junior Preachers Schools were held there. By 1938 the facility was rented to the Pennsylvania State Police as a training school, and the former football field was used to train the K-9 corps. When the police relocated their school to Hershey PA, Old Main was abandoned again, except for use as a warehouse by a local shirt factory. Some repair work provided by state funds had been done, but the ravages of weather were making the property unsightly. After supporting missions and the work of local churches, there was little money left to launch a school, but this did not dim the vision of those who wanted an EC school of theology. Too many Evangelical Congregational pastors had no theological training, and those who did were attending a wide range of seminaries, many with views of Scripture and theology not congenial to the EC Church.

In 1942 Bishop Mengel called for a "corporation" to be formed to take over the "unused properties" at Myerstown. Following the War in 1946 the Board of Education endorsed a plan at General Conference for establishing a governing body with permission to raise funds and recruit a faculty and students. No longer was the Board to oversee the training of ministers through a conference-endorsed course of study; it was to become caretaker of a theological institution. Of course, not everyone agreed with this plan, and several hurdles had to be overcome before the mandate could become a reality. As funds slowly trickled in, Pennsylvania state inspectors evaluated Old Main with its chapel and dormitory addition and determined that it could be satisfactorily renovated but at a cost in excess of $50,000. In addition, the state required a minimum of eight full-time faculty members for a seminary, and this was more than the church could afford. The issue was resolved when Temple School of Theology in Philadelphia offered to accept degree students from the projected school for their final two years of instruction at Temple with the Temple faculty considered instructors at the EC school. The vision was on the verge of becoming reality.[46]

Ecumenical Relations

The United Evangelical Church had been a member of the Federal Council of Churches, although there were some who had misgivings about this association. The EC Church did not maintain this relationship, but sessions of both Annual Conferences received greetings and/or devotional talks each year from representatives of the Federal Council of Churches or a state Council of Churches; the 1942 General Conference, for example, listened to a strong anti-Communist message from a member of the American Council of Christian Churches. Use of the International Sunday School lessons continued; indeed, an entire page in the weekly denominational periodical contained comments on these lessons. Youth and adult affiliates of the International Society of Christian Endeavor with their motto "For Christ and the Church" were active in most EC churches. The denomination cooperated with the Pennsylvania Sabbath School Association and the Anti-Saloon League (later the Pennsylvania Council on Alcohol Problems). Participation in the work of the American Bible Society gave the church a voice in and commitment to the translation, printing, and distribution of Bibles throughout the world. In 1950 the Evangelical Congregational Church first participated in the nation's military chaplaincy. Some local congregations also participated in community councils of churches and the National Week of Prayer each January.

Still, many in the EC Church, especially those scarred in the merger battle of 1922, feared loss of identity or independence in some "super church." In 1938 Bishop Mengel told the General Conference, "It seems to me the time is ripe to establish closer fraternal relations with other Churches. Isolation is not the best policy, but merger is taboo."[47] It was from the West, where large distances and relatively meager resources were constant reminders that Christ's work is bigger than any particular denomination, that the initiative for cooperation with other churches came. In 1942 Rev. Robert S. Wilson, pastor at Dixon IL, became aware of efforts to form the National Association of Evangelicals and established contact with the organizers. The General Conference Committee on Church Federation asked him to attend the Constitutional Convention for United Evangelical Action in Chicago as an observer in May 1943, but it was the Western Conference that first joined the NAE in 1947, naming its Presiding Elder, N. J. Broadway, as its representative.[48]

Bishop Cooper's vision for Christian unity made him an advocate for closer ties to other like-minded churches. He called for federation with the United Brethren in Christ (Old Constitution) and the Primitive Methodists, for association with the Pennsylvania Council of Churches, and membership in the National Association of Evangelicals. His appeals continued at each Annual Conference session from 1947 to 1949. Cooper in 1948 expressed a hope for union with sister denominations like the United Brethren and Primitive Methodists.[49] He was aware that "organic unions," especially "forced unions," could damage a church. (He had been a delegate at Detroit!) However, he wanted the Evangelical Congregational Church to develop a strategy creating local cooperation between denominations based on the Lordship of Christ. A Council on Church Fellowship began negotiations among the three churches with the understanding that the churches would continue to be independent of one another. A *limited* General Assembly representing each church would give direction to a common Sunday school curriculum, a "united missionary program...and a common hymn book."[50] Movement towards Cooper's goals was minimal, and his untimely death in the summer of 1950 interrupted momentum toward cooperation with other bodies. His successor, Bishop John Smith, sought to develop the Evangelical Congregational church rather than merge it. The three denominations agreed to cooperate in ventures of mutual advantage without actual merger.

Preacher's Aid Society and Support of Retired Clergy

The Charitable Society of the United Evangelical Church never succeeded in raising adequate funds for the support of clergy after retirement. In 1921 its total resources amounted to $33,154.85,[51] and this was
one of the great benefits seen in merger with the wealthier Evangelical
Association, that UE ministers would be able to join the EA
Superannuation Fund (assets $675,338.72) and receive a pension upon
retirement, even if they had contributed to it only a few years.[52] The East
Pennsylvania Conference, however, along with a few other annual conferences had its own Preachers' Aid Society, which was replenished from
conference apportionments, Children's Day offerings, member dues, and
investment income. Claimants included ministers' widows and orphans
who were minors, as well as retired clergy. In 1924 its by-laws were
amended to admit non-merging ministers from other conferences,[53] and
on April 7, 1930, it became "The Preachers' Aid Society of the
Evangelical Congregational Church." [54] Group insurance for EC ministers was first approved in 1928, and in 1936 new rates of pension support were set: to a retired minister—$14 for each year in the ministry to
a maximum of $600 per year; to a widow—$7 for each year of husband's
service in the ministry to a maximum of $300 per year; and to orphan
children under 16—$3 for each year of father's service to a maximum of
$120 per year.[55] Congregations began making contributions into the
fund for their pastors (1 % of pastor's salary) in 1938.

In 1948 retired pastors still received an annual pension of only $14
per year of service as an itinerant in active ministry[56] and widows half
that amount, even though costs had risen dramatically since 1936.
Because this pension was so meager many pastors chose not to retire,
but continued in ministry until deteriorating health forced them to step
aside. In an attempt to help retirees the Society in 1946 assumed the lia-
bility for the pastor's life insurance coverage previously held by a commercial insurance company.[57] Under the new arrangement a retired pastor could make a periodic withdrawal on the value of the policy during
his lifetime to supplement his pension benefits.[58] A total of $2,000 was
available for each retired pastor either as a death benefit or as additional pension aid. Two years later the Society raised the defined benefit rate
to $ 20 per credit year for pastors and $ 10 for widows.[59] In 1950 the
Society paid over $16,000 to claimants and ended the year with assets
of over $71,000.[60] Rev. C. D. Huber served as Secretary of the Preachers'

Aid Society from 1922 to 1941, and Rev. C. J. Yoder served from 1941 to 1977.

Historical Interests

The growing historical collection at the United Evangelical Church center in Harrisburg, of course, became the property of the Evangelical Church at the merger of 1922, but interest in Evangelical history was strong in the Evangelical Congregational Church, which saw itself as the most loyal of Albright's children. Bishop Heil served as Conference Historian of the East Pennsylvania Conference in its early years. After his death, however, no successor was appointed, and interest in history was overshadowed by other concerns for a decade. Then, in 1938 at the urging of Rev. Robert S. Wilson the Western Conference proposed an amendment to the *Discipline* to the General Conference:

> Whereas, there is a need for historical material of our church for the Conference Course of Study, as well as of suitable tracts concerning our church, her doctrine and mode of worship, the Western Conference humbly petitions the General Conference to appoint a committee to prepare an up-to-date history of the Evangelical Congregational Church, as well as other historical material, and tracts suitable for use in church, as the committee may deem advisable.[61]

The 1938 General Conference appointed the first Special Historical Committee, consisting of G. A. Maurey, H. E. Messersmith, and E. S. Woodring. This Committee reviewed and approved a manuscript by Wilson, *Jacob Albright: the Evangelical Pioneer,* which was published by the EC Church Center Press in 1940.[62] In its report to the 1946 General Conference the Historical Committee asked permission to receive historical material "to be made available for a library if and when a school is opened at the Church Center" and to assemble material for a short history of the Evangelical Congregational Church. At this time the Committee consisted of Messersmith, Woodring, and Wilson.[63] Four years later, the Committee's three priorities were the same: collecting historical documents and books, forming these materials into a historical section of a seminary library, and publishing historical manuscripts. Wilson was writing a series of historical articles in *The United Evangelical* that would be published in 1953 as *A Brief History of the Evangelical Congregational Church* (85 pp.).[64]

Church Life

The Pastorate

Appointment

In a system carried over from the traveling (itinerant) preachers on the early American frontier, pastors received their assignments for the coming year on the final day of each session of Annual Conference. The Stationing Committee (the Bishop and the Presiding Elders in the Conference) positioned ministers based on the Committee's sense of the church's needs after careful prayer for divine guidance. Bishop Mengel claimed that this system was a stabilizing influence on the denomination. Congregations with "the old age complex" might prefer young energetic preachers over older, seasoned men, he said, but church leaders could insure that age never prevented the use of an individual. Mengel listed eight factors to be weighed in stationing: 1. Denominational loyalty and interest; 2. The personality of the minister and "possibly his wife's"; 3. Diligence in ministry; 4. Religious experience; 5. Adaptability and success in administration; 6. Training and preparation; 7. Preaching ability; and 8. Years of service.[65]

Itinerancy also meant that preachers were kept on the move, if only over periods of years, but moving was often unpleasant, especially for clergy families, and the limit on the number of years a pastor was allowed to remain at one church was raised from five years to eight in 1934.[66] Changing the East Pennsylvania Conference session from February to April in 1923 also made the "move," usually by railroad, a bit easier, but children in clergy families often stayed with friends or relatives to complete their school year. Nevertheless, the stationing system remained largely intact through the period, though dissatisfaction with the system was developing in the Western Conference and would bring pressure on administrators to revise the process.

Salaries

"Advancement" by the stationing committee to a larger church might mean a larger salary, and salaries during this period were very meager. The 650-member Seibert church in Allentown PA, for example, paid $2900 plus parsonage in 1928, and only a few others met this standard. Some regular appointments paid $1,765 in 1928, an increase of 2.5% over the year 1920. Most of the churches, however, listed one hundred members or less and paid only $500 to $1200.[67]

Both salaries and prices remained relatively stable during the lean years of the Depression and World War II wage and price controls. After the War, however, the church entered a period in which it struggled to provide pastors with adequate income. The lay delegates of the East Pennsylvania Conference recommended that the pastors be given an increase in salary in 1944,[68] and the Conference authorized an increase of $200 in each of the three ministerial categories, bringing the annual minimum salaries to $1,200 for licentiates, $1,300 for deacons, and $1,500 for elders.[69] Two years later the laity proposed an increase of $200 for licentiates and $300 each for deacons and elders.[70] Further raises were passed in 1948 and 1950. In that year the minimum salaries were $2,100 for licentiates, $2,300 for deacons, and $2,400 for elders. Students serving a church received a minimum of $1,300.[71]

The first change in the Western Conference salary standards came in 1946 as a response to a recommendation by Bishop Cooper.[72] In 1950 salary minimums were set at $1,800 for licentiates, $2,000 for deacons, and $2,200 for elders.[73]

Sunday Services

Society's attack on the sanctity of the Lord's Day continued and intensified during this period; now there were *other* things to do on Sunday besides church. The Evangelical Congregational Church did its best to defend Sabbath observance and provided many Sunday activities, including large and active Sunday schools, morning and evening worship services, and Christian Endeavor, originally a youth movement but now including weekly meetings for all age groups.

Afternoon services were held in churches without electricity and in multi-church charges where the pastor was at another church in the morning. Many members walked lengthy distances to the place of worship, sometimes twice on the same day. Most pastors had automobiles in order to make their rounds, but some, for instance Rev. H. E. Samuels, never owned a car and relied on public transportation or "borrowing a ride" even to do hospital visits! During World War II the rationing of fuel and tires limited auto travel and so caused canceling of services. These conditions even forced rescheduling of the proposed 1942 sessions of the General Conference from Johnstown PA in the Western Conference to Allentown PA in the East.[74]

Evangelical Congregational worship remained a mixture of revival informality and civilized decorum, particularly at the Sunday morning service. Clergy attire remained a simple but dignified suit, but pipe organs and choir gowns reinforced the formal side of morning worship.

Some old-timers felt out of place in city churches with choir procession-als and candles and warned against creeping formalism, but in many country churches worship had changed little from the Evangelical Association days. Even in larger churches evening services tended to be less structured, often evolving into times of testimony and chorus singing.

Preaching

Preaching was one of the pastor's most important duties and received much attention in the early EC Church. The Course of Study required for aspiring pastors listed books on evangelistic preaching, including Broadus' *Preparation and Delivery of Sermons*, Jowett's *The Passion for Souls*, and Conant's *Every Member Evangelism*. Every prospective pastor had to pass an examination on preaching, as well as theology, pastoral work, and Bible, and was required to submit a sermon to the Board of Examiners for its approval. His grades were published in the annual Conference *Journal*.[75] Responding to a request from lay delegates for better training of preachers, the Board of Examiners organized a School for Junior Preachers to be held at Waldheim Park near Allentown PA beginning July 7-12, 1924, and required all preachers-in-training to attend.[76] This School was held annually and featured notable lecturers. Ministers, both inexperienced and experienced, also had opportunities every summer at campmeeting to hear great preachers like Dr. Robert G. Lee and Bishop Arthur Moore. Lee's sermon entitled "Pay Day, Some Day" brought many to their knees at Waldheim Campmeeting.

It is difficult to provide a general description of preaching throughout an entire denomination over a generation. Some preachers were educat-ed and polished; many during this period had only a high school edu-cation, and their preaching was rather rough. Some preachers were calm and dignified; others were emotional and very lively in the pulpit. Sermons tended to exceed thirty minutes. Many preachers stayed very close to the biblical texts in their sermons; sermons were often verse-by-verse Bible studies.[77] Most preachers used evangelistic sermons each Sunday, and the altar was "open" for seekers to come to Christ after the *Evangel* sounded. A denomination of 20-27,000 members consistently reported between 5500 and 8500 conversions each quadrennium in this period.[78] Bishop A. W. Cooper excelled in the pulpit; in the words of his conference obituary: "His pulpit utterances were marked by clari-ty and backed by conviction."[79] Other exceptional preachers of this peri-od were Allen Z. Bodey, Kenneth Maurer, J. S. Harper, and J. R. Weaver.

Weaver was well-known as a Bible expositor and like others preached series of sermons covering a book of the Bible.[80]

Sacraments

Holy Communion

Every year Annual Conference sessions, which were the heart of denominational life, began with a service of Holy Communion. After a strong devotional message lay delegates and clergy would make their way to the altar railing to be served by their leaders. This impressive devotional practice was repeated in local churches generally four times per year, as stipulated by the *Discipline,* although some churches also offered Communion during Holy Week as well as Easter. In the EC Church, as in its ancestor denominations, only preachers who were ordained elders were permitted to administer the sacrament. Where a church was served by a licensed but non-ordained minister, Communion had to be postponed until the Presiding Elder of the district could be present. The hardship this placed on the sprawling Western Conference led to the division of that Conference into two Presiding Elder districts in 1941, so that churches served by student pastors could receive the Lord's Supper more frequently.[81] Private communion provided elderly and shut-in members with the Lord's Supper in what might be thought of as an extension of the Lord's Table beyond the walls of the church. When a large parish had many homebound persons, pastors visited each shut-in with the emblems four times a year. In a denomination not particularly inclined to ceremony and ritual, the Lord's Supper occupied a large place as a tradition with meaning.

Baptism

Baptism continued according to the rites of the United Evangelical Church with a brief ceremony for infant baptism and an adult baptismal service based on the Apostles' Creed. Adults were sometimes baptized by immersion, but infants and children were baptized by sprinkling or pouring. During the period three-quarters of all reported baptisms were infant baptisms. Adults converted at EC altars were often subsequently baptized, but there is no correlation in the statistical reports between number of conversions and number of baptisms. Some of those converted in EC churches actually joined other churches, and some of the converted had already been baptized years before. In any case, the EC practice of baptism remained true to the church's Reformation heritage, Methodist tradition, and its interpretation of the Bible.

Music

The Evangelical Congregational Church continued its great Evangelical heritage of spirited singing. Some urban churches had fine choirs and excellent organists who presided at instruments as good as any in the city. Many smaller and rural congregations used pianos, reed organs, or the newer electric models and had smaller, less polished choirs. ECers formed singing and musical groups, quartets, male choruses, choral associations, Sunday school orchestras, and bands. Hymns and gospel songs were joined by the occasional "Pennsylvania Dutch" chorus, like "*O wie lieblich ist Jesu*" (O how lovely is Jesus), especially at testimony meetings. The great biblical truths of doctrine, spirituality, and life were perpetuated in the songs of faith. Many a great sermon was lost on the memories of God's people, but they sang E. A. Hoffman's "Leaning on the Everlasting Arms" again and again.

The first EC General Conference (adjourned session Jan. 10, 1928) appointed a Hymn Book Committee to prepare a new hymnal for the new denomination. The Committee surveyed the congregations and determined that: 46 of 81 congregations responding were using the United Evangelical Hymnal exclusively; 10 of 81 were using the UE Hymnal and another song book; 23 charges that were not using the UE Hymnal at all were using 18 other song books; a total of 7072 UE Hymnals and 5045 other song books were in use in the denominations. The Committee conferred with George Sanville, general manager of the Rodeheaver Co., one of the leading publishers of evangelical hymnals, and learned that compiling and publishing a new denominational hymnal would be prohibitively expensive. Sanville, however, offered to publish a special edition of his company's *Standard Church Hymns and Gospel Songs* with the addition of ninety-six hymns to be chosen by the Committee under the title *Evangelical Congregational Hymnal* for a very reasonable price. The 1930 General Conference accepted this offer, and the Committee surveyed the churches to determine which additional hymns and gospel songs to include, providing in their letter a list of recommended additions from the old UE Hymnal. The Committee worked quickly to provide Rodeheaver with a list of additions (including newer gospel songs and Pennsylvania Dutch choruses as well as old United Evangelical hymns), and the new hymnal covered in black silk was published in 1931.[82]

An essay in the *United Evangelical* on "Music in the Church" described the function of music as "bringing the congregation into an attitude of worship." The author, Dr. Henry Stermer, organist and choir director at Trinity church, Allentown PA, and a member of the Hymn Book Committee, detailed the origins of music, especially in the Psalms of David. The primary role of music in revival and church, he said, is praise and celebration. Many hymns "do not contain a single note of praise," while too many lean toward secular types, some with "a decided jazz rhythm." Choral music, Stermer wrote should not be elaborate but understandable to the people. The central purpose is to worship God.[83]

Church Buildings

The 1922 merger maelstrom was certainly over an "ideal," but it had strong physical ramifications. Hundreds of church buildings and parsonages, as well as denominational sites like campmeeting grounds, the publishing house at Harrisburg, and the United Evangelical colleges in Iowa and Pennsylvania were claimed by both the merged and the non-merging UEs. The issuance of the "quit claim" deeds by the Evangelical Church in 1927[84] gave congregations that had voted not to merge into that church uncontested title to the buildings, but many properties had already been lost, and struggles over land and buildings split families and left many people embittered.

Large sanctuaries of stone and brick had been constructed during the United Evangelical period, and several large churches were built in the 1920s. In Allentown Morris Bastian gave unstintingly to the building of the monumental new Seibert Church, which was completed only after his death in 1932.[85] Lancaster Grace and Reading First in Pennsylvania and Columbus First and Akron First in Ohio also had commodious worship and Sunday school facilities.

Smaller congregations in Ohio and Illinois, however, had lost their properties in the merger, and many had to lease rooms in which to worship. One of these churches began by meeting in a funeral parlor, and another (Mansfield OH) met first in an auto display room and then in a Moose Hall.[86] At Johnstown PA the Evangelical Church took control of the church building when the congregation voted not to join the merger. Those members who organized to perpetuate the United Evangelical Church rented rooms in the old UE church recently vacated when the merged congregation built a new church; it was by this time a gas station! Frustrated in their attempts to purchase this building, they built a new church and dedicated it as soon as it was under roof, "without a rostrum, without carpets, without…opera chairs."[87] Many pastors, equipped with hammer and saw, assisted in constructing places of worship. Large debts were incurred, but when at last a debt was paid off, as for example at Dixon IL, churches immediately launched into building more rooms.

The United Evangelical published a constant stream of articles by the Bishop and the Presiding Elders from each Conference describing dedicatory services, mortgage burnings, and ground breaking ceremonies. These local church properties, of course, belonged to the local congregation and not to the Annual Conference in which the church was located. However, all new building projects needed the approval of a special committee of the Annual Conference to assure the Conference that unmanageable debts would not be incurred. Permission to solicit contributions from other local churches was also allowed, because conference Church Extension Societies had little money to loan for building repairs or new construction.

Class Meetings/Prayer Meetings

"The class leaders, as a rule, report the meetings are spiritual but not many come," Presiding Elder J. S. Heisler stated in 1934. "Before conducting an election for a class leader a certain pastor read the disciplinary requirements for a class leader. One of the surprised members, who never heard anything about such requirements, declared, 'Well, we don't have an animal around here that meets such requirements.' Perhaps our prayer meetings would be better attended if more leaders would meet the disciplinary requirements." In the same year, however, Presiding Elder C. D. Huber reported a country church of 116 members with an average prayer meeting attendance of 112."[88] Church leaders contended that the "prayer meeting continues to be the strong right arm of the spiritual church" but admitted that only a minority of members attended prayer meeting, some congregations had discontinued them entirely, and even some preachers and lay delegates to conference "seldom if ever attend a prayer meeting."[89] Such was the state of prayer meetings, the leading of which remained the class leader's chief responsibility; along with other church activities prayer meetings could thrive or wither during these decades. Each year Presiding Elders would admonish churches to do "something" about the midweek service, but the denomination gave no help or suggestions to the local church as to how this might be done.

Church Year

For the Evangelical Congregational Church, like the United

Evangelical, the church calendar was a mixture of civil holidays, special Sunday School days, and seasonal activities with remnants of the liturgical year observed in older denominations. Lenten services were popular in some churches, replacing the midweek service in spring. Christmas and Easter Sundays, including Holy Communion on Easter, attracted huge crowds, and elaborate decorations accompanied each of these holy days, although Christmas decorations might include Santa Claus! Advent and Pentecost, however, were little observed, and the big days were most likely to be Boys' Day and Girls' Day in Sunday School, Rally Days (spring and fall), Christian Endeavor Sunday in February, Mother's Day, and of course Children's Day in June, which often brought lavish fresh flower displays and smiles from admiring parents who came to hear recitations by their offspring. Harvest Home in the fall featured colorful and abundant displays of home-canned goods and fresh vegetables and fruits, which went to the pastor's family. In Pitman PA, for example, Pastor Dan Draper received so many items each Harvest Home that he traveled about the neighborhood huckstering them from a hearse he had borrowed!

Civil holidays, like New Year's Day, Memorial Day, Independence Day, Labor Day, and Armistice (Veterans) Day, were observed in churches. The campmeeting season and revival services, culminating in Decision Day, remained special times for the Evangelical Congregational Church.

Campmeetings

The United Evangelical campmeeting groves were independently owned by stockholders and controlled by Boards of Directors independent of the church hierarchy. When the merger of 1922 was disputed in eastern Pennsylvania, it was up to each campmeeting board to determine which way the campmeeting would go. Waldheim, near Allentown, remained solidly with the East Pennsylvania Conference.[90] The Herndon campmeeting north of Harrisburg was sidetracked by merger issues in the summer of 1923, when pro-merger members of the Board of Directors attempted to bring the camp into the merger. The majority of the stockholders were, however, anti-merger and elected a new Board under whose auspices campmeeting services resumed in 1924.[91] Perkasie, near Quakertown, was lost in the merger, so the people of the Reading churches led by the pastor of Bethany Church purchased a beer garden and dance hall in 1924 that became Rosedale Grove.[92]

The campmeetings remained in this period unique places of spiritual uplift and evangelism. Spiritual revival in the local church often followed a summer of active soul winning at the camps. Rev. J. S. Heisler reported eighty decisions among children at Rosedale Campmeeting in 1928.[93] The Presiding Elders were responsible for conducting the ten days of campmeetings and selecting the preachers for the services. In earlier years pastors were expected to attend the entire session, and members of their churches came by auto, bus, or train, especially to the closing Sunday night rally. Beginning with Morning Watch and concluding with the Evening Rally, a full day was spent in the things of God. Cottages and tents at Waldheim housed entire families. Allentown (PA) Zion church, for example, had eleven families staying the entire week in 1925. Stories about the shoes that floated downhill from beneath the tents during a torrential rainstorm are the "stuff" from which campmeeting lore is made.

The churches that formed the Western Conference retained no UE campmeetings and, realizing the effectiveness of this summer evangelistic effort, sought to provide new ones for their people. The 1937 Annual Conference appointed a Campmeeting Committee, which investigated the possibility of a camp in the vicinity of Akron OH. Unable to find an affordable site the Committee disbanded in 1941 "for the duration of the war."[94] After World War II these efforts in the West were redirected into establishing a youth camp.

Revivals and Evangelistic Meetings

Revival continued to be the pivot on which the Evangelical Congregational Church moved forward. EC churches held up to four weeks of revival services every year. The local pastor, neighboring pastors, or a professional evangelist preached, and local or touring groups provided special music. Rev. William Rhoda, a blind preacher of great power, was East Pennsylvania Conference Evangelist during the United Evangelical Church period and the early EC days, and Harry Carmichael served as Western Conference Evangelist from 1940 to 1942. Traveling musical groups like the "Happy Clarks" of Philadelphia and the Kutch Gloria Singers of Lebanon PA added their voices. These meetings were often "protracted" until the Lord "broke through" to bless; nightly the same persons would go forward to the altar railing to seek victory over sin. Evangelistic services continued to include a "Decision Day" in the Sunday School to reach children and young people for Christ, and these resulted in many converts.[95] Hearts were changed, men were called to pastoral ministries, and local churches added teachers and workers.

Whole congregations were added to the church through evangelistic services, particularly in the West. In 1927 Presiding Elder H. D. Shultz reported that

> For several years we felt that there were places within the territory of this conference where our church could find opening for new work. We secured the services of Evangelist Rev. J. M. Huff who came with his tent to help us in testing out several places. We pitched the tent for a ten day's campaign in the city of Lancaster. Brother Huff delivered faithful gospel messages. But the time was right in vacation and the park-visiting season, and the very parties who were the most enthusiastic in urging our coming, failed us, and we closed without any visible results. On August 3rd, we opened a campaign in Mansfield....And the results are the organization of a Sunday School.... The tent was pitched next in Akron. Our people and pastor joined with the Evangelistic party, rendering energetic support in the effort.[96]

Cottage Grove EC Church in Akron OH had its origin in a three-week series of evangelistic services led by Rev. Cyrus Hartman in 1927. This congregation erected a building in 1929 and planted two additional congregations, Talmage Ave. and Turkeyfoot EC churches. The first mission in Mansfield OH died after the people lost their meeting place at a local school, but the Conference sent Evangelist H. A. James back to town in 1931. After six weeks of services in an outdoor tabernacle, fifty persons united to form a congregation. In December 1931 James moved on to Youngstown OH and held services. In June 1932 those he had gathered purchased a former dance hall ("taken from the devil and dedicated to God"), and in October a congregation of over one hundred members was accepted into Western Conference.[97]

Revival and evangelistic services were held in every season of the year. In winter families might walk to church each night in the hip-deep snow with only a lantern to light the way. In summer several rural churches, like Steelstown and Dayton PA, held summer "woods meetings" in nearby wooded groves. The Reading District churches rented a tent in 1935 and made it available for summer campaigns in addition to Rosedale Campmeeting. The Western Conference secured a tent in 1937 for its churches to use in starting new congregations.[98]

As early as 1939 former Bishop E. S. Woodring sensed that "the old-fashioned revival meeting seems to be on the decline. [Yet,] until we find a better way to lead people into a personal experience of salvation we cannot afford to discard or to neglect such means of grace."[99] Bishop Cooper was convinced, however, that the church had to find better ways to reach the lost. "Evangelism must be restored to its former place as the main business of the Church," he said in appeals to the Annual Conferences in 1944. "It must be the normal expression of believers."[100] Western Conference responded by appointing Rev. Paul Gordon full-time Conference Director of Evangelism, and East Pennsylvania appointed a Special Committee on Evangelism. In its report to the 1945 session of the East Pennsylvania Conference the Committee recommended continuation of revival meetings and altar worship services, recognizing that "despite all their limitations and weaknesses, the old time revival meetings did engender a dynamic spiritual power that seems lacking in so many of our churches today," but it also outlined a new, more systematic approach to evangelism. The Committee recommended appointment of an Evangelistic Committee in each church to identify unsaved persons among families and organizations of the church and organize a Personal Workers' Group to contact these persons. The Committee also recommended an Evangelistic Campaign of Twelve Sunday Evenings to precede and culminate in Holy Week. Evangelistic services would be coordinated with visitation of church families, three Decision Days in Sunday School, religious instruction classes, weekly prayer meetings, and articles on evangelism in *The United Evangelical*.[101] A "Crusade of Evangelism" was inaugurated by the East Pennsylvania Conference and adopted by the Western Conference, and the church made a special effort to conduct twenty-one meetings in September 1946 promoting evangelism. Bishop Cooper issued another impassioned plea for the Crusade at the 1946 General Conference, and the General Conference Committee on Evangelism first appointed in 1942 endorsed it and promised to outline a strong program for the church.[102] Yet, the church as a whole does not seem to have caught the vision at that time. Gordon remained in his evangelism position only one year before being assigned to a church, and the East Pennsylvania and General Conference Committees on Evangelism made no further reports after their initial ones.

Catechetical Instruction

The Evangelical Congregational Church continued to use United Evangelical catechetical manuals to teach converts about the faith and history of the church before admission to it. Hartzler's adult catechism was required reading for the Course of Study throughout the period, but several attempts were made to provide new materials for children and youth. Rev. Clarence J. Yoder prepared "A Course in Catechetical

Instruction for Juniors, Intermediates, Young People" in 1940 that was published as a forty-four-page pamphlet by order of the Board of Publication on October 4, 1944, with the title "A Help for Catechetical Classes." It consisted of questions with hints for looking up answers in the Bible. Rev. Kenneth R. Maurer initiated an attempt to prepare "a complete catechetical manual for use with children and youth of our Church" in 1945, but the project was not completed at this time.[103] Between 1946 and 1950 a total of 231 catechetical classes with 1935 catechumens were held in the 136 organized congregations of the East Pennsylvania Conference and 15 classes with 138 catechumens were held in the 27 congregations of the Western Conference for a total of 2,073 catechumens, an increase of 156 over the previous quadrennium.[104]

Sunday School

Sunday School was a very important component of the Evangelical Congregational Church during this period, even overshadowing worship services in many congregations. Indeed, for many people Sunday School was *the* way to express devotion to God; hearty singing (accompanied by the Sunday School orchestra), reading of the scripture lesson, checking the attendance and offering, teaching by a beloved teacher, and the final reading of the secretary's report were all parts of a dynamic movement. Weekly Sunday School teaching, the annual picnic, Boys' Day, Girls' Day, Rally Days, and many other special days filled the entire year. The Sunday School year culminated in the blessed climax of conversion at Decision Day! Could more be asked?

The 1926 General Conference reported 150 Sunday Schools in 155 organized congregations with a total enrollment of 33,685 (church membership was 21,216) and an average attendance of 17,698. In 1950 163 schools reported an enrollment of 33,818 (church membership was 27,376) with attendance of 18,729. The intervening years were anything but "status quo" years, and many converts were reported each year, but denominational leaders were disturbed that strenuous efforts seemed to result in little or no net gain in members.[105]

School of Methods

The School of Methods at Waldheim Campmeeting in Allentown PA, founded in the waning days of the United Evangelical Church, continued to flourish in the early days of the Evangelical Congregational Church. School of Methods Clubs, the first of which was organized at

Ashland PA in 1924, met in the months between the summer sessions to study, maintain friendships, and build enthusiasm for the School. Soon, the clubs banded together into Groups (Anthracite Group in 1926, followed by Lehigh Valley, Garden Spot, Schuylkill Valley, and Lebanon Valley Groups). Later, an Alumni Association for those who had graduated with a School of Methods Diploma became very helpful in the growth of the School. Notable speakers (Robert G. Lee and Samuel Zwemer) and musicians (Homer Rodeheaver and Benton Ackley, Billy Sunday's chorister and pianist) were brought in year after year. Waldheim Park was soon overcrowded during School of Methods week, even though most of the cottages were used for student housing. By 1945 over 700 attendees had to be housed in the grove and fed in the dining hall.

During the early years of the School the great majority of the students were young adults or adults. Gradually the starting age for attending the School was reduced to include children in their lower teens and later pre-teens. By the 1940s it was obvious that effective teaching could not be done in lectures to groups of 700 to 1,000 and ranging in age from 10 to 70. Beginning in 1943 two simultaneous courses were offered, one for juniors and one for adults. Children and adults attended separate classes during the day but joined for the evening rallies and evangelistic services. This was better pedagogy, but it did nothing to relieve the problem of accommodations, so in 1946 two weeks of School were offered, one for juniors and one for older students. About 400 attended the first week and about 300 the second. Two years later the program expanded to three weeks (Junior, Intermediate, and Senior) plus a Labor Day weekend (Young Married Couples Retreat). By 1950 the expanded program was attracting over 3,000 registrants. Superintendents during this period were: E. S. Woodring (1921-27), H. S. Heffner (1927-37), C. P. Kichline (1938-42), H. H. Scanlin (1943-52).[106]

The Western Conference had no summer conferences or camps of any kind after 1922. Resources were not available for purchase of a camp grounds and efforts to rent camps of other groups were unsuccessful until 1946. In 1945 the Executive Committee of the Sunday School and Christian Endeavor Federation of the Western Conference appointed a committee under R. S. Wilson to organize a summer conference "to meet in conjunction with the W.M.S. and Ministers." Wilson set to work and located a Christian and Missionary Alliance camp at Beulah Beach OH that might be available for rent. When another group canceled for July 9-14, 1946, his Committee took the dates and planned a camp in conjunction with the Church of the United Brethren in Christ. Called a "youth camp," its 215 campers included children, teenagers, and adults.[107] The Western Conference continued to hold youth camps at Beulah Beach until 1955.

Women

Women retained the positions they had held in the United Evangelical Church: Sunday School teachers, missionary society leaders, musicians, and to a lesser extent stewards, lay delegates, and class leaders. The Western Conference provided women with more opportunities for leadership, but even the East Pennsylvania Conference had four women lay delegates at its first two sessions after the merger. The first woman to serve as a regular delegate to General Conference was Marguerite Hauser from Delightful OH in 1942.[108] Pastor's wives were expected to be active leaders in education, missions, and/or music and were recognized as true partners in ministry with their husbands, being memorialized like pastors in annual conference *Journals* and *The United Evangelical*. This was a period in which one salary (the pastor's) often got a church two full-time leaders.

The Western Conference, handicapped by shortages in pastors and evangelists, grappled with expanding the ministerial roles of women. The Conference licensed Amy Deck, the daughter of Rev. Q. A. Deck, as a "minister" in 1930. She was listed among the "Preachers in their Order" as a licentiate and as a Quarterly Conference member in the Stationing Committee report. The minute states: "Miss Amy Deck was granted the license to preach the Gospel on condition that the General Conference does not take an adverse position on the question of licensing women to preach."[109] She, like other ministers, declared her "willingness to travel." She was never appointed as a pastor, but she did serve successfully as an evangelist in both Conferences of the Evangelical Congregational Church and as a writer of denominational Sunday School materials, even after her marriage to a Presbyterian pastor.

Attempts were made by some in both Annual Conferences in 1934 to allow women to move toward ordination, but nothing came from these efforts. A proposed amendment to the *Discipline* stipulating that "In the granting of licenses, no discrimination shall be made between men and women" was defeated 0-123 in voting among the Annual Conferences. After much discussion the 1934 General Conference approved an amended amendment permitting "devout women and men" to be licensed "as Christian Workers and Evangelists by a vote of three-fourths of an Annual Conference, This license is to be granted only to those who complete the course of study as prescribed" and "shall give authority to preach the Gospel as Evangelists on trial, to conduct and assist in Evangelistic services, but shall not give authority to baptize, unite in matrimony, administer the Lord's Supper or to function as a preacher in charge" of a congregation. The approval was 20-5.[110] Female Christian Workers and Evangelists in Western Conference during this period were: Amy Deck Faust (1935) Roberta Craig (1937-38), Marguerite Hauser Stine (1941), Lois Crowl (1946), and Violet Sheffer Hanna (1947).

Youth

The Evangelical Congregational Church continued to support Sunday School classes, Christian Endeavor groups, and Missionary Societies for children and teenagers as well as adults, and all three of these programs played important roles in the lives of the denomination and of individual ECers, often over-shadowing the worship services of the church. Many EC pastors, notably R. C. Steinhart, had a great love for work with children, and many pastors' wives worked in this area of service. The East Pennsylvania and Western Conference Sunday School and Keystone League of Christian Endeavor (S. S. and K.L.C.E.) Federations continued to thrive during this period, providing training and support for youth and those who worked with them. Their Annual Conventions were important dates on the EC calendar.

The S.S. and K.L.C.E. Federations also supported a new form of outreach to children, the Vacation Bible School. The East Pennsylvania Federation created the office of Superintendent of Church Vacation Schools in 1924, and in 1928 churches were required to include VBS in their statistical reports. That year nine churches conducted Vacation Bible Schools, and seventeen churches participated in community VBS programs. In 1950 the totals were forty-four and twenty-seven out of a total of 136 churches.[111]

Also at this time, some pastors and congregations took advantage of the opportunity to provide religious instruction in the Released Time program under which students were dismissed from public school to attend an hour of religious instruction. The curriculum was of the pastor's choosing, and sometimes several pastors in a community cooperated to offer several grade levels of instruction in locations convenient to the schools.

Beliefs

Theology

Theological issues played no part in the controversy of 1922, except to the extent that those opposed to the merger believed that the United Evangelical *Articles of Faith* were being diluted by union with the *Articles* of the Evangelical Association. The Evangelical Congregational Church kept the unaltered *Articles* of the United Evangelical Church, including the statement on "Christian Perfection."

Still, the Evangelical Congregational Church was not isolated from the theological controversies of its time. It was born at the height of the Fundamentalist - Modernist controversy, and many of its early leaders, including Bishop Woodring, had attended Moody Bible Institute, an early bastion of fundamentalism. Rev. C. G. Unangst of Dixon IL reported on the meetings of the Chicago Fundamentals Ministers' Union in *The United Evangelical* and wrote that, "Fundamentalism stands for Apostolic Christianity in these latter days."[112] A strong Fundamentalist strain would run through the church during this entire period. Of course, Woodring's interests evidenced a much broader scope than the stereotypes of Fundamentalism, and the movement at its beginning was not as narrow and anti-intellectual as some of its later adherents. However, doctrines such as biblical inerrancy came to be the assumed position of the church, even though the *Articles of Faith* retained the traditional Anglican and Methodist position affirming only that Scripture contains all that is needed for salvation.[113]

Throughout the period EC pastors were educated in a wide variety of institutions, including Eastern Baptist, Moravian, Temple, and Princeton Theological Seminaries. The church's Wesleyan heritage faded further into the background as a more generic conservative, evangelical mindset prevailed.

Christian Conduct

The Wesleyan doctrine of Christian Perfection did not grip the EC Church like it did the Holiness Churches of the period, but the intent of sanctification NEVER dropped out of the EC vocabulary. Though evangelism, prayer and Bible study were important, Christian conduct was a vital concern. Bishop Heil in his closing Episcopal message in 1926 listed seven positive reasons for the Evangelical Congregational Church to continue. Then he concluded, "The key to our future is character,"[114] and character meant purity and holy living. Articles in the pages of *The United*

Evangelical called upon believers to show their faith by their works – complete devotion to God. Both Western and East Pennsylvania Conferences had active Committees on Temperance, Sabbath, and Spiritual State of the Church, and their reports constantly stressed Sunday observance, abstinence from alcohol, and non-participation in worldly activities. The reports and articles in *The United Evangelical* cited movies and the theater, smoking, dancing, and sporting events as evil and urged proper attire at beaches and swimming pools. Hollywood and divorce were frowned upon, and games of chance including bingo were criticized. The repeal of Prohibition was seen as victory for the forces of evil, and the emancipation of women and the automobile did not escape criticism. Presiding Elders and Bishops cited these matters in their reports to the General and Annual Conferences, bemoaning the loosening of rigorous biblical standards, and calling upon the faithful to resist the extremes to which society was leaning. The church was in a battle with Satan, and he was unwelcome in EC churches and families.

Church Organization (Polity)

The first Evangelical Congregational *Discipline* was not prepared until 1929, and the East Pennsylvania Conference strictly followed the United Evangelical Church polity during its early years. The organization of the General, Annual, and local Quarterly Conferences, the functions of trustees and stewards, and tasks of the class meetings and class leaders were identical in the new church. The only changes made in the Temporal Economy section of the *Discipline* (i.e. the section describing church institutions) were those designed to further safeguard the rights of individual congregations. Amendments proposed to the General Conference that affected the local church, and especially the congregation's right to own, sell, and vote on property issues, were referred to each Annual Conference, since lay delegates were present there to cast votes. A congregation's local Quarterly Conference was even allowed to stipulate how its lay delegate should vote on such matters, and congregations had the right to reject any change in the *Articles of Faith*.[115]

Conclusion

Lloyd Brownback, layman and financial adviser to many agencies of the Evangelical Congregational Church, said on one occasion, "In 1922 they took from us everything but Jacob Albright's saddlebags!" Yet, Albright's legacy was successfully maintained despite a national Depression and tragic World War. Campmeetings and a splendid retirement home, though legally independent of the annual conferences, were mightily supported by them. The issue of women in the ministry was addressed, then put aside. The new name "Evangelical Congregational," though confusing to outsiders, asserted the conditions under which the new denomination felt the *Evangel* could usher forth. Fear of merger and even alliance with other churches was felt deeply by the founding generation, despite the verbal efforts of Bishop Cooper to stress cooperation at the same time that the Evangelical Church was merging with the Church of the United Brethren in Christ (New Constitution) in 1946. Yet, by the end of the period postwar laity and clergy were no longer responding to traditional organizational patterns, and it was becoming evident that new structures would have to be explored.

During the period 1922-1950 the East Pennsylvania Conference saw few church plants, while the Western Conference increased significantly. Western Conference Presiding Elders' reports give a "blow-by-blow" account of the hard work and tenacity of the people in Ohio and Illinois to align, reconstitute, and nurture churches. In both conferences strong leadership led the way. Laity and clergy, scarred by 1922, stepped forward to preserve the strengths that existed within a body of believers, and later in the period exceptional people reaffirmed their stand. Each held to the stabilizing effects of the autonomous Annual Conferences, a time limit on episcopal terms, congregational property rights to ownership, and the itineracy as a safeguard. The purchase of the Myerstown property and the wise use of the printed page in a linear age re-enforced the work. The "faith mission" concept encouraged missionary candidates. Local revivals, including camp and tent meetings, won lost souls. A spirit of friendship and fellowship was nurtured by School of Methods clubs and Field Days. Annual conferences highlighted the years, bringing eastern representatives to the West to encourage and plan for growth. Youth, the future of the church, were served through catechetical training, Christian Endeavor, School of Methods, released time, and a strong Sunday school program. Many were called to the mission field and the pastorate; local churches were assured of future workers through teacher training programs, strong preaching, and an emphasis on family values. Brownback recognized these factors when he made his statement: he knew the Kingdom is not composed of flesh and blood. Human hearts preserved the ideal that 1922 symbolized.

Notes

1. R. S. Wilson, *History of the Evangelical Congregational Church* (Myerstown, PA: Church Center Press, 1976), 19.

2. J. E. Moyer, *A History of the Evangelical Congregational Church and Growth Strategies for the Twenty-first Century* (unpublished thesis), 57, n. 5.

3. "The Court of Appeals in the Ninth Judicial Dictrict in the State of Ohio Decided the Greensburg Case in Favor of the Merger," UE, July 22, 1924, 9.

4. Moyer, 60.

5. Included among the names were Albright Evangelical Church and Evangelical Missionary Church.

6. In a personal interview Rev. Robert Wilson stated that Rev. Henry Messersmith, the denomination's publisher, suggested the name. (It was not included among the original names submitted.) No documentation exists to verify this statement.

7. Wilson, 36–37; ECGenConf], 1930, 19.

8. Moyer, 61.

9. L .0. Hynson, "Congregational! Evangelical! Wesleyan?: The Evangelical Congregational Church, 1922–1950," *Methodist History* 36 (July 1998), 209, n 4.

10. R. S. Wilson, (Myerstown PA: Church Center Press 1953), 37.

11. W. F. Heil, "A Bit of Personal History," UE, November 14, 1924, 5.

12. "Episcopal Address," ECGenConf], 1934, 25.

13. "Report of the Presiding Elder, Harrisburg District," UEEPAConf], 1923, 43.

14. "Report of the Presiding Elder, Harrisburg District," UEEPAConf], 1924, 42.

15. "Episcopal Address," ECGenConf], 1934, 36, 37.

16. Hynson, 212.

17. ECEPAConf], 1938, 41; ECEPAConf], 1939, 40; ECEPAConf], 1942, 43; ECGenConf], 1942, 35–38.

18. ECGenConf], 1938, 28–36; ECGenConf], 1942, 30–31.

19. Robert G. Hower, *From Vision to Reality. The Story of Evangelical School of Theology, 1953–1993* (unpublished monograph, 1993), 94

20. Editorial, "Outstanding Ministry," *Allentown Morning Call.* January 10, 1964.

21. "Minutes," UEEPAConf], 1922, 34.

22. ECGenConf], 51, 88.

23. "Episcopal Address," ECGenConf], 1943,41–43.

24. "Episcopal Address," ECGenConf], 1946, 45–47.

25. "Episcopal Address," ECGenConf], 1938, 36.

26. W. F. Heil, "Episcopal Message," UEGenConf], 1926, 44.

27. A 1932 brochure titled "Church Center Campaign" outlines with photos, text, and financial goals the plans for creating a Church Center. Target groups

from eastern Pennsylvania churches headed the drive for funding to develop a school, orphanage and publishing plant in the heart of Myerstown.

28. Wilson, *History*, 48.

29. S. L. Wiest, "Sanctification," UE, March 13, 1923, 2–3.

30. *Twentieth Anniversary – 1925–1945 – Burd and Rogers Memorial Home* (Myerstown, PA: Church Center Press, 1945?), 2.

31. Interview with Rev. C. C. Reeder.

32. "Our Early Years at Herndon 1925–1941," *The Voice*, 1 (Summer, 1985), 1–4.

33. Wilson, *History*, 49.

34. "Board of Church Extension" UEGenConf], 1926, 51.

35. "Report of the Corresponding Secretary of the Board of Church Extension," ECGenConf], 1946, 97–98.

36. Robert S. Wilson, "Fifty Years of the Western Conference," ECWConf], 1972, 128–139.

37. Wilson, *History*, 39–40.

38. The Beckers' story is told in William J. Petersen, *Another Hand on Mine* (New York: McGraw-Hill, 1967); Mae Royer wrote of her work in *In the Heart of Mexico* (Lititz, PA: F.J. Klopp, 1984).

39. "How the Gospel Reached the Hill People," *Tidings from Christian Missions in North East India,* August 1984, [1–2]; "India Mission Workers," *Tidings*, June 1985, [2–3].

40. Robert S. Wilson, *History of Women's Missionary Societies: East Pennsylvania Branch, Evangelical Congregational Church – Fifty Years of Missions, 1922–1972* ([Myerstown, PA]: Eastern Branch Missionary Fellowship of the Evangelical Congregational Church, 1976), 49–50.

41. "Missionary Committee," ECGenConf], 1934, 51–52; J. A. Smith, "Report of the Corresponding Secretary of the Board of Missions," ECGenConf], 1950, 86–87; Wilson, *History of Women's Missionary Societies*, 10–12.

42. Moyer, 71.

43. A. W. Cooper, "Thirty First Annual Report of the Corresponding Secretary of the East Pennsylvania Conference Missionary Society of the United Evangelical Church, UEEPAConf], 1925, 88.

44. Smith, "Report," ECGenConf], 1950, 86–87.

45. "Episcopal Message," ECGenConf], 1934, 37.

46. Hower, chapters 1–2.

47. "Episcopal Message," ECGenConf], 1938, 38.

48. R. S. Wilson, "New Evangelical Movement Starts in Chicago—A Committee Report," UE, July 27, 1943; R. S. Wilson, "Report of Delegate to the NAE Conv." UE, Nov. 2, 1948, 7.

49. The United Brethren Church (Old Constitution) was the denomination formed by conservatives under Bishop Milton Wright in 1899 after a bitter disagreement over the adoption of a new constitution. As such it was, like the E.C. Church, a conservative remnant of a "German Methodist" church. The Primitive

Methodist denomination was concentrated in the Northeast and especially the coal fields of Pennsylvania. It was of British background but within the Wesleyan heritage.

50. "Episcopal Message," ECEPAConfJ, 1948, 46–49 ; "Committee on Church Federation," ECGenConfJ, 1950, 55 –

51. "Report of William W. Fetter, Treasurer of the Charitable Society of the United Evangelical Church," UEGenConfJ, 1926, 49–50. Fetter, a layman from Reading PA, kept control of the funds until the courts ruled that they had to be turned over to the Evangelical Church in 1928.

52. "The Superannuation Fund" (Harrisburg, PA: Inter-Conference Committee for the Promotion of Church Union, 1923), 5.

53. "Preacher's Aid Society," UEEPAConfJ, 1924, 89.

54. "Preachers Aid Society," ECEPAConfJ, 1929, 91–92.

55. "Preachers' Aid Society," ECEPAConfJ, 1936, 94.

56. "Committee on Ministerial Aid," in ECGenConfJ, 1946,75.

57. "Preacher's Aid Society," in ECEPAConfJ, 1946, 113.

58. "Report of the Preachers' Aid Society of the Evangelical Congregational Church," in ECGenConfJ, 1946, 121.

59. "Preachers' Aid Society," in ECEPAConfJ, 1948, 124–125.

60. "Charter of the Preacher's Aid Society of the Evangelical Congregational Church," 1930; "Report of the Preachers' Aid Society of the Evangelical Congregational Church," ECGenConfJ, 107.

61. "Committee Reports," ECGenConfJ, 1938, 43.

62. "The Historical Committee," ECGenConfJ, 1942, 44.

63. "Report of Historical Committee," ECGenConfJ, 1946, 69–70.

64. "Historical Committee Report," ECGenConfJ, 1950, 58.

65. "Abstract of Episcopal Address," ECEPAConfJ, 1938, 41; "Abstract of Episcopal Address," ECEPAConfJ, 1941, 41.

66. ECGenConfJ, 1934, 18.

67. ECEPAConfJ, 1928, 103–130.

68. "The Layman's Committee," in ECEPAConfJ, 1944, 88.

69. "Ways and Means Committee," in ECEPAConfJ, 1944, 106.

70. "Laymen's Committee," in ECEPAConfJ, 1946, 84.

71. "Layman's Committee Report," in ECEPAConfJ, 1950, 93.

72. "Ways and Means Committee," in ECWConfJ, 1946, 49.

73. "Laymen's Committee," in ECWConfJ, 1950, 50.

74. Personal remembrance of Robert Hower; C. H. Mengel, "General Conference Address," ECGenConfJ, 1942, 29.

75. See for example "Examination Classes for 1933–34," ECEPAConfJ, 1934, 56–57; the 1922 East Pennsylvania Conference Journal gives a particularly detailed list of all assignments and readings (pp. 60–63).

76. "Board of Examiners," UEEPAConfJ, 1924, 59–60.

77. Interviews with Dr. William Sailer, Marlin and Dorothy Heisey, and Dr. John Moyer.

78. "Quadrennial Statistical Reports," E.C. General Conference Journals, 1926–1950.

79. "Memorial Committee – Bishop A. W. Cooper," ECEPAConfJ, 1951, 97.

80. Interview with Dr. John E. Moyer. Weaver's "Romance of Redemption series" on Ruth was especially well-known.

81. "Bishop's Message," ECWConfJ, 1941, 29.

82. "Report of the Hymn Book Committee," ECGenConfJ, 1930, 45–46; form letter from C. J. Yoder, Committee Secreatary, Oct. 24, 1930; "Preface," *Standard Church Hymns and Gospel Songs–Evangelical Congregational Church Edition* (Myerstown, PA: Church Center Press, 193–?).

83. H. R. Stermer, "Music in the Church," UE, May 30, 1939, 8.

84. See above "The Crisis of 1922."

85. "Seibert's Golden Jubilee" (Allentown. PA: Seibert E. C. Church, 1944). Bastian gave over $150,000 to the project before 1932.

86. W. E. Seesholtz, "Presiding Elder's Report–1932," ECOConfJ, 1932, 26.

87. Q. A. Deck, "Presiding Elder's Report, Eastern District, Western Conference," ECWConfJ, 1943, 36.

88. "Presiding Elders' Reports–Eastern District," ECEPAConfJ, 1934, 42; "Presiding Elders' Reports–Western District," ECEPAConfJ, 1934, 45.

89. John Smith, "Presiding Elders' Reports–Western District," ECEPAConfJ, 1942, 60; N. N. Lower, "Presiding Elders' Reports–Western District," ECEPAConfJ, 1945, 59.

90. See H. P. Scanlin, *Waldheim Park: A Centennial History* (Allentown, PA: E. C. Waldheim Park Association, n.y.p.

91. I. C. Burd, and E. S. Woodring, "The Herndon Campmeeting Situation," UE, August 14, 1923, 6–8; *Herndon Camp Grove–Centennial 1901–2001* (n.p. : Herndon Camp Meeting Association, 2001), 44–47.

92. Anniversary Booklet Committee, "The Fiftieth Anniversary – Rosedale Grove" (n.p.: Rosedale Grove Association, 1973).

93. "Reading District," ECEPAConfJ, 1928, 50.

94. ECWConfJ, 1937, 24; reports of the Special Committee on Campmeeting, ECWConfJ, 1938–41.

95. "Presiding Elders' Reports–Western District," ECEPAConfJ, 1940, 56.

96. "Presiding Elder's Report," ECOConfJ, 1927, 19–20.

97. E. S. Woodring, "A Report Submitted by Bishop E. S. Woodring, as Substitute for that of a Presiding Elder," ECOConfJ, 23–24; W. E. Seesholtz, "Presiding Elder Report–1933," ECWConfJ, 26.

98. Moyer, 85.

99. "Presiding Elders' Reports–Eastern District," ECEPAConfJ, 1939, 47.

100. "Bishop's Address," ECWConfJ, 1944, 30.

101. ECEPAConfJ, 1944, 38; "Special Committee on Evangelism," ECEPAConfJ, 1945, 88=89.

102. A. W. Cooper, "Episcopal Message," ECGenConfJ, 1946, 52; "Committee on Evangelism," ECGenConfJ, 1946, 69; Moyer, 87.

103. Letter from A. R. Kratzer to Kenneth Maurer, Nov. 27, 1945.

104. "Officers Reports," ECGenConf], 1950, 62.

105. "Quadrennial Statistical Report of the United Evangelical Church 1922–1926," ECGenConf], 1926, 74; "Officers Reports–Statistical Secretary," ECGenConf], 1950, 62.

106. "Christian Camping–Evangelical Congregational Church–East Pennsylvania Conference–Golden Anniversary–1920–1970" (n.p.: Twin Pines Camp, 1970).

107. M. E. Detterline, "The Story Behind Beulah Beach Camp," UE, June 18, 1946, 7–8; Paul D. Dunn, "Beulah Beach Camp Report," UE, July 30, 1946, 9.

108. UEEPAConf], 1922, 23–25; ECGenConf], 1942, 3.

109. ECOConf], 1930, 3, 14.

110. ECGenConf], 1934, 20–21.

111. "Committee on Sunday School and K.L.C.E.," UEEPAConf], 1924, 78; Statistical Reports, ECEPAConf], 1928 and 1950.

112. "The Best Way to Recommend the Fundamental Movement," UE, July 3, 1923, 2; see also June 12, 1923, 12 and July 3, 1923, 12.

113. Hynson, 213.

114. UEGenConf], 1926, 46.

115. Wilson, *History of the E. C. Church*, 37. The *Discipline* was amended in 1932 and 1948. Each Annual Conference had to approve an amendment (or revise it) in order for it to return to the General Conference for its "final reading." The provision only became part of the Discipline if both Conferences approved it. If no agreement was reached the legislation might be adopted as a Special Rule of an annual Conference.

5

Evangelical Idealism and Advance:
The Evangelical Congregational Church
(1950–1973)

Overview

A Church in a Changing Society

The Evangelical Congregational Church began the sixth decade of the century confident of its evangelical moorings. Its doctrine was rooted in Articles of Faith that articulated an experience–based faith in Christ, a message consistently preached since the days of Albright. Evangelistic fervor, another mark of the evangelical, was an integral part of congregational life. For the first time in its history the Evangelical Congregational Church actively cooperated with other denominations to further the cause of Christ. With an evangelical ideal firmly established, the denomination made significant advances both in its institutions and in its local congregations.

The advances were short-lived, however, because the society in which the church was embedded was undergoing a drastic transformation. Coming out of World War II the United States was embroiled in a cold war involving the democracies of the West and the communist countries of Eastern Europe and Asia. Americans were united in their opposition to atheistic communism, making it patriotic to embrace a faith in God. When the United States joined other members of the United Nations in resisting the invasion of South Korea by North Korea, the churches did not oppose the conflict. Three years of strife ended when the combatants signed a truce at Panmunjom in July 1953. The next time the United States was involved in armed conflict abroad, however, it was not so united. The long war in Viet Nam that ended in 1973 left the nation bitterly divided, and a secular society emerged that had less time for organized religion.

During the 1950s Evangelical Congregational churches along with the majority of American churches experienced significant growth. The mood of the nation changed radically, however, during the 1960s. All authority, including the authority of the church, was challenged. In the closing years of this period the Church was under attack and local congregations turned inward. The gains of the 1950s began to evaporate. After the Evangelical Congregational Church reached a peak in membership and attendances in the mid-1960s, a decline set in that still needs to be reversed.

The Bishops

Bishop Smith

Following the death of Bishop Cooper in the summer of 1950, the General Conference selected John A. Smith (1890–1983) to serve as the fifth Bishop of the Evangelical Congregational Church. He assumed the office of Bishop at the opening of the East Pennsylvania Conference in April 1951. When Bishop Smith was elected to this office he was completing his second term as Presiding Elder of the Eastern District of the East Pennsylvania Conference. In addition to two terms as Presiding Elder of the Eastern District, he had previously served one term as Western

Bishop John A. Smith, 1951–1959

District Presiding Elder. Smith had served on all of the denomination's major boards, acting as chairman of three, and was one of the dwindling number of denominational leaders to provide a bridge from the United Evangelical period. During his eight years as Bishop the Evangelical Congregational School of Theology was established and the Burd and Rogers Memorial Home expanded by adding an infirmary. The Victory Through Loyalty to Christ campaign (1946–1954) was brought to a successful conclusion, and the Greater E. C. Rally (1954–1958) campaign was prosecuted with vigor. These were years of growth within the churches, and building projects multiplied as local churches tried to conserve the gains they experienced.

Bishop Scanlin

Harold H. Scanlin (1906–1982) was chosen to be Bishop by the 1958 General Conference. He was the first person in the Episcopal office who had begun his ministry within the Evangelical Congregational Church. After receiving a license to preach from the East Pennsylvania Conference in 1929 he ministered in five churches within the conference and then replaced Smith as Presiding Elder of the Eastern District in 1951. Scanlin was an able administrator, and the denomination recognized this talent by placing him in numerous positions of leadership in both the Annual and General Conferences. He served as Superintendent of the School of Methods, as a member of the Board of Missions, as a trustee of the School of Theology, and as a member of the Board of the Burd and Rogers Memorial Home.

Bishop Harold H. Scanlin, 1959–1967

As Scanlin relinquished the leadership of the Church in 1967, he could look back on eight years of significant achievement. He had given leadership to The Extra Mile Crusade fund-raising campaign. An Administrative Council had been organized to care for the work of the general church between the sessions of the General Conference. The Episcopal residence had been moved to Reading, and the Board of Missions had begun operating out of an office building in Shillington. The work of the Burd and Rogers Memorial Home was consolidated in Myerstown upon the completion of a new residential facility. The East Pennsylvania Conference School of Methods had moved to a new site at Twin Pines Camp near Stroudsburg.

In a lengthy report to the Administrative Council in March 1967 Scanlin voiced his concern for the future of the denomination. He felt that the actions taken by the General Conference in 1966 and those that were to come before the East Pennsylvania Conference in 1967 would place a heavy strain on the financial resources of the churches. The East Pennsylvania Conference was considering adding a third District Superintendent. The 1966 General Conference had given authorization to the Board of Christian Education to employ a Director of Christian Education. General Conference had also urged the Board of Church Extension to be more aggressive in starting new churches. After reviewing the past efforts at church extension Scanlin urged caution and stated, "If we have had *only one* venture that would have measured up to our expectations we might more enthusiastically plan for the future."[1] More than a decade passed before the Evangelical Congregational Church aggressively pursued the planting of new churches.

Bishop Cressman

The seventh Bishop of the Evangelical Congregational Church was Paul K. Cressman (1905–1972). He interrupted a teaching career to respond to a call to pastoral ministry in 1931 and served five churches. In 1958 his Conference chose him to serve as Presiding Elder and assigned him to the Western District, a position he held for eight years. He had just returned to the pastorate when he was elected Bishop in 1966. Cressman was an active member of the Board of Missions and served for thirteen years as the corresponding secretary of the Conference Missionary Society. He also served on the Board of Trustees of the Evangelical Congregational School of Theology.

Bishop Paul K. Cressman, 1967–1972

In his tenure as Bishop, Cressman witnessed the construction of a library at the School of Theology and a health care center at the Evangelical Congregational Church Retirement Village, the new name for the Burd and Rogers Memorial Home. Within the Board of Missions there was a transition of leadership following the death of Thomas Paul. The greatest challenge Cressman faced, however, was the financial condition of the Board of Publication. He appealed to the members of the churches to assist in paying the burdensome indebtedness that the publishing house had accumulated.[2]

Bishop Cressman died on December 18, 1972, after a brief illness. Bishop Scanlin, who was vice chairman of the General Conference, presided at the spring meeting of the Administrative Council and the 1973 session of the East Pennsylvania Conference. A special General Conference was called for May 15, 1973, the day before the opening of the East Pennsylvania Conference. On that day Herbert D. Wittmaier (1909–1992) was elected to the office to fill the unexpired term of Bishop Cressman.

Denominational Growth and Decline

Early in his second term Bishop Scanlin addressed the East Pennsylvania Conference under the theme "A Year of Crises." He was prompted to use that title because of the critical events that had transpired within the United States and in other parts of the world in the previous year, 1963. He defined the word "crisis" as "as a decisively or vitally important stage in the course of anything; a turning point; a critical time or occasion."[3] The Evangelical Congregational Church was facing such a crisis, the full extent of which would not become apparent for a number of years. Unknown to Scanlin, the Church had reached its numerical peak that very year. In 1963 the total membership of the Church was 30,172,[4] an increase of nearly ten thousand since 1924. Of this total 3,515 were in the Western Conference and 26,657 in the East Pennsylvania Conference. After this the church began a slow decline in membership. At the General Conference of 1974 the churches reported a total of 29,331, a loss of 841.

Several environmental conditions contributed to the downturn experienced after 1963. The anthracite coal region of east-central Pennsylvania, an area of strength from the earliest years of the new denomination, went through drastic changes from 1940 through 1960. Technological advances in mining along with the decrease in the use of coal resulted in a reduction of those employed in mining. By 1954 the unemployment rate in the anthracite coal region was 11 %,[5] and many people moved out of the region to find work elsewhere. The cutback in coal production and the decrease in population in the anthracite coal region resulted in membership losses in the Evangelical Congregational churches in that area. In 1950 twenty-four churches with a membership of 4,294 were located in the hard coal regions of Pennsylvania. By 1973 the membership of these churches dropped to 3,222. During the twenty-four years that followed 1973 four of these churches were closed, two merged, and in 1998 the remaining nineteen congregations reported a membership of 2,360, a forty-five percent loss since 1950.

Pennsylvania cities also lost wealth and population during this period, which contributed to the decline.[6] Many of the Evangelical Congregational congregations located in urban centers traced their origins back to the Evangelical Association era and the disruptions of 1894, when the United Evangelical Church was formed. Five other urban churches in the East Pennsylvania Conference were established during the United Evangelical period. Only three city congregations, Allentown Boulevard, Reading Greenmont, and Lancaster Trinity, were planted after 1922. In 1950 twenty-five East Pennsylvania Conference churches located in cities with a population of twenty-five thousand or more had a total membership of 9,447. Between 1950 and 1973 two of these churches merged and relocated in the suburbs, and one new church was planted. The resulting twenty-four churches reported a total membership of 8,038 in 1973. These urban churches were no longer neighborhood churches as they were when they were founded. Members were scattered throughout the suburban communities that surround the cities. The church found it difficult to reach their new neighbors, who in some instances were of a different ethnic origin.

Denominational Activities

Publishing

Just as the Board of Publication was the first denominational group to become operative in 1922, it became the first to undergo a change of direction and effectiveness forty years later. Through the years the Board was responsible for the publication of the *United Evangelical*, Sunday school literature, and other material authorized by the conference. It operated its own printing plant, the Church Center Press, and solicited commercial business to help subsidize the denomination's publications, but in the mid-sixties the Board of Publication faced serious financial pressures. The profits from printing were declining, and the funds received from the denominational financial campaigns were insufficient to make needed upgrades in equipment. Since the Church Center Press could not keep up with the technological advances in printing, it lost much of its commercial business.

The Board of Publication reported to the 1970 General Conference that it intended to discontinue the printing department and to liquidate its assets in order to pay its outstanding indebtedness.[7] As one cost-cutting measure the Conference accepted a resolution to terminate the full-time position of editor and employ a part-time editorial staff to edit the *United Evangelical*.[8] Under the direction of Coordinating Editor William S. Sailer the paper took on a new look and new life. In 1972 the *United Evangelical* received an award for "the most improved periodical" from the Evangelical Press Association.[9]

While the Boyer Printing and Binding Company in Lebanon PA printed the *United Evangelical*, the Board of Publication asked the United Brethren in Christ Publishing House in Huntington IN to print the Sunday school literature.[10] The result of this later action was the cooperative publication of the Venture Series, in which writers from both denominations shared in producing the material for their Sunday schools. Within the next quadrennium the Church Center Press building was sold to the Evangelical Congregational Church Retirement Village, and private individuals purchased the adjoining homes previously used as residences for the editor and publisher.[11] The operations of the Board of Publication had been cut to a bare minimum.

The *United Evangelical*, whose editorials and informative articles on church life played such an important part in the reorganization after the merger, gradually faded in effectiveness, in spite of its new image. The number of subscribers fell from 5200 in 1962 to under 2700 in 1982.[12] The Board attempted to offset rising costs by cutting the number of issues, and in January 1965 the *United Evangelical* became a biweekly magazine.[13]

The long involvement of Editor Harry E. Messersmith (1881–1973) ended in 1954, when he retired and Robert S. Wilson (1907–1993) was elected Editor of Publications. In the capacity of Editor of Publications Wilson was not only responsible for the *United Evangelical*, but also the Sunday school literature published by the Church. Clarence J. Yoder (1891–1978) occupied the position of Publisher from 1943 until his retirement in 1959. Under Yoder's leadership an addition was attached to the Church Center building in 1957 to house the print shop. Lloyd A. Eshbach filled the post of Publisher from 1959 through 1963, after which the Board of Publications selected Clarence C. Reeder (1909–1991) to manage the Church Center Press. He filled that position for the next six years.

In the seventies the Board of Publications made the transition to more limited activities. Beginning in 1970 an editorial staff handled the editing task, while the business affairs were managed by Donald E. Emig, Clarence J. Yoder, H. Arlington Gerhart (1896–1971) and, finally, Edward J. H. Flexer (1902–1974).

Church Home

The Burd and Rogers Memorial Home maintained buildings at both Herndon and Myerstown until 1961, but the emphasis was now definitely on the Myerstown property. The former Albright College Science Building was converted into an infirmary in 1954 to add health care to the residential care previously provided.[14] Two wings were added to this building in 1955 and 1957, and in 1961 the Home constructed a modern unit (the Burd and Rogers Residential Care Center) with rooms for thirty residents plus dining room, chapel, beauty salon, and lounge.[15] Albert R. Kratzer (1907–1992) remained Superintendent until 1970, when he became Home Chaplain and Russell H. Wise (1914–1990) was named Superintendent.[16] Annual Home anniversary celebrations continued to bring hundreds of people to the Myerstown campus.[17]

Church Extension

One of the key elements in the EC Church's evangelical heritage has been the deliberate effort to establish new congregations. During the twenty-three years covered in this chapter the Evangelical Congregational Church made six attempts to plant new churches, three in the Western Conference and an equal number in the East Pennsylvania Conference. Seven previously established congregations also affiliated with the denomination during this period.

The Western Conference added six churches between 1950 and 1973. In 1950 Fred J. Fink (1906–1992), pastor of the four-church Venango charge in western Pennsylvania, responded to a request from a few families in Emlenton to hold weekly services in their community.[18] The new Emlenton mission was linked with New Zion, one of the Venango churches, to form a separate charge in August 1951.[19] However, the life of the new work was brief. It was merged with New Zion one year later.[20] Also in 1950 two young pastors, Duane Ray (1923–1996) and Jack Foster, held tent meetings in a new housing development in Rock Falls IL.[21] When the Western Conference met in August, Duane Ray was assigned to serve this new mission along with St. James Church near Dixon IL.[22] He held weekly worship services in the tent until the conference purchased an army barracks and placed it on a lot in the Rock Falls housing development. This extensively renovated building was dedicated in April 1951.[23] Later that year members of Cottage Grove Evangelical Congregational Church south of Akron OH undertook the third new church start, beginning a Sunday school in a public school building on Turkeyfoot Lake Road, eight miles from their church. The new congregation was chartered in May 1954 with twenty-eight members.[24] Four years later a church building was erected.[25]

The Western Conference received three established churches during this period: the Mount Forrest Bible Church of Willow Springs, IL (1952),[26] the Community Church of Shaw Station, IL (1953),[27] and the Nelson Memorial Church in Chicago, IL (1959). Benjamin A. Nelson had started the Chicago congregation as an independent church. His son, Eddie, was pastor of the congregation when it affiliated with the Evangelical Congregational Church.[28] In 1962 the church moved from a small building on south side of Chicago to new facilities purchased from the Christian Reformed Church.[29] However, the population in the neighborhood in which the church was located underwent a transition. In 1971 the congregation voted to disband, and the conference sold the facilities.[30]

In May 1956 the Stationing Committee of the East Pennsylvania Conference assigned Henry A. Minnich (1908–1999) to a mission in the expanding western section of the city of Lancaster PA, the first target of the East Pennsylvania Conference church planting efforts during this period. He began to hold services in a local elementary school one month later.[31] The resulting congregation, Trinity Evangelical Congregational Church, was received into the Conference in 1957 with a charter membership of twenty-four.[32] A sanctuary for the new church was dedicated on January 26, 1958.[33] The pastor and lay members of Grace Evangelical Congregational Church in Lancaster provided significant assistance in the birth of Trinity Church.

David P. Heil, Pastor of St. Paul Evangelical Congregational Church in York PA, initiated the second church-planting endeavor within the East Pennsylvania Conference in this period. He and members of his church held Sunday School services on Sunday afternoons in a fire hall in Weigelstown, a growing suburban community north of York PA.[34] In the spring of 1961 the East Pennsylvania Conference received the Weigelstown congregation, with twenty-two charter members, and instructed the Conference Trustees to purchase a designated parcel of land and oversee the construction of a sanctuary.[35] The building was dedicated on December 9, 1962.[36] By 1991 St. David's Evangelical Congregational Church had a membership of over four hundred.

Nine years after starting the work in Weigelstown, David Heil, now pastor of Grace Evangelical Congregational Church in Lancaster, saw another growing suburban area that needed the ministry of his denomination. In September 1968 he and members of his church began holding Sunday services in the Locust Grove Mennonite School east of Lancaster City.[37] The work expanded rapidly and had a membership of forty-three when the East Pennsylvania Conference appointed David R. Heffner as pastor of the newly organized Faith Evangelical Congregational Church in 1969.[38] On March 19, 1972, the growing congregation east of Lancaster dedicated its new church building.[39]

The East Pennsylvania Conference also received two unaffiliated community churches in Pine Beach NJ (1956)[40] and Bair, York County, PA (1959).[41] In addition, an Evangelical United Brethren congregation in Clarksburg WV identified with the Evangelical Congregational Church in 1968 rather than enter into the Evangelical United Brethren-Methodist merger.[42] Finally, the former St. John's Lutheran Church, Bartonsville, united with the East Pennsylvania Conference in 1973.[43]

Missions

As it entered the decade of the fifties the Board of Missions continued to pursue the worldwide spread of the gospel through interdenominational missions boards (faith boards). This enabled the EC Church to place missionaries on all the major continents of the world and in a wide variety of missionary activities, including medicine, education, technology, and evangelism. Between 1950 and 1958 the Evangelical Congregational Board of Missions commissioned twenty-one missionaries.[44] By 1962 the Board was working with eight different faith boards[45] in fourteen countries.[46]

Rev. Thomas E. Paul continued to direct the work of the Board of Missions from the home provided for him and his family in Shillington in 1949. The Board constructed a separate office building on the Shillington property in 1961, but the house remained as a residence for the Pauls with an upstairs apartment available for EC missionaries on furlough from their mission fields.[47] Paul died in February 1969 after twenty-seven years as Secretary to the Board of Missions, and his wife, Marian, served as acting Secretary until a successor could be named.[48] Richard A. Cattermole, pastor of Grace EC Church in Schuylkill Haven PA, assumed the post of Secretary soon after the 1970 East Pennsylvania Conference and served until 1980.[49]

Beginning in the mid-sixties the Board of Missions broadened its involvement further by assuming responsibility for mission fields that were directly under its supervision. In 1966 the General Conference amended the *Discipline* to provide for the creation of missionary conferences,[50] and the first missionary conference was established in Liberia. EC missionaries Herschel and Ruth "Sammie" Ries had met Clara Baines Wilson, a Liberian pastor directing a cluster of churches among the Bassa people, in Africa and suggested that she visit EC churches on her 1962

Liberians reading the newly published
Bassa New Testament

trip to the United States. On her next American visit in 1966 "Aunt Clara" (as she was known throughout the EC Church) was commissioned as an Evangelical Congregational missionary,[51] and in 1973 the thirty-four churches she embraced were organized as the Liberia Conference of the Evangelical Congregational Church.[52]

Mae Royer's work in Mexico continued to flourish, and she was commissioned as a missionary by the Evangelical Congregational Church in 1958. The orphanage she founded near Montemorelos[53] became the base around which churches were planted by young men from the orphanage who received their training in the Rio Grande Bible Institute.[54] The Latin American Conference of the Evangelical Congregational Church was organized in 1977 with nine congregations, one of which was located in Edinburgh TX.[55]

The partnership between the Evangelical Congregational Church and the North East India General Mission continued to strengthen during this period. The NEIGM Board selected the Secretary of the EC Board of Missions, Thomas E. Paul, as its General Secretary.[56] Secretary Paul and Bishop Smith visited the North East India field in 1961.[57] A new mission field was opened in Japan in 1962, when the EC Church commissioned John and Machi Masuda in 1962 as missionaries to their native country.[58]

Throughout the period the Eastern and Western Branches of the Women's Missionary Society provided vital support to the missionary program of the church. In annual spring conventions and (after 1954) fall mission rallies they kept the cause of missions to the forefront of the church's attention, raised essential funds for missions, and provided means for the laypeople of the church to meet missionaries personally. In 1953 the Eastern Branch devised the first missionary commissioning service. A renewed Spend-a-Day program encouraged laypeople to become personally involved with missions by signing up to support a specific missionary with $1 and pray for that missionary while the missionary prayed for the supporter.

Toward the end of this period the "men's liberation" movement caught up with the Branches. In 1971 both Branches voted to give men full rights as members and change the names of local societies to "Adult Missionary Societies." This change was approved by the 1974 General Conference. Presidents of the Branches during this period were: Eastern – Helen Manwiller (1952–1958) and Mary Elizabeth Detterline (1958–1972); Western – Stella Mineely (1942–1958), Isabel Wilson (1958–1966), and Irma Taubenheim (1966–1974).[59]

Higher Education

After years of planning and preparation, the Evangelical Congregational School of Theology (ECST) opened on September 22, 1953, with twelve students,[60] none of whom had attended college but all of whom had completed the conference reading course and were already serving churches.[61] In its first year the faculty of the school consisted of two full-time professors, Dr. Kenneth R. Maurer (1918–1977) and Dr. James D. Yoder, and two part-time instructors, John R. Waser and G. Robert Booth.[62] At first, seminary students with a baccalaureate degree from an accredited college had to transfer to Temple University School of Theology upon completion of their first year at ECST in order to receive a Bachelor of Sacred Theology degree.[63] In 1957, however, the Commonwealth of Pennsylvania granted Evangelical Congregational

School of Theology permission to confer the degree of Bachelor of Divinity, and the relationship with Temple University was terminated.[64] A year later Edward J. Vondran became the first person to receive a Bachelor of Divinity degree from ECST.[65] Since 1953 the seminary has had a profound effect on the life of the denomination; the vast majority of pastors presently serving Evangelical Congregational churches received their theological training at Myerstown.

With seminary education available to prospective pastors, the church realized that its reading course was unnecessary. In 1964 the East Pennsylvania Conference took action to discontinue the conference course of study and required all ministerial candidates to attend seminary.[66] The Committee on Scholastic Requirements for Ministers urged those called to pastoral ministry to secure a bachelor's degree from college before attending the School of Theology. However, ministerial candidates twenty-two years of age and older could still enroll at ECST in the Diploma of Theology program.[67] An extra year was added for the diploma students to provide some courses normally taken in college.[68]

In its infancy the leadership of the School was in the capable hands of Dean Kenneth Maurer, who served as both sole administrator and full-time professor of church history. The Board of Trustees asked Harold Scanlin to accept the position of President of the School when his second term as Bishop was completed in the spring of 1967, and Scanlin served in this capacity from 1967 until his retirement in 1975. Dr. Maurer continued to serve as Dean until his resignation for health reasons in 1971. He was succeeded by J. Creighton Christman (1970–1980).

When President Scanlin reported to the Annual Conferences in 1968, he stated that, although the enrollment of the School had increased from twelve to forty-two in its brief fifteen-year history, it faced a serious predicament. In order to continue to provide the training needed by the ministerial candidates the School had to find additional sources of income. A capital fund drive was needed to meet immediate needs. Long-term growth would require reaching out to other denominations and receiving accreditation from the American Association of Theological Schools (AATS).[69] Scanlin set about reaching these goals. He launched the Forward Fund Campaign in the fall of 1968 with a goal of $300,000. A year later, the School of Theology received nearly $100,000 from the estate of Paul and Ella Rostad, former missionaries to northeast India. With this bequest and the proceeds of the fund drive the trustees erected a new library building and made extensive renova-

Cornerstone Laying for the Rostad Library

tions to Old Main.[70] At the same time, Scanlin secured approval from the EC General Conference to admit non-EC members to the Board of Trustees. He proposed changing the name of the School from "Evangelical Congregational School of Theology" to the less-sectarian "Evangelical School of Theology"; this was finally accomplished in May 1975. He hired non-EC faculty, including Kirby N. Keller from the Church of the United Brethren in Christ in 1974. Accreditation, however, was beyond his grasp. AATS granted the School only "associate" status in 1970. Faculty set to work approving needed expansions of the curriculum, and Dean Christman prepared the necessary studies, but the School's application for accreditation was rejected in 1974.[71] Soon afterward, Scanlin announced his retirement.

Ecumenical Relations

From 1951 through 1960 representatives of the Pennsylvania Council of Churches visited the East Pennsylvania Conference and urged the delegates to participate in a united witness in the Commonwealth. However, the ties with the National Association of Evangelicals were stronger, and by the action of the 1962 General

Conference the Evangelical Congregational Church became a cooperating denomination of this national organization[72] rather than affiliate with the state council. Bishop Scanlin represented the Evangelical Congregational Church as a member of the NAE Board of Administration.[73]

After Bishop Cooper's death in 1950 the General Conference took action to discontinue sending representatives to meet with the United Brethren Church (Old Constitution) and the Primitive Methodist Church.[74] For the next eight years cooperative efforts with these two denominations were confined to the use of some of the Evangelical Congregational Sunday School materials by Primitive Methodist and United Brethren churches. In 1958, however, William A. Smith of the Primitive Methodist Church wrote a letter to the Evangelical Congregational Administrative Council suggesting the appointment of a committee to study merging the two denominations.[75] Within a year Bishop Scanlin received a communication from the United Brethren Church (Old Constitution) also mentioning possible church union.[76] The Administrative Council authorized its executive committee plus Kenneth Maurer to write a reply.[77] It was not until March 1962, three years later, that representatives of the Primitive Methodist Church and the Evangelical Congregational Church met together to discuss organic union.[78] The Primitive Methodist Church was facing two major problems that made consideration of merger with another body critical. The first was a dwindling population base in areas in which the denomination was strongest, and the second was failure of the general church to provide the local churches with supervision. The outcome of this meeting was agreement that the churches should continue to fellowship together and that informal meetings of representatives from the various boards of the two churches should share ideas and keep alert to opportunities for cooperation.[79]

The Evangelical Congregational representatives reported back to their Administrative Council in May 1962, and the Council encouraged further cooperation with the Primitive Methodist Church that could lead to future union.[80] A year later Bishop Scanlin gave a detailed report on the relationships with the Primitive Methodist Church. In this statement to the Council he mentioned the problems that the Evangelical Congregational Church would face in considering merger; he felt, however, that permitting the Primitive Methodist churches to affiliate with the Evangelical Congregational denomination would be acceptable. He went on to list the advantages the absorption of these churches would have on the boards and institutions of the Evangelical Congregational Church.[81] Apparently the Primitive Methodist Church did not receive this approach favorably, because in the spring of 1964 the Administrative Council learned that the Primitive Methodists were no longer considering merger, and that they were experimenting with a paid administrator.[82]

Preacher's Aid Society and Support of Retired Clergy

Providing adequate pensions for retired clergy continued to be a challenge for the church in the second half of the century. In 1954 the federal government amended the Social Security Act to allow clergy to elect social security coverage, and the General Conference that year urged the pastors to choose this benefit.[83] The amount pastors were asked to pay to the Preachers' Aid Society for their pension was reduced in anticipation of the cost of the tax paid to social security, and the Society raised the amount congregations paid into its fund to make up for the deficiency.[84] The Preachers' Aid Society used its resources to offset the corrosive effect inflation had on investments and permit periodic increases in the amount of pension per year of service in the ministry that it paid to retired pastors and pastors' widows.[85] By 1974 the Society paid retired pastors $ 58 a year per year of active ministry and widows $ 36 per year.[86] The 1974 pension benefit represented a 314% increase in twenty-nine years, almost double the increase of the cost of living for the same period. In 1974 the pastor with forty-five years of pension credit received an annual pension of $2,610. The combination of pension benefits and receipts from social security made it possible for an increasing number of pastors to consider retirement at sixty-five years of age.

Clarence J. Yoder served as the secretary and assistant treasurer of the Preachers' Aid Society for 1941 to 1971. He was responsible for compensating the beneficiaries, implementing the decisions of the trustees, and guiding the investment policies of the Trustee Board.

> By continuous planning and watchfulness he [Yoder] led the trustees and assisted the treasurer in making recommendations which enlarged the assets from a meager $34,763.46 in 1941 to a robust $274,328.47 in 1971. Generations of ministers and widows will be in his debt for establishing this sound financial foundation for the Board of Pensions.[87]

In 1971 the Preachers' Aid Society became the Board of Pensions, and the new Board selected James D. Yoder to succeed his father as the secretary and assistant treasurer.[88]

Historical Interests

The establishment of Evangelical School of Theology with a library to include historical materials and the publication of R. S. Wilson's *A Brief History of the Evangelical Congregational Church* in 1953 fulfilled long-time goals of the General Conference Historical Committee, but the 1950s saw a new awakening of interest in historical matters in the church. A service to commemorate the 150th anniversary of the death of Jacob Albright planned by the Historical Committees of the General Conference and the East Pennsylvania Conference and held at Albright's grave at Kleinfeltersville PA on May 18, 1958, was a great success with over three hundred people in attendance.[89] The Committees immediately began work on a commemoration of two hundredth anniversary of Albright's birth in 1959, and this became a major event jointly sponsored by the EC Historical Committee and the Northeastern Conference Historical Society of the Evangelical United Brethren Church (successor to the Evangelical Church). Then, on October 25, 1961, Bishop Scanlin wrote to the chairman of the Historical Committee, J. C. Christman, asking him to activate his committee to establish an archives at the School of Theology so that valuable historical papers of the first generation of EC leaders, who were passing away, would not be lost.[90] At its next meeting, on February 7, 1962, the Committee made plans to set up an archives and appointed a temporary curator but also voted to recommend the establishment of a denominational historical society.[91]

The Historical Committee adopted a Constitution and By-laws for a Historical Society of the Evangelical Congregational Church on July 23, 1964, and these were approved by the 1966 General Conference. The Society was originally intended to be self-supporting, and the By-laws provided for four classes of sustaining sponsors ($ 5 to $ 50 annual dues) and memorial or honorary sponsors (single payment of $ 100). The By-laws also provided for auxiliary societies in each Annual Conference and the selection of Conference Historians.[92] The Board of Trustees of the Historical Society held its first meeting on October 18, 1966, and elected its first officers: H. S. Heffner, President; Walter Q. Bunderman, Vice President; J. C. Christman, Secretary; and R. S. Wilson, Treasurer.[93]

The new Society's first years were busy ones. The Board secured the selection of Conference Historians for the East Pennsylvania (Ralph H. Bornman) and Western (C. F. Rissmiller) Conferences. It established the

Archives in a former library room at Evangelical School of Theology with help of expertise and donations from Dr. John H. Ness, Jr., last Curator of the Historical Society of the Evangelical United Brethren Church and first holder of that office in the United Methodist Church. It secured incorporation of the Society as a non-profit corporation of the Commonwealth of Pennsylvania on July 11, 1968. Historical Pilgrimage services at the grave of Jacob Albright at Kleinfeltersville PA were held in 1970 and 1972 under the co-sponsorship of the Society and the General Commission on Archives and History of the United Methodist Church. The Conference Historians worked to secure Local Church Historians in every congregation. Ralph Bornman succeeded Heffner as President of the Board in 1971.[94]

Church Life

The Pastorate

Appointment

The eight-year limit on length of pastorates was often unpopular with clergy families, but by the late 1940s the small number of churches in the Western Conference had made continually shuffling pastors among them within the limit a real problem, so in 1950 it was this Conference that petitioned the General Conference to eliminate the restriction.[95] The General Conference adopted an amendment to the *Discipline* making unlimited reassignment of pastors possible, but the East Pennsylvania Conference failed to approve this amendment at its next session.[96] The proposal was reintroduced to the East Pennsylvania Conference 1953.[97] In his Episcopal address Bishop Smith urged the delegates to approve the request coming from the sister conference; he stated, "Our time limit is causing us increasing hardships and we can't go on much longer without suffering greatly."[98] The Conference abolished the time limit, but the strictly enforced system of clergy placement (the itinerancy) was still in place.

During the decade of the fifties thirty-five pastors withdrew from the ministry of the Evangelical Congregational Church to accept pulpits in other denominations.[99] Although a number of reasons were advanced for this loss, the itinerant system seemed to be at the root of the problem. Bishop Scanlin in his address to the East Pennsylvania Conference in 1961 listed two items of significant concern to pastors: first, "the right to exercise a reasonable degree of leadership in the functioning of the local church," and second, "the assurance of a reasonable tenure of office in a particular congregation."[100]

Pastors perceived that strong, entrenched laypersons could prevent the exercise of firm pastoral leadership by appealing to the denominational Stationing Committee for a change of pastor. The pastor had little recourse but to either submit to the wishes of the laity or accept reassignment. Bishop Scanlin sought to alleviate this problem by appealing to the laity to permit the clergy to lead more aggressively.[101] The Bishop and District Superintendents from both Conferences met at the seat of the General Conference in 1962 and agreed on a policy that they felt would cultivate harmony between the pastors and officials and congregation. They urged each congregation to appoint a Pastor-Church Relations Committee to channel requests for a change of pastor to the Stationing Committee. The District Superintendent could also meet with the committee to deal with controversies and make sure that all sides in a dispute were heard.[102] Pastors and churches, however, remained without voice in stationing decisions and had to wait for the reading of the report of the Stationing Committee at the closing session of the Annual Conference to learn of any change in pastoral assignment.

Salaries

In 1957 the Special Committee on Pastoral Compensation of the East Pennsylvania Conference compared the salaries of pastors in the Conference with those of other denominations. The Committee found a striking deficiency and recommended that increases be given in each of the next three years. The Committee also found that the salaries of pastors serving the larger churches had not kept up with increases in the cost of living. In order to encourage larger churches to make significant advances in wages the Conference established a range of salaries for the churches paying more than the minimum.[103] The 1958 Conference received word that 93 % of the churches paying above the minimum had met or exceeded the goals set by the Conference the year before.[104]

In addition to salary increases, the East Pennsylvania Conference began adding fringe benefits to the clergy compensation package. In 1964 it asked local congregations to begin paying the utilities for the parsonage.[105] Two years later, the Annual Conference required the churches to pay an additional amount of cash equal to one half of their pastor's social security payment.[106] In 1972 churches were asked to consider paying all or part of the pastor's hospitalization insurance.[107]

The Western Conference followed the lead of its sister conference in 1957, proposing a three-year program of increased minimum wages. The

Conference also established salary goals for the larger churches.[108] However, the Western Conference did not go along with the mandated fringe benefits. Instead, the Western Conference delegates recommended that cash salaries be large enough for the pastor to afford the items provided by the churches in the East.

By 1968 the Western Conference no longer listed minimum salaries for each category. The Conference proposed one minimum for "full-time licentiates" amounting to $5,000.[109] One year later this salary standard was referred to as a starting salary.[110] The Conference chose to mandate the entry-level salary for full-time pastors and anticipated that the churches would properly compensate pastors according to the years served and the size of the congregation. In 1973 the starting salary for Western Conference pastors was set at $6,100.[111]

During the sixties the East Pennsylvania Conference Committee on Pastors' Salaries recommended annual increases to keep up with the rising cost of living. The minimum salaries in 1973 stood at $5,600 for licentiates, $5,820 for deacons, and $6,050 for elders.[112] This was an increase in cash salary of over 150% above the 1950 minimums. Since the compensation for East Pennsylvania pastors also included utilities, one half of Social Security, and hospitalization, the increase over 1950 was closer to 200 %.

Sunday Services

Most Evangelical Congregational churches during this period followed the same schedule every Sunday: Sunday school and worship in the morning and a youth meeting (primarily Christian Endeavor) and worship service in the evening. In earlier years the evening service was used as an opportunity to preach an evangelistic message and invite the unsaved to the altar. Indeed, this was the chief on-going evangelistic effort of local churches. In the 1950s and 1960s, however, evening attendances began to dwindle, and those who did attend were long-time members. Pastors began to experiment with other programming options, such as concerts and special speakers, to attract a larger audience. District Superintendent Paul D. Dunn, addressing the Western Conference in 1961, stated,

> If the evening service is to be helpful and inspiring it must be given the same emphasis as the morning service in choir music, pulpit preparation and publicity. It must not be just another service.[113]

Some churches, especially those without a Sunday evening youth program, gave up on evening services. Yet, in 1973 slightly more than three quarters of the churches of both conferences still reported holding evening services.

Preaching

"A Servant of the Word," the title of a popular work on preaching by Herbert H. Farmer (1892–1981), is a fitting description of Evangelical Congregational preachers during this period. Through personal study and formal training these preachers became committed to expository preaching, in which a message arose from the Scripture and was in agreement with the intent of the biblical author rather than starting with a subject that was later tied to a likely Bible passage (a "prooftext"). During these years Evangelical Congregational preachers began to acquire books by Andrew W. Blackwood (1882–1966), best known as the professor of preaching at Princeton Theological Seminary. He concluded his teaching career at Temple University School of Theology, where the earliest students of Evangelical Congregational School of Theology went to complete their degrees under him. Blackwood emphasized the importance of preaching through entire books of the Bible and planning sermons a year at a time. Instead of randomly selecting biblical passages for preaching week after week, Blackwood's students were encouraged to "set apart in the study a place for a homiletical garden," in which sermon seeds that are planted grow and bloom at appropriate times during the year.[114]

A sermon preached by one of the highly respected expository preachers of the EC Church, Allen Z. Bodey (1903–1977), appeared in the *United Evangelical* in 1956. The message, entitled "I Believe God—or god!" concluded:

> You want to know what God is like? You say, 'I believe in God, I believe God is a Spirit, I believe that He is one nevertheless that He is a Trinity. I believe that He is a personal being, that He is eternal, all-wise, all-powerful, present everywhere. I do believe it. But I need more than this. All of these things are sublime but still I am not satisfied. Tell me, what is God like?" And the reply is simply this, "If you would really know God look to Jesus Christ. When you see Him you behold the living and true God."[115]

Sacraments

Holy Communion

Whether worshipping in large urban sanctuaries or in small rural churches, EC people continued to gather around the altar railing for communion four times every year. In most churches the people knelt at the altar railing and received the bread and the cup from their pastor, though some churches constructed altar railings with holders for the bread and cups so people would not have to wait to be served individually. Those people in the pews sang hymns focused on Christ's sacrifice on the cross or meditated reverently as the organ or piano played. The communion service was longer than the normal Sunday morning worship service, but this service drew larger attendances than the other Sundays of the year. The only deviation from this standard practice occurred when pastors held "Upper Room" communion services on Maundy Thursday. Here the worshippers sat around tables and received the emblems in much the same way they were distributed by Jesus in the Upper Room.

The administration of the sacrament of the Lord's Supper was reserved for the ordained clergy of the Church. Licentiates serving churches either called on their Presiding Elder or an ordained elder from a neighboring EC church to administer the communion in the worship service and to shut-ins in their homes. A disciplinary amendment approved in 1958 granted licentiates permission to assist the elder and "in emergencies" to administer the sacrament themselves.[116] Fourteen years later the *Discipline* was amended to allow a licentiate serving as pastor to "exercise of all ministerial functions including ... administering the Lord's Supper."[117]

Baptism

In 1955 former Bishop Edwin S. Woodring (1892–1957) at the request of an Annual Conference Committee wrote two articles for *The United Evangelical* under the title, "Baptism—Its Value and Importance to the Denomination."[118] While recognizing that there were differing opinions within the church concerning the subject of baptism and that a discussion on the subject was needed, he presented his view of the position of the Evangelical Congregational Church. Woodring began by quoting the Article of Faith on Baptism. Then he stated,

> We notice...[t]hat our church looks upon Baptism as a Sacrament instituted by our Lord, and by Sacrament we mean, "an outward and visible sign of an inward and spiritual grace." Baptism may be considered the initiatory rite of introduction into the Christian Church and a sign and seal of the new covenant, as circumcision was of the old.[119]

His first article was largely a defense of infant baptism and reached the conclusion that "all children by virtue of unconditional benefits of the atonement are included in the covenant and are members of the kingdom of God and are therefore entitled to baptism, the sign of the covenant."[120] His second article discussed the mode of baptism; he concluded that "Parents should be taught the significance of infant baptism and their duty in connection with the baptism of their children."[121]

> Let the church recognize its duty. The names of all children who have been baptized should be enrolled, not as members of the church, but as prospective members, and the church should feel its duty to watch over them and nurture them, until they will, of their own accord, apply for full membership."[122]

In order to emphasize the covenant nature of infant baptism the conferences of 1958 amended the infant baptism ritual in the *Discipline* to include the words, "and is a sign of the covenant relationship of this child to God through the atoning work of Christ."[123] An editorial discussing this proposed amendment appeared in the *United Evangelical* in June 1958,[124] and this prompted a vigorous debate on baptism in the church paper in the following months. Letters to the editor presented arguments for and against infant baptism because in some portions of the Evangelical Congregational Church the Anabaptist influence was strong, and some parents choose to postpone baptism until their children had made a profession of faith in Christ. These parents asked for some type of service to enable them to dedicate newborn children to God without submitting them to baptism. The Administrative Council took up this request in 1964, appointing a committee to study the matter and to make a recommendation to the Council.[125] The committee, chaired by Kenneth R. Maurer, made its recommendation in April 1965 against including a service of infant dedication in the *Discipline*. The committee also strongly urged pastors not to adapt the infant baptism ritual for purposes of infant dedication.[126]

Yet, denominational statistics provide an indication of continuing discomfort with infant baptism. In 1954 the General Conference noted that nearly seventy-five per cent of all baptisms in the prior quadrennium were infant baptisms. By 1974 this percentage had dropped to sixty-five per cent. In the Western Conference more adults were baptized than infants in the four-year period 1970–1974. While the number of baptisms decreased by thirty per cent between 1950 and 1974, the number of infant baptisms diminished by thirty-seven per cent during the same period, indicating that pastors were performing a larger percentage of adult baptisms than was the case twenty-four years previously.

Music

By 1958 the supply of the *Hymnal* published in 1930 was nearly exhausted. Rather than direct another printing, the General Conference authorized the appointment of a committee to investigate the publication of a new hymnal. Bishop Scanlin appointed Norman N. Lower (1883–1976) chair of the committee; Harrison S. Heffner (1893–1971) later assumed leadership. Early in their deliberation the committee members decided to compile and publish their own hymnal rather that adopt one that was currently in publication. The 1958 committee felt that to repeat the procedure followed in 1930 would result in "two books under one cover."[127]

The new red *Evangelical Congregational Hymnal*, the culmination of nearly seven years' work, arrived in churches in time for the 1965 Christmas season. Church musicians and pastors could choose from nearly twice as many Advent and Christmas carols and hymns than could be found in the previous hymnal. The *Hymnal* was a blend of stately old hymns and evangelistic camp meeting songs. Eighteen hymns by Charles Wesley are included and twelve by Isaac Watts. Gospel songs by the Evangelical Association hymnist Elisha A. Hoffman and United Evangelical Bishop Henry B. Hartzler were also contained among the 558 entries. However, because of financial constraints the committee could include only a small number of songs written in the twentieth century that were still under copyright restrictions and chose the majority of selections from among older songs that were within the public domain. Committee members were disappointed to find that it was too costly to use the popular hymn, "How Great Thou Art," but they included "O Lord Most High," Norman Clayton's translation of the original Swedish hymn set to the same tune.[128] The initial order of fifteen thousand copies sold rapidly, and by the fall of 1966 only two thousand copies were left. An additional seventy-five hundred hymnals were ordered two years later.

Evangelical Congregational churches eagerly anticipated the publication of a new hymnal because singing was an important part of congregational life. The stately hymns of the Church and a smattering of gospel songs were used on Sunday in the morning worship service accompanied by an organ in many of the churches. Anthems sung by robed choirs were a regular feature of the worship experience.[129] Gospel songs were used nearly exclusively in Sunday school "opening exercises" accompanied by a piano. Some Sunday schools were able to put together Sunday school orchestras; noteworthy was the twenty-seven-piece orchestra of St. Paul Evangelical Congregational Church, York.[130] Occasionally, as a part of the altar services that concluded evangelistic services, the old German choruses were still sung.

The youth of the church found popular choruses to be a welcome change from the traditional gospel songs, but their use did not meet with universal approval. The East Pennsylvania Conference Committee on the Spiritual State of the Church expressed concern in its 1965 report

> when we learn of some music in the church which tends to obscure the majesty and greatness of God and substitutes instead something resembling a "hit parade of songs." We read of jazz combinations participating in Worship programs....The majesty of the "Hallelujah Chorus" has given way to the "Off-beat."
>
> The din and noise of modern music does not testify to the saving Grace of the Lord Jesus Christ as the One who satisfies the longing of the human soul.[131]

Church Buildings

During the fifties and early sixties many local congregations experienced significant growth that taxed their facilities. Some, like Lancaster PA Grace (1952),[132] Royersford PA (1961),[133] Highland Park IL (1963),[134] Lititz PA (1970),[135] and Emmaus PA (1971),[136] responded to the increase by constructing new Christian education structures. Others, such as Sunbury PA (1955),[137] Canton OH (1960),[138] Akron OH Cottage Grove (1960),[139] Allentown PA Zion (1962),[140] Reedsville PA (1969),[141] and Cedarville IL (1973),[142] built new sanctuaries to provide additional space for worship. Three churches that struggled with temporary quarters in basements were finally able to build sanctuaries above ground. These churches were Reading PA Greenmont (1955),[143] Norwood Heights IL (1955),[144] and Mansfield OH (1960).[145]

Some congregations responded to the need for housing an expanding ministry by relocating. Akron OH First (1955),[146] Palmyra PA (1956),[147] Ephrata PA (1958),[148] Youngstown OH (1962),[149] Pottsville PA (1969),[150] Steelton PA (1969),[151] Annville PA (1971),[152] and Dixon IL Bethel (1971)[153] were among the congregations that moved to new sites during this period. The East Pennsylvania Conference saw relocation as a way to help two small mission churches become self-supporting;[154] it provided substantial financial aid for this purpose to congregations in Birdsboro (1952)[155] and Temple (1957).[156]

Bethesda EC Church, Reedsville, PA

The sanctuaries constructed during this period continued to place the pulpit in the center of a raised platform with the communion table in front of the pulpit on the same level as the congregation. The platforms in the new churches were larger in order to accommodate musical instruments, choirs, and worship participants. Most new worship facilities exhibited the clean simple lines of contemporary architecture, with less Gothic ornamentation and less emphasis on art glass windows.

Class Meetings/Prayer Meetings

In the 1950s and 1960s participation in the midweek prayer service remained steady in Evangelical Congregational churches, running at approximately ten percent of the membership of the churches. The leadership of the prayer meeting was the chief responsibility of the class leaders, even though other responsibilities were also mentioned in the *Discipline*. Pastors and class leaders stressed the importance of this prayer experience, and Seibert Evangelical Congregational Church in Allentown PA referred to it as the "Hour of Power." Larger EC churches, including Seibert, had prayer meetings for teens and children, as well as adult meetings each Wednesday evening. The format of the services continued to include singing, a devotional message, and a period of prayer.

By the early 1970s, however, many churches were beginning to look at other approaches to corporate prayer. A standing committee of the 1970 General Conference recommended that churches consider "the establishment of home-centered prayer cells."[157] "Cottage prayer meetings," which earlier were used to prepare for evangelistic services, now became an established program in some churches under names such as "prayer, share, prepare groups" or "little churches." Congregations that took seriously the need to involve as many members as possible in corporate prayer no longer considered the midweek prayer meeting as the only valid means to bring their people together to commune with God.

Church Year

Each season of the church year offered unique opportunities for worship and fellowship within local churches. For Evangelical Congregational churches the year began in fall when members returned from summer vacations and children began school. The children of the Sunday school were promoted to new classes or departments and Rally Days restored the momentum lost to the summer slump. Samples of the fall harvest were displayed in the sanctuary. In the Eastern Conference those churches that did not give the produce to their pastors sent the items on display to the Burd and Rogers Memorial Home. Harvest home among the Western Conference churches was often celebrated with a congregational dinner. In 1954, for example, the Norwood Heights EC Church in Chicago IL held a harvest home banquet for the benefit of its building fund; within a few months construction began on the church's sanctuary on top of the basement in which they had been worshipping.[158]

The weeks leading up to winter were the busiest of the year. Christmas parties, cantata rehearsals, and hanging of the greens seemed to fill every spare moment. Following the Christmas festivities the members of many EC churches gathered on New Year's Eve for a Watch Night Service. This evening's activities began with a time of fellowship and refreshments and ended as those present gathered around the altar railing of the church to welcome in the New Year on their knees praying for God's blessing. In February many churches observed the birthday of Christian Endeavor by featuring young people in leadership of all the services on Anniversary Sunday. When Christian Endeavor celebrated its seventy-third birthday in 1954, members of the three societies in St. Luke's EC Church in Shillington PA took part in services throughout the week.[159]

The high point of the church's year was Holy Week. On Palm Sunday new members, including young people who completed catechetical instruction, were welcomed into the church.[160] On Good Friday afternoon many EC churches either held three-hour services focused on the seven last words of Christ from the Cross or participated in similar community services. Easter Sunday morning began with a dawn service followed by worship services honoring the risen Christ.

While the regular services were held in local churches during the summer, the young people of both conferences participated in one of the three EC youth camps. The Sunday Schools of the Eastern Conference competed with one another for the honor of having the best attendance on Sunday School night at their campmeeting. All of the Western Conference churches were well represented at the combined missionary and Christian education conventions that were held each summer at Huntington College in Huntington IN. Missionaries and nationally known Christian education leaders mixed with the 184 delegates who attended the conference in 1967. At that gathering the quiz team from the Cedarville IL church won the Bible quiz competition that was based on the book of Acts.[161]

Campmeetings

As the second half of the century began, the campmeeting groves in the East Pennsylvania Conference still played a prominent role in the life of churches. Waldheim Park in Allentown was the seat of an effective School of Methods program with weeklong sessions for junior, intermediate, and senior youth, and indeed the facilities at Waldheim were expanded to accommodate increased use. Two chapels were added, and in 1957 a swimming pool was constructed[162] to replace the quarry swimming hole, which was no longer safe. In addition to campmeeting services, the Rosedale Grove in Reading hosted the Annual Bible Conference that was preceded by a one-day Junior Preachers' School.

By 1973 much had changed. School of Methods found a new home in Twin Pines Camp near Stroudsburg PA, and the Bible Conference followed the youth camp to its new location.[163] The seminary at Myerstown made the Junior Preachers' School unnecessary. Yet, throughout the period the ten days of campmeeting services remained the primary summer evangelistic thrust of the Evangelical Congregational churches in eastern Pennsylvania. The Herndon Campmeeting followed a daily schedule similar to that used in the early years of its operation: early morning prayer service, morning Bible study and worship, followed by worship in the afternoon, and concluding with the evening evangelistic service. Special services dealing with temperance and missions were held on designated days, and because the Burd and Rogers Memorial Home was situated on an adjoining property, the home anniversary celebration was included on the campmeeting program.[164] Each year the Herndon Campmeeting attendees observed the Lord's Supper on the concluding Sunday morning. The *Discipline* directed the Presiding Elders to be "in charge of the spiritual interests of the Camp Meetings."[165]

In the early fifties the Rosedale and Waldheim Campmeetings also had a full compliment of daily services. These groves were close to urban centers, however, and more people could commute to the campgrounds for individual services rather than staying for the entire duration of the campmeeting, so participation in the daytime meetings began to decline. Rosedale continued to make tents available to those who chose to stay on the grounds and maintained morning Bible study, vacation Bible school for children, youth Bible study, and an afternoon Bible discussion group.[166] By 1973 at Waldheim, however, only the morning Bible study remained of an extensive weekday daily schedule. Even the missions service was moved to Sunday.[167] During the years that School of Methods shared the facilities at Waldheim the campmeeting and the senior camp held joint services.

Revivals/Evangelism

Evangelism in Evangelical Congregational churches was effective in the fifties because society seemed open to the call to faith in Christ. The successful Billy Graham crusades provided a model that was eagerly adopted by other professional evangelists. Local churches found renewed interest in weeks of evangelistic services that had been such a significant part of church life in the early years of the century. While many churches used their own pastors to preach these local evangelistic crusades, others employed full-time evangelists.

Regular reports of evangelistic efforts appeared in *The United Evangelical*. One such report told of the seven Evangelical Congregational churches in Allentown PA cooperating in a week of evangelistic services in November 1954 with the local pastors preaching. In the week prior to the cooperative endeavor Robert Gamber served as the evangelist in services held in Zion Church. Seventeen persons came to the altar railing on the concluding night. James K. Rapp (1910–1980), pastor of Zion Church, spoke at the Decision Day service held in the Junior Department of the Sunday School on the Sunday between these two weeks of services, and fifteen children responded to the invitation.[168]

The United Evangelical also reported that in January 1955 Curt Wetzel, the flying evangelist from Lock Haven, was the preacher at two weeks of services held in Trinity Evangelical Congregational Church in Fern PA. Each day he took off in his plane spending an hour in the air playing hymns, quoting Scripture, and advertising the services over a public address system.[169] That same year Richard Christman, a licentiate in the East Pennsylvania Conference, put together the EC Boys Gospel Team made up of young men from his home church, Bethany in Allentown PA, to assist local area churches in their outreach efforts.[170] Later, in 1967 Christman, after serving several conference churches, formed an evangelistic association and spent the next sixteen years as a traveling evangelist.[171] Another Pennsylvania pastor, Kenneth M. Weaver, pursued a full-time evangelistic ministry from 1968–1980.[172]

Yet, early in this period it was becoming clear that churches could not rely solely on weeks of evangelistic services to reach the unsaved. In 1954 the General Conference Evangelism Committee outlined an extensive four-year program of outreach. This report was the most comprehensive program of evangelism that had been prepared by the Evangelical Congregational Church. It provided annual themes, conference goals, detailed directions on various evangelistic methods, and advice for local churches who implemented an evangelistic thrust.[173] Eight years later the General Conference supplied a list of evangelistic material currently available or proposed for publication.[174] The Annual Conferences and local congregations only minimally implemented these proposals, however, and as a result the churches made negligible gains in evangelistic effectiveness.

Other new evangelistic strategies involving entire congregations in soul winning were, nonetheless, beginning to permeate the broader evangelical community. As the decade of the sixties closed a faith mission group, Latin America Mission, developed a program called Evangelism in Depth for mobilizing churches on the mission field for outreach. Forrest Schwalm, a staff member of the Latin America Mission, was brought to eastern Pennsylvania to adapt the Evangelism in Depth model for local congregations, forming a group called Christ for Eastern Pennsylvania.[175] The organization utilized three goals, total mobilization, total evangelization, and visible unity of the Church, to help individual congregations prepare for reaching the unchurched. Through congregational surveys designed to determine felt needs, the establishment of small "Prayer, Share and Prepare" groups, and instruction in personal evangelism, cooperating Evangelical Congregational churches embarked on evangelistic efforts that produced significant results.[176] Many churches also participated in "Key '73," which was an attempt to apply the Evangelism in Depth principles in churches throughout the North American continent. Local congregations were mobilized in a united evangelistic effort aimed at "calling our continent to Christ."[177]

Catechetical Instruction

After World War II the nation's focus turned to starting families and educating children. The Sunday School and Keystone League of Christian Endeavor Federation of the East Pennsylvania Conference took on new life and activities, including a new catechism for children. In 1951 a group of ministers involved in the Federation (J. Creighton Christman, Donald Floyd, Elvin Groff, Raymond Wolfgang) formed a Catechism Committee, and in September of 1953 the first mimeographed edition of *The Threshold of the Church* (148 pp.) was presented to the church.[178] The 1954 General Conference appointed a Special Committee on Catechism (Bishop Smith, H. H. Scanlin, H. S. Heffner, J. C. Christman, R. S. Wolfgang, and R. S. Wilson) to revise the *Threshold*, and the first printed edition of *Threshold* was published by the Board of Publication in 1956. This manual discussed the church's history, theology (Lord's Prayer, Apostles' Creed, and Articles of Faith), polity, and missions and the catechumen's spiritual life.[179] The *Threshold* sold well (about 1000 copies per year), and in 1962 the Catechism Committee began plans for a revised edition. R. S. Wilson chaired the revision sub-committee and James Yoder chaired a sub-committee to prepare a version for younger children.[180] The second revised edition of *Threshold* was published in 1965 and a third revised edition in 1971. Discussion continued on producing a Junior Catechism.[181]

Sunday Schools

From its beginning the Evangelical Congregational Church counted more people in Sunday School than in any other activity of the church. Sunday School in the EC Church had always functioned as the chief recruiting arm of the church, with new people introduced to the life of the congregation first through attendance at Sunday school. Attendances declined during the war years but rebounded afterward. As the Baby Boomers reached school-age, the 1950s saw unprecedented growth within the denomination's Sunday schools, but the leaders of the Sunday

School and Keystone League of Christian Endeavor Federations recognized that if the growth was to be maintained the educational quality within local Sunday schools had to improve. The East Pennsylvania Conference selected Raymond Wolfgang to serve as part-time Secretary of Christian Education in 1949[182] and a year later recommended that the General Conference employ a General Conference Secretary of Christian Education,[183] but the General Conference was not ready to make such a commitment. The next year the East Pennsylvania Conference eliminated even the part-time Christian education position, but employment of a denominational Secretary of Christian Education was on the agenda of the Board of Christian Leadership and Education (later named the Board of Christian Education) from the time it was established in 1954. It was increasingly evident that local churches needed to evaluate their Christian education programs. Sunday schools came under criticism in the closing years of the 1950s when a national magazine characterized the Sunday morning teaching effort as the "most wasted hour of the week."[184] Sunday School enrollment in the EC Church reached an all-time high in 1959, and average attendance peaked one year later.

The Western Conference tried to address these issues with a conference-wide Sunday School evaluation program in 1960. Two years later, the Christian Education Committee of the General Conference recommended that the program be used by the entire denomination. The 1966 General Conference approved the selection of a Director of Christian Education with the provision that the Board of Christian Education submit details to the Administrative Council before employing anyone.[185] The next year the Board of Christian Education requested financial support for the office of Director of Christian Education from the East Pennsylvania Conference, but the Conference narrowly defeated the recommendation, and the effort to provide a denominational Christian education position was abandoned once again. When the 1970 General Conference convened, the Committee on Christian Education submitted the following: "We recommend that the Board seek alternative methods of meeting the challenge of extending and enlarging the effectiveness of our Christian education program."[186] By that time the denomination's Sunday schools had experienced ten years of decline. The Sunday school attendances reported to the conferences in 1973 were below those of 1950. All the gains of the fifties had been lost.

The Sunday Schools of each Conference depended on their respective Sunday School and Keystone League of Christian Endeavor Federation for training and resources. A high point of the conference year was the Sunday School and Keystone League of Christian Endeavor Convention that included workshops to assist Sunday schools and youth groups to be more effective in their ministries. In order to encourage the use of new teaching methods the Federations acquired a library of visual aids (filmstrips, movies, records) and loaned them to congregations.[187] In 1950 the Evangelical Congregational Church affiliated with the Evangelical Teacher Training Association,[188] and from that time the Federations encouraged pastors to offer teacher-training courses within their churches in order to certify their teachers. The Federation in the Western Conference sponsored annual contests, awarding Sunday schools for significant growth. The East Pennsylvania Conference Federation accepted the responsibility of putting together bulletin covers for the local congregations of both conferences, and a committee within the Federation faithfully fulfilled this task for more than twenty years.

The East Pennsylvania Conference Federation also sponsored Daily Vacation Bible School workshops in Myerstown. During these workshops the materials from various publishing houses were evaluated, and seminars were held on different facets of the DVBS ministry. These workshops were well attended, and boosted interest in this venture. By the early seventies local Bible bookstores held their own DVBS workshops, so this conference-sponsored activity was no longer needed. Generally, Vacation Bible Schools were held on weekday mornings for two weeks immediately after the conclusion of the public school year in early summer and concluded with a program on the Sunday evening following the final weekday session. As an increasing number of women from the churches entered the workforce, however, it became difficult to find staff for morning schools, so many churches began to hold the Vacation Bible School in the evening and cut the length of the Schools to one week. At first the schools were confined to children three years of age through sixth grade and junior high students were only occasionally included in the programming. When VBS moved to the evenings, however, the age span increased to include high school students and even adults.

Youth Camps (School of Methods)

The School of Methods of the East Pennsylvania Conference continued to grow in the 1950s. In the summer of 1959, for example, 1,372 people attended four camps and a married couples retreat at Waldheim

Park. During these weeks ninety-four conversions were recorded, plus 136 reconsecrations and twenty-eight dedications to full-time service.[189] In July 1955 Dr. Robert G. Lee (1886–1978), a popular Southern Baptist preacher, made his twentieth visit to Waldheim to help celebrate the thirty-fifth anniversary of School of Methods.[190] School of Methods Booster Clubs also continued to thrive.

The focus of School of Methods was changing, however, from leadership training and study to a less-structured recreation-based camping program. The leaders of the School of Methods now found the facilities at Waldheim less suitable for their purposes, and since they did not have direct control of the property they could not make the alterations they considered necessary. In 1961 the Christian Education Society of the East Pennsylvania Conference (formerly the Sunday School and Keystone League of Christian Endeavor Federation) authorized the appointment of a committee "to investigate the matter of obtaining information relating to prospective camp sites for the promotion of School of Methods."[191] After one attempt to secure a developed campsite failed, the Committee proposed the acquisition of Twin Pine Ranch near Stroudsburg for $110,000. On May 15, 1963, the Society approved the purchase of the property for use as a year-round camp and conference center for the East Pennsylvania Conference to be known as Twin Pines Camp.[192] Among the renovations needed to turn the former dude ranch into a Christian youth camp was the conversion of the stable into a chapel. Kenneth M. Weaver was the General Superintendent of School of Methods following the transition to the new site.[193] By 1972 Twin Pines was in use every week from June 25 to September 2 hosting four junior camps (ages 9–11), three intermediate camps (ages 12–14), one senior camp (age 15 and up), one adult camp, and one family camp with a total attendance of over 2,000.

Meanwhile, the Eastern District of the Western Conference continued to hold its School of Methods at Beulah Beach Camp until 1955. In 1956, however, EC campers were unable to reserve the Camp for the weeks that they wanted it, so this School of Methods was transferred to a campgrounds owned by the Church of God near Butler OH called Camp Otyokwah.[194] The long-term solution for an expanding program was, of course, owning a campsite, and in 1959 the churches of the District were able to purchase a suitable tract of land near Carrolton OH.[195] Camp EccO opened with three weeks of camping in the summer of 1961.[196]

The churches in Illinois began holding youth camps in 1950 in rented facilities along the shores of Lake Geneva WI.[197] They used the camp owned by the Evangelical Free Church at Williams Bay, Lake Geneva WI, from 1951 to 1956.[198] In 1956 the churches in the Western District purchased sixteen acres of land along the Rock River near Dixon IL,[199] and in the summer of 1958 Rock River Bible Camp was ready for occupancy by the young people of the Illinois churches.[200]

Women

In the 1950s and 1960s women continued to teach Sunday school classes, minister through Ladies Aid Societies, serve on Official Boards, and represent their churches as lay delegates to the Annual and General Conferences. Women provided vital support for missions through local Women's Missionary Societies and Conference Missionary Branch Fellowships. These women made the Evangelical Congregational Church a mission-minded church through their meetings, rallies, and writings. The following served as presidents of the Western Conference Branch: Rebecca Shultz (1882–1941) from 1923 to 1927; Jennie Wilson (1870–1960) from 1927 to 1942; Stella Mineely (1899–1981) from 1942 to 1958; Isabel Wilson (1909–1992) from 1958 to 1966; and Irma Taubenheim (1911–1990) from 1966 to 1974. The presidents of the East Pennsylvania Branch were Carrie Neitz (1852–1939) from 1923 to 1934; Alice Schlappich (1884–1958) from 1934 to 1952; Helen Manwiller (1896–1978) from 1952 to 1958; and Mary Elizabeth Detterline (1900–1978) from 1958 to 1974.

Missions also provided opportunities for EC women to fulfill the call of Christ to full-time service. Between 1950 and 1973 forty-nine women either began missionary service or were commissioned as Evangelical Congregational missionaries.[201] Nearly two-thirds of these were single women, and they served largely in teaching, nursing, or clerical work. Whether or not women could assume pastoral responsibilities, however, was still not clear. The East Pennsylvania Conference sought to clarify the issue of women in pastoral ministry in 1966 when an amendment to the *Discipline* was proposed which limited applicants for ministerial credentials to men,[202] but this amendment was defeated. In 1967 Irene Reiber of Wiconisco PA applied for a Local Preacher's License. She had been serving as pastor of two small churches in Halifax since 1964, and before that she had ministered to a church in Kansas under Village Missions, Inc. The East Pennsylvania Conference Relations Committee felt that this application might cause dissension if it was presented to the Annual Conference. The Committee conveyed its sentiments to Miss

Reiber in a letter advising that she seek missionary credentials from the Board of Missions, and serve as pastor of the churches as a home missionary.[203] She sought and received the Board's approval and was commissioned in November 1967.[204] However, her pastoral service was cut short when she was injured in an automobile accident in January 1968.[205] It would remain for a future generation to define more clearly the call of women to pastoral ministry.

Youth

In 1950 Christian Endeavor was firmly planted in East Pennsylvania Conference churches with large congregations reporting five CE societies for young children through adults. In churches with multiple societies the senior (adult) societies frequently provided the leadership and financial support for the other groups, and as long as the adult society remained strong the younger groups flourished. During the period 1950–1973, however, the number of senior societies declined dramatically from a high of sixty-two societies (1770 members) in 1952 to twenty-four societies (570 members) in 1973. At the same time high school societies increased from twenty-nine in 1951 to sixty-seven in 1973. With the lessening of the influence of the adult groups the churches depended either on the pastor or the Sunday School Board to provide leadership for the youth and children's societies.

The majority of Christian Endeavor societies met on Sunday evening before the evening worship service. The leaders used topics and resources provided by the International Society of Christian Endeavor headquartered in Columbus OH. Each week the *United Evangelical* devoted a page to commentary on the upcoming CE topics for the various age groups. In 1960 the Board of Christian Education of the Evangelical Congregational Church began publishing a quarterly entitled, *The Endeavorer,* to further assist societies.[206] Two years later the Board also embarked on a Christian Endeavor promotional campaign called "New Horizons."[207] Young People and adults regularly attended area and state Christian Endeavor conventions.

The churches in the Western Conference were not able to generate the same support for Christian Endeavor as their sister conference in the East. Frequent references appeared in the reports of the Conference Sunday School and Keystone League of Christian Endeavor Committee encouraging churches to organize Christian Endeavor societies for various age groups,[208] but congregations were only marginally successful in providing a Christian Endeavor type of ministry for their youth. By 1963 the Western Conference had begun utilizing Bible quizzing as an approach to youth ministry. Youth would be given a book of the Bible to study at the beginning of each quiz season and then organized into teams to answer questions about that book in a game-show setting. This quickly revitalized the youth program of the churches,[209] and "quiz offs" became regular features of the district youth gatherings and of the annual Christian Education Convention held at Huntington College, Huntington IN.[210]

In 1972 the East Pennsylvania Conference joined the Western Conference in promoting Bible quizzing. The first denominational-wide youth rally held in Huntington IN on August 8–10, 1972, was the site of an inter-conference quiz-off in which Bethel Church of Dixon IL, the "best of the West," defeated the team from Zion Church of Dauphin PA, "the best of the East."[211]

Beliefs

Theology

In the first three decades of its existence the leaders of the Evangelical Congregational Church struggled to maintain a consistent theological position within the churches. Guest preachers, who were brought to camp meetings, youth camps, and Bible conferences, often personally held doctrinal positions at variance with the Evangelical Congregational Church. Local churches also used evangelists and Bible teachers who were not in sympathy with the Wesleyan/Arminian position of the denomination, even though they were advised of the denomination's doctrines and instructed to avoid controversy.

In 1958, in an attempt to curb the use of evangelists and Bible teachers that disseminated doctrine that it deemed divisive, the Church adopted an amendment to the *Discipline* requiring pastors to investigate thoroughly the doctrinal beliefs of visiting preachers and consult with the District Superintendent before the speaker was engaged.[212] To guide pastors in selecting speakers the East Pennsylvania Conference attempted to compile a list of approved evangelists.[213]

The Conferences sought to secure compliance to the Articles of Faith among the clergy through a rigid screening process, but this task was challenging because ministerial candidates were often trained at institutions with various doctrinal views. In Pennsylvania pastors attended colleges and seminaries sponsored by the Presbyterian, Baptist, Lutheran, and Moravian Churches; in Ohio and Illinois pastors who desired a formal training utilized Bible institutes. The strong desire to develop a consistent theological stance among the clergy was one of the reasons for establishing a school of theology in Myerstown.[214] Since the founding of the Evangelical Congregational School of Theology, the conferences have experienced greater theological stability.

As neo-orthodoxy gained a broad acceptance among theologians in western Christendom the Evangelical Congregational Church scrutinized more closely its doctrine of inspiration of Scripture and especially its view of inerrancy. The Article of Faith "Of the Holy Scriptures" does not address the infallibility issue, but the first catalog of the Evangelical Congregational School of Theology in 1953 was accurate when it stated: "The School, in harmony with the denomination, believes the Holy Bible to be inerrant in the original languages, and uses this as the basis for biblical teaching."[215] Candidates for pastoral ministry were closely examined to determine whether they agreed with this position on inspiration.

The inerrant Bible and the unalterable twenty-five Articles of Faith formed a stable theological base for instructing new members of the Evangelical Congregational Church. Biblical doctrines accepted since the days of Albright still occupy the prevailing place in the faith standards of the Evangelical Congregational Church. These doctrines include a commitment to the authoritative and inspired Word of God, the proclamation of salvation by grace through faith in Christ as the only hope for sinful humanity, and the availability of Holy Spirit power to live a changed life that is pleasing to God. Defending these beliefs is not simply speaking out for abstract Wesleyan traditions; it is defending the very pattern and substance of the denomination's life.

Social Issues

In the early years of the EC Church both the East Pennsylvania Conference and the Western Conference continued to focus concern on society's use of alcohol and the use/abuse of the Lord's Day. This focus remained in the East. Meetings of the Temperance Reform and Social Service Society were held during annual sessions of East Pennsylvania Conference, and the Conference maintained a close affiliation with the Pennsylvania Temperance League (later, Pennsylvanians Concerned about Alcohol Problems) and the Lord's Day Alliance of Pennsylvania. Even though the Federal Supreme Court upheld the constitutionality of the Sunday blue laws in Pennsylvania, Massachusetts, and Maryland, the Pennsylvania legislature began passing laws permitting sports and limited liquor sales on Sunday. The Conference drafted resolutions and urged constituents to write the legislators to curb the weakening of the observance of the Christian Sabbath,[216] but by the early 1970s the Sunday blue laws had been eliminated. As this period progressed, gambling in Pennsylvania became a prominent issue. A referendum was placed before the voters to permit pari-mutuel betting at harness horse races in 1960, and in spite of the rigorous objection of the Christian community the referendum passed.[217] This was followed in 1971 by the passage of a bill to initiate a lottery in Pennsylvania.

The Western Conference, on the other hand, not being tied to any particular state, often took the lead in addressing broader social problems. Both Conferences voiced strong opposition to atheistic communism and supported the participation of the United States in the Korean conflict and the war in Viet Nam. Throughout this period members of Evangelical Congregational churches supported the public school system and opposed any use of tax money for private or parochial education because they believed that such funding would increase the influence of the Roman Catholic Church. The Western Conference Committee on Lord's Day, Temperance and Spiritual State of the Church wrote in 1960, "We note with concern and great alarm the under-current movements of the Roman Catholic Church in its effort to control the educational system and our political and temporal affairs of state and union."[218] The churches began to rethink their support of the public school system, however, when in 1963 the United States Supreme Court ruled that prayer and Bible reading in tax-supported schools was unconstitutional.[219] The East Pennsylvania Conference got behind efforts to amend the United States Constitution to permit voluntary devotions in the public schools.

Civil rights became a major topic of discussion during the 1950s and 1960s. In 1956 the East Pennsylvania Conference stated, "It is the position of our church that we set forth and defend the teaching of equality of all people in the sight of God regardless of race or color."[220] Subsequent actions by the conferences bolstered this stand and called on the churches to open their doors to minority segments of the population. In the mid-1960s relationships between African Americans and whites broke down and erupted into violence. The Western Conference appointed a special committee to study the civil rights movement and provide educational materials for local churches. The urgency of such a study was reflected in the words that appeared in the report of the committee to the 1966 Western Conference. "Just three miles from our Chicago Kimball Avenue Church an explosion of violence and destruction brought us face to face with the reality that it could happen 'here.'"[221]

Church Organization (Polity)

Annual Conferences

In the Evangelical Congregational Church the central administrative organization was the Annual Conference. The *Discipline* stated, "The Annual Conference is possessed with all powers, legislative, judicial, and administrative, which it has not surrendered to the General Conference by legislative enactment and which have not been reserved to the congregation."[222] Each of the denomination's congregations was represented at the sessions of an Annual Conference.

From 1950 to 1973 there was no change in the requirements for membership in the Annual Conference. All itinerant ministers plus one lay delegate from each charge were members of the Annual Conferences to which they belonged. In spite of this fact, the number of lay and ministerial delegates increased twenty-four percent in each Conference due to the break up of many of the multi-church charges and the significant increase of the number of retired pastors. The lay presence in the Conference sessions also increased because in 1966 provision was made for the selection of a reserve or alternate lay delegate in addition to the regular lay delegate from each charge.[223] Although not voting members of the Conference, the reserve or alternate delegates frequently accompanied the lay delegates to the seat of Conference.

Legislative actions were presented to the delegates as recommendations from either special or standing committees. Standing committees composed of both lay and clergy members were appointed on the first day of Conference and functioned until the Conference adjourned. The Bishop appointed special committees at the direction of the Conference to deal with specific tasks. These committees functioned largely between the sessions of the Conference. Any proposals contained in the reports of the Bishop or Presiding Elders were channeled through committees before reaching the delegates for action. In 1950 the East Pennsylvania Conference had eighteen standing committees and nine special committees. That same year the Western Conference had fourteen standing and nine special committees.

Other organizations called "societies" held their business meetings at the seat of the Annual Conference. Two of the societies, the Conference Missionary Society and the Church Extension Society, were Annual

Conference branches of General Conference boards. The membership of these auxiliary bodies was identical to the membership of the Annual Conference. The East Pennsylvania Conference had a third society, the Temperance Reform and Social Service Society, to deal with matters of social concern.

The Sunday School and Keystone League of Christian Endeavor Federations also functioned at the Annual Conference level. The membership of these bodies differed somewhat from that of the Annual Conference, because they contained representatives of the Sunday Schools and youth groups from the conference churches. The Federation business sessions were conducted during annual conventions held each year on a date and at a location that differed from the sessions of the Annual Conference. In 1960 the federations changed their names to Christian Education Societies. In the East Pennsylvania Conference the Christian Education Society began to function as the other Conference societies with a membership composed of the delegates to the Annual Conference and business held during the Annual Conference. The Western Conference Christian Education Society continued to meet at the annual convention and transact its business at that time.

Until 1952 the Western Conference met in August, but in 1951 the opening date of conference was moved to the "Thursday preceding the third Sunday in June."[224] This change gave reassigned pastors of school age children an opportunity to settle into their appointments before the school year in fall. The East Pennsylvania Conference convened at the end of April with sessions lasting from Wednesday through Monday. By 1954 the length of conference was shortened with the concluding service, including the reading of the Stationing Committee's report, on Sunday evening. In 1961 the Conference moved its opening date to the Wednesday following Mothers' Day in May. This change somewhat alleviated the need for school children of newly appointed pastors to be either separated from their parents until the school term ended or to miss the concluding days of school. The sessions of both Conferences were held in local Evangelical Congregational churches with the host church arranging meals for the delegates and housing ministers in members' homes.

The supervision of churches remained the responsibility of the Presiding Elders, a title that was changed to District Superintendent in 1958.[225] The Presiding Elder conducted four Quarterly Conferences in each charge on his district and preached on a Sunday in each congregation every year. The fall Quarterly Conference eventually became a group conference with fifteen to twenty churches gathering together in a convenient location. In an age of instantaneous communication, however, these visits seemed to be more perfunctory than necessary and were seen as diverting time from intensive involvement in churches that really needed close supervision.

In 1967 an East Pennsylvania Conference committee charged with considering the election of a third District Superintendent to share the burden of overseeing the 129 churches in the Conference proposed instead an extensive revision of the role of District Superintendent.[226] Under the new arrangement adopted by the Conference the District Superintendent was responsible for attending only one of the four Quarterly Conferences, renamed "Local Conferences," held by each charge. He continued to make a Sunday visit to each church, and he was to have a personal conference with every pastor on his district. Freedom from attending the other Local Conferences, however, made it possible for the District Superintendent to be available to individual churches when they needed assistance.[227] Both District Superintendents reported to the 1968 Eastern Annual Conference that they were pleased with the new procedure and recommended that the appropriate disciplinary amendments be made to make it permanent.[228]

The Presiding Elders/District Superintendents in the East Pennsylvania/Eastern Conference after 1950 were: Eastern District—Harold H Scanlin (1951–1959), Earl D. Ehrig (1959–1967), J. Karl Harper (1967–1975); Western District—Harrison S. Heffner (1950–1958), Paul K. Cressman (1958–1966), Herbert W. Wittmaier (1966–1973). Presiding Elders/District Superintendents in the Western Conference were: entire Conference—Norman J. Broadway assisted by Robert S. Wilson in Illinois (1948–1951); Eastern District—Norman J. Broadway (1947–1955), Paul D. Dunn (1955–1962), George E. Ralph (1963–1968); Western District—Paul D. Gordon (1952–1960), George E. Ralph (1960–1963), Paul D. Gordon (1963–1971).

General Conference

The General Conference, which met every four years, was charged with the responsibility of promoting and supervising the denominational interests of the Evangelical Congregational Church. In the early years of the denomination special sessions of the General Conference were called to care for items that needed attention between the quadrennial meetings. As the years passed it became increasingly apparent that a more structured way of dealing with these emergency matters was needed.

In 1954 the Western Conference proposed that the *Discipline* be amended to provide for a Council of Administration "to coordinate the work and program of the entire denomination and implement the general program of the Church."[229] The 1954 General Conference decided to appoint a Council of Administration in the new quadrennium and asked the Amendments Committee to consider including such a council in the *Discipline* at a later date.[230] The Council of Administration authorized by the 1954 conference finally met for the first time in April 1957 with only one item of business, determining the place for the next General Conference. One additional meeting was held prior to the General Conference to discuss the progress of the Greater E. C. Rally fund-raising campaign.

The Greater E. C. Rally was a successor to the Victory Through Loyalty to Christ campaign initiated by the 1942 General Conference.[231] The Victory campaign was designed to run from 1944 to 1947 and had a financial goal of $110,000, but collecting all the monies pledged had dragged on into the early 1950s. Bishop Smith recommended starting an entirely new campaign in 1954, the Greater E. C. Rally, with a four year financial goal of $113,000.[232] This was a great success, and by 1958 it was oversubscribed by $10,000.

The Council, now under the name "Administrative Council," brought to the 1958 General Conference an enabling act that defined its areas of responsibility. The Conference decided to place the composition of the Administrative Council in the special rules of conference rather than in the *Discipline*.[233] The newly constituted Council consisted of the Bishop, the District Superintendents of both Annual Conferences, the Editor, the Treasurer of the General Conference, the Dean of the School of Theology, the Superintendent of the Burd and Rogers Memorial Home, and two representatives from each general board and benevolent agency.

Although the mandate given to the Council was broad, i.e. "to implement and administer the actions of the General Conference,"[234] in its meetings immediately after the General Conference it focused narrowly on the financial needs of the boards and agencies. At the 1958 General Conference the Bishop requested that some type of ongoing financial support for the institutions be developed, preferably without another fund drive. [235] The Council agreed to employ a financial agent with responsibility to seek out persons from Evangelical Congregational churches to personally support the institutions,[236] but it could not find anyone to take this position or even personnel for a fund-raising committee. As a last resort the Council turned again to the fund drive format, and the Extra Mile Crusade was born.[237] As in the case of the Greater E. C. Rally offering goals for local congregations were set. This time, however, hearty support was not forthcoming. By the time the

Promotional Materials for the Extra Mile Crusade

1962 General Conference met only 57 % of the $164,000 goal had been reached.[238] The crusade was extended for another four years to give local churches an opportunity to reach their goals. Four years later the Extra Mile Crusade was permitted to die with 76 % of its goal received. This was the last time the denomination attempted a general church fund drive.[239]

Once the initial organizational issues were settled, the Administrative Council set a pattern of meeting twice a year, in spring and fall. Each of the boards and agencies gave reports, and special committees authorized by the General Conference gave accounts of their progress. Early in each session the Bishop shared his view of developments within the Church since the last meeting.

Various crises requiring immediate action repeatedly demonstrated the wisdom of creating the Administrative Council. In 1964 First

Evangelical Congregational Church in Canton OH faced the possibility of default on its mortgage and the loss of its property,[240] and Western Conference leaders turned to the Administrative Council for aid in meeting this need. With the sessions of the Council serving as a forum a unique cooperative plan was forged involving various general church boards and Annual Conference bodies. These agencies provided the funds needed to satisfy the requests of the Ohio financial institutions and helped the church become solvent. After the 1970 General Conference, which took action to close the print shop of the Church Center Press, the Administrative Council monitored the Board of Publication's progress in making the transition and provided assistance when needed. It arranged for the trustees of the Evangelical Congregational Retirement Village to purchase the Church Center Press building[241] and for the Board of Christian Education to make funds available to finance a new edition of the *Discipline* when the Board of Publications was not able to come up with the money.[242] Again the Administrative Council provided the forum for this cooperation.

Then, in early 1973 the Council was required to take charge following the death of Bishop Cressman. The *Discipline* made no provision for caring for the many details in preparation for an Annual Conference, the denominational representation at interdenominational gatherings, and the preliminary work of stationing pastors in the event of the death or incapacity of the Bishop. The March meeting of the Council dealt with these matters,[243] and a smooth transition occurred with Herbert Wittmaier being elected Bishop at a special session of the General Conference held on the day before the opening of the Eastern Annual Conference.

Local Church Governance

EC congregations had been effectively administered by Official Boards since the early twentieth century, but with an amendment to the *Discipline* in 1954 Boards became mandatory.[244] Further amendments presented to the 1958 General Conference clarified the operation of the Official Board[245] and made the trustees of the local church amenable to the Official Board,[246] rather than operating as a separate board reporting to the Quarterly Conference and the annual congregational meeting.

The amendments to the *Discipline* in 1958 also provided local congregations with an orderly way of updating their membership rolls.[247] This action was needed because in the prior quadrenniums churches had pared their church membership lists in order to reduce their apportionment obligations to the Annual Conferences. Local church membership was one of the factors along with total giving that was included in the formula used to assess congregations.

Conclusion

When the Evangelical Congregational Church celebrated its fiftieth anniversary in 1972, it could look back on years of significant advance since that November day when a special session of the East Pennsylvania Conference resolved to continue under the *Discipline* of the United Evangelical Church even though the UE Church had merged into another denomination. Two institutions, the Evangelical Congregational Church Retirement Village and the Evangelical School of Theology, were firmly established and growing. A missionary thrust was developed that reached around the world and included four mission fields directly under the Board of Missions. Membership in the denomination's churches had increased by nine thousand in this half-century, and there had been a net gain of twelve congregations.

However, as it observed its golden anniversary the Evangelical Congregational Church faced challenges unprecedented in its previous history. The society in which it ministered had become increasingly unfriendly. Local congregations were experiencing declining participation, and many of them were located in transitioning neighborhoods. There were stirrings among the clergy and laity to provide new administrative structures to meet the challenges.

Notes

1. Harold H. Scanlin, "Final Report of the Chairman of the Administrative Council," in AdCoun, March 16, 1967, 6, mimeograph, emphasis added.

2. Paul K. Cressman, "Episcopal Address," in ECEPAConfJ, 1971, 80.

3. Harold H. Scanlin, "Episcopal Address," in ECEPAConfJ, 1964, 80.

4. The membership and attendance statistics quoted in this chapter are taken from the reports of the statistical secretary in the respective General Conference Journals and the sections on Statistics in the respective Annual Conference Journals.

5. Sylvester K. Stevens, *Pennsylvania, Birthplace of a Nation* (New York: Random House, 1964), 348–349.

6. See John E. Moyer, "Episcopal Address," in ECEPAConfJ, 1984, 91–95.

7. John E. Moyer, "Report of the Board of Publications," in ECGenConfJ, 1970, 159–160.

8. "Minutes of the Sessions," in ECGenConfJ, 1970, 43.

9. [William S. Sailer], "Editorial: We Won!" UE, May 30, 1972, 3.

10. "Committee on Publishing Interests," in ECGenConfJ, 1970, 82.

11. Ralph T. Baily, "Report of the Secretary of the Board of Publications," in ECGenConfJ, 1974, 134.

12. Richard A. Cattermole, "Report of the Administrative Secretary," in ECGenConfJ, 1982, 89.

13. [Ronald B. Kuntz], "Editor's Note," UE, August 26, 1977, 2.

14. "Home Echos," UE, April 5. 1965, 9.

15. "To Dedicate $365,000 Addition to E. C. Church Home at Myerstown," Lebanon Daily News, June 24, 1961, 9.

16. "Home Superintendent Retires," UE, June 2, 1970, 12.

17. "Our Denomination: Home Anniversary," UE, October 2, 1955, 8.

18. Robert S. Wilson, "Western Conference Churches," in ECWConfJ, 1972, 138.

19. "Committee on Boundaries," in ECWConfJ, 1951, 53.

20. "Committee on Boundaries," in ECWConfJ, 1952, 52.

21. Robert S. Wilson, "Tent Meeting in Rock Falls, Ill.," UE, August 15, 1950, 8.

22. "Stationing Committee Report," in ECWConfJ, 1950, 45.

23. Robert S. Wilson, "Rock Falls, Illinois Dedicates New Church," UE, May 1, 1951, 7.

24. Norman J. Broadway, "Presiding Elder's Report," in ECWConfJ, 1954, 50–51.

25. Paul D. Dunn, "Presiding Elder's Report," in ECWConfJ, 1958, 50.

26. "Conference Relations Committee Report," in ECWConfJ, 1952, 53.

27. "Conference Relations Committee Report," in ECWConfJ, 1953, 57.

28. Paul D. Dunn, "Presiding Elder's Report," in ECWConfJ, 1959, 58.

29. George E. Ralph, "District Superintendent's Report," in ECWConfJ, 1962, 63.

30. Paul D. Gordon, "Western District Superintendent's Report," in ECWConfJ, 1971, 59–60.

31. Harrison S. Heffner, "Presiding Elder's Report," in ECEPAConfJ, 1957, 74.

32. "Report of the Special Committee on the Lancaster Mission," in ECEPAConfJ, 1957, 127.

33. Harrison S. Heffner, "Presiding Elder's Report," in ECEPAConfJ, 1958, 81.

34. Paul K. Cressman, "District Superintendent's Report," in ECEPAConfJ, 1961,98.

35. Ibid., 98–100.

36. Paul K. Cressman, "District Superintendent's Report," in ECEPAConfJ, 1963, 78.

37. David P. Heil, "New Congregation at Lancaster, PA," UE, March 25, 1969, 15.

38. Herbert D. Wittmaier, "District Superintendent's Report," in

ECEPAConf], 1969, 98.

39. Herbert D. Wittmaier, "Report of Superintendent Western District," in ECEPAConf], 1972, 89.

40. "The Journal," in ECEPAConf], 1956, 38.

41. "The Journal," in ECEPAConf], 1959, 37.

42. "The Journal," in ECEPAConf], 1968, 90.

43. "Official Minutes," in ECEPAConf], 1973, 66.

44. Thomas E. Paul, "Board of Missions Report," in ECGenConf], 1954, 107; Thomas E. Paul, "Board of Missions Report," in ECGenConf], 1958, 142.

45. Thomas E. Paul, "Report of the Corresponding Secretary of the Board of Missions," in ECGenConf], 1962, 134.

46. Thomas E. Paul, "Report of the General Secretary of the Board of Missions," in ECGenConf], 1966, 144.

47. "Our Missions Base," UE, September 19, 1961, 1.

48. "Our Departed Missions Secretary," UE, March 11, 1969, 15.

49. "Missionary Committee," in ECEPAConf], 1970, 149.

50. "Committee on Amendments," in ECGenConf], 1966, 98–99.

51. Thomas E. Paul, "Board of Missions' Report," in ECGenConf], 1966, 150.

52. Richard A. Cattermole, "Report of the Board of Missions," in ECGenConf], 1974, 123.

53. Robert S. Wilson, *History of Women's Missionary Societies: East Pennsylvania Branch, Evangelical Congregational Church—Fifty Years of Missions, 1922-1972* ([Myerstown, PA]: Eastern Branch Missionary Fellowship of the Evangelical Congregational Church, 1976), 43-44.

54. "Report of the Texas-Mexico Committee to the Board of Missions," Minutes of the Board of Missions, October 10, 1973, 279, mimeographed.

55. Richard A. Cattermole, "Report of the General Secretary to the Board of Missions," Minutes of the Board of Missions, October 26, 1977, 3, mimeographed.

56. "Minutes of the Organization Meeting of the North East India General Conference, Inc.," June 23, 1959, 1, mimeographed.

57. Thomas E. Paul, "We Traveled East," UE, January 16, 1962, 6–7.

58. Wilson, *History of the Women's Missionary Societies*, 48.

59. Wilson, *History of the Women's Missionary Societies*; R. A. Cattermole, "Report of the Board of Missions," ECGenConf], 1974, 124; Robert S. Wilson, "Fifty Years for the Western Conference" (Myerstown, PA: The Author, 1972), 134.

60. Charles H. Mengel, "Report of the Board of Education and the E. C. School of Theology," in ECGenConf], 1954, 104.

61. Robert G. Hower, "From Vision to Reality: the Story of the Evangelical School of Theology," (Myerstown: Evangelical School of Theology, 1995), 11.

62. Ibid., 10.

63. Ibid., 9.

64. Kenneth R. Maurer, "Report of the Dean of the E. C. School of

Theology," in ECGenConf], 1958, 135.

65. Kenneth R. Maurer, "Report of the Dean of the E. C. School of Theology," in ECEPAConf], 1959, 109.

66. "Scholastic Requirements of Ministry," in ECEPAConf], 1964, 130.

67. Ibid.

68. Robert G. Hower, "From Vision to Reality . . ." [12].

69. Harold H. Scanlin, "School of Theology President's Report," in ECEPAConf], 1968, 225–229.

70. Harold H. Scanlin, "School of Theology President's Report," in ECEPAConf], 1971, 178–179.

71. Robert G. Hower, "From Vision to Reality: The Story of the Evangelical School of Theology" [rev. ed.] (Myerstown: Evangelical School of Theology, 2003), 65–69.

72. "Minutes of the Sessions," in ECGenConf], 1962, 28.

73. "Minutes of the Sessions," in ECGenConf], 1962, 30.

74. Ibid., 54.

75. AdCoun, September 25, 1958, 3, mimeographed.

76. AdCoun, October 16, 1959, 23, mimeographed.

77. AdCoun, April 2, 1959, 16, mimeographed.

78. George A. Raker, secretary, "Committee Minutes," March 30, 1962, 1, mimeographed.

79. Ibid., 3.

80. AdCoun, May 2, 1962, 48, mimeographed.

81. Harold H. Scanlin, "Report to the Administrative Council...Relations of E. C. Church to P. M. Church," AdCoun, April 4, 1963, 57–62, mimeographed.

82. AdCoun, April 30, 1964, 75, mimeographed.

83. "Report of the Ministerial Aid Committee," in ECGenConf], 1954, 66.

84. Ibid., 67.

85. "Board of Pensions," in ECEConf], 1979, 181.

86. "Board of Pensions," in ECGenConf], 1974, 129.

87. "Board of Pensions," in ECGenConf], 1974, 128.

88. Ibid., 129.

89. "Report of the Historical Committee," ECGenConf], 1958, 114.

90. Harold H. Scanlin to J. C. Christman, October 25, 1961, typescript, papers of the Historical Society, E.C. Archives, Evangelical School of Theology, Myerstown, PA.

91. "Minutes of the General Conference Historical Committee, 2/7/62," Archives of the EC Church.

92. "Historical Committee," ECGenConf], 1966, 112–114.

93. "Minutes: Board of Trustees of the Historical Society, October 18, 1966," Archives of the EC Church.

94. "The Historical Society," ECGenConf], 1970, 139–141; "Historical Society," ECEPAConf], 1972, 108.

95. "General Conference Committee Report," in ECWConf], 1950, 49.

96. "The Journal," in ECEPAConfJ, 1951, 38.

97. "The Journal," in ECEPAConfJ, 1953, 33.

98. John A. Smith, "Episcopal Address," in ECEPAConfJ, 1953, 53.

99. Harold H. Scanlin, "Episcopal Address," in ECEPAConfJ, 1961, 66.

100. Ibid.

101. Ibid., 68.

102. Harold H. Scanlin, "Episcopal Address," in ECEPAConfJ, 1963, 68–69.

103. "Special Committee on Pastors' Salaries," in ECEPAConfJ, 1957, 133–139.

104. "Committee on Pastors' Salaries," in ECEPAConfJ, 1958, 139.

105. "Pastors' Salaries," in ECEPAConfJ, 1964, 127.

106. "Pastors' Salaries," in ECEPAConfJ, 1966, 137–138.

107. "Pastors' Salaries Committee," in ECEPAConfJ, 1972, 123.

108. "Ways and Means Committee," in ECWConfJ, 1957, 68–69.

109. "Special Rules of Conference, XII, Salaries," in ECWConfJ, 1968, 31.

110. "Pastor's Salary Committee", in ECWConfJ, 1969,84.

111. "Pastor's Salary Committee," in ECWConfJ, 1973, 73.

112. "Pastors' Salaries Committee," in ECEPAConfJ, 1973, 107.

113. Paul D. Dunn, "District Superintendent's Report," ECWConfJ, 1961,57.

114. Andrew W. Blackwood, The Preparation of Sermons, (New York: Abingdon Press, 1948), 39.

115. Allen Zartman Bodey, "I Believe God—or god!" UE, July 10, 1956, 2–3, 15.

116. "Report of the Committee on Amendments to the Discipline," ECGenConfJ, 1958, 104.

117. ECDisc, 1972, 121.

118. UE, September 6, 1955, 2–3; September 13, 1955, 2–3.

119. Ibid., 2.

120. Ibid., 3.

121. Edwin S. Woodring, "Baptism, Part II, The Mode of Baptism," UE, September 13, 1955, 3.

122. Ibid.

123. "Report of the Committee on Amendments to the Discipline," in ECGenConfJ, 1958, 89.

124. Robert S. Wilson, "Editorial: Our Baptismal Ritual," UE, June 3, 1958, 4–5.

125. AdCoun, November 20, 1964, 81, mimeographed.

126. AdCoun, April 12, 1965, 89–90, mimeographed.

127. "Church Hymnal Committee," in ECGenConfJ, 1962, 89.

128. [Robert S. Wilson], "Our New Hymnal," UE, December 20, 1965, 4.

129. [Robert S. Wilson], "Robes for Your Choir," UE, December 8, 1964, 6–7.

130. "Orchestra—St. Paul's Church, York, PA," UE, July 17, 1956, 1.

131. "Spiritual State of the Church," ECEPAConfJ, 1965, 162.

132. "Grace E. C. Lancaster, PA, Will Dedicate $200,000 Addition June 22,"

UE, June 17, 1953.

133. "Education Annex at Royersford Dedicated," UE, November 14, 1961, 10.

134. "Addition Dedicated at Highland Park, Illinois," UE, August 6, 1963, 1, 10.

135. Herbert D. Wittmaier, "Report of Superintendent Western District," in ECEPAConf], 1971, 90.

136. "Emmaus Church Dedicates," UE, April 6, 1971, 1, 9.

137. John A. Smith, "Dedication of New Church, Sunbury, Pennsylvania," UE, May 15, 1956, 1,6–7.

138. "New Church at Canton, Ohio," UE, June 6, 1961, 1, 11.

139. Paul D. Dunn, "District Superintendent's Report," in ECWConf], 1961, 55.

140. "Zion Allentown to Dedicate New Sanctuary," UE, April 14, 1964, 1, 10.

141. "Bethesda Church Dedication," UE, September 9, 1969, 1, 9.

142. "Faith Builds Cedarville, " UE, May 2, 1972, 8.

143. John A. Smith, "Greenmont Dedication, Reading, Pa," UE, October 4, 1955, 10.

144. Richard G. Gordon, "A Thank You, from Norwood Heights," UE, June 4, 1955, 5.

145. Paul D. Dunn, "District Superintendent's Report," in ECWConf], 1961, 55.

146. Glenna Pilpott, "Laying of the Cornerstone," UE, April 5, 1955, 9.

147. "Palmyra Dedication," UE, October 2, 1956, 9–10.

148. H. Arlington Gerhart, "New Church Planned for Ephrata, PA," UE, October 9, 1956, 9.

149. "Ground Breaking at Youngstown, Ohio," UE, August 15, 1961, 10.

150. "Pottsville Dedication," UE, May 6, 1969, 11.

151. "Chambers Hill Dedication," UE, October 7, 1969, 7.

152. Herbert D. Wittmaier, "Report of Superintendent Western District," in ECPAConf], 1972, 89.

153. Paul D. Gordon, "Western District Superintendent's Report," in ECWConf], 1971, 59.

154. John A. Smith, "Episcopal Address," in ECEPAConf], 1954, 64.

155. "Birdsboro Ground Breaking," UE, September 18, 1956, 11.

156. Harold H. Scanlin, "Presiding Elder's Report," in ECEPAConf], 1959, 84.

157. "Prayer, Family Life and Social Concern," ECGenConf], 1970, 80.

158. "Norwood Heights: Fifth Annual Harvest Home Banquet," UE, January 4, 1955, 3.

159. "C. E. in St. Luke's Shillington, Pa." UE, February 16, 1954, 7.

160. This seems to be a faint echo of the Easter Vigil service of the ancient church, in which converts who had completed catechetical instruction culminating in Lent were baptized on the eve of Easter, passing from death to life

with Christ.

161 "Western Convention," UE, August 15, 1967, 15.

162. "Waldheim Swimming Pool a Reality," UE, December 18, 1956, 9–10.

163. "Bible Conference Directors," in ECEPAConf], 1966, 130.

164. Earl A. Troup, "Herndon Camp Meeting," UE, August 29, 1950, 7.

165. ECDisc, 1948, 112.

166. See the "Fiftieth Anniversary Rosedale Camp Meeting, July 13–22, 1973," brochure.

167. See the "Sixty-Eighth Session of Waldheim Camp Meeting, July 7–15, 1973," brochure.

168. James K. Rapp, "Zion Allentown Activities," UE, January 18, 1955, 10–11.

169. Robert S. Wilson, "Western Conference News Items," UE, February 15, 1955, 7.

170. "E. C. Boys Gospel Team," UE, February 22, 1955, 3.

171. "The East Pennsylvania Conference," UE, June 6, 1967, 12.

172. Herbert D. Wittmaier, "District Superintendent's Report," in ECEPAConf], 1968, 124.

173. "Evangelism Committee," in ECGenConf], 1954, 83–91.

174. "Evangelism Committee," in ECGenConf], 1962, 93–96.

175. William Wortman, "In-Depth Evangelism's New Strategy for North American Churches," *Latin America Evangelist*, 52, no. 2 (March-April 1972): 1–4.

176. John E. Moyer, "Six Churches Involved: In-Depth Evangelism," UE, March 21, 1972, 8.

177. David R. Wolfe, "Calling Our Continent to Christ," UE, February 22, 1971, 6–7.

178. Kenneth R. Maurer, "Acknowledgements," The Threshold of the Church (Myerstown, PA: S.S. and K.L.C.E. Federation of the E.C. Church, 1953), [1].

179. The Threshold of the Church: A Catechetical Manual of the Evangelical Congregational Church (Myerstown, PA: Board of Publication of the Evangelical Congregational Church, 1956).

180. R. S. Wilson, letter, August 16, 1962; Kenneth M. Weaver, letter to R. S. Wilson, January 22, 1965.

181. R. S. Wilson, letter to Paul D. Dunn, April 6, 1971.

182. Donald T. Floyd, "Another Evangelical Pioneer," UE, January 31, 1950, 3.

183. "Sunday School and Keystone League of Christian Endeavor Committee," in ECEPAConf], 1950, 113.

184. Wesley Shrader, "Our Troubled Sunday Schools," Life, XLII, (11 February 1957): 110.

185. "Minutes of the Sessions," in ECGenConf], 1966, 34.

186. "Christian Education Committee," in ECGenConf], 1970, 69.

187. "Report of the Sunday School and Keystone League of Christian Endeavor Committee," in ECEPAConf], 1956, 159.

188. "Sunday School and Keystone League of Christian Endeavor Committee," in ECGenConf], 1950, 50–51.

189. "Waldheim School of Methods," UE, September 8, 1959, 10.

190. Edwin S. Woodring, "Twentieth Visit of Dr. Lee to School of Methods, Waldheim," UE, May 17, 1955, 6–8.

191. "Christian Education Society," in ECEPAConf], 1961, 170.

192. "Christian Education Society," in ECEPAConf], 1963, 149.

193. "Christian Education Society," in ECEPAConf], 1964, 169–170.

194. "Sunday School and KLCE Federation Report," in ECWConf], 1956, 78.

195. Paul D. Dunn, "Presiding Elder's Report," in ECWConf], 1959, 62–63.

196. "Camp EccO Report," in ECWConf], 1961, 86.

197. "Sunday School and KLCE Federation Report," in ECWConf], 1950, 57.

198. "Sunday School and KLCE Federation Report," in ECWConf], 1951, 81.

199. Paul D. Gordon, "Presiding Elder's Report," in ECWConf], 1956, 55–56.

200. Paul D. Gordon, "Presiding Elder's Report," in ECWConf], 1958, 45–46.

201. In 1953 the Board of Missions began using a commissioning service for missionaries it supported. Some missionaries who had begun service prior to 1953 were commissioned when they returned home for furlough.

202. "Amendments to the Discipline," in ECEPAConf], 1966, 206.

203. Paul K. Cressman to K. Irene Reiber, March 27, 1967, transcript in the Archives of the Historical Society, Myerstown, PA.

204. "Commissioning Service for Miss Reiber," UE, December 19, 1967, 7.

205. "Personals," UE, February 13, 1968, 10.

206. "Christian Education Report," in ECEPAConf], 1960, 131.

207. "The Christian Education Committee," in ECEPAConf], 1962, 127.

208. "Sunday School and KLCE Committee Report," in ECWConf], 1952, 60.

209. Paul D. Dunn, "District Superintendent's Report," in ECWConf], 1963, 60.

210. "Quiz Team Wins," UE, September 1, 1964, 10.

211. "Best of the East," UE, October 3, 1972, 9.

212. "Report of the Committee on Amendments to the Discipline," in ECGenConf], 1958, 106.

213. "Annual Conference Special Committee on Evangelism," in ECEPAConf], 1960, 134.

214. John A. Smith, "Episcopal Address," in ECEPAConf], 1954, 47–48.

215. "Bulletin of the Evangelical Congregational School of Theology: Announcements for the Session 1953–54," August 15, 1953, 5–6.

216/ "Report of the Committee on Sabbath and Spiritual State of the Church," in ECEPAConf], 1953, 96–98.

217. "Lord's Day and Spiritual State of the Church," in ECEPAConf], 1961,

145.

218. "Lord's Day, Temperance and Spiritual State of the Church Committee," in ECWConfJ, 1960, 66–67.

219. "Lord's Day and Spiritual State of the Church," in ECEPAConfJ, 1963, 127.

220. "Lord's Day and Spiritual State of the Church," in ECEPAConfJ, 1956, 138.

221. Social Action Committee, Special Study," in ECWConfJ, 1966, 92–96.

222. "418–Powers of the Annual Conference," ECDisc, 1994, 106.

223. "Committee on Amendments," in ECGenConfJ, 1966, 93.

224. "The Ways and Means Committee," in ECWConfJ, 1951, 62.

225. "The Report of the Committee on Amendments," in ECGenConfJ, 1958, 106.

226. "Possible Third District Superintendent," in ECEPAConfJ, 1967, 126.

227. "Special Report of the Stationing Committee," in ECEPAConfJ, 1967, 131–140.

228. J. Karl Harper, Herbert D. Wittmaier, "District Superintendents' Reports," in ECEPAConfJ, 1968, 122, 125.

229. "Amendments to the Discipline Committee," in ECWConfJ, 1954, 65.

230. "Official Proceedings," in ECGenConfJ, 1954, 35.

231. "Committee on Ways and Means," in ECGenConfJ, 1942, 60.

232. John A. Smith, "Episcopal Address," in ECGenConfJ, 1954, 54.

233. "Administrative Council," in ECGenConfJ, 1958, 85.

234.. Ibid.

235.. John A. Smith, "Episcopal Address," in ECGenConfJ, 1958, 58-59.

236. AdCoun, October 20, 1958, 2, mimeographed.

237. AdCoun, May 22, 1959, 20, mimeographed.

238. "Extra Mile Crusade," in ECGenConfJ, 1962, 71-75.

239. "Extra Mile Campaign Receipts," in ECGenConfJ, 1966, 71.

240. "Report to the Administrative Council–Emergency Problems at Canton, Ohio," AdCoun, April 30, 1964, 68-74, mimeographed.

241. AdCoun, March 18, 1971, 168, mimeographed.

242. AdCoun, October 7, 1971, 171, mimeographed.

243. AdCoun, March 22, 1973, 197-202, mimeographed.

244. "Committee on Amendments," in ECGenConfJ, 1954, 79.

245. "Report of the Committee on Amendments," in ECGenConfJ, 1958, 94-95.

246. Ibid., 97.

247. Ibid., 89-91.

6

In Search of Evangelical Roots:
Reappraisal, Restructuring, and Advance
(1973–2002)

Overview

A Time of Change

Watergate, "the Year of the Evangelical," the release of US prisoners from Iranian captivity, economic downturns, the demise of Soviet communism, the HIV epidemic and the sexual revolution, greenhouse warming, terrorism, and the 9/11 attack—these are some of the events that engaged America and the world in the period 1973–2002. The Christian church faced a spectrum of issues ranging from legalized abortion and ordination of practicing homosexuals to persecution of foreign missionaries and the teaching of evolution in public schools. The Evangelical Congregational Church did not escape these turbulent times. Like many denominations, it continued to lose members. The peak membership of 30,172 had been reached in 1963; in 2002 the churches reported a total membership of 21,208—a loss of 8,964. Much of this decline could be blamed on demographics. The populations of Pennsylvania, Ohio, and Illinois were declining, and this decline was most severe in the anthracite coal region of Pennsylvania, where many small EC churches were located. Yet, there were also weaknesses in the structure and vision of the church that hampered its witness to the unsaved.

The Board of Missions was most aware of this and asked Christian Service Fellowship (CSF) in 1972 to study how it might increase its effectiveness. CSF declined to undertake the evaluation unless it included the entire denominational structure, so the 1974 General Conference approved the expanded evaluation, and CSF gathered data throughout 1975, monitoring board meetings and church services, visiting denominational institutions, interviewing members, and conducting surveys.

The final report issued in 1976 provided guidelines for restructuring the Administrative Council, revamping the denominational structure inherited from the United Evangelical Church, and ultimately for strengthening the local church.[1] Changes would affect Christian education, church planting initiatives, church leadership, stewardship, church publications, and even denominational property and investments. Those who longed for growth were encouraged.

The Administrative Council adapted the CSF recommendations to nurture growth from mere "maintenance ministry" to outreach ministry. Although some members and congregations hesitated, unsure about change, both the Annual and General Conferences took on a freshness of intent, and frustrations were met with creative thinking and action. Bishop John E. Moyer (1979-1987) took the lead in helping the church through its growing pains.

During the years 1982-1987 organizational change reached down to the local churches, where there was evidence of increased fervor for missions, educational work, and new methods of evangelism. New church buildings, larger budgets, and higher expectations in Christian living marked these years. Bishop Moyer ended his term with a challenge called "Vision 21," a look into the twenty-first century where he envisioned an EC Church enlarging its borders. He called for a return to a fervor for evangelism capable of motivating the church to reach contemporary ethnic cultures, particularly inner-city Hispanics.

Bishop Richard A. Cattermole (1987–1991) did much to continue earlier initiatives, but church planting efforts suffered from inadequate financial support, and lingering losses in membership created a crisis situation early in the administration of Bishop Richard W. Kohl (1991-1999). Kohl's leadership brought results, however, and the decade and century ended with strong ventures toward restoring denominational vitality. Church leaders never lost sight of "Vision 21," and with the election of Michael W. Sigman as Bishop in 1999 a stronger urgency seemed to possess the church. Under his leadership the church developed "Vision 20/20," a comprehensive plan to create "healthy" churches.

The Bishops

Bishop Wittmaier

The death of Bishop Paul K. Cressman on December 18, 1972, saddened the entire church in the midst of its fiftieth-anniversary celebrations. Cressman had been a successful and pastoral leader. A special session of General Conference held at St. Paul's Church in York PA on May

15, 1973, unanimously elected Herbert D. Wittmaier, District Superintendent of the Western District of the East Pennsylvania Conference, as the new leader of the church. This session also approved several changes in the *Discipline* governing succession in office.[2]

Wittmaier had pastored seven churches, including First Church in Reading PA, and taught theology and philosophy at Evangelical (Congregational) School of Theology from 1954 to 1961 while stationed at Plymouth Meeting PA. The tall, angular Wittmaier was known for his pleasant smile and his love of puns. While District Superintendent he sent many warm and caring typewritten letters to the men on his district, always adding personal greetings and a promise to pray for the recipient. Wittmaier completed

Bishop Herbert D. Wittmaier,
(1973–1979)

Cressman's term as Bishop and was elected to a full term, serving from 1973 to 1979. He was assisted by Eastern Conference District Superintendents John Moyer, Karl Harper, and David Heil and Western Conference Superintendents Dr. Paul Dunn, Fred Fink, and Albert E. Anderson. Near the close of his tenure, the issue of church reorganization suggested by Christian Service Fellowship (CSF) and endorsed by the Administrative Council and the General Conference concerned Wittmaier. His forty-eight-year ministry ended as his successor inherited those changes. Wittmaier continued to serve the church as President of the Board of the ECC Retirement Village.

Bishop Moyer

John E. Moyer (1979-1987) had succeeded Wittmaier as District Superintendent after serving four congregations in Pennsylvania and now followed him as Bishop. At the outset of his first term as Bishop Moyer pointed back to Wittmaier as an administrator whose decisions came only after time in Bible study and prayer. That example, and the leadership style of Moyer's former pastor, Bishop Harold H. Scanlin, helped him in his administration. Strength in leadership was needed for the organizational changes suggested by CSF, and Moyer had a fully developed theology of leadership:

> The type of leadership with which I am most comfortable is a shared
> leadership....'Let us love one another for love is of God, and he who
> loves is born of God and knows God' (I John 4:7).[3]

In quoting John, the apostle of
love, John Moyer set the tone for the
decade of the 1980s. Under the CSF
structure the Bishop chaired the
Commission on Evangelism and
Spiritual Care, and naturally as
Bishop he gave this assignment con-
siderable time and effort. Other
administrative duties were carried
out by Administrative Secretary
Richard Cattermole (later Director of
Church   Ministries,   or   DCM),
Director of Missions Duane Ray,
Eastern Conference Superintendents
David C. Greulich and David R.
Wolfe, and Western Conference
Superintendents Paul Dunn and
Robert Zetterberg.

Bishop John E. Moyer, 1979 -1987

At the end of his first term Bishop Moyer felt that the church was "still
struggling with our identity,"[4] but near the end of his tenure in 1986 he
was ready to challenge the church to a new vision, "Vision 21." Based on
responses obtained from clergy and lay delegates, Moyer presented his
"legacy" as Bishop for the twenty-first century by calling for a renewed
commitment from the churches. Vision 21 included four goals: (1) twenty-one new churches, seven of which were to be ethnic; (2) twenty-one
new pastors plus twenty-one more for replacement and expansion; (3)
twenty-one percent increase in average attendance in worship and
Sunday school (from 1986 - 1990); and (4) a twenty-one percent
increase in professions of faith (1986 - 1990).[5] Already, during a seven-
month period in 1985-6, ninety-five visitation/evangelism teams composed of 240 persons made 3,001 contacts as a start of the "new" evangelism.[6] Upon his retirement as Bishop, Moyer undertook further studies at Fuller Theological Seminary (D.Min. 1995) and served as Professor
of Pastoral Ministry at Evangelical School of Theology from 1987 to
1998. There, he trained hundreds of pastors and church workers, inspir-

ing them with his vision of church growth and advancement. He also conducted Church Growth Seminars throughout the conferences of the EC Church.

Bishop Cattermole

To bring "Vision 21" into focus, the church elected Richard A. Cattermole as Bishop (1987-1991). Cattermole grew up in Trinity Church, Royersford PA, and received his Master of Divinity degree from Evangelical School of Theology at Reading PA. He was especially active in camping and Christian Endeavor. Cattermole was selected to head the Board of Missions (1970–1980) and then served as Administrative Secretary and Director of Church Ministries (1980-1986) before his election to the episcopacy. Cattermole's leadership style involved

Bishop Richard A. Cattermole, 1987–1991

> getting into the churches to not only explain what we were doing, but also letting people know that we were available to them…to listen, to respond personally was and is vital. Having traveled ten years and contacting local churches with regard to mission concerns was, for me, the basis of easy contact in the new responsibility. The people began to realize leadership in the denomination was servant leadership, and we tried at every turn to inspire that motive through our communication.[7]

He worked to facilitate the changes CSF had recommended by holding workshops on stewardship and leadership at the local level and gathered teams of church workers. Resistance to change was evident in some places, especially when various organizations were asked to merge their treasuries. The Church Extension Society, Church Builder's Fellowship, Conference Missionary Societies, and the Board of Missions, for example, all had small funds for church planting, none of which was sufficient to undertake major projects. It was only when treasuries were pooled (and one group refused to do so) that effective church planting efforts could be undertaken. As Director of Church Ministries Cattermole accomplished a monumental task in completing the reorganization envisioned by CSF and coordinating and supervising the commissions on which the new structure was based. He utilized persons with expertise and experience who also offered guidance to him in bringing about these changes. His style combined humor, congeniality, and hard work.

Bishop Cattermole's episcopal address to the 1990 General Conference reflected both his vision for church expansion and the financial realities of his term. Introducing a "Decade for Decision," Cattermole said:

> Our accountability is usually based on financial solvency—not to spiritual maturity. This must change so that evangelism and faithful prayer will be engaged in to meet spiritual needs of people in the 90's....The question remains, "How do we reach people with spiritual needs who see the Church as irrelevant, or behind the times?[8]

He praised his mentors, the late Harold H. Scanlin and John E. Moyer. He recounted his travels to almost every EC church in the United States and to twenty-five countries during his twenty-one years as an administrator. He urged the denomination to utilize the Church Information and Development Service (CIDS), which shares demographic information to local churches about the surrounding community to help them know what ministries are needed. "Vision 21" had so far birthed only seven new church plants, and none of these were ethnic congregations. Fifteen additional churches in the 1990s would achieve the goals of the vision. Finally, he organized the Conference into a "committee of the whole" to pray together, think aloud, and work to determine the path the denomination should take in the 1990s. Cattermole was aided in his work by Director of Church Ministries Keith Miller, Director of Missions David Hornberger, and District/Conference Superintendents Richard Zetterberg, David Roof, and Robert M. Daneker, Sr. After his retirement, Bishop Cattermole worked with Director of Church Ministries Keith Miller to help congregations use CIDS research. He continued to advise EC leaders and served as President of International Christian Endeavor.

Bishop Kohl

Bishop Cattermole declined to stand for re-election, and the new vision of the church was reflected in the choice of his successor. Current administrators were passed over in favor of a pastor who had been a successful church planter. Richard W. Kohl, eleventh Bishop of the Evangelical Congregational Church (1991 - 1999), had one favorite question, "What is the name of the last person you introduced to Jesus and when did that happen?"

Bishop Kohl grew up in Zion EC Church of Allentown and was edu-

Bishop Richard W. Kohl, 1991–1999

cated at Moravian College and Seminary with graduate studies at New York University and the University of Kansas. Licensed in 1952, he pastored several EC churches before serving as a U.S. Army Chaplain for twenty years beginning in 1961. Upon his retirement he accepted the challenge of starting an EC church west of Harrisburg PA. Its success marked Kohl as a man who could help the church reach the goals of "Vision 21."

Unfortunately, mounting financial problems due to declining memberships and contributions reached a crisis point early in Kohl's first term. The Eastern Conference cut costs by replacing its two District Superintendents with one Conference Minister, Ronald Miller. Even though he did not have all the duties of the District Superintendents, Miller still had more than 120 churches to serve. Of necessity, Kohl had to add more pastoral duties to his administrative ones. Western Conference also took steps in 1993 to reduce its deficit, and further belt-tightening measures at the General Conference level helped the financial picture. Delinquent churches paid their apportionments, and those who could not afford to received help. It was the change of local church *attitudes*, however, that had the most dramatic and positive impact.[9] Congregations, organizations, and individuals responded to the crisis with increased contributions and matching fund challenges.

Kohl also called for a change in attitude regarding pastors. The supply of candidates for the ministry was dwindling. Kohl attributed this to the decline of Christian Endeavor in the denomination since 1982 and to the way pastoral ministry was presented to young men, but he also blamed the lack of spiritual "life" in many congregations and the harsh criticism of pastors by believers, even though pastors spent long hours caring for congregations while receiving relatively low salaries. Kohl urged pastors to preach on the "call" to ministry while personally guiding and encouraging young men to accept the call, and he called on congregations to develop a supportive environment. Within three years the situation turned around as more young men accepted the call to ministry, many ministers were received from other denominations, and older men began choosing ministry as a "second career." Still, no church failed to receive a pastor during the "dry time." Kohl summarized his term in office as follows:

> Our struggles, new depths of prayer experience, responses, uniting in spirit and focus, changes (temporary and permanent), the faithful following of the leading of the Holy Spirit—are all contributing aspects of what continues to happen within the E.C. Church.[10]

Bishop Sigman

Following Bishop Kohl, the General Conference again elected a successful church planter without denominational administrative experience. The youngest Bishop in the history of the EC Church, Michael W. Sigman, was thirty-six at the time of his election in September 1998. Sigman grew up in Conestoga (PA) EC Church and was led to Christ in Vacation Bible School by Art Davis (later an EC missionary). After serving in youth ministry at two EC churches, Sigman was assigned to a church planting project in Rosedale MD in 1986. The congregation was chartered in 1988 and experienced phenomenal growth under Sigman's strong leadership. Sigman

Bishop Michael W. Sigman, 1999–

writes that the work at Rosedale "forced me into the homes of the unchurched and unsaved thereby cultivating a passion to share my faith and see folks become disciples of Jesus Christ."[11]

Financial concerns also beset Sigman's first year as Bishop, but this time the cause was something beyond the church's control: increased costs of health insurance for pastors and retirees, which increased the expenses of local churches. Moreover, Sigman was charged by the 1998 General Conference to delineate a vision for the future of the church, so that it would be more pro-active rather than re-active in fulfilling its mission. Twenty-six leaders gathered in November, 1999, to begin the discernment process. This gathering named a "Vision 20/20" Task Force including laity, clergy, missionaries, and conference personnel under the leadership of Rev. James Shields. The Task Force gathered and analyzed data on every aspect of the denomination, and Sigman traveled "intensively" seeking "grass roots" involvement and support. A prayer team of more than three hundred intercessors upheld the project! The emphasis on planting new churches was replaced by a desire to make existing churches "healthy." Vision 20/20 emphasized five core values: passion for Christ, compassion for the lost, servant leadership, healthy ministries, and unity in the Body of Christ. It gave the Evangelical Congregational Church a statement of purpose (To know Christ and to make him known) and a statement of mission (To raise up healthy churches proclaiming Christ to a hurting world). [12]

Sigman was a student of history; he believed that the study of history was "critical to effectively lead the church seeking to embrace the future." [13] He looked to the future, however, even more than the past. As he is "Mission driven," he set "mission" as the church's future goal. A "Basis of Union" forged by the Committee became the "compass" for twenty-first century ECs. It proposed "[a] united denomination that concentrates on building strong partnerships among churches ...a truly mission-driven movement of God." [14] and was quickly approved by both Annual Conferences. Sigman also led the development of a Pastoral Assessment Center in 2002 to enhance leadership recruitment and increase pastoral standards. His goal was a church with a new vision.

Denominational Activities

Publishing

The 1970s and 1980s were not good years for denominational publications. Visual media like television were supplanting print media, while the cost of printing was skyrocketing. The Board of Publication tried to keep *The United Evangelical* viable after the Church Center Press print shop was closed. Color printing was introduced in 1974, and the editorial staff was cut to one editor, David Reed, plus minimally paid contributing editors. Frequency was cut from biweekly to monthly in 1977. Kids Korner and Youth Outreach pages were added in an attempt to draw younger readers. Joint publishing with the Federation editors of the *Primitive Methodist Journal* and *The United Brethren* magazine produced a "Triventure" quarterly, which survived from 1977 to 1982. [15] The first computer-generated issue appeared in 1983. Still, the circulation of *The*

United Evangelical dropped from 4,736 readers in 1973 to half of that in 1983. Under the reorganization mandated by the Christian Service Fellowship Report a Publication Services Commission of the Administrative Council was responsible for printing and selling materials for the denomination. The refurbished Church Center in Myerstown that opened on July 12, 1976, contained an expanded bookstore operated by Martha Metz and Stanley Heimbach, but the store was never profitable and had to be subsidized by the Division of Missions, the Retirement Village, and the Eastern Branch of the Adult Missionary Society.

Finally, in September 1989, with subscribers continuing to dwindle, *The United Evangelical* was replaced by *E.C. Doors and Windows*, a newsletter distributed without charge to EC congregations.[16] In the early 1990s various pastors prepared issues of *Doors and Windows*, and beginning in 1996 Carol Kline coordinated a staff of pastors and laity who contributed to the issues. The number of copies increased from 8,000 to 17,000, but in 2000 this was replaced by an e-magazine called *ConnECtions*.

Of course, the various administrative divisions, church camps, and ECC Retirement Village continued to produce a steady stream of pamphlets, newsletters, brochures, bulletin inserts, and other publications. Evangelical School of Theology began a scholarly journal, *Evangelical Journal*, in 1983 under the editorship of Dr. William Sailer. Rev. Richard D. Miles produced a *Church Directory: Eastern Conference of the Evangelical Congregational Church* (283 p.) in 1989 that provided a brief history, list of pastors, illustration, location, and historical statistics for each congregation in the Eastern Conference.

Yet, denominational headquarters persevered in its conversion from communication by print to communication via Internet. By 2002 the primary source for information about the church was the website http://www.eccenter.com. This site contains news about the denomination and its divisions. Division-sponsored publications, such as *Heartcry* and *Windows on the World*, can be downloaded for distribution to the local congregation. Local churches linked to it can publicize their worship, youth and special events.

Church Home

The early 1970s saw a transformation of the Burd and Rogers Home in Myerstown. The old Infirmary no longer met changing state regulations, and at the forty-seventh Home Anniversary on June 17, 1972, ground was broken for a four-story Health Care Center, which was named for Bishop C. H. Mengel. Construction on a new Central Kitchen began on December 22, 1972. Then, historic Mohn Hall, the main residential building, was condemned, and the Home (now renamed the Evangelical Congregational Church Retirement Village) began construction of the seventy-bed David S. Warfel Personal Care Center, which was dedicated on Anniversary Day, June 14, 1975. When the dust settled, the E.C.C.R.V. had a capacity of 203 beds and a debt of $8,000,000.[17]

The Village Auxiliary was formed in 1974 to promote and coordinate volunteer aid to E.C.C.R.V. and to raise funds for special projects like a transportation van and video equipment for transmitting worship services to the guests' rooms.[18] Anniversary Day became the annual Bazaar, and a year-end recognition banquet honored volunteers from EC congregations and the community. By the end of the decade volunteers were clocking more than 10,000 hours of service per year.

Rev. Franklin H. Schock succeeded Rev. Russell Wise as Superintendent in 1977. Rev. Clarence C. Reeder served as chaplain until 1982, when Rev. David Reed took the position, and Floyd Leonard was the Director of Financial Services. In 1979 the Trustee Board changed its Charter and By-laws to allow the 1982 General Conference to elect a majority of the Board of Trustees, thus making the Village a bona fide denominational institution for the first time. Ten additional trustees were selected by the Board, five of which were to be chosen from the denomination. The Executive Director (formerly Superintendent) was also made a Board member.

The Village began the 1980s with an evaluation by Health Care Resources, Inc. Federal and state assistance funds were drying up, and the changes in organizational and administrative structure recommended in the evaluation produced needed savings. Additional savings came from more efficient heating, cooling, and kitchen equipment. The Village hired a Director of Community Affairs, John McKillop, in an attempt to gain greater visibility in the donor community and seek broader public support. Increased contributions from the annual Mother's Day offering helped the financial picture, and the annual Life Care Fund increased every year. Yet, the Village resisted the temptation to raise its fees; daily rates in 1982, for example, were only $27, $46, and $57 respectively for residential, personal, and health care.

Unfortunately, Pennsylvania state regulations continued to create new challenges. New regulations in 1983 made it harder for people to qualify for health care in nursing facilities, and the Village suffered a 9 % loss in reimbursements when the state unilaterally reclassified many in-house patients from "skilled" to "intermediate" level of care to lower their state assistance payments. Private assets of over one hundred residents ran out before their health care needs, and the Village assumed responsibility for raising the money to pay for their care. The Auxiliary continued to provide funds for sewing machines, large print books, and draperies for residents' rooms, and in 1986 the Life Care Fund reached $137,00 (up from $66,000 in 1981), but federal funding continued to decline.[19] The new Alzheimer care unit was established in 1985 for people with special needs, but this also added to expenses. Then, the Village had to face a costly ($238,000) lawsuit brought by some residents over the terms of their long-term care agreements. The Village replaced its daily fee structure with a "pay as you go" policy for residents, while the $8,000,000 debt was amortized during this time.

The Village staff provided therapy, craft work, inspirational meetings, personal grooming services, and recreation for hundreds of people, but it was hampered by its constricted half-block site from providing what seniors with greater incomes were looking for: apartments, spacious cottages, state-of-the-art health care, and recreational amenities. The Village purchased a sixty-five-acre site on a major highway outside of Myerstown and drew up plans for the Cross Timbers community. Construction was planned for the Fall of 1990, but the project never generated sufficient response, and it was dropped, resulting in additional losses to the Village.

Rev. Bruce Hill assumed the position of Executive Director in 1995. His first quadrennial report in 1998 told of the complex nature of running an institution from which government demanded ever more but provided less. The Village had become even more dependent on the gifts of private supporters. Still, it was debt-free, with 90 % of every dollar being used for "program services" and only 10 % for administration. An ElderCare program was launched to assist elderly ECers in their own communities outside Myerstown through information and "hands on" help for seniors. [20]

Then, in 2000 the Village got the opportunity to realize many of its goals. An up-to-date retirement community in Myerstown became available for purchase at a bankruptcy sale, and the Village was able to buy the fifteen-acre campus with 31 cottages, 150 apartments, a 60-bed skilled nursing area, 30 assisted living suites, and large common areas for $8,355,750.[21] The StoneRidge campus was dedicated at the Village's

Seventy-fifth Anniversary celebration in August 2000. The former properties of the Village became the Albright Campus of E.C.C.R.V. By 2002, 3,654 volunteers were putting in over 14,000 hours at the two facilities. Even though the Mother's Day offerings decreased, the Benevolent Care Fund reached over $120,000. Five hundred staff members provide care for five hundred seniors.

Church Extension

Church Planting in the 1970s

In the early 1970s starting a new church was a complex procedure in the Evangelical Congregational Church, involving several separate agencies with overlapping jurisdictions. District Survey Committees within the East Pennsylvania Conference Missionary Society tried to find target areas for new churches. The Church Builders' Fellowship operating under the East Pennsylvania Conference solicited money for the new churches and the relocation of established churches. The Board of Church Extension and the Eastern and Western Conference Societies of Church Extension made interest-free loans to new churches and churches engaged in renovations or building projects. The Western Conference received some funds through a Church Extension Offering and the Inner Mission Committee of the Conference attempted to identify potential areas for new church starts. Anyone hoping to plant a new church had to approach each of these groups separately for assistance. The Church Extension Committee of the 1966 General Conference had urged a cooperative effort to bring an expanded home mission program under the Board of Missions. The 1970 General Conference instructed the Boards of Church Extension and Missions to provide "a more adequate home missions emphasis concerning the establishment of new churches as well as assisting in relocating churches."[22] The two boards studied the possibility of coordinating the work, but failed to take any action.

The 1974 General Conference tried to coordinate church planting under the denominational Board of Church Extension by inserting in its charter the statement that the Board was "to initiate and to engage in church planting in conjunction with other responsible agencies of our conference."[23] The next year the Council of Church Expansion was organized to bring together representatives of the Annual and General Conference groups involved in starting new churches. Fundamental change, however, came in 1978, when the General Conference received a report from the Administrative Policy Committee detailing a new organizational structure for the church. Under this structure the EC Administrative Secretary chaired a Church Planting Committee within the Division of Church Ministry, and the General Conference Administrative Council established guidelines for the initiation of a new work, the length and extent of financial assistance to it, and the procedure for chartering the church. The groundwork was laid for successful church planting.

Four new churches had been launched prior to the establishment of the Church Planting Committee, two in the Eastern Conference and two in the Western Conference. Crestwood Village EC had its origins when Richard E. Kern, pastor of the Pine Beach NJ church, saw a potential for ministry in a new retirement community composed of three thousand homes not far from his church. The 1973 Eastern Conference sent Milton E. Detterline, Sr. (1904-1989) to start a church in Crestwood Village, the church was chartered in 1975 with an average attendance of eighty,[24] and a church building was dedicated in 1976.[25] The EC Church in Winter Springs FL was launched in 1978 by the Council on Church Expansion under the pastoral leadership of Robert E. Burns. One year later the congregation was chartered with an initial membership of twenty-five.[26] Property was purchased in September 1979, and the house on the property was renovated to serve as a place of worship. After a period of growth the church stagnated, however, and was not able to provide full pastoral support. In 1993 the congregation voted to disaffiliate with the Evangelical Congregational Church and became a part of the United Brethren in Christ Church.[27] The Seneca (PA) EC

Trinity EC Church, Seneca, PA, constructed 1975

Evangelical Fellowship, Winnebago, IL

Church began when a group of laypersons meeting for Bible study and prayer requested affiliation with the Western Conference in 1974.[28] The Stationing Committee assigned John C. Ward as pastor of the new congregation, and a year later the church was organized with a charter membership of thirty-one. Two laymen from the church donated a parcel of land, and a new building was dedicated on February 29, 1976. Finally, the Winebago (IL) EC Church began as an extension ministry of the Afolkey IL church. Duane M. Ray served as pastor of both congregations starting in 1976 until the Winnebago Church was received into the Western Conference three years later with a charter membership of sixteen. Ray continued as the pastor of the new church. The first phase of a building program was begun in 1987 and dedicated in June 1988.

Reaching Out in the 1980s

When the Church Planting Committee under the restructured church began to meet in early 1980, the Committee assumed the supervision of the Florida church and began to lay plans for opening other churches. A survey indicated substantial potential in Dallastown PA, and the Committee initiated a Sunday school there in June of 1980. A year later, the Eastern Conference assigned Sterling I. Trimmer as the first pastor of the congregation, and the Arlington Evangelical Congregational Church was chartered in 1982 with an initial membership of twenty-two. The infant congregation moved from a room in the Arlington Plaza to the Community Building in Red Lion. By March 1990 the first phase of an extensive building program was completed and the congregation continued to experience encouraging growth. One year later the church dedicated a newly constructed educational unit.

In 1981 the Eastern Conference attempted a church plant on the west shore of the Susquehanna River across from Harrisburg PA. The Evangelical Congregational churches in the Harrisburg provided significant support to the project led by Chaplain Richard W. Kohl, who had retired from military service in August 1981 and was able to devote himself fulltime to church planting. The new congregation met in the Villa Leo Motel each Sunday morning for the next seven years. One year after its launch, the West Shore congregation was received into the Eastern Conference with fifty-seven members. The church, now under the name of Wyndamere Heights Evangelical Congregational Church, dedicated its new church building in May 1987 with more than 360 persons attending the service.[29]

The next opportunity for church planting came when Scott Shaffer, a United Methodist pastor in western Pennsylvania, applied for admission into the Western Conference in early 1982. With the approval of the Bishop and Conference Superintendent and under the supervision of the Administrative Secretary, Pastor Shaffer held Sunday worship services in a motel near Clark PA. At the next session of the Western Conference the Shenango Valley Evangelical Congregational Church was received into the conference with a membership of thirty-nine.[30] In January 1983 the renamed Lakeside Evangelical Congregational Church dedicated a newly constructed sanctuary.[31]

Also in 1982 the Eastern Conference authorized the start of a new church in Pottstown PA composed of the remnants of the Greater Pottstown Community Church that had filed for bankruptcy and closed.[32] Dr. James D. Yoder provided pastoral leadership to a group of forty attendees. The new Pottstown congregation, St. Andrews Evangelical Congregational Church, was received into the Eastern Conference in 1986 with twenty-six charter members. That year the Conference assigned Lewis H. Bollinger as the church's first full time pastor, but in spite of extensive efforts by the leaders of the church and conference, the congregation failed to experience adequate growth, and in 1993 the members petitioned the Conference to discontinue the work.

Meanwhile, in October 1983 the young Lakeside congregation began an extension ministry at the nearby community of Hadley PA. Kenneth Shaffer, brother of the Lakeside pastor, was assigned to serve the church plant in 1984. One year later the newly established congregation of Countryside Evangelical Congregational Church moved into a new church building and was received into the Western Conference with a charter membership of fifty-nine.

The church seized another opportunity in 1986, when the Rosedale Community Church northeast of Baltimore MD asked the Eastern Conference for assistance. Michael W. Sigman was assigned to provide leadership to the congregation,[33] and in June 1988 the church was received into the conference. By 1998 the Rosedale Evangelical Congregational Church had grown to a membership of 219 with an average morning worship attendance of 243.

The EC church in Shrewsbury PA began in 1981 as an extension of the ministry of St. David's Church in Weigelstown PA. Frank E. Miller, a layperson from Weigelstown, led a Bible study early in the year and at the sessions of the Eastern Conference he was licensed to preach and assigned as pastor. In March 1989 the church held its first worship service in a renovated machine shop. One hundred, ninety-eight persons attended this initial service. The congregation was received into the conference in 1992 with a membership of twenty-two.

The Clarion PA church began when the 1990 session of Western Conference sent Maurice Friedlund to start a church there. The first service was held in November of that year, and at the next session of the Western Conference the new congregation was received with a membership of forty-eight. In December 1993 the congregation moved into the newly renovated facility it had purchased.

Consolidation and Advances in the 1990s

The 1980s had been good years for church planting, but at this point further efforts had to be curtailed until additional sources of funding could be secured. Up until this time financial support had come from the annual Church Builders Fellowship Offering in February and the Church Planting Partners program in which individuals contributed $100 a year to the church expansion effort. The Annual Conferences also assigned a portion of the proceeds received from the sale of closed churches to church planting. When the new church thrust began in 1980 the Church Planting Committee agreed to provide full funding for each new project in its first year, with a reduction of twenty per cent per year until the church became self-supporting in the sixth year. As the number of new works increased, this commitment placed a heavy financial burden on the program, and by 1992 the church-planting program faced a deficit of $200,000.

A generous response to the Church Builders Fellowship appeal, receipts from the Vacation Bible School Missions Offering, and a substantial contribution from the Western Conference reduced the shortfall to $70,000 by 1994, and the 1994 General Conference did its part by redirecting the annual World Wide Missionary Offering to church planting. As a long-term solution, the Church Planting Committee revised its financial policies to reduce subsidies for each new project and also began to use bi-vocational church planters. By 1995 the deficit was erased.

While struggling to clear its debt, the leaders of the Church had received appeals for pastoral assistance from a group of Christians in Wilmington DE. Dr. Cattermole provided the necessary pastoral care until the Eastern Conference convened in 1994 and assigned Rev. F. Kenneth Hoffer to this project. A year later Rev. Leslie D. Cool assumed the leadership of the new work, and the infant congregation moved to rented facilities near Newark DE. Although this mission experienced initial losses resulting from a change in ministry focus, the newly named Hope Community Church welcomed new converts and started to grow again. At the first session of the newly restructured National Conference in 2003 the Newark Hope Community Church was received as a chartered member with fifty-four members.[34]

Another Hope Community Church held its first public worship service on Easter Sunday 1995 in rented facilities west of Allentown PA. This church was the vision of Rev. Robert M. Daneker, Sr., and a core of approximately twenty members of Evangelical Congregational churches in the Allentown area. The congregation initially worshipped in one of the buildings on the Penn State-Allentown campus, but in 1997 Hope community Church united with the Eastern Conference with a membership of fifty-one, and eleven acres of land were purchased for a building.

In Lancaster PA Grace Evangelical Congregational Church, already the mother church of Lancaster Trinity and Lancaster Faith churches, lent its support to the forming of another EC church when a group of its members began holding services in a former antique car museum in Willow Street, a town south of Lancaster city, in August 1995. By the spring of 1996 attendances had reached 140, and the new congregation petitioned the Eastern Conference to be received as a member church.

Wilmer R. Martin, while pastor of Grace Church, was instrumental in establishing the new work, and he assumed the pastoral supervision at the 1996 Eastern Conference.

Soon afterward, St. David's EC Church in Weigelstown helped launch another church when in June 1997 Rev. Richard Christman and his wife Shirley opened their home in East Berlin PA to public worship services. The infant congregation quickly outgrew the basement of the Christman home and began meeting in their renovated garage. In July 1998 the Countryside Evangelical Congregational Fellowship purchased a facility to house its growing congregation, and two years later, when the Eastern Conference received this congregation, the charter membership stood at fifty.

Finally, Paul and Linda Miller, at the direction of the Church Planting Committee, launched a new work in the Bushkill area of Pennsylvania in October 2001.[35] The new congregation experienced significant growth and was received into the National Conference in 2003 with the charter membership of forty-four.

Urban Churches and Ethnic Ministries

From its beginning the Evangelical Congregational Church was a denomination with strong and influential city churches. In the peak year of 1963 it had forty city congregations with a total membership of 11,140, or 37 % of the entire church. By 2003, however, the number of city churches had dropped to twenty-one with a membership of 3,532, only 17 % of the denomination's membership. This, of course, was the result of the massive movement of the white middle classes from cities to suburbs. Yet, the denomination and the city congregations themselves did make attempts to reach out to the new ethnic populations that now surrounded their monumental urban churches.

In 1975 the Board of Missions launched ECCO (Evangelical Congregational Community Outreach) in cooperation with the churches in Reading PA. An EC missionary, Edmund J. Reitz, attempted to provide church members with opportunities to minister to the residents of inner-city Reading.[36] This initiative was short-lived, but the need was not forgotten. In the early 1980s a fellowship of Christians known as "Servants of the Great I Am" began meeting in Grace Evangelical Congregational Church in Reading. The Mohn's Hill EC Church located outside of Reading saw an opportunity to partner with city residents to evangelize the Latino population surrounding Grace Church. Two local pastors from Mohn's Hill, Alton A. Hoffman and Carl H. Fisher, moved into the neighborhood with their families and began an outreach ministry. The ministry continued after Grace Church closed in 1984[37] but was discontinued by 1990, and the former Grace Church building was sold.[38]

The Kimball Avenue Evangelical Congregational Church in Chicago IL had a long history of direct involvement in ministry to the residents of Logan Square, the neighborhood in which the church is located. In 1990 Jane Heck, an EC missionary, began an after-school program for children in the area of the church. Known as the Christian Care Center, this state-licensed program secured funding from the community and from other churches[39] and for the next eleven years effectively served the children and families of the Logan Square as a ministry of the church. Today, it is a non-denominational family assistance agency with a mission "to holistically address the spiritual needs of children and families."[40]

In Allentown PA a Syrian native named Ghosoub Al-Khal was actively involved in a ministry to the poor and homeless based at Bethany EC Church. He felt a deep concern for the Arabic-speaking community of the Lehigh Valley and in 1997 asked the Committee for approval to plant an Arabic church. Al-Khal was licensed to preach by the Eastern Conference and began holding services in St. John's Evangelical Congregational Church in Allentown in August 1998. A year later, the congregation moved into the building formerly occupied by Olivet Evangelical Congregational Church in Bethlehem PA. Attendances had grown to 110 when in 2001 the Arabic Living Evangelical Congregational Church was received into the Eastern Conference.[41]

Additional ethnic congregations grew out of the "Project Samaria" launched by the Division of Missions in 1995. (A more complete description of this effort can be found under "Missions" later in this chapter.) This effort has been successful in planting urban churches, especially among Hispanics, in several cities in Pennsylvania and Illinois.

New Directions

Many factors influence the success of church planting efforts. Adequate support by a denomination and established congregations, in terms of money and personnel, is important. Adequate planning and preparation help too, but the commitment and capabilities of the church planting leaders can be crucial. The Church Planting Committee realized that one of its crucial tasks was the evaluation of the ministry skills of potential church planters. In 1995 the Committee began using

Church Planting Assessment Centers as a guide to determine the call of candidates. The first Center held in the spring of 1995 was jointly sponsored by the Mission Northeast of the Free Methodist Church and the Evangelical Congregational Church. In the years that followed numerous Assessment Centers have been successfully used in preparation for new churches. The three-day Assessment Center places the candidate and spouse in a variety of settings, which provide some indication of future effectiveness in church planting. Participants who receive a "green light" are then sent to a church planting boot camp along with a coach for intensive training before the new church is launched.

The Church Planting Committee under the leadership of Keith Miller also began to look at older churches that were no longer healthy and in 2001 initiated a "restart" program designed to restore failing ministries. As Bishop Sigman put it, "Restarting a church means that the old methods and structures pass away and the church begins a new life with a church planting–plus pastor and an aggressive plan for evangelistic outreach to the community."[42] A congregation suffering serious financial and attendance problems could be disbanded and a new pastor who was dedicated to a new approach and specially trained in church planting assigned to build a new congregation in the church building. The first two restarts were New Bethany Church, a multicultural ministry to inner-city Allentown PA with Ghosoub Al-Khal as pastor, and Living Hope Lighthouse, a vibrant ministry in the former home of Trinity Church in Palmerton with Nathan Fry as pastor.

Between 1974 and 2002 twenty-four church planting projects were successfully launched. Eighteen became chartered churches within the Annual Conferences, and the other six were discontinued.[43] Church leadership also took an active role in closing or merging non-viable churches. The following Eastern Conference churches, all in Pennsylvania, were closed during this period: Clark's Valley Grace (1973), Harrisburg Sixth Street (1973), Lebanon Grace (1978), Cetronia, (1979), Pottstown Greater Community (1982), Pillow (1982), Richland (1983), Reading Grace (1984), Newmanstown (1987), Reading Greenmont (1988), Barry (1991), Pottstown St. Andrew's (1993), Egypt (1994), Palmerton (2000), and Allentown Bethany (2001). The Wiconisco and Dayton churches in Pennsylvania merged in 1992 to form William's Valley Faith Church. Three Reading PA churches (Trinity, St. Paul's, and Bethany) merged in 1995 to become the Reading Community Evangelical Church. One year later the Berrysburg (PA) and Gratz (PA) congregations merged. In 1999 the Trappe congregation combined with Zieglerville and the two Bethlehem PA congregations, Olivet and Emmanuel, merged.[44] The churches in Pine Swamp PA (1983), Pine Beach NJ (1988), Winter Springs FL (1993), Dauphin PA (1997), and Locust Dale PA (1999) disaffiliated with the Evangelical Congregational Church. The Clarksburg WV church was transferred to the Western Conference in 1975, but a year later this congregation disaffiliated with the Evangelical Congregational church.[45] Five Western Conference churches closed during this period: Willow Springs IL (1986), Hubbard OH (1988), Turkeyfoot OH (1991), Mansfield OH (1994), and Norwood Heights IL (1997). Two of the Akron OH churches, Airport Chapel and Chapel Hill, merged to form United Evangelical Congregational Church in 1988.

Missions

The Board and Division of Missions

Richard Cattermole's years as Secretary of the Board of Missions (1970 to 1980) saw many new ventures. The Board of Missions joined the Evangelical Foreign Missions Association and took on the commitment of guaranteeing support to all approved EC missionaries if they were not able to raise sufficient support on their own, a commitment unique to the Evangelical Congregational Church. Missionaries were accepted into the pension and hospitalization plan of the denomination in 1978.[46] A missions newsletter "It's Happening Now" joined *The United Evangelical* in spreading the missionary cause. Cattermole also produced a brochure entitled "Qualifications and Preparation of Missionary Candidates," containing EC "doctrinal convictions" along with "desirable character traits" for applicants. The first denominationally-advertised tours of missions for EC laypeople visited the work of the Masudas in Japan and the new Liberian Conference, and lay work teams built a parsonage and church at the Canyon Falls KY mission. The Missions Office was moved to the new EC Church Center in Myerstown in 1976, and the proceeds from the sale of the Shillington missions property were put into a fund to help missionaries on furlough meet their housing needs. A program was inaugurated for joint support of missionaries by the Federation of the Evangelical Congregational Church, the Church of the United Brethren in Christ, and the Primitive Methodist Church.[47]

During this time EC missionaries spread to the far corners of the world. Wycliffe translators John and Carolyn Miller, working among the Bru people in Vietnam, received national attention when they were captured by the Viet Cong. They were treated well in the POW camp and released in 1975. Their ordeal became the basis of a best-selling book, *Captured*, published by Word Books in 1978.[48] A "Project Philip" fund to purchase Bibles for India, in conjunction with the World Home Bible League, collected more than $145,000.

In 1979 the Board of Missions became the Division of Missions, and Rev. Duane Ray succeeded Cattermole as Secretary in 1980, becoming Director in 1982. Ray was a successful pastor from Winnebago IL who had served at the Canyon Falls KY mission for thirteen years. His first project was directing one of the largest EC work teams ever assembled, forty men and women from all parts of the denomination, in building Faith EC Church in Edinburg TX. In fact, the 1980s saw a stream of "short term" workers visit EC mission projects and conferences. In 1982 Ray could report that EC missionaries were serving in more than forty areas of the world under twenty inter-denominational agencies, but he challenged the 1982 General Conference to develop urban ministries and support work with unreached people groups, and he challenged local churches to become involved with EC missionaries on a personal level.[49] The missions newsletter was still being published under the title "It's Happening," but Ray also began distributing tape-recorded "Monthly Missions Moments" to better communicate with local congregations. Like Cattermole, Ray and Bishop Moyer visited missions conferences regularly. In 1983, for example, Moyer and Ray visited Japan, India, and Liberia and in 1984 Mexico, Japan, and India.

Ray's call for urban missions was answered by Joe and Wendy Toy, who worked briefly in Reading PA before affiliating with Open Air Campaigners in Philadelphia in 1987. Rev. Eugene Madeira, assisted financially by Grace Church in Lancaster PA, worked with Spanish-speaking people in that city, but neither of these efforts led to establishing congregations. Contact with unreached peoples (cultural groups of which fewer than 20 % have any understanding of the Gospel) began in 1984, when Art and Mary Ellen Davis began work with the Pokot people of northern Kenya. The whole denomination got involved with Pokot project, cooperating with Africa Inland Mission to raise funds to drill wells in that arid region. Perhaps Ray summarized this vital period in EC missions best when he wrote,

> Appropriately this quadrennium closes with the theme adopted by the denomination—Exalting Christ Through the Church in World Outreach....All are lost apart from the life Jesus Christ imparts by faith. That is why outreach is the premier challenge in every generation.[50]

Ray was succeeded as Director of Missions in 1988 by Rev. David Hornberger. Pastor Hornberger and his wife had served fifteen years in Kenya, and he had written "Nature-ally Speaking" mission articles for *The United Evangelical*. He had also worked as Africa Inland Mission's Director of U. S. Ministries. Hornberger's first challenge was financial; computerization expenses and the increasing cost of guaranteeing support to all EC missionaries had left the Division of Missions with a large deficit. The Director addressed the immediate problem through intensive fundraising, leaving more managerial tasks to his Administrative Assistant, Patricia Strain. He addressed long-term problems by encouraging EC missionaries to work directly with the EC Division of Missions, instead of specialized mission boards, and by requiring EC missionaries to have three months of support on deposit with the Division of Missions and the remainder of their support pledged before leaving for the mission field. The Canyon Falls KY church was told that its mission support would be ending. By the end of 1989 the financial deficit was erased.

Hornberger suffered a heart attack in 1991, and though he returned to work, continuing health problems required an emergency leave of absence in 1993 and his resignation in 1994. During his tenure the Division approved its first "non-resident missionaries," and opened up new EC missions in Belize and the Caribbean. Hornberger was succeeded by Dr. John Ragsdale (1994 - 2005), former missionary to Africa, professor, President of United Wesleyan College, and Vice President for Development at Evangelical School of Theology. Dr. Ragsdale began with a vision for missions to foreign nationals resident in cities with EC churches; he called this "Project Samaria."[51] As Jacob Albright had reached out to German Americans, Duane and Mary Ray were reaching out to Hispanic Americans. Eventually, Latino congregations were started in Lancaster PA, Myerstown PA, Allentown PA, Reading PA, York PA, Hazleton PA, and Highland Park IL. The Administrative Council approved the concept of a North American Mission Conference for these congregations in 1995. Ragsdale also developed a concept he called TEACH International to bring together leaders of all foreign mission conferences and representatives from major cooperating mission boards for a two-day convention to be held in conjunction with General Conference sessions. In addition, Ragsdale reorganized the committee structure of the Division and developed a Missionary Retreat at Twin Pines Camp in 1995 to bring EC missionaries together. The quarterly missions newsletter *E.C. World Outreach* was renamed *Window on the*

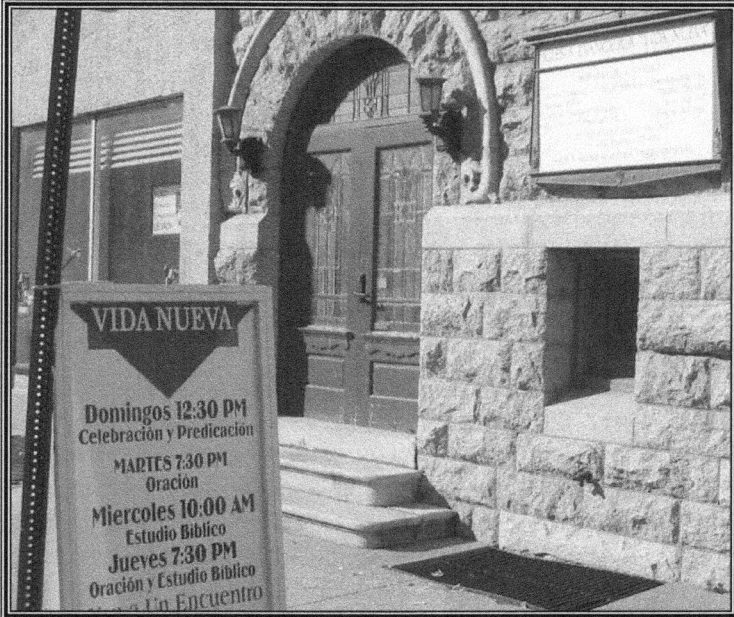

First EC Church, Reading PA.
Our Latino congregation meets in this historic downtown church

World, and a monthly newsletter and prayer guide called *E.C. Scene* began in 1995. A new EC mission field was started in 1995 in Costa Rica, when Rev. Luis Lluberes, a member of Seibert EC Church in Allentown PA, returned to his native land to plant churches. By 1999, when they were organized as the newest EC missions conference, there were fifteen churches and four hundred members in Costa Rica.

In 1998 Dr. Ragsdale requested that the offices of Director and Chairman of the Division of Missions be separated, and Rev. Ralph Owens assumed the position of Chairman in 2000. The missions office moved into new quarters on the third floor of the refurbished Church Center building in 2001. By 2002 the Evangelical Congregational Church was supporting seventy-five active missionaries in seventeen countries. The Division of Missions received almost $2,000,000 that year to spread the *Evangel* in the United States and around the world. Long-term missionaries continue to receive support, and work teams continue to provide short-term mission opportunities for many in the EC Church.

Adult Missionary Fellowship

The Eastern and Western Branches of the newly expanded Adult Missionary Fellowship remained a driving force behind the missionary activities of the church. Their area representatives provided vital links between missionaries, local churches, and the Branches. The Branches also provided program materials for Vacation Bible Schools and Youth for Missions groups (formerly YPMS), who studied about and raised funds for different projects each year: 1978-Mexico, 1979-Europe, 1980-Alaska, 1981-South America, 1982-Edinburg TX (van), 1984-Kenya (autoclave), 1985-Mexico (minivan), 1986-European Christian Mission (radio transmitter), 1987-Honduras (plane).

In 1984 the Eastern Branch organized the first EC Festival of Mission on the Myerstown campuses of the Church Center, the School of Theology, and the Retirement Village. The Festival was designed to showcase not only missions but all the various ministries of the EC Church and bring people from all over the denomination together at Church Center as Field Days had done in the 1930s. Probably the best-attended gathering of the denomination in EC history, the Festival provided entertainment, inspiration, food, and fellowship. Similar Festivals of Mission were held in 1988, 1992, 1996, and 2001.

Annual mission society dues remained the same as they had been for 150 years ($2.00), but other things were changing. Men were gradually becoming integrated into the organization. In 1999, at Dr. Ragsdale's suggestion, the Branches became the Eastern and Western Committees on Missions, and in 2000 the Eastern Committee elected its first male president. Branch Presidents during the period were: Eastern — Mary Brandt (1974-1979), Mary Good (1979-1991), Betty Hughes (1991-2000), and Norman Harner, ECOM (2000-); Western — Norma Carr (1974-1982), Helen Theobald (1982-1990), Dorothy Bissenden (1990-1995), Ann Brown (1995-).

Mission Conferences

Liberia

The first Mission Conference (1973) suffered from the years of civil war in Liberia that destroyed churches and schools, uprooted congregations, and prevented communication with American church leaders. Rev. Jacob Higgins was elected "Bishop" of the church during a peaceful interlude in 1996 and reported a membership of nearly 9000 in 1998, but in December 1998 Higgins was found guilty of misappropriation of church funds. The Division of Missions revoked his status as an EC missionary, and the Liberia Conference deposed him from office. A new Field Superintendent, Matthew Gueh, was elected. In 2000 the Conference commissioned a minister to Liberian expatriates living in Ghana.[52]

Latin American

The Mexico Mission Conference became the Latin American Mission Conference in 1980 when the first church on the American side of the border (Edinburg TX) was built. By 1986 eleven churches were reporting an attendance of 555 in Sunday School and 467 in Evening Service, but Dr. Ragsdale on his first visit to Mexico in 1995 expressed concern about the lack of outreach or movement toward self-support. He proposed a ten year plan in 1998 that was not received with great enthusiasm to end dependence on missionary support. On the other hand, two new church planting projects were started in Monterrey, Mexico, and one among Mexican immigrants in south Texas.[53]

Japan

The Kyodo Grace Church under Rev. John Masuda dates from 1974. In 1983 it declared its intention to become an EC church, and the next year the Japan Conference was organized with Masuda as Field Superintendent. At that time his wife, Machi, was ordained a deacon at his request, becoming the first women to receive ordination in the Evangelical Congregational Church. A second church was organized at Machida in 1985 and relocated to Sagamihara in 1997.[54]

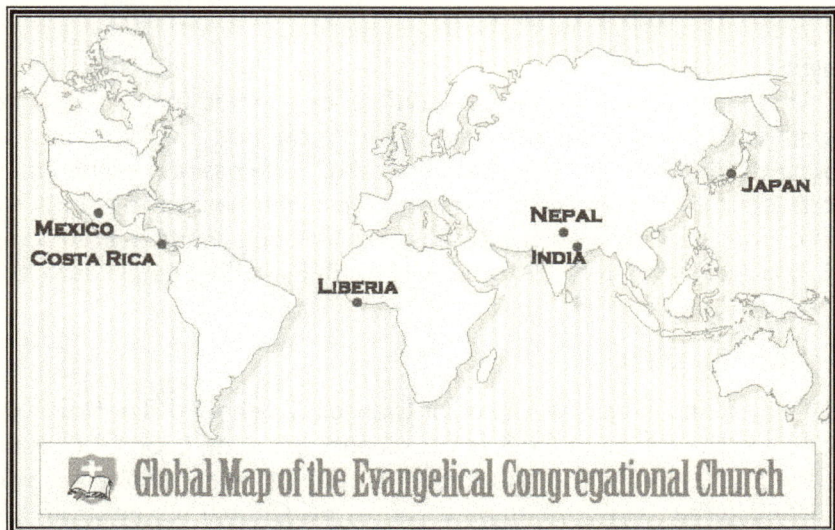

Global Map of the Evangelical Congregational Church

India

By the 1980s all the U. S. board members and the chairman of the Northeast India General Mission Board were members of the Evangelical Congregational Church and 90 % of its funding was coming from EC sources. In 1984 John Moyer and Duane Ray went to India to propose merger with the EC Church. The Evangelical Congregational Church of India was formally established in September 1986, becoming the fourth EC Mission Conference. Unfortunately, the same attitude of dependence that Ragsdale found on his first visits to other Mission Conferences was evident in India. When he replaced specific contributions with a single block grant and announced a fifteen-year plan to phase out the grant, one of the largest presbyteries in the Conference left it to affiliate with another denomination. Tribal fighting in the late 1990s also resulted in destruction of churches and schools, mass slaughter, and disruption of congregations. Still, in 1998 the Conference reported a membership of 57,008. Rostad High School was closed in 1999, but the first E.C.C.I. Missions Conference was held in Churachandpur in December 1999 with Dr. Ragsdale as keynote speaker. When Bishop Sigman visited India in 2000 he found over 63,000 members in India, Myanmar (Burma), and Nepal. While he was there, Dinwiddie Bible College became Evangelical College of Theology.[55]

Costa Rica

The churches in Costa Rica were formally organized as an EC Mission Conference on April 10, 1999. By 2000 the Conference had fifteen churches with 400 members.[56]

Latino

The North American Mission Conference adopted the name Latino Conference when it was formally organized on June 2, 1999, with five churches and five pastors. In 2000 several of these pastors resigned their posts, but new opportunities continue to present themselves.[57] In 2002 the Latino Conference, which by this time included churches in Reading PA, Hazleton PA, York PA, and Highland Park IL, merged into the National Conference.[58]

Higher Education

Dr. Scanlin's expansive vision for Evangelical School of Theology was evident in the choice of the School's second president, Leon O. Hynson (1975-1982). Dr. Hynson was already a noted Wesley scholar. He was squarely in the theological tradition of the EC Church but not from the denomination itself, although he joined the Evangelical Congregational Church after his selection. Hynson immediately brought to conclusion development of an academic degree (Master of Arts in Religion) to stand beside the professional degree (Master of Divinity) previously granted by the School. Working with Librarian Harold P. Scanlin he doubled the size of the library through purchase of 28,000 volumes from Garrett-Evangelical Theological School in Chicago in 1976. The School's first development officer, Glenn Irwin, was hired in 1978 and its first Business Manager, Carl K. Becker, Jr., in 1980. Also in 1980, J. Duane Beals became Academic Dean upon the resignation of Dean Christman. Faculty salaries and benefits were increased. Renovation of Old Main continued under the sponsorship of Kathryn Dech and the Joel Zinn family. Enrollment increased from 83 in 1976 to 97 in 1979, with seventeen denominations represented.[59] The School purchased Albright Field in 1980, adding four acres to the campus.

After seven years as president Dr. Hynson resigned to return to teaching, and in 1982 Dr. Ray A. Seilhamer, Senior Pastor of the Huntingdon (IN) United Brethren in Christ church, was chosen as Evangelical's third President. His immediate concerns were financial because fund raising was not keeping pace with rising costs. After weathering the initial crisis, Seilhamer launched a five-year capital improvements campaign called "Sowing for Leaders" (1984-1989) that brought in $2,500,000 for endowment, student aid, parking facilities, a new kitchen, and thirteen townhouses for student housing. This was succeeded immediately by the "Step Up to the Future" campaign with a four-year goal of $2,750,000 for annual expenses. The efforts toward accreditation continued also, and on December 8, 1984, Evangelical was accredited by the Middle States Association of Schools and Colleges. The following June, the Association of Theological Schools once again agreed to evaluate Evangelical and finally awarded the School accreditation in January 1987.[60]

Meanwhile, a member of the faculty, Kirby N. Keller, had been chosen to succeed Dr. Beals as Dean in 1987. While the seminary *seems* at times to be "bricks and mortar," it is the training of lives for the ministry that remains primary. The 1980s saw new courses, new faculty, and a new emphasis on Christian education. Student internships under a successful pastor mentor became a requirement for graduation with a Master of Divinity degree by 1986, and internships in Clinical Pastoral Education were also available for counseling majors. Nancy Johnson was named first Dean of Students in 1993.[61]

Dr. Kirby N. Keller became Evangelical's fourth President in 1994, while remaining as Dean, upon Dr. Seilhamer's election as Bishop of the Church of the United Brethren in Christ. Once again, a new president faced a financial crisis as static support from the EC Church compounded a decline in tuition revenue and rising costs. Faculty cuts were combined with greater emphasis on student recruitment, and in 1995 the University Senate of the United Methodist Church approved Evangelical as a seminary for training its pastors. Gradually, the financial picture improved, and in 1998 the School was once again able to hire an Academic Dean, Dr. Rodney H. Shearer, pastor of Ono United Methodist Church and former Chaplain of Lebanon Valley College. Dr. Shearer accepted appointment as a District Superintendent of the United Methodist Church in 2002, and Dr. Kenneth Miller, Professor of Systematic Theology at Evangelical, was selected as sixth Academic Dean.[62]

A generous and faithful Board of Trustees, dedicated and caring faculty, and an efficient administration brought Evangelical into the twenty-first century facing the challenges of technological innovations in teaching, a growing but changing student body, and an enlarged curriculum. The approval of the Master of Arts in Marriage and Family Therapy program in 2002 marked a major expansion of the School into new areas of service. In the Fall 2002 semester Evangelical School of Theology enrolled 161 credit students (118 men and 43 women) from twenty denominations. United Methodist students made up 34 % of the total, Evangelical Congregational students 13 %.

Ecumenical Relations

Even though the movement toward the merger of the Evangelical Congregational, United Brethren in Christ, and Primitive Methodist Churches was halted in the 1960s, representatives of the three denominations continued to meet informally at the annual convention of the National Association of Evangelicals and other interdenominational gatherings. In 1972 the Boards of Missions of the United Brethren in Christ and the Evangelical Congregational Churches jointly sponsored a Men's Congress at Huntington IN. The popularity of this event prompted Bishop Cressman to initiate a meeting with leaders of the United Brethren in Christ, Brethren in Christ, and Evangelical Mennonite Congregational denominations to facilitate further cooperation. This was the beginning of an organization that later adopted the name "Consortium for Evangelical Action."

The denominations that eventually became active in the Consortium were: Church of the United Brethren in Christ, Primitive Methodist Church, Evangelical Congregational Church, Brethren Church of Ashland OH, Conservative Congregational Christian Church, and Churches in Christian Union. At semiannual meetings held from 1972 through 1977 the leaders of these groups of Churches planned four Men's Congresses: Grove City PA (1973), Muncy Terrace PA (1974), Winona Lake IN (1976), and Angola IN (1977). The Consortium also sponsored a Church Extension Seminar in 1973 and a Christian Leadership Workshop in 1975. When the United Brethren in Christ, Primitive Methodist, and Evangelical Congregational Churches became deeply involved in a Federation in 1974 the Consortium was no longer needed, and in 1977 it was finally disbanded.

Leaders from the Evangelical Congregational Church, the Church of the United Brethren in Christ and the Primitive Methodist Church began a new round of talks promoting cooperation in Youngstown OH on February 14, 1974. In this initial meeting the attendees dismissed the idea of merging the three bodies and concentrated on the concept of federation.[63] When the representatives met again in October 1974, articles of organization were adopted. The group approved a definition of federation: "a group of autonomous bodies forming a unit of function which will assess the needs and resources in various ministries and explore and implement procedures most fully to meet these needs and most economically use these resources."[64] Under this definition the three denominations entered into a productive period of cooperation.

Each of five sub-committees met independently of the Joint Commission on Federation to explore areas in which the three denominations could work together. The Sub-Commission on Christian Education and Publications developed unified Sunday school curriculum material called "The Venture Series," which was marketed among the churches of the Federation and other denominations. This group also produced two issues of a combined denominational paper, named *Triventure*, which highlighted the work of each communion, building an appreciation for the ministries of the participating bodies. In addition to sharing information on the work of the representative Boards of Missions, the Missions Sub-Commission recommended that the three denominations share in the support of designated missionaries. Ron and Brenda Anderson from the Primitive Methodist Church were the first commissioned Federation Missionaries. In 1977 the three denominations took action to financially back their work in Spain.[65] The other three sub-commissions, Higher Education, Evangelism and Church Growth, and Stewardship, met regularly to build bridges of cooperation between the three Churches.

By 1981 the three denominations seemed ready to take a further step in cooperation. The Western Conference of the Evangelical Congregational Church in two separate resolutions urged the Evangelical Congregational members of the Federation to work toward a merger of the three groups.[66] When the General Conference of the United Brethren Church met later in June the following motion was adopted, "that the General Conference go on record as being in favor of aggressively pursuing a merger with the Evangelical Congregational Church and/or the Primitive Methodist Church."[67] Representatives of the three groups met in Myerstown in December of that year and prepared a joint statement that briefly sketched the history of federated activity and outlined the procedure needed to explore organic union.[68]

The Administrative Council encouraged the leaders of the Evangelical Congregational Church to enter into merger talks in spite of the barriers that the provisions in the *Discipline* put in the way. In 1975 when the Christian Service Fellowship surveyed the pastors and laity of the Church, a heartening sixty-nine percent of those that responded were favorable to merger. Eighty-five percent of the pastors were open to union with another denomination.[69] The good relations maintained with the other two denominations seemed to build on that positive feeling during the years that followed. The 1982 General Conference of the Evangelical Congregational Church approved the continued merger talks and instructed the Administrative Council to prepare a questionnaire about merger similar to the 1975 survey to determine the attitude of the constituency.

Delegates representing the three denominations met again in October 1982. The focus of that gathering was to consider the way in which uniting the Churches would impact the various boards and institutions of the cooperating communions. The group decided that in preparation for the January 1983 meeting of the Steering Committee on Merger Discussion the delegates would entertain the question, "What are the benefits that would come as a result of merger that could not be achieved through federation?"[70]

The Steering Committee met in Huntington IN on January 14, 1983. Each group shared its views concerning the advantages of merger over federation. Both the United Brethren and the Primitive Methodist delegates felt that there was no appreciable advantage of merger over federation. The Evangelical Congregational representatives reflected on the administrative benefits of merger and the extension of ministry that would be possible if the three denominations were one. The United Brethren position on secret societies, however, became the roadblock to union. Since the constitution of the United Brethren Church forbids any connection with those who are members of secret societies the United Brethren delegates felt that "to proceed with merger discussions is a divisive issue and probably not a viable situation with the three denominations."[71] Action was taken to discontinue the efforts toward a merger. Three months later the executive committee of the federation prepared a joint statement on the merger question and began exploring ways of strengthening the work of the federation.[72]

In the decade that followed the three denominations continued to share in various federated activities. By 1986 three missionary families were supported jointly by the three groups.[73] Each fall a seminar, sponsored cooperatively, dealt with various topics of mutual interest such as, evangelism, conflict management, youth ministries, and pastoral transitions. In 1990 a fourth denomination, the Southern Methodist Church, joined the Federation.[74] This group is a dissenting remnant of one the denominations that merged in 1939 to form the Methodist Church. By 2001 the members of the federation felt that the usefulness of the organization was passed and in March of that year the leaders of the four denominations took action to disband "with thanksgiving to God for many fruitful years of ministry we shared together."[75]

On a broader scale, the EC Church continued to maintain its affiliation with the National Association of Evangelicals, and in 2001 at the urging of Bishop Sigman the church affiliated with the Christian Holiness Partnership, "a network of churches that espouse the Wesleyan doctrine of entire sanctification or holiness."[76]

Board of Pensions

The Board of Pensions struggled in the last years of the century to provide E.C. ministers with adequate protection from the vagaries of illness, disability, and old age. Presidents of the Board during this period included Rev. David Heil, Homer Luckenbill, and William Kautz. Dr. James Yoder continued to oversee day-to-day operations throughout the period, with the title after 1990 of Business Manager.

Retirement Benefits.

The pension program for retired ministers came under intense scrutiny in the mid-1970s when it was determined that the defined benefit plan could no longer provide adequately for the needs of the retired pastors. The program was not "funded"; that is, the financial reserves were not sufficient to cover obligations to present and future beneficiaries. Annual income was used to cover annual obligations to retired pastors, and very little was set-aside for those who would retire in the future. In addition, the plan provided little flexibility for the participants.

The Board of Pensions reported to the 1978 General Conference that they were considering moving from a "defined benefit" plan to a "defined contribution" plan. This meant that pastors could make personal contributions into individual accounts, and they would receive credit for some of the funds contributed by their churches. In order to make the transition the Board of Pensions pooled the funds received from the churches and used a portion of the total to pay the current beneficiaries and part of the balance was credited to the active participants. Gradually those persons under the defined benefit plan decreased, and more of the church's contribution was credited to individual accounts. In 1982 the Additional Aid Fund, established in 1946 to replace group insurance, was phased out, and the proceeds were placed in individual pastors' accounts. By 1986 the rates per credit year in the defined benefit program were frozen at $ 90 per credit year for the pastors and $ 62 per credit year for the widows. Some of the retired pastors experienced financial hardship as inflation crept upward and the benefits did not increase. To provide financial aid for these pastors and widows the Manna Fund became operational in 1989; this fund is financed through annual contributions from individuals and churches.

Expansion in the eligibility for participation in the pension program began in 1977, when career missionaries employed under the Board of Missions were added to the program hitherto reserved for itinerant pastors. By 1998 membership included all ministers licensed by the Evangelical Congregational Church and employed by a conference, church, or division/board of the denomination, full-time or part-time ministers in related fields, and career missionaries employed by the denomination's Board of Missions. In 1998 the combined assets of the Board totaled more than $ 8,000,000, the bulk of which was credited to the accounts of individual participants.

Health Insurance.

In 1957 "the Society invited the active ministers of the Evangelical Congregational Church to provide health insurance for themselves and their dependents by purchasing Blue Cross and Blue Shield contracts through group contracts arranged for by the Society. The Society agreed to pay one dollar per month per contract to help defray the cost of the same."[77] The financial obligation of the Preachers' Aid Society/ Board of Pensions for health care coverage remained small until 1974 when the Board accepted the responsibility for receiving an additional apportionment to cover Blue Cross/Blue Shield for all active pastors and for subsidizing the cost for all retirees and their widows in addition to purchasing major medical protection for all active and retired ministers.

Unfortunately, during the 1980s and 1990s the cost of health insurance soared. In order to minimize the increased obligation the Board raised the co-payments and deductibles for pastors. In 1997 the Board began offering a managed health care plan or HMO. Savings to the Board permitted reimbursement of pastors for any out-of-pocket expenses consisting of deductibles, co-payments, and amounts paid to non-participating Blue Shield doctors in excess of seven hundred dollars.

Disability Fund

In 1980 the Eastern Conference initiated a Disability Contingency Fund that came under the Board of Pensions when the Western Conference adopted the program in 1981. Participants were guaranteed an income for a maximum of two years in the event of total disability. Assets of the fund exceeded $ 300,000 by the year 2000.[78]

Historical Society

The Board of Trustees of the Historical Society of the Evangelical Congregational Church continued its work during the last decades of the twentieth century in four areas: archives and records preservation, historical publications, commemorative celebrations and services, and education and outreach.[79] Board Presidents during this time were Rev. Ralph H. Bornman (1971-1983), Dr. Thomas H. Leininger (1983-1998), and Dr. Robert G. Hower (1998-2003). Conference Historians were: Eastern Conference—Rev. Ralph Bornman (1967-1983), Rev. Lloyd Eshbach (1983-1985), Sylvia Bixler (1985-1987), Dr. Thomas Leininger (1988-1998), Dr. Robert Hower (1998-2002); Western Conference—Rev. C. F. Rissmiller (1967-1981), Rev. Stephen Cramer (1981-1988), Rev. Gary Brown (1988-2002).

Archives and Records Preservation

Accumulation and preservation of records of the Evangelical Congregational Church and its predecessor denominations were always high priorities for the Historical Society Board. Church records of viable congregations remain in local churches, but records of discontinued congregations are to be deposited in the Archives. The Board also arranged for the Church of Jesus Christ of Latter-day Saints to microfilm local church records at the 1981 Annual Conference sessions and acquired copies of the microfilms for the Archives. Members of the Board recorded invaluable interviews with elder church leaders in the 1980s for the Archives cassette collection. The Archives found a permanent home in protected quarters in the Rostad Library of Evangelical School of Theology in 1979, and the Board worked continuously to add to its holdings, keep its holdings safe, and make its holdings accessible to researchers. The following persons have served as Archivist: Harold P. Scanlin (1973-77), Lloyd Eshbach (1977-1985), J. Creighton Christman (1985-1992), Terry Heisey (1992-).

Historical Publications

In the 1970s the Board approved the publication of R. S. Wilson's *History of the Evangelical Congregational Church,* and Ralph and Mildred Bornman compiled a "Pictorial History of Evangelical Congregational Churches and Pastors." In the early 1980s the Board sponsored publication of the section on the Evangelical Congregational Church Wilson wrote for a volume commemorating the tercentennial of religion in Pennsylvania, *The Holy Experiment.* The Board initiated the writing of the present book in 1987 and produced a series of church bulletin inserts on various historical topics beginning in 1989. In addition, the Board produced a slide-and-cassette-tape multi-media kit on the history of the Evangelical Congregational Church for use by local churches in the 1980s.

Commemorative Celebrations and Services

The EC Historical Society continued to co-sponsor historical pilgrimages to the Albright Chapel in Kleinfeltersville with the General Commission on Archives and History of the United Methodist Church, commemorating anniversaries in 1976, 1982, 1983, 1988, and 1989. It produced a historical video and information packet for local churches and planned a service at the 1994 Eastern Conference to commemorate the centennial of the founding of the United Evangelical Church. On October 3, 2000, the Society celebrated the bicentennial of Albright's first three class meetings with a special class meeting at Evangelical School of Theology; Charles Yrigoyen, General Secretary of the United Methodist General Commission on Archives and History, was the speaker.

Education and Outreach

The Board constantly strove to focus attention of the church and its members on history. The Historical Society had displays and interactive exhibits at the denominational Family Conventions, the Festivals of Mission, and sessions of the Annual Conferences. Conference Historians worked to secure congregational historians in every local church, and the Board hosted a biennial fall symposium for congregational historians to aid in their education and training. In 2000 former Bishop Richard Cattermole produced a records retention guide, "Record Keeping for the Local Church," and a booklet, "Guidelines for Congregational Church Historians," that were distributed by the denomination.

Church Life

The Pastorate

Appointment

The process of appointing pastors continued to evolve during the 1970s. In its 1976 report to the Eastern Conference the Special Committee on the Study of the Itinerant System presented a definition of the itinerant system that acknowledged the implied guarantee of placement of each itinerant pastor in good standing and the implied guarantee of pastoral ministry for each congregation. While still placing the right of appointment in the hands of the Supervisory Committee, the Conference gave approval for pastors and churches to express their preferences in regards to stationing. The policy was further modified a year later by urging the Supervisory Committee to be ready to announce the changes in stationing on the opening day of Conference, rather than at its conclusion. The gradual opening up of the process to consultation between the pastors and churches was inaugurated during the years that followed. At a special session of the Eastern Conference in November 1993 the delegates approved open negotiation between pastors who are recommended by the Stationing Committee and the churches requesting a change. Since the office of District Superintendent was eliminated in 1993 and the new Conference Minister had no role in stationing pastors, two Stationing Elders were selected in June 1994 to assist the Bishop in finalizing appointments. In 2001 the number of Stationing Elders was increased to four.

Ordination

During the last decades of the twentieth century the Eastern

Conference Relations Committee inaugurated a re-examination of the dual ordination process the Evangelical Congregational Church had inherited from its predecessor denominations. Traditionally, ministerial candidates were ordained first as deacons and then a few years later ordained as elders. The Special Committee on Pastoral Ministry assigned to examine the issue came to feel, however, that the preponderance of Scriptural evidence favored a singe ordination as elder. In 1986 the Annual Conferences approved the recommendations of the Committee and began to prepare amendments to the *Discipline* that would implement the single ordination of ministers. Under the new system candidates would now move from approved candidacy to licentiate status to ordination as an elder after completion of educational requirements plus at least three years of pastoral service, one of which had to be full-time after completion of classwork. Following ordination two additional years of service would be required for admission to the itinerancy. The new standards attempted to heighten the significance of the ordination experience and make provision for gaining experience, maturation, and examination of the candidate before final acceptance as an EC pastor.

The amendments were ready in 1990 and approved by both the Eastern Conference and the General Conference. When the Western Conference considered the amendments in 1991, however, the delegates failed to concur with them. The Western Conference objected to the two-year trial period between ordination and reception into the itinerancy, believing that the two should be concurrent. Failure to approve this key amendment meant that single ordination could not be implemented in 1991. A year later, the Western Conference approved a compromise amendment, which, with minor revisions, was adopted by the conferences in 1994. A special rule of the Eastern Conference provided for a two-year wait for newly ordained elders prior to being received into the itinerancy, while in the West the two actions are frequently concurrent. The Annual Conferences of 1994 were the last conferences in which the Evangelical Congregational Church ordained deacons.

Chaplaincy Ministry

By the early 1980s Evangelical Congregational pastors were serving in diverse areas, and chaplaincy in the Armed Forces of the United States figured prominently among the alternatives to pastoral ministry. During World War II some EC pastors had taken their place along side of their parishioners who were called into military service. Other itinerant elders enlisted as chaplains. Three of them were from the East Pennsylvania

Conference, and one came from the Western Conference.[80]

Most of these men returned to the pastorate after the War, but Rev. Thomas G. Hepner reenlisted and had an eminent twenty-eight year career as a chaplain in the United States Air Force. Chaplain Hepner was the only Evangelical Congregational pastor serving as chaplain in active military service until 1961, when Richard E. Kohl was endorsed by the church to serve on active duty in the United States Army Reserves. Five years later Ronald D. Miller joined Chaplain Kohl in ministry to the military. By 1982 the Chaplaincy Committee of the General Conference could report four Evangelical Congregational chaplains serving in the U. S. Army, two in the U. S. Navy, and one in the U. S. Air Force. An additional two were chaplains in the U. S. Army Reserves, one in the Army National Guard, and one in the Navy Reserve, for a total of eleven pastors in military chaplaincy.[81]

Chaplaincy ministries were not confined to the military. Pastors in both conferences volunteered as chaplains in community hospitals, fire and police departments, and the Civil Air Patrol. In 1982 the Evangelical Congregational Retirement Village employed David H. Reed as its first full-time chaplain, a post he held until 2002.

Salaries

The churches in both conferences struggled to maintain their pastors' salaries at a livable level during a period of crippling inflation. The consumer price index rose 305 % from 1973 to 2002, with nearly half of that increase between 1973 and 1985.[82] The recommended increases in the minimum salaries in the Eastern Conference closely matched the anticipated inflation rate each year. The impact of inflation was somewhat ameliorated in 1974, when each church began covering the cost of the pastor's health insurance through apportionment. A year later the Eastern Conference asked each congregation to pay the cost of health insurance for its pastor's family as a fringe benefit. By 2002 the salary standards in the Eastern Conference were: licentiates - $25,250, deacons/licentiate II - $26,940, and elders - $27,814. This came to a 360% increase in the elder's minimum over the 1973 standard.

The Western Conference continued to recommend a minimum starting salary and a percentage increase for other pastors in line with the rise in the consumer price index. Because the minimum was set only for entry-level pastors the Conference felt no obligation to increase this minimum each year. For four years (1979-1983) the minimum remained at $10,214. In 1986 the Conference reversed its position and began recommending a minimum salary for full-time ministers rather than only for starting pastors. Three years later the Western Conference followed the practice of Eastern Conference and listed minimum salaries for each of the three classifications of pastors. By 2002 the minimums recommended by the Pastors' Salary Committee were: licentiates - $25,250 and elders - $27,331. The Western Conference no longer listed the classification of deacon. The Pastors' Salary Committee of the Western Conference recommended in 1980 that churches either assume the cost of the parsonage utilities or give their pastors a ten percent increase in salary. By 2002 seventy per cent of the congregations were paying the utilities as a fringe benefit. The Western Conference also provided for health insurance coverage for the pastors and families through the Annual Conference apportionment beginning in 1977.

As inflation began to cut the value of the monetary savings pastors had set aside for retirement, they began to request housing allowances, rather than church-owned parsonages, so that they could purchase homes and begin building equity in them. The report of the Committee on Pastors' Compensation of the 1980 Eastern Conference contained a set of guidelines for churches considering this option. By 1998 twenty-eight full-time pastors were receiving a housing allowance and purchasing their own homes.

Sunday Services

The last quarter of the twentieth century was a time of many changes in the worship practices of Evangelical Congregational churches. In the 1970s Sunday evening attendances were declining,[83] but the EC church remained committed to these services. District Superintendent David P. Heil urged in 1976 that "whenever possible, and even at the cost of great effort, Sunday evening services be continued and developed into a very vital part of our faithful witness for Christ."[84] Congregations searched for creative ways to cultivate interest. Grace Church in Schuylkill Haven PA, for example, held "drive-in" services on summer Sunday evenings; on June 1, 1975, one hundred cars, holding more than 400 people, crowded bumper to bumper on the church's parking lot to hear the Jacob Brothers in concert.[85] By 2002, on the other hand, most EC churches had given up this effort. Only a little more than one third of the churches held evening services and just as few scheduled Sunday evening youth programs.

As the other Sunday services lessened in significance the morning worship service became more prominent. More and more the life of the congregation came to revolve around this one service on a Sunday morning, and everything from worship and Bible study to announcements and fellowship had to be packed into one hour. Prayer needs of the members previously shared in the midweek prayer service, for example, were now gathered prior to the pastoral prayer on Sunday morning. Bible study previously done in Sunday School had to become part of the sermon. Even the annual congregational meeting was frequently moved to Sunday after the morning worship service. Pastors increasingly recognized that this was their one and only chance to equip people to serve in Christ's name for the rest of the week

Preaching

At one time, it was almost accurate to call EC pastors simply "preachers." Preaching two sermons each Sunday was their primary task. By the 1980s, however, pastors were expected to do much more than preach and visit the sick. Annual Conference reports included not only morning and evening service attendance and number of baptisms, conversions, and visitations but also number of pastoral counseling sessions, discipleship/growth groups, and evangelism/visitation teams (plus number of persons involved). Yet, the importance of preaching remained. In 1985 the Division of Evangelism and Spiritual Care formulated a program calling for an "increased incidence of preaching and teaching for decision ," "energetically and expositionally" correct preaching with a clear call for commitment. Evangelistic meetings were held as preachers exchanged pulpits, preaching on the theme "Christ, Our Hope."[86]

At the dawn of the twenty-first century, EC sermons were shorter than those of a century before. A growing number of pastors were adding a visual element to their sermons with illustrations and text projected on screens behind them while they preached. As in Albright's day, preachers could no longer assume that those who heard them were familiar with biblical stories and theological jargon; many preachers were recasting their message to reach a new generation of spiritual "seekers."

Sacraments

In the 1980s professors at Evangelical School of Theology prepared a series of seven pamphlets outlining the EC position on various theological topics, including "Authority and Inspiration of Holy Scriptures," "Sanctification," "Trinity," "Assurance and Apostasy," "The Church," "Salvation," and "The Sacraments."[87] In "The Sacraments" the Lord's Supper was portrayed as a memorial and Baptism explained with a dual stress on covenant and symbolism in the administration of water to the infant of believing parents.

The baptismal rite was re-formulated in 1978 to include a section calling for congregational involvement in the nurture of the baptized infant. At the same time, General Conference finally approved a "Service of Presentation of Infants" for use with believing parents who wished to postpone baptism until their child had personally received Christ as Savior.[88] This "Service" was not, however, placed in the *Discipline*.

The church's doctrines of the sacraments again came under review in connection with preparation of Vision 20/20. A committee to examine the Ritual recommended new rites for the Consecration of a Bishop and the Installation of a Local Church Pastor. In the Service of Holy Communion several changes were adopted to reflect current practice in the churches, including an option for pew communion and the distribution of the emblems by laity with an ordained minister officiating.

Music

Music in Evangelical Congregational churches changed perceptively over the last quarter of the twentieth century. The singing of choruses had been standard practice in Christian Endeavor, prayer meeting, and Sunday School, but as the popularity of these meetings waned in the 1970s their music found a new home in Sunday morning worship services. Baby boomers found the music of the Gaithers, Ralph Carmichael, Andraé Crouch, and Kurt Kaiser more congenial than traditional hymns, gospel songs, and even older choruses, and the *Evangelical Congregational Hymnal* (1965) already seemed dated. In 1982 the stock of hymnals was running low, and the publisher (Lillenas) indicated that a new printing would cost more than double the price of the previous one, so Bishop Moyer asked Rev. David Heil, chair of the Hymnal Committee, to convene his Committee and investigate alternatives. The Committee sent a questionnaire to the churches,[89] which indicated that 76 of the 115 responding churches were using the 1965 *Evangelical Congregational Hymnal* but elicited over 400 suggestions for additional songs.[90] The Committee decided not to reprint the 1965 hymnal "since interests have changed"[91] but to recommend adoption of the new hymnal being prepared by Hope Publishing Co. called *The Singing Church* with the EC name and logo imprinted on the cover and the Lord's Prayer and the Apostles' Creed printed in the front.[92] This eclectic collection featured "scripture songs" and choruses, folk songs, classic hymns, and gospel songs with more selections than previous EC hymnals for the seasons of the church year. Ten thousand copies of the new hymnal arrived on January 28, 1985.[93]

Most EC churches purchased the new hymnal, but music in the EC church continued to evolve rapidly. Praise teams and bands with guitars, drums, and electronic instruments joined pianos and organs in morning worship services. Song books of any description were replaced by words projected onto screens. Devotional periods at both Annual Conference sessions each year featured the introduction of the new trends. Sometimes congregations were torn apart by "worship wars" between adherents of traditional and modern styles of music, and the solution for some was separate "contemporary" services in addition to the "traditional" Sunday morning service. In other places, worship evolved into a blend of old and new, each congregation finding its own unique blend.

Church Buildings

Many congregations enlarged their facilities during the last years of the twentieth century. In Pennsylvania, for example, Bethlehem Emmanuel spent $275,000 and Rutherford Heights $150,000 on additions. Lancaster Grace did extensive renovations ($300,000), and Mohn's Hill purchased a mobile classroom unit. Boyertown purchased land and relocated in 1974, while Pottstown moved into a new church. The General Conference sessions of 1974 were held in a refurbished Allentown Boulevard Church. In 1976 the denomination established its headquarters in the renovated Church Center Building at 100 W. Park Ave. in Myerstown, formerly home of the Church Center Press. This brought together offices for the Bishop, Director of Church Ministries, Eastern Conference Western District Superintendent (later Regional Elder), Director of Missions, and their staffs plus a remodeled bookstore.

Floods in June of 1972 caused destruction to Clark's Valley Grace that forced the congregation to close in 1973. In that year Cedarville IL dedicated its new church,[94] and the Western Conference met there in 1974. Other new construction in the Western Conference included Venango PA Bethany (1975 with a Christian Day School in 1977), Venango PA Grace (1975), Seneca PA (1975), Findlay OH (1976), Afolkey IL (parsonage 1979 and mobile home classroom 1983, Lakeside (1982),[95] Seneca PA (parsonage 1985), Dixon OH Bethel (a $225,000 Christian High School 1984), Columbus OH (1983), and Winnebago IL (1986).

Trinity EC Church, Boyertown, PA, sanctuary constructed 1992

Church Builder's Fellowship continued to solicit funds annually from the churches to help congregations with their building projects, and a personal solicitation component called Church Builder's Partners netted $55,000 in 1986.[96] From 1990 through 2000, however, the pattern began to change with increasing emphasis on planting new churches. Director of Church Ministries Keith Miller pioneered the work in both conferences. His annual reports told of slow but sure growth in many places, as Bible study groups met or children's meetings were held in order to attract families. Ethnic ministries and "restarts" of new congregations in old buildings were attempted. Church *planting* loomed large, while church *building* had to wait until congregations grew enough to sustain costly construction programs.

Class Meetings/Prayer Meetings

In the 1970s and 1980s churches continued to experiment with different forms of small group meetings. The 1983 statistics of the Annual Conferences reflect the presence of multiple prayer and Bible study groups in addition to the midweek prayer service; that year a total of 229 prayer and discipleship groups were reported. By 2002 the Cedarville IL congregation reported thirteen such groups, Trinity Church in Boyertown PA reported twenty-five Bible study/discipleship groups, and the newly planted church in Willow Street PA reported fourteen.

Indeed, the Evangelical Congregational Church experienced a revival of interest in prayer on many levels. David Bryant's book *With Concerts of Prayer* provided a new model of corporate prayer for the church, and by 1985 "prayer partner" churches were developing across the conferences.[97] The first Wednesday of each month was set aside for prayer and fasting, an activity that many continue to follow. Rev. Robert Zetterberg developed materials in 1987 to assist in the prayer service while conducting workshops/seminars on his Ohio and Illinois districts, and Rev. John Ward produced a packet of helps for prayer time in 1995. At the 1994 General Conference delegates took Henry Blackaby's words, "Find out what God is doing, and join it," to heart and spent significant time in confession, weeping, and decisive prayer for each other. These prayers were answered in "winds of renewal."[98] Bishop Sigman encouraged the creation of a Prayer Network in 1998 that spread from the Eastern Conference to become a beacon in raising the level of prayer in the denomination. Sixty pastors and lay leaders attended the first EC Prayer Summit at Franklin PA in August 1999, and in the words of one of those pastors, Richard Reigle,

> There is no adequate means by which to describe that meeting with God. We struggle to define it because it is spiritual and personal …It's foundation was established by the Word of God and supported with times of worship and praise.[99]

Other successful prayer events followed on the denominational level and in local congregations that provided vital support for the "Vision 21" and "Vision 20/20" efforts.

Heartcry, a monthly newsletter of the EC Prayer Intercessors Network, provided motivation and inspiration for individual prayer warriors and for small prayer groups. In the September 2002 issue Rev. Kevin Leibensperger, Prayer Coordinator for the denomination, offered five suggestions for persons "interested in 'nudging' Prayer Meeting back to its primary purpose or spawning new prayer focused gatherings":

1. Challenge—the other members of the group with the need to pray more.

2. Commit—to devoting at least 45 minutes of an hour long prayer meeting to praying.
3. Channel—the conversation back to prayer & suggest themes to pray about.
4. Collect—prayer resources. If a lesson is to be taught make it prayer/worship focused.
5. Confirm—that even times of silence before God have value; don't fear the gaps.[100]

The EC Church also took steps to revitalize the class meeting, so essential in the days of Wesley and Albright but so long neglected. A pamphlet "So You're a Class Leader" (1990) and a newsletter from the Division of Evangelism and Pastoral Care, *Class LEADERship*, attempted to inform and encourage these lay leaders.[101] In the spring of 2002 Bishop Sigman appointed a Class Leader/Class Meeting Exploratory Committee (Class Leader Task Force), which was charged to: "Discover the functional equivalent of the Class Meeting with its emphasis on discipleship, mutual care, and discipline by redesigning Official Board polity and addressing the matter of church discipline."[102] The committee, chaired by Brian Garner, made its first report to the National Conference in 2004. Out of the committee's deliberation has come the recognition that each church must have wholistic small groups, gatherings that offer "a safe place for intimacy, accountability, and service."[103]

Church Year

Evangelical Congregational churches continued to observe a mix of civil holidays and liturgical holy days, though some adopted the liturgical year more or less completely and many changed the colors of paraments with the liturgical seasons. Midweek Lenten services, especially in a community setting, continued to gain in popularity, as did three-hour Good Friday services. Candlelight Christmas Eve services and Advent wreaths were common. Protracted revival series remained a fixture in some churches but in other places were replaced by Lay Witness and Missionary Weekends. Summer campmeetings were still held in the Eastern Conference, but they had little impact on most congregations and pastors. The denomination began to observe national days of prayer and fasting set by the President of the United States and began to set its own days of prayer and fasting. Weekly Days of Prayer and Fasting were set for April 1980, for example, in preparation for denomination's "Year of Evangelism"(1981).[104]

Campmeetings

In the late twentieth century the Evangelical Congregational Church continued to maintain the campmeeting tradition. Waldheim, Herndon, and Rosedale held ten-day sessions (Friday through Sunday of the following weekend) in July or August each year. Outstanding evangelists and musical groups presented the Gospel, and daily Bible studies were led by EC ministers. Yearly attendances remained steady, and additional people came to the campmeeting sites for weekend conferences, Saturday seminars, and Sunday services and concerts. In 1994 leadership of the campmeetings was transferred from the District Superintendents to the Boards of Directors of each campmeeting, but the campmeeting programs were little changed. A new generation of cottage owners at each site provided energy and motivation to continue the traditions of former years.

Rosedale Campmeeting celebrated its fiftieth anniversary in 1973. Herndon replaced its ancient dining hall with a new building, the Mary Henning Brandt Memorial Hall, in 1989 and celebrated its centennial in 2001 with special services and an anniversary book.[105] Waldheim lost two of its major structures when the dining hall was destroyed by fire on January 10, 1987, and its unique tabernacle collapsed under the weight of a snow on its aging timbers on March 13, 1994. The new tabernacle, dedicated June 25, 1995, was designed to replicate the original as closely as possible. Waldheim's centennial celebration was planned for 2004.[106] Finally, in the summer of 1990 EC churches began supporting a fourth campmeeting, the Susquehanna Valley Campmeeting at New Freedom PA, on a regular basis.

Revivals and Evangelistic Services

The denominational restructuring in 1978 assigned evangelism a prominent place. The Special Committee on Evangelism of the General Conference recommended that the responsibility for evangelism be brought under the direct supervision of the Bishop and that the division he headed be named the Division of Evangelism and Spiritual Care.[107] The first meeting of the new Division was held on September 18, 1979, and the members of the Division immediately gave attention to putting together a program of evangelism for the churches. By the time the Administrative Council met in March 1980, the program entitled REAP (Reach Every Available Person) was ready. The year 1981 was designated as a year of evangelism. Seminars were scheduled throughout the territory of both Annual Conferences, and local congregations were asked to make evangelism a priority for the year.[108]

After REAP the Division continued to provide material and programs to assist local congregations in outreach, and these efforts met with varying degrees of acceptance. The 1986 General Conference noted that Church Growth clinics were held in conjunction with the two Annual Conferences. Win Arn conducted a one-day seminar prior to the sessions of the Eastern Conference, and the Bishop met with local congregations in both Conferences to acquaint the leaders with church growth principles. By the fall of 1984 he had conducted twenty-nine such workshops. [109]

In the next quadrennium the Division of Evangelism and Spiritual Care was instrumental in involving churches in the evangelistic program developed by John Maxwell, pastor of the Skyline Wesleyan Church in Lemon Grove CA. Clinics featuring John Maxwell were held in both Conferences, and attendance by pastors was strongly urged. Staff from the Department of Extension and Evangelism of the Wesleyan Church trained the leaders of five pilot churches in the use of the GRADE material. Growth Resulting After Discipleship Evangelism (GRADE), which was called a ministry lifestyle rather than a program, was used effectively by churches within both Conferences. In the GRADE strategy four teams are recruited: "Abrahams" whose task it is to pray for the lost, "Barnabas" workers who make friendly contacts with first time visitors, "Andrews" who engage in visitation evangelism, and a team that provides instruction for new converts through a "Timothy" discipleship course. Trinity Evangelical Congregational Church in Boyertown PA reported that in 1990 there were nineteen conversions and that the majority of them were linked to the GRADE effort. [110]

Trinity EC Church, Royersford, PA, constructed 2002

Some churches continued to rely on the traditional week of evangelistic services as the main outreach thrust of the year. These congregations utilized professional evangelists, denominational officials, and fellow pastors as the featured speakers. Frequently appearing in the advertisements for local Spiritual Life Crusades were names such as Harvey Copperwheat, Duane Beals, Neville West, and John DeBrine. Denominational leaders, however, perceived that the evangelistic strategies of the past were becoming less effective in reaching an increasingly secular generation and tried to encourage alternative evangelistic methods. In 1982 the General Conference added new items to the annual statistics received from local churches in order "to reflect extended ministries of the church."[111] Pastors were required to report on the activity of evangelistic visitation teams and the number and attendance at prayer and Bible study groups.

In 1997 the Evangelical Congregational Church began a productive relationship with Mission America Coalition, an organization established in this country as an outgrowth of the Laussane Consultation on Evangelism. The focus of MAC was Celebrate Jesus 2000, which had as its goal "to pray for and share Christ with every person in America before the end of 2000." In order to reach this goal Mission America Coalition sought to recruit Christians to establish lighthouses of prayer throughout the country. "A 'lighthouse' is defined as a person or family committed to pray and care for people within their neighborhood, work place, or school community and to share Jesus as God leads."[112] The Division of Evangelism and Spiritual Care set a denominational goal of three thousand lighthouses. By 2001 the Division reported that 62.5 % of the churches were involved and that 1,773 lighthouses were established.[113]

The last years of the twentieth century, however, saw a fundamental change in the way people came to join a church. In the past, most people found salvation and a church home through special revival crusades, personal evangelism, or through the Sunday School. In the latter twentieth century, spiritual seekers were more apt to sample Christianity by attending a worship service. If these first-time visitors were to come back, it was felt that the worship services had to be "seeker friendly," that is appealing to the "baby boom generation." EC churches began reshaping their principal worship services on Sunday mornings along the model of those at Willow Creek Community Church in Barrington IL to feature upbeat music and short thematic preaching, possibly introduced by drama and accompanied by colorful visuals. The worship service became the outreach service. The Second Service Planning Team at

Seibert Church in Allentown PA expressed as its goal, "to increase our outreach efforts directed at contemporary people by offering an alternative to the traditional worship service."[114]

Catechetical Instruction

The church's catechism, *The Threshold of the Church*, continued to receive wide acceptance, so that by 1973 the stock of available copies was nearly depleted. The Board of Christian Education appointed a committee chaired by Duane M. Ray and Robert G. Hower to revise the manual, but further revision had to await completion of the denominational restructuring begun in 1979. Pastors also continued to feel the need for a simpler manual of instruction in church history and doctrine for younger converts. In the fall of the 1981 the church released a new junior high catechism entitled "The Mystery of the Hidden Treasure." It was based on Paul's epistle to the Colossians and came with a leader's guide and visual aids as well as the student manual.[115]

The new junior high catechetical manual was not as widely used as its predecessor. Pastors were finding it more difficult to schedule extended series of sessions for young people seeking church membership; the competition from extra-curricular school activities and television was proving too hard to overcome. Pastors continued to rely on the *Threshold* even for the more abbreviated instruction sessions, but copies of this were again in very short supply. In 1984 the denomination even issued an appeal to churches for any available unused copies, and some pastors photocopied their own copies.[116]

In 1986 *Threshold* was revised and reprinted again as part of an enlarged study packet targeted for adult study groups. Two years later the church released a high school catechism entitled "This I Believe." In 2001 Bishop Sigman appointed a task force to write a new edition of *The Threshold of the Church* reflecting current teaching techniques and the newly articulated core values of the Evangelical Congregational Church.[117]

Sunday School

In 1980 Sunday Schools throughout the world celebrated the two hundredth anniversary of the first Sunday School, but the celebration was somewhat muted by the fact that in a majority of churches Sunday Schools were experiencing what seemed to be an irreversible decline. Within Evangelical Congregational churches Sunday schools had experienced two decades of dropping attendances by 1980. The 1978

Eastern Conference heard Richard Osberg's sobering assessment of Christian education in the churches and recognized that immediate and focused attention needed to be given to reverse the trend. The General Conference of 1982 accepted the recommendation of the Church Development Committee to appoint a task force to assess the Christian Education program, giving attention to the areas of leadership development and youth ministries.[118]

The task force met in 1984, and a year later held workshops for the pastors of each district under the title "Breaking the Cycle for Growth." It unveiled a program of leadership training called ECSEL (Evangelical Congregational Servants Embracing Leadership) in the April 1986 issue of *The United Evangelical*.[119] The purpose of ECSEL was to "stimulate all E. C.'s to embrace leadership development in all areas of the local church." ECSEL workshops were held at the site of both Annual Conferences that spring to further highlight the work of the task force and intensive training sessions were scheduled for later that year.

The task force also issued a renewed call for employment of a denominational director of Christian education.[120] The Administrative Council adopted a job description for the position in March 1987, and a year-long search resulted in the selection of Donald W. Metz, pastor of Grace Church in Knox PA, as Director of Christian Education in the spring of 1988. Metz was completing a Doctor of Ministries degree program at Trinity Evangelical Divinity School in Deerfield IL. He had served as a member of the Christian education task force and was the architect of the ECSEL program.[121] In the five years that followed, the Director of Christian Education was actively involved in visiting local congregations, observing their Sunday schools, and giving workshops dealing with Sunday school management, leadership motivation, and conflict management. The strong emphasis on improving the Sunday schools began to have its effect on the statistics. By the time the General Conference met in 1994 the decline in Sunday school enrollment and attendance had slowed to its lowest level in twenty years.

The denomination's experiment with a Director of Christian Education, however, had already come to an end in 1993. The previous year the Eastern Conference had faced a serious financial shortfall that compelled the Conference to make substantial cuts in its budget. The Bishop noted in a report to a special session of the Eastern Conference held in December 1992 that the General Conference Administrative Council was recommending the elimination of the position of Director of Christian Education, and Eastern Conference endorsed this action.

Metz submitted his resignation "so that a special session of General Conference need not be convened and so that when the financial base is restored sufficiently another Director of Christian Education can be hired."[122]

With Metz's resignation the responsibility for Christian education was placed on the Church Development Committee of the Church Ministries Division and each Conference's Special Committee on Christian Education. One new venture that came out of the work of the Church Development Committee was a program of workshops for children's ministries workers called E3CW (Evangelical Congregational Church Children's Workers). Well-attended workshops for local church children's workers were held over the next three years.[123] Both Conference Committees on Christian Education provided occasional seminars for leaders of the Sunday Schools, but no coordinated program of Sunday school promotion was developed.

The Sunday School emerged from this period in 2002 decidedly weakened, but pastors know that creating disciples is still an essential task of the local church. Evangelical Congregational Sunday Schools of the twenty-first century stand with prayer and Bible study groups targeting children, youth, men, and women in an attempt to provide "life to life" relationship-based experiences that stimulate Christian growth. Today, in strong churches Christian education is very different from the heyday of large adult Bible classes, Sunday school orchestras, and rally days, but the new Christian education emphases may be as effective at fulfilling the Great Commission charge to "make disciples" than even the best Sunday schools of yesterday.

Camping and Retreats

By 1973 the $110,000 debt on the Twin Pines property near Bartonsville PA had been cleared, and the date of the mortgage burning, June 8, 1973, became the yearly time for festive activities at the site. The Camp immediately developed a Master Plan and fund raising campaign for new buildings and needed equipment. Rev. James Shields became General Director of Twin Pines Camp in 1973[124] and started adding programs and activities. Already in 1976 Twin Pines hosted 1,088 summer campers, of whom 350 made decisions for Christ, and 1600 persons on weekend and other short-term retreats throughout the year.[125] Special music camps, nature camps, basketball camps, outdoor (tent) camps, bike camps, hunters camps, singles camps, and "Golden Agers" camps brought in more people and used more of the camp site.

Twin Pines also continued to host the annual East Pennsylvania Bible Conference in September of each year. Thirty-five acres were added to the site in 1982, and new facilities were developed. The Camp announced plans for a new conference and retreat center, Aspen Lodge, in 1995; construction on this facility began in 2002.

Rock River Bible Camp at Dixon IL continued to flourish as the century came to an end with camps for grades 4 to 12. Camp ECCO at Carrolltown OH suffered the lost of its main building when its roof collapsed in 1979, but out of this calamity grew a new master plan for future growth.[126] Over two hundred youth attended the Camp during its thirtieth anniversary year (1989).[127] The "You Lead" program designed by Rev. John Ward was successfully revived in the late 1990s to train youth at both camps for future roles in the denomination. All EC camps received accreditation by the National Association of Camps and Conferences.

Lay Men and Women in the Church

Lay men always had prominent roles in the Evangelical Congregational Church. Indeed, it may be said that the church was founded to safeguard the rights of lay men to control their own church properties and to have an equal voice with clergy in denominational affairs. Local church officials (at least until recently mostly men) have over the years given thousands of hours to meetings and administrative activities. Lay men also provided countless hours of volunteer labor maintaining and improving church properties, and men's Sunday School classes have undertaken many worthwhile projects. In the latter part of the twentieth century, however, as in the latter part of the nineteenth century, churches made special efforts to reach men with the Gospel and provide support for male spirituality. The Federation of the Evangelical Congregational Church, the United Brethren in Christ, and the Primitive Methodist Church sponsored Men's Congresses beginning at Grove City College in 1973. Later, in the 1990s the non-denominational Promise Keepers movement attempted to develop "men of integrity" and increased from 280,000 participants in 1994 to 1,200,000 in 1996. Sixty-two EC pastors attended the February 1996 Promise Keeper Clergy Conference, and Eastern Conference Minister Ronald Miller gave it hearty support.[128] This movement, though not always meeting with EC approval, gave inspiration and encouragement to many men from the church.

Lay women have had prominent roles in missions, Christian education, music, and hospitality throughout the history of the church. Late-twentieth-century examples of women with noteworthy denominational roles include women with prominent or administrative roles on a denominational level: Mrs. Dean Graham, a lay delegate from Akron OH who served on the Board of Christian Education; Kathryn Dech, the first female member of the Board of Trustees of Evangelical School of Theology; Mary Good, Missions Society Branch President and lay delegate; and Martha Metz, book store manager at Church Center. Involvement of pastors' wives in their husbands' ministries was long assumed, but more recently the church has acted to explicitly include wives of candidates for ordination and church planting pastors in the assessment and preparation process because of the key roles these women have in ministry. A Pastors' Wives Seminar was held in conjunction with the 1980 session of Western Conference, and from this grew the *Pastor's Wife Newsletter*, which provided continuing encouragement and a sense of community to clergy spouses in the Conference. As the century drew to a close, women found ever more places in the leadership of churches and the church. The Women's Ministry Network was established in 2000 to intensify partnerships in prayer and planning through "Vision 20/20."

The latter years of the twentieth century also saw a new emphasis on family. Much effort went into organizing Family Conventions at Grove City College every three years between 1975 and 1990. These were times of fellowship, recreation, and inspiration for hundreds of people. In general, Evangelical Congregational laity (men, women, boys, and girls together) have done most of the ministry in the Evangelical Congregational Church over its history, and that is as it should be. The late twentieth century saw a new recognition of the role of the pastor as facilitator, leader, and enabler of the real ministers—the people in the pews.

Youth

Vestiges of the EC/CE (Evangelical Congregational/ Christian Endeavor) connection remained in the latter part of the twentieth century. Two EC pastors served as CE officers during this time: Franklin Schock as Field Secretary of Pennsylvania CE and Charles Barner as General Secretary of International CE. Bishop Wittmaier commended CE for its contribution through the decades by bringing youth "toward Christian maturity and leadership."[129] The tie in many local churches, however, was unraveling. Christian Endeavor attendances dwindled and societies disbanded. The General Conference of 1974 approved the creation of Evangelical Congregational Youth Ministries (E.C.Y.M.), which could maintain use of Christian Endeavor materials and membership but were free to use other formats. Still, traditional youth activities continued to lose their hold in the 1970s; while Bible quizzing continued in the West, its popularity in the East was brief.[130] The Spiritual State of the Church Committee in the Western Conference lamented in 1982 the lack of youth involvement in church leadership.[131]

As the century drew to a close more EC churches began to hire youth pastors to provide professional leadership for young people's programs, and some clergy were stationed as youth pastors. Young people got valuable training and experience as counselors at summer camps in both Conferences.[132] Youth traveled to Central America and Mexico on mission work teams. Churches organized weekend retreats for teens, contemporary Christian music concerts, and other activities. The EC Youth Network was established in 2000 to develop cooperation between large and small youth ministries as part of "Vision 20/20."[133]

Beliefs

Charismatic Movement

In the late nineteenth century the Evangelical Association was torn by controversy between those whose primary concern was conversion and those who believed a "second blessing" was necessary. Eventually the church reaffirmed its Wesleyan belief in Christian perfection but not necessarily an instantaneous experience of it, and the controversy died down. The "second blessing" idea remained alive in other "holiness churches," however, and gave rise to "pentecostal churches" like the Assemblies of God who experienced "baptism in the Holy Spirit" in the early 1900s. Around 1960 a second wave of Pentecostalism broke into the mainstream denominations as many groups experienced baptism in the Holy Spirit and claimed the Gifts of the Spirit, including speaking in tongues, as the right and requirement of all genuine Christians. This aroused the same reaction as the advocacy of second blessing a century before, threatening to disrupt congregations in the EC Church. The 1975 Eastern Conference appointed a committee to study the issue. In its report to the 1976 Conference the committee compared charismatic teaching with Scripture and concluded that it can not be convincingly asserted that the Bible teaches a post-conversion baptism in the Holy Spirit. Instead, the committee concluded that:

1). We are baptized in the Spirit as believers.

2). Fullness of the Spirit refers to sanctification or Christian growth.

3). Speaking in tongues is NOT a sign of fullness of the Holy Spirit, nor a sign of genuine Christian commitment and should not be encouraged.

4). The Gifts of the Spirit are possible, but it is the Fruit of the Spirit (Christian character) that is expected of every Christian.[134]

This understanding was consistent with that of the East Pennsylvania Conference during the height of the sanctification controversy one hundred years before: holiness was equated with right living, not special blessing. The "Spiritual State of the Church Report" in 1983 called on pastors and congregations to prayerfully review the Biblical and Disciplinary statements concerning holiness of life.[135] In 2001, however, Bishop Sigman secured church membership in the Christian Holiness Partnership (CHP) (formerly the Christian Holiness Association), a network of churches dedicated to maintaining the holiness tradition in the Wesleyan heritage.

Social Issues

In the 1970s the Eastern Conference continued to show concern for alcohol use and Sunday observance, though Prohibition and Sunday blue laws were no longer even possibilities. The church also continued to look for ways to respond to the Supreme Court's ruling prohibiting prayer and Bible reading in the public schools. Evangelical Congregational churches aligned with other congregations sponsoring released time religious training for children in public schools, and with a growing conviction that "our schools are being invaded by secular humanism,"[136] some local churches attempted to provide alternative Christian education for their children. In 1984 Bethel Evangelical Congregational Church in Dixon IL in cooperation with a neighboring church sponsored a Christian High School and erected a multipurpose building to house the students. Evangelical Congregational pastors and lay members began to "home school" their children during the nineties, and this trend accelerated in the new century.

More and more, however, the church was preoccupied with issues involving sexuality and reproduction. On January 22, 1973, the Supreme Court of the United States announced its decision on the constitutionality of state laws that prohibited or limited abortions and in "Roe vs. Wade" decided that these laws were unconstitutional. At first, church leaders seemed to acquiesce to the decision. An editorial in the *United Evangelical* entitled "It's Up to You" pointed to the number of previously illegal abortions as evidence of the difficulty of legislating morality; it is up to each Christian, the editor said, to teach and model personal morality and not depend on the government to do so.[137] A few months later, a new Coordinating Editor wrote a summary of an interview he had with Dr. Don C. Folmer, Chair of the Northampton County Medical Society's Committee on Medicine and Religion, in which the doctor presented a position that emphasized the importance of the health and well-being of the mother in considering an abortion.[138] This rather liberal view of abortion did not, however, pass unnoticed by the readers. In a letter to the editor, "Abortion Rebuttal," one reader challenged the view expressed in the earlier article and strongly supported what has become the "pro-life" position.[139] In the fall of 1973 the *United Evangelical* printed a National Association of Evangelicals resolution stating that "We affirm our conviction that abortion on demand for social adjustment or to solve economic problems is morally wrong," while also expressing an openness to "therapeutic abortion" and advising that religious, medical and psychological counseling precede any decision to curtail a pregnancy caused by incest or rape.[140]

By 1982 the General Conference was ready to declare the position of the church on the issue. A greatly expanded section of the *Discipline* dealing with Christian practice mirrored the NAE position and presented biblical support of "the value of life prior to birth."[141] The "pro-life" movement continued to gain strength in the 1980s, however, and the Annual Conferences passed resolutions taking even firmer stands. The Social Action Committee of Western Conference stated in 1985 that "the ultimate child abuse is abortion." It recommended support for local crisis pregnancy centers and a boycott of pharmaceutical firms that manufacture abortion agents. The 1990 Eastern Conference took a stand against abortion, even when a mother's life is threatened. While permitting abortion after thoroughly sensitive counsel, their Resolution states, "We affirm the power of God to preserve the life of both mother and child even in uncertain medical situations."[142] In 1995 a detailed description of the ministry of crisis pregnancy centers appeared in the Western Conference Journal, and churches were encouraged " to view their local CPC as a home mission."[143]

Temperance, abstinence, drug abuse and alcohol were major divisions in the *Discipline* under "Moral Standards," but as the century drew to a close there were also sections on divorce, responsible parenthood, AIDS, pornography, adoption, adultery, pre-marital sex, and homosexuality. The church sponsored many forums, seminars, and collegial opportunities for pastors and laity to study and discuss these issues. In fact, many Annual Conference sessions took on the shape of forums intended to equip delegates with answers to the issues. In 1996 each church was urged to develop a policy on child abuse, and in 2000 the EC Church joined the Pennsylvania Family Institute, a group working to stabilize the Christian family.

Church Organization (Polity)

The years 1973-2002 are bracketed by two of the most sweeping reorganizations the Evangelical Congregational Church experienced. The first resulted in the restructuring of the boards and agencies of the Church, the selection of a denominational administrative officer, and the reconstitution of the Administrative Council. This Plan of Restructuring was completed in 1982 with the adoption of disciplinary amendments that formalized the new organization. The second reorganization effort brought about the union of the Annual and General Conferences, the establishment of a new National Conference, the reformulation of the Administrative Council as the National Ministry Team, and the realignment of the churches into districts. This effort culminated in 2002, when the twentieth General Conference adopted the necessary amendments to the *Discipline* and launched a refreshed vision for the Church.

General Conference and Administrative Council

The initial restructuring began when the Administrative Council met in October 1973 and Richard Cattermole, General Secretary of the Board of Missions, shared his desire to have an independent missionary foundation, the Christian Service Fellowship (CSF), evaluate the Board of Missions. CSF, however, was willing to undertake this project only if it could evaluate the administrative structure of the entire denomination. The Council endorsed the expanded proposal, and one year later General Conference authorized the issuance of a formal application to CSF for a denominational-wide evaluation. For the next two years CSF representatives made extensive studies of the church through surveys, interviews, and observations.

During this time the church completed efforts to physically centralize the denominational offices in Myerstown PA. A special session of the General Conference in May 1975 adopted the report of the Committee on Coordination of Business Operations and authorized the purchase and renovation of the former Church Center Press building in

Myerstown to accommodate offices for the Bishop, Board of Missions, and the Western District Superintendent of the Eastern Conference and a bookstore operated by the Board of Publication. The Bishop also moved from Reading PA to Myerstown in 1975.[144] The EC Church Center was dedicated on June 2, 1976.[145]

CSF issued its report in mid-1976 and recommended structural streamlining and a similar centralization of denominational administrative structures. The report concluded that "the Evangelical Congregational Church is experiencing diminishing returns as a result of the burden of its own administrative complexity."[146] It suggested ways of reducing overlapping responsibilities so as to achieve the ministry goals of the church without needlessly burdening pastors and laity and proposed a new administrative office to more adequately direct those areas that related to the ministry of local churches. The Fall 1976 session of the Administrative Council asked the General Conference Administrative Policy Committee to examine the report and make appropriate recommendations. Subcommittees worked to fit specific recommendations to the structure of the EC Church. A draft of a restructuring plan was presented to the Administrative Council in February 1978, and the Council presented a revised version to the General Conference of 1978, recommending "that it consider and approve said plan for a trial period until the General Conference of 1982 such trial period to begin after the approval of the plan by both conferences."[147]

Since the plan reduced the number of committees and boards and effected a greater centralization of administrative responsibility, the General Conference reconstituted the Administrative Council so that local churches would be more adequately represented. Up to this time, the Council had consisted of representatives from various boards and agencies. Now, pastors and lay representatives were elected by the Annual Conferences to serve with denominational administrators as members of the Council. The old and the new Administrative Councils met in joint session in March 1979; from that time on the Administrative Council held biennial meetings for the purpose of reviewing the work of the Divisions and "the coordination and implementation of the general church program of the denomination between the sessions of the General Conference."[148]

Richard Cattermole was elected in November 1979 to serve as the first Administrative Secretary (the title was changed to Director of Church Ministries in 1982). As chair of the Divisions of Church

Ministries and Services the Administrative Secretary had a diverse range of responsibilities ranging from Christian education and church planting to finances and property and office management. In the eight years he served in this capacity Cattermole launched an aggressive church planting program and provided very effective leadership in each of the other areas. The other two divisions of the Administrative Council were the Division of Evangelism and Spiritual Care chaired by the Bishop and the Division of Missions under the supervision of its own General Secretary (later known as the Director of Missions).

Annual Conferences

There was little to indicate that dramatic changes were coming as the Annual Conferences met in 1974. Both Conference sessions were held in local churches, as Evangelical conferences had been since the first Evangelical Association church was built. Conference societies continued to convene during the week of conference, and legislative initiatives came before the delegates through reports from standing and special committees. Conference membership remained limited to itinerant clergy and duly elected lay delegates representing churches. It was not until 1986 that local preachers who were serving churches were given the opportunity to vote,[149] and licentiates assigned to churches were denied that privilege until the *Discipline* was amended in 1994.[150]

District Superintendents continued to provide supervision and support for churches. District Superintendents in the Eastern Conference were: Eastern District—David P. Heil (1975-1983), David R. Wolfe (1983-1986), Robert M. Daneker, Sr. (1986-1994); Western District—John E. Moyer (1973-1979), David C. Greulich (1979-1987), David G. Roof (1987-1994). District superintendents in the Western Conference were: Eastern District—Fred T. Fink (1968-1976) and Western District—Alfred E. Anderson (1971-1975). A Study Committee on Supervisory Needs recommended to the 1974 Western Conference session that when the Western District Superintendent's term ended in 1975 the Conference not fill the office but elect only one superintendent for the entire conference,[151] since the second District Superintendent position was being supported by the Board of Missions and the Conference felt this could no longer be justified. For the next two years Fink supervised all of the Conference churches, and the 1975 Conference took action to select an itinerant elder to serve as third member of the Stationing Committee with the Conference Superintendent and the Bishop. Western Conference Superintendents were: Paul D. Dunn (1976-1984), Robert

W. Zettterberg (1984-1992), John C. Ward (1992-2000), and Gary M. Brown (2000-2002). During Ward's tenure his position was made a part-time position, so that he could be assigned to the Cedarville IL church, and three itinerant elders were appointed as State Superintendents to assist him.[152]

The 1978 Eastern Conference acted to provide a year of preparation between the election of the District Superintendents and the beginning of their terms,[153] but greater change came with the approval of the Plan of Restructuring in 1979. Under this Plan administrative divisions assumed the functions of the denominational and conference societies, and when the restructuring trial period ended in 1982 the societies were formally merged into the Annual Conferences. Both the Eastern and Western Conferences took action in 1990 to create Conference Administrative Councils to plan and coordinate the work of the Annual Conference between sessions. The first report of the Eastern Conference Administrative Council recommended streamlining the Conference sessions so that Conference could be held from Thursday through Sunday.[154] The Western Conference Administrative Committee originally included eleven members, but two years later the number was reduced to six, and the committee began functioning as the Conference executive committee.[155]

The Eastern Conference Administrative Council dealt with its first major crisis in 1991. Conference apportionment requisitions had been rising steadily, and some local congregations were finding it difficult to make their contributions to the denominational treasury. As the number of delinquent churches grew, surpluses in the conference treasury melted away, and the Conference faced a deficit. The Conference Administrative Council made recommendations to a special session of the Annual Conference in December 1992, which, although it took no dramatic action to reduce the budget, heightened awareness of the problem, convinced delinquent churches to bring their apportionment payments up-to-date, and prompted other churches to make contributions to assist struggling congregations.

The increasing financial pressure on the Conference and its churches was one of the underlying reasons the 1992 Eastern Conference instructed the Bishop to appoint a special committee "to review the structure of the Annual Conference and its relationship to the General Conference administrative positions."[156] This committee made some sweeping recommendations to the next regular session of the Eastern Conference. First, the standing committee structure of conference was to be discontinued, and during the time normally set aside for committee meetings discussion groups would meet to address some of the issues on the Conference agenda. Second, the two District Superintendents were to be replaced by one Conference Minister, who would have no stationing responsibilities but would serve as a "church growth catalyst" for local congregations and provide pastoral care for the ministers. Third, two Stationing Elders were to be elected to assist the Bishop with stationing pastors, and the stationing process was to be changed to allow more consultation with ministers and congregations prior to finalizing appointments.[157] The Eastern Conference adopted the recommendations and instructed the committee to fine-tune the proposals for presentation at a special session of the Annual Conference to be held on November 20, 1993, and provide a nominee for the position of Conference Minister. This Conference first took action to suspend the disciplinary provision for the election of a District Superintendent so that the Conference Minister could be selected. Then, the Conference elected Ronald D. Miller, pastor of Zion Church in Annville PA, to serve as Conference Minister for a trial period of three years. Since the term of District Superintendent Daneker expired in 1994, no election was held to fill his position, and District Superintendent Roof was asked to step down one year early to make it possible for Miller to assume the office in July 1994.[158]

The new arrangement saved money for the conference, but it placed a heavy burden on the Bishop. In his episcopal address to the Eastern Conference Bishop Kohl stated,

> The temporary laying aside of the two positions of District Superintendents, and the removal of all administrative responsibilities from the Conference Minister has made the Bishop vulnerable to the direct access of 121 pastors, churches, PRC's [Pastoral Relations Committee] and officials ... These and other administrative requirements meant many meetings, personal counseling, consultations, telephone conversations and letters, all matters previously cared for by the DS's [District Superintendent].[159]

The Conference Administrative Council recommended the creation of a new post of Conference Administrative Secretary, but the Eastern Conference asked the Council to consider "all possible options" and report to a special session of the Conference.[160] The delegates to the special conference held in October 1996 decided to employ two Regional Elders instead of continuing the Conference Minister's position. Two months later at another special Conference session, Gerald E.

Baum, Pastor of Faith EC Church in Temple PA, and Frederick J. Moury, Associate Pastor at Trinity EC Church in Lititz PA, were elected to this position, and they assumed office in June 1997.

The job description of the Regional Elder that was adopted in 1997 specified three areas of responsibility: pastoral care for clergy and their families, including visiting each at least once per year; support of local churches, including provision of resources for growth and encouragement through visits to congregations; and administration, including aid to local church Pastoral Relations Committees and handling applicants for ministry. The Regional Elders were not, however, to have any responsibilities for stationing and were to participate in other committees only with the prior consent of the Bishop.[161]

While the administrative structure of Eastern Conference was evolving, changes were also occurring in the Conference sessions themselves. In 1978 the Bishop began reading the report of pastoral changes on the opening evening of the Eastern Conference instead of at the closing session. The 1985 Eastern Conference took action to convene future sessions on the "Wednesday following the last Sunday of May," two weeks later than previously. By the 1990s local churches were finding it increasingly difficult to host the Conference sessions in church facilities, and in 1991 the motion that stipulated the location of the next Eastern Conference also stated, "These sessions may take place on a college campus."[162] The 1992 Eastern Conference was hosted by Trinity Church of Lititz PA but held at Messiah College in Grantham PA, with the closing denominational rally at Lancaster Bible College on Sunday evening. Subsequent Eastern Conference sessions were held at Messiah College, though the closing rallies were held at various other locations. The Western Conference began meeting on a college campus in 1998, when they convened at Bluffton College in Bluffton OH.

The Eastern Conference took on a new look when it moved to a college campus. In the years that followed, the ordination service was scheduled for either Wednesday or Thursday evening instead of Sunday afternoon. Informative, lively forums were held during the day. The wives of the pastors accompanied their husbands to conference and participated in special programs prepared for them. A much larger percentage of delegates were lodged at the seat of Conference. The Western Conference was also gradually streamlined and restructured. Starting in 1989 the Bishop read the Stationing Committee's report early in the session. The number of standing and special committees was reduced, ordination was held earlier in the week, and by 1995 no Conference services were held on Sunday.

Local Church Organization

The Evangelical Congregational *Discipline* of 2000 provided for a model of congregational organization that was little changed from the United Evangelical Church. Indeed, although some of the titles were changed, the basic pattern had its roots in Wesley's church. The "highest judicial or legislative body" was still the Local Conference (formerly Quarterly Conference) chaired by an officer of the Annual Conference (now the Conference Superintendent or Regional Elder). Its business was still to examine the moral conduct of the congregation's officials and "those who may come to celebrate the Lord's Supper," examine candidates for ministry, fix the pastor's salary, elect a lay delegate to Annual Conference, and receive quarterly reports from the pastor and church leaders for the benefit of the Conference Superintendent or Regional Elder.

The Official Board was to serve as the principal administrative body of the congregation, but, reflecting the concerns of church leaders when such Boards first developed in the early twentieth century, the *Discipline* was very clear that it not "usurp or infringe upon the duties and powers...vested ...in the Local Conference." The Official Board was to consist of: the pastor, the lay delegate to the Annual Conference, the class leaders, the trustees, the stewards, the general superintendent of the Sunday School, the president of the senior Christian Endeavor Society, the Youth Ministries representative, the president of the Adult Missionary Fellowship or the chairperson of the local Missionary Committee, the church treasurer, and the chairman of the local Board of Christian Education, plus any additional members elected by the Board. Some of these titles were relatively new and reflected new options in congregational life: "Adult Missionary Fellowship" replaced "Women's Missionary Society" in 1975, the local Missionary Committee was an option added in 1983 for congregations without an Adult Missionary Fellowship, the Youth Ministries position added in 1975 recognized the presence of alternatives to Christian Endeavor in many EC congregations, and the local Board of Christian Education was an optional body including representatives of Sunday School, youth ministries, and missionary organizations to structure and oversee the total Christian education program of a congregation. The basic structure and most of the offices, however, had long histories. As in Wesley's day the class leaders and classes were charged with ascertaining the spiritual condition of individual members, developing the members in spirituality, and providing weekly times for prayer, praise, and testimony. The stewards still had financial duties (to develop with the pastor his salary and benefit package for recommendation to the Local Conference, to provide living quarters for the pastor, to promote the financial program of the church) and were charged as always with providing the bread and grape juice for Holy Communion. The trustees were to care for the church properties. As in the days of Dubs and Heil, Sunday School, youth, and missionary organizations were well-represented. The *Discipline* also provided for an annual congregational meeting to hear reports, consider local opportunities and needs, and elect officers.[163]

Yet, two concepts were introduced in the late twentieth century that will have long-range effects on how local EC churches are governed. The first of these was the modification of the Pastoral Relations Committee (PRC), a body that was introduced by Bishop Scanlin in 1963 in order to assist in the stationing process. [See Chapter Five, "Church Life: The Pastorate."] Initially, the concept of Pastoral Relations Committee was not widely understood or even accepted. Even though the appointment of a PRC was made a rule of the Eastern Conference in 1968, pastors were suspicious of a committee that they saw as functioning only when there was unrest in the congregation. In 1976, therefore, the Policy Committee of the Eastern Conference developed guidelines and resource materials in an attempt to alleviate these suspicions and reinforce the view that "the primary function of this committee shall be to aid the pastor, and any pastoral assistants, to effectively serve the needs and program of the local congregation."[164] The next General Conference (1978) approved an amendment to the *Discipline* making Pastoral Relations Committees, which up until this time had been found only in the Eastern Conference, mandatory for all Evangelical Congregational churches.

Further change came with the new stationing procedures introduced to the Eastern Conference in 1993. In the event of a pastoral change the PRC is now to prepare a Church Self-Study (Church Information Profile) "to assist the church and stationing committee in knowing the strengths and weaknesses of the church body, ministry, as well as in knowing what gifts are required in a pastor for effective ministry." [165] The Stationing Committee gives the name of a prospective pastor to the PRC, and arrangements are made for the committee to interview the pastor. After the interview, the committee decides on the acceptability of the pastor and conveys its decision to the Stationing Committee. The position of the PRC in stationing was formalized in the Vision 20/20 proposal approved in 2002.[166]

The second new concept that will have long lasting results is the optional "alternative church structure for local church organizations" approved by the 1998 General Conference.[167] Coming out of a study by the Church Development Commission of the Administrative Council, this option is an attempt to make church governance less property/finance-centered and more ministry-oriented.[168] In this structure a Ministry Council replaces the Official Board as the local governing body. The membership of the Council does not have to conform to the representative model of the Board but may be stipulated by a congregation at its annual meeting or by the Ministry Council itself. Instead of committees, the Council works through commissions, including those for evangelism, missions, Christian education (including Sunday school and youth ministries), worship, music, and pastoral relations, each with well-defined goals. Each commission is free to make decisions and plans without prior approval from the Ministry Council as a whole. Both Annual Conferences accepted the new system, and several churches, including Boyertown PA and Dixon IL, have restructured successfully.

Toward the National Conference

As the twentieth century drew to a close, the Evangelical Congregational Church was experiencing change at all levels of its organization. Some changes were reactive, *ad hoc* adaptations to circumstances beyond the control of the church. Some changes were proactive, attempts to analyze weaknesses and address fundamental problems. Some changes were the result of careful planning and preparation. Some changes were spontaneous, a response to the leading of the Holy Spirit. At the 1994 General Conference the devotional leader, a noted Southern Baptist author named Henry Blackaby, concluded his final message to the Conference by calling the delegates to a season of prayer.[169] The prayer time became a prolonged time of soul searching, confession, and reconciliation, in which the Holy Spirit softened the hearts of all who were present and prepared the soil for new visions of cooperative ministry. At its conclusion a minister from the Western Conference, Richard Osberg from Knox PA, made a motion

> that the Eastern and Western Conferences of the Evangelical Congregational Church consider merging to form one Conference. That the Boundaries Committee of the General Conference prepare an impact and feasibility study of this proposal to be presented at both

Annual Conferences in 1996 for discussion and revision. That both Annual Conferences vote on a proposal in 1997. That the General Conference adopt or reject any final proposal in 1998.[170]

His motion was adopted, and a new chapter began for the EC Church.

The Boundaries Committee met on September 18, 1995, but reports were not made at the 1996 Annual Conference sessions nor was a vote taken on a proposal in 1997. On March 24, 1998, however, the Conference Relations Committees of both Annual Conferences met to discuss credentialing differences, and on April 22, 1998, Bishop Kohl convened a meeting of Annual Conference representatives and the Bishops Emeriti to further discuss merger. The conclusion drawn at these meetings was that "there are no insurmountables" to merger. The Boundaries Committee offered the following motion at the 1998 General Conference held at Wyndamere Heights Church in Lewisberry PA:

> The merger of the Eastern and Western Conferences is a viable option to be further considered and that committees be assigned to make such further study for presentation to the General Conference of 2002. Reports to be made to the Annual Conference in 2001 (and 2002 if necessary).[171]

The Standing Committee on Church Development recommended "that the Bishop-elect appoint a task force for visioning the future so that we may be more 'pro-active' rather than largely 're-active.'"[172]

Bishop Sigman appointed the Vision 20/20 Core Committee and Task Force in the summer of 1999 with Rev. James Shields, Executive Director of Twin Pines Camp, as Chair. The Task Force began by formulating Purpose, Mission, Values, and Vision (PMVV) Statements for the denomination, and the General Conference Administrative Council approved these in October 2000. The next step in the "pro-active process" envisioned by Bishop Sigman was to measure current denominational structures against PMVV statements so as to make restructuring a transformative process. The Council directed Bishop Sigman to convene a General Conference Transformation Team to begin restructuring work. When the Team met January 8-10, 2001, the merger proposal was reintroduced as a logical "next step" in denominational transformation.

The 2001 Annual Conferences received an extensive report from the Vision 20/20 Transformation Team. This report was the result of work of countless hours of deliberation and the input of hundreds of ECers working together and was bathed in prayer by a network of intercessors directed by Kevin Leibensperger as prayer coordinator. It outlined steps necessary to unite not only both Annual Conferences but also the General Conference and the Latino Conference. Both Annual Conferences adopted the report and authorized the appointment of Eastern and Western Transformation Teams, which met in joint session on August 29-31, 2001. The Annual Conference Teams affirmed the work of the General Conference Team and expanded it by developing new structures to replace the current structures of the Eastern and Western Conferences. The report of the three teams was made to the General Conference Administrative Council in October 2001. The Council affirmed the report and directed Bishop Sigman to coordinate the writing of a *Basis of Union* setting forth the new structures needed to advance the mission and realize the vision of a "united" Evangelical Congregational Church.[173]

The Basis of Union proposed that the Annual Conferences and the General Conference be merged into a new National Conference. All of the functions previously reserved for the General Conference, such as election of a Bishop and amending the Discipline, were to be assumed by the National Conference in which all itinerant ministers and lay delegates were members. Churches were to be grouped into districts, "ten (10) to twenty-five (25) congregations in a variety of geographical areas [which] are organized to accomplish the Lord's commission."[174] The goal is that over time districts will develop a sense of district identity, so that churches will give each other the care and assistance previously provided by the Annual Conferences and find ways to cooperate in reaching new areas with the Gospel. At the time of the adoption of the Basis of Union in 2002 there were thirteen districts divided into three regions. The tasks undertaken by the Divisions under the old structure now became the responsibility of Commissions, each of which is "charged with the implementation and oversight of one aspect of our church's purpose, mission, values, and vision."[175] Commissions of Church Health, Church Planting, Church Services, Evangelism and Discipleship, Global Missions, and Leadership would function under the authority of a National Ministry Team. Like the former General Conference and Annual Conference Administrative Councils, which handled matters between the sessions of their respective conferences, the National Ministry Team "attends to all matters that arise between the sessions of the Conference as well as carrying out tasks assigned to it by the Conference."[176] Unlike the previous Administrative Councils, the National Ministry Team would have no ex-officio members; the membership would be composed exclusively of pastors and lay delegates representing districts.

The Basis of Union was approved by the 2002 General Conference and sent to the Annual Conferences. The Western Conference met in special session on October 31 and November 1, 2002. Business sessions were mixed with services of celebration in three different locations, First and Cottage Grove Churches in Akron OH and First Church in Canton OH. Members of the Western Conference looked back on eighty years of fruitful ministry for Christ and overwhelmingly approved the Basis. The final business session of the Eastern Conference was held on March 29, 2003, at New Bethany EC Church in Allentown PA. At this session the amendments to the Discipline approved at the 2002 General Conference were adopted, and the conference became part of the new National Conference of the Evangelical Congregational Church. One month later clergy and laity from all areas of the Eastern Conference gathered in First Church in Reading PA for a service of celebration and thanksgiving.

As this new structure was worked out the Task Force prayed that the following vision statement would be a reality.

> The Evangelical Congregational Church will be a dynamic movement of God that is led by pastors and laity who have a burning passion for God and a missionary zeal to reach the lost. We will creatively obey the Great Commission by transforming plateaued and declining churches into healthy, disciple-making churches that are committed to evangelizing the communities to which God has called them. Healthy churches will reproduce themselves by planting churches in least reached communities. Interdependence will be the distinguishing mark of the Evangelical Congregational Church as local churches network with one another and ministries beyond the E.C. family to proclaim the Gospel to the world.[177]

Conclusion

The "Albright People" have been "evangelical" from the beginning. For two centuries children of Jacob Albright, whether they were called the *Evangelische Gemeinschaft*, the Evangelical Association, the United Evangelical Church, or the Evangelical Congregational Church, have had the same Gospel mandate: "take the Gospel to every person everywhere."[178] Fulfilling an unchanging mandate has meant, however, changing methods as the culture surrounding the church has changed with increasing rapidity. Missions, ministry, Christian education, and worship in 2002 are quite different from the way they were in 1802, but the Evangelical Congregational Church remains zealous in pursuit of the holy life and the worship of God, committed to viable traditions like campmeeting and to benevolent care of those in need, and attentive to the views and needs of the local congregation.

In a new millennium the Evangelical Congregational Church continues to do its part in spreading the *evangel*. It is an "old, old, story" but always told in new ways by new voices. Albright's parting words are still being fulfilled today:

> If it is God's will that you shall be a permanent association, He will also provide the elements necessary to success. He will rise up men from among you who will take up the burden I can no longer bear, and consummate the work. It is of God and in His hands, and He will provide."[179]

Notes

1. Christian Service Fellowship, *Evaluation Study Report of Evangelical Congregational Church* (Minneapolis: Christian Service Fellowship, 1976), section I.

2. In the event of a bishop's death a special session of the General Conference "within three months of the time the vacancy occurs shall elect a bishop for the unexpired term." In addition, if a bishop's death "should occur within the last year of his term of office" the District Superintendent shall have the option of not calling for a special election. Furthermore, if a bishop is expected to be incapacitated for "a prolonged and indefinite period of time" the Administrative Council shall meet and "determine the means by which the duties of the office shall be handled." The Council also could declare the office of bishop vacant by reason of the bishop's incapacity. ECGenConfJ, 1973, 145.

3. "Episcopal Address," ECGenConfJ, 1979, 87.

4. "Episcopal Address," ECGenConfJ, 1982, 52.

5. "Episcopal Address," ECGenConfJ, 1986, 101–115.

6. Ibid, 112.

7. E-mail response to questionnaire, November 2003.

8. "Episcopal Address," ECGenConfJ, 1990, 33.

9. "Episcopal Address," ECGenConfJ, 1994, 31.

10. E-mail response to questionnaire, November 2003.

11. Ibid.

12. From a brochure entitled, "Vision 20/20. The future is NOW!" December 2000.

13. Sigman, E-mail.

14. "Episcopal Address," ECEConfJ, 2002, 105.

15. Notice, UE, July 29, 1977, 14.

16. Keith R. Miller, "Report of the Director of Church Ministries," in ECGenConf], 1990, 54.

17. "A History of the Evangelical Congregational Church Retirement Village 1925–1985" (Myerstown, PA: 60th Anniversary Committee of the Evangelical Congregational Retirement Village, 1985), 12–14.

18. See for example "Retirement Village Acquires Bus," UE, October 27, 1977, 12.

19. Franklin H. Schock,"E.C.C. Retirement Village Board," ECGenConf], 1986, 154–163.

20. "E.C.C. Retirement Village," ECGenConf], 1998, 127–135.

21. Bruce D. Hill, "Evangelical Congregational Church Retirement Village," ECEConf], 2001, 141.

22. "Missions Committee," ECGenf], 1970, 79.

23. "Missionary Committtee and Church Extension Committee," ECGenf], 1974, 67.

24. J. Karl Harper, "Report of the Superintendent Eastern District," ECEConf], 1975, 165.

25. David P. Heil, "Report of Eastern District Superintendent," ECEConf], 1977, 83.

26. David P. Heil, "District Superintendent Report," ECEConf], 1978, 93.

27. "Official Minutes," ECEConf], 1993, 60.

28. "Western Conference Missionary Society," ECWConf], 1974, 92.

29. David C. Greulich, "Western District Superintendent's Report," ECEConf], 1987, 123.

30. "Official Minutes." 1982 ECWConf], 69.

31. Paul D. Dunn, "District Superintendent's Report," ECWConf], 1983, 72.

32. See [James D. Yoder], "Pottstown Profile," ECEConf], 1984, 153–154.

33. Richard A. Cattermole, "Director of Church Ministries Report," ECEConf], 1986, 208.

34. "Official Minutes," ECNConf], 2003,Section 4–7.

35. Keith Miller, "Director of Church Ministries," ECEConf], 2001, 133.

36. Edmund J. Reitz, "ECCO: A New Venture for Christ and Church Growth," UE, May 30, 1975, 1, 4–6.

37. David C. Greulich, "Report of Western District Superintendent," ECEConf], 1984, 105.

38. "Trustees of Conference," ECEConf], 1990, 90.

39. Karren L. Ray, "Christian Care Center of Logan Square," ECWConf], 2000, 78.

40. Bruce A. Ray, e-mail to John E. Moyer, November 12, 2004.

41. "Official Minutes," ECEConf], 2001, 85.

42. Michael W., Sigman, "Episcopal Address," ECEConf], 2001, 95.

43. Other church planting projects that were started, but were discontinued before being chartered, are: Lordstown, OH (1981), Burlington, VT (1985), Marion OH, (1985), Perry Hall, MD (1988), Lafayette, IN (1989), and Largo

MD (1997).

44. "Boundary Committee," ECEConfJ, 1999, 91.

45. Fred Fink, "Conference Superintendent's Report," ECWConfJ, 1976, 44.

46. "E. C. Board of Missions—Report to the 14th General Conference of the Evangelical Congregational Church—September 22, 1978," ECGenConfJ, 1978, 107.

47. Patricia Strain, "A History of the Missions Program of the Evangelical Congregational Church From 1975–2000" (ME 795 Guided Research Paper, Evangelical School of Theology, 2001), 4–5.

48. Ibid., 6.

49. "E. C. Division of Missions," ECGenConfJ, 1982, 95.

50. "Division of Missions," ECGenConfJ, 1986, 132.

51. Strain, 16–19.

52. John P. Ragsdale, "Division of Missions," ECGenConfJ, 1998, 110; Strain, 9, 26–27, 30–31.

53. Juan Obando, "Latin American Conference," ECGenConfJ, 1986, 142; Strain, 19, 25, 31.

54. Jean Buss, "Japan Conference," ECGenConfJ, 1986, 140–141; Strain, 7–8, 24.

55. Strain, 10, 21, 23, 28–29, 32.

56. Strain, 21, 30.

57. Strain, 28, 31.

58. John P. Ragsdale, "Global Ministries Commission," ECNConfJ, 2003, section 7, 9.

59. Robert G. Hower, "From Vision to Reality: The Story of the Evangelical School of Theology" [rev. ed.] (Myerstown: Evangelical School of Theology, 2003), 74–79.

60. Ibid., 97–100.

61. Ibid., 96, 100.

62. Ibid., 123–132.

63. "Minutes of the Joint Commission on Federation," (2–3 October, 1974): 1.

64. Ibid.

65. "Minutes of the Joint Commission on Federation," (22–23 September 1977): 6.

66. "Church Federation," "Lay Delegates," ECWConfJ, 1981, 61,62.

67. "Minutes of the Joint Commission on Federation," (28–29 October, 1981): 1.

68. "Joint Statement Concerning Exploration of Merger," AdCoun, March 31, 1982, 336.

69. "Evaluation Study Report of the Evangelical Congregational Church," Part One. (Minneapolis, MN: Prepared by the Christian Service Fellowship, 1976), A–21.

70. "Minutes of the Joint Commission on Federation," (28–29 October,

1982): 9.

71. "Minutes of the Steering Committee on Merger Discussion," (14 January 1983): 2.

72. "Minutes of the Administrative Council of the Joint Commission on Federation," (7 April 1983): 1.

73. "Church Federation Committee," ECGenConfJ, 1986, 225.

74. "Church Federation Committee," ECGenConfJ, 1990, 106.

75. Michael W. Sigman, "Episcopal Address," ECEConfJ, 2001, 98.

76. Michael Sigman, "Episcopal Address," ECWConfJ, 2000,40; AdCoun, March 21, 2001,11, mimeographed..

77. "Report of the Preachers' Aid Society," ECGenConfJ, 1958, 150.

78. "Board of Pensions," ECGenConfJ, 1998, 142; 1982, 97; 1990, 67

79. R. H. Bornman, "The Historical Society," ECGenConfJ, 1978, 100; R. H. Bornman, "Historical Society Trustees," ECGenConfJ, 1982, 114; Thomas Leininger, "Historical Society Trustees," ECGenConfJ, 1986, 182–184; Thomas Leininger, "Historical Society Trustees," ECGenConfJ, 1990, 85–86; Thomas Leininger, "Historical Society," ECGenConfJ, 1994, 81–82; Robert Hower, "Historical Society," ECGenConfJ, 1998, 139–140.

80. Clarence R. Robson, John K. Bergman (1897–1987), and Thomas G. Hepner in the U. S. Army and Robert S. Wilson in the United States Navy.

81. "Chaplaincy Committee," ECGenConfJ, 1982, 193. The eleven pastors listed are: CH(MAJ) David E. Myers, CH(CPT) Robert H. Gresh, CH(CPT) Robert L. Bast, CH(CPT) Philip T. Guistwite, LT Robert A. Brown, CHC USNR, LT Paul W. Steel, CHC USNR, CH(CPT) William C. Christian, CH(LTC) Ronald D. Miller, CH(CPT) Craig Nagle, CH(CPT) Robert L. Nissly, and LT William J. McEllroy, Jr.

82. The consumer price index information was taken from the Bureau of Labor Statistics web page, www.bls.gov/pub/special.requests/cpi/cpiai.txt.

83. Editorial, "P. M. Obit," UE, March 21, 1975, 2–3.

84. "Report of Superintendent—Eastern District," ECEConfJ, 1976, 85.

85. UE, June 27, 1975, 15.

86. ECEConfJ, 1985, p 160,161.

87. The series is available along with a companion pamphlet, "The Evangelical Congregational Church is…" (formerly "Followers of the Way").

88. A copy of the service is found in ECGenConfJ, 1978, p 33.

89. Hymnal Committee, [Minutes], November 30, 1982.

90. Hymnal Committee, [Minutes], April 8, 1983.

91. Hymnal Committee, [Minutes], June 21, 1983,

92. Hymnal Committee, [Minutes], October 25, 1983; August 8, 1984.

93. Hymnal Committee, [Minutes], January 29, 1985.

94. UE, Nov 16, 1973, p 12.

95. ECWConfJ, 1982, p 62.

96. See Annual Conference Journal District Superintendent's Report. These reports annually highlighted local church improvements, additions, etc. of a

large and not so large nature.

97. Division of Evangelism and Spiritual Care, "A Denominational Day of Prayer and Fasting," UE, April 1980, 17.

98. The Minutes state: "During and following Dr. Blackaby's message there was a mighty moving of the Holy Spirit, which lead [sic] to a time of repentance, and prayer, of such magnitude, that it is impossible for these minutes to capture what happened in our midst. The conducting of business was put aside for an extended time as God continued to work among us." ECGenConf], 1994, 28.

99. Michael Sigman, "Vision 20/20," *Doors and Windows* 10, no. 5 (1999–2000), 1.

100. "Heartcry," September, 2002, 1.

101. David G. Roof, "Division of Evangelism & Spiritual Care," ECGenConf], 1990, 51.

102. "Vision 20/20 Report," section VII.B.1, 4.

103. "Class Leader's Task Force," 1.

104. See UE, April, 1980 and UE, May, 1985.

105. *Herndon Camp Grove, Centennial 1901–2001* (n.p.: Herndon Camp Meeting Association, 2002). (335 pp.)

106. "E.C. Waldheim Park Association 1904–2004—100th Anniversary Souvenir Booklet."

107. "Committee on Evangelism," ECGenConf], 1978, 161.

108. Report of the Division of Evangelism and Spiritual Care," AdCoun, (18 September 1982): 2

109. "The Division of Evangelism and Spiritual Care," ECGenConf], 1986, 113.

110. "Short Takes: How Evangelism Works in Boyertown," E. C. Doors and Windows, Winter, 1991, 15.

111. "Minutes of the Sessions," ECGenConf], 1982, 29.

112. Richard W. Kohl, "Episcopal Address," ECWConf], 1999, 40.

113. "Evangelism and Spiritual Care Report," ECEConf], 2001, 131.

114. "Second Service News," 1 #4, (14 November 1999): 3, Archives, Evangelical Congregational Church, Myerstown, PA.

115. "Administrative Secretary," ECEConf], 1982, 178.

116. "Administrative Secretary," ECEConf], 1984, 171.

117. "Church Development Committee," ECGenConf], 2002, 168.

118. "Church Development," ECGenConf], 1982, 128.

119. "ECSEL! Know What It Means? How Is It Pronounced? What Is It For?" UE, April 1986, 14–15.

120. "Task Force on Christian Education," ECGenConf], 1986, 231.

121. See Donald W. Metz, "Institution of a Leadership Program for the Sunday Schools of the Evangelical Congregational Church," (M.Div. diss. Trinity Divinity School, Deerfield, IL, 1989).

122 "Director of Christian Education," ECWConf], 1993, 48.

123. "Director of Church Ministries," ECEConfJ, 1997, 115.

124. William S. Ryan, "Past-Present-Future," UE, June 29, 1973, 6.

125. "Twin Pines Camp," UE, October 8, 1976, 7.

126. Paul D. Dunn, "Presiding Elder's Report," ECWConfJ, 1979, 50, 51.

127. "Camp ECCO," UE, March 1989, 7.

128. Ronald D. Miller, "Conference Minister's Report," ECEConfJ, 1996, 75.

129. Herbert D. Wittmaier, "Episcopal Address," ECGenConfJ, 1978, 45.

130. ECGenConfJ, 1974, 83–84.

131. "Spiritual State of the Church," ECWConfJ, 1982, 102.

132. *Pine Lines,* January 2003, 1; September 2003, 1.

133. Michael W. Sigman, "Episcopal Address," ECEConfJ, 2000, 95.

134. "Committee to Study the Implications of the Charismatic Movement on and in our Churches," ECEConfJ, 1976, 112–119.

135. "Spiritual State of the Church," ECEConfJ, 1983, 155.

136. "Social Action Committee," ECWConfJ, 1980, 64.

137. [William S. Sailer,] "It's Up to You," UE, February 20, 1973, 2–3.

138. Ronald B. Kuntz, "The Abortion Revolution," UE, June 29, 1973, 13–16.

139. Mrs. Robert L. Michell, Sr., "Abortion Rebuttal," "Letters to the Editor," July 27, 1973, 15.

140. "Resolution," UE, November 30, 1973, 11.

141. "143.1.2.5–Abortion," ECDisc, 2000, 16.

142. "Committee on Social Concern and Action," ECEConfJ, 1990, 113.

143. "Social Action Committee," ECWConfJ, 1995, 82–83.

144. "Excerpts from the Report of the Committee for Coordination of Business Operations," "Minutes of the Special Session of the Thirteenth Quadrennial General Conference of the Evangelical Congregational Church, May 22, 1975," ECGenConfJ, 1978, 170.

145. "Our New Church Center," UE, August 27, 1976, A–D.

146. Christian Service Fellowship, "Part One—Evaluation Study of Evangelical Congregational Church, Myerstown, Pennsylvania, 17067," 13.

147. "Minutes," AdCoun, April 6, 1978, 288.

148. "Administrative Council of the General Conference," ECDisc, 2000, 105.

149. "Amendments to the *Discipline* Committee," ECGenConfJ, 1986, 214.

150. "Amendments," ECGenConfJ, 1994, 92.

151. "Study Committee on Supervisory Needs," ECWConfJ, 1974, 74.

152. "Administrative Committee," ECWConfJ, 1999, 64.

153. "Policy," ECEConfJ, 1975, 101.

154. "Administrative Council," ECEConfJ, 1991, Gray, 15.

155. "Revision of Rules," ECWConfJ, 1992, 88.

156. "Official Minutes," ECEConfJ, 1992, Green, 9.

157. "Study of the Structure of Annual Conference," ECGenConfJ, 1993, Grey 95–103.

158. "Minutes," ECEConf], special session, November 20, 1993, 1–2.

159. Richard W. Kohl, "Episcopal Address," ECEConf], 1996, 72.

160. "Eastern Conference Administrative Council," ECEConf], 1997, 102.

161. "Special Rules," ECEConf], 1997, 63–64.

162. "Official Minutes," ECEConf], 1991, 9.

163. *The Creed, Ritual and Discipline of the Evangelical Congregational Church,* 2000 ed. (Myerstown, PA: Evangelical Congregational Church, 2000), 36–50.

164. "Policy Committee," ECEConf], 1976, 110–111.

165. "Special Session of the Eastern Annual Conference," November 20, 1993.

166. *Basis of Union,* 57–60.

167. "Amendments," ECGenConf], 1998, 158–160.

168. Ibid., p. 145

169. "Official Minutes of the Sessions," ECGenConf], 1994, 22.

170. ECGenConf], 1994, 28.

171. "Boundaries Committee," ECEConf], 1998, 95.

172. "Church Development," ECGenConf], 1998, 145.

173. Basis of Union, section two, "Introduction," 2.

174. "Amendments," ECGenConf], 2002, 189.

175. "Amendments, ECGenConf], 2002, 196.

176. "Special Rules," ECNatConf], 2003, Section 3, 7.

177. "Purpose, Mission, Values and Vision," Basis of Union, 15.

178. "Episcopal Address, ECEConf], 2002, p. 103.

179. R. W. Albright, *A History of the Evangelical Church* (Harrisburg: Evangelical Press, 1942), 84.

Afterword

by

Bishop Michael Sigman

Evangelical Christians are united in their declaration that belief must be reflected in practice and that practice should give witness to belief. This conviction holds true both for individual believers and a body of believers. When a body of believers, whether it is a local congregation or a national denomination, sets forth Purpose, Mission, Values and Vision (PMVV) statements, one should expect that these statements will determine the course and shape the structures of the body. The message a Church proclaims should be reflected in the life of that Church.

When the Administrative Council of the General Conference adopted the PMVV statements recommended by the Vision 20/20 Task Force in October 2000, it was clear that our work was far from complete. If "raising up healthy churches that proclaim Christ to a hurting world" is truly our mission, then our structures must advance that mission. If we believe that the five values identified are truly the "core of our being," then our structures should grow out of these values. If our vision is to become a movement of God, then denominational structures should help us realize this vision. In brief, the purpose, mission, values, and vision the Evangelical Congregational Church proclaims should be reflected in the daily life of the denomination. For this to happen, restructuring was essential.

The restructuring which culminated in the uniting of the conferences in 2003 was a process whereby the current denominational structures were examined in light of the PMVV statements. Changes were recommended so that the structures would reflect these statements. To understand why certain changes were made, one must understand the foundational principles that guided us. These principles really are the "foundation" upon which the new structures are built.

1. Foundational Principle: Being Mission-Driven

The decisions and direction of the early Church were driven by the mission of the Church. The mission was simple and aggressive: make disciples of Jesus Christ of all people everywhere (Matthew 28:16-20). Church leaders like Paul, Peter, and John were driven by their desire to fulfill this mission. They lived to introduce men and women to the Savior. Bill Easum captures the mission-driven spirit of the early Church well when he writes:

> Christianity lives and breathes for this cause: the redemption of creation. Christians will do whatever will assist in achieving that mission. The clash between Paul and the Jerusalem Church gives some help here. When the church leaders heard that Paul had been baptizing converts without first circumcising them, they rebuked him. But after hearing of the marvelous work occurring in people's lives, the council members changed their minds. The guiding principle: If it transforms lives, you do it even if it is illegal - because redeeming people is more important then keeping institutional traditions. The early Christians didn't let a little thing like legality get in the way of their radical devotion to Jesus.[1]

The Evangelical Congregational Church adopted a denominational mission statement: "to raise up healthy churches proclaiming Christ to a hurting world." This mission must determine our structures and drive our decisions. When it does, the denomination becomes a servant to local congregations with an emphasis on resourcing rather than regulating. The focus is not on preserving the institutional denomination but on proclaiming the transformational Gospel and doing so by raising up healthy communities of faith that will powerfully penetrate the dark corners of the world. In brief, it is not the survival of a denomination that is paramount. It is the salvation of a world of people! This mission must drive EVERYTHING we do.

2. Foundational Principle: Becoming a Movement of God

The Acts of the Apostles is a book about church. Its author, the physician Luke, records the birth of the church, describes the church's first attempts at holding annual (!) Conferences, and shows how God handled stationing in the early years. From this book, we learn about church conflict, cultural relevancy, and successful missionary strategies. It really is quite an exciting book with action scenes from chapter 1 to chapter

28. The sense that one has when reading the book of Acts is that the church was on the move for God - always expanding the boundaries, boldly taking risks, and fearlessly confronting modern (maybe even "post-modern") sensibilities. This church—the church in the book of Acts— was a dynamic, vibrant, visionary church possessing a burning passion for God and a missionary zeal for the lost. This church should be the church that the world sees today. This is the church God wants the Evangelical Congregational Church to become!

Too often, the church behaves more like a settled institution on earth than a dynamic movement of God. "Institution" evokes the image of an immovable building to which people are invited to come, while "movement" evokes the image of an active body of people influencing the cultures to which they go.

An institution preserves boundaries; a movement pursues new frontiers. An institution is marked by caution; a movement is marked by risk. An institution has its eyes fixed on itself and is content with itself; a movement has its eyes fixed on a goal and is moving toward it. An institution has many essentials and few negotiables; a movement has many negotiables and few essentials. An institution is law-based; a movement is grace-based. An institution operates with a highly defined hierarchy and a low level of trust; a movement draws its life from a finely tuned team and a high level of trust.

The Evangelical Congregational Church must again become a movement of God. We say "again" because it is our conviction that Jacob Albright led a movement of God in the year 1800 when he raised up the first three class meetings and launched an itinerant ministry that we inherited from Albright's co-laborers. Bishop John Seybert energized the pace of our movement in the mid-nineteenth century as he inspired a generation of evangelical preachers to unashamedly preach the gospel of Jesus Christ and plant the church in new territory. Evangelicals weren't content to keep the home fires burning; Evangelicals fanned the flames of revival at every crossroads that was without a witness for Christ.

The structures we adopted as we entered the 21st century must return us to this course and accelerate us as we seek to realize the vision of becoming a movement of God.

3. Foundational Principle: Cultivating Trust

Dr. Jay Desko of the Philadelphia Biblical University observes that "the mission and performance of the (Christian) organization will ultimately be limited or sacrificed without a culture of trust."[2]

Sadly, the history of the Evangelical Congregational Church is rooted in a culture of distrust that began in 1887 with the schism of our parent denomination, the Evangelical Association (EA). While there were very good reasons to separate and form the United Evangelical Church (and ultimately the Evangelical Congregational Church), the climate of suspicion and distrust influenced the design of denominational structures. At times, "checks and balances" took precedence over mission and vision. For example, Annual Conferences were originally designed to efficiently and expeditiously advance God's kingdom into new territory. Over time, they became mere instruments of political power in denominational struggles.

The new denominational structures have been designed to recapture and cultivate trust. Several factors that contribute to a higher level of trust were incorporated into the design of new structures. They are:

- Regular time together as a denominational family
- Positive and enjoyable environment
- Freedom and encouragement to raise questions in a spirit of Christian love
- Mutual participation and support for most significant decisions
- Carefully appointed committees that represent a cross-section of the denomination
- Information freely shared between people and groups
- Minimal suspicion regarding motives and decisions, deepening level of dialogue over time[3]

Of course, the most significant "trust cultivator" was the union of the conferences which resulted in the historic first National Conference in May 2003. This was the first time every EC pastor and lay delegate gathered together under one roof to do the work of the Church.

These then are the key foundational principles upon which the new structures were built. These principles formed our thinking and planning and, as a result, were woven throughout the *Basis of Union*, the document that outlined the proposed restructuring.

Of course, key foundational principles may be solid and the proposals that flow from them may be popular, but if our hearts are not convinced, our union will not be complete. Reflecting upon the weaknesses of the merger between the United Evangelical Church and Evangelical Association, Bishop W.F. Heil wrote,

A heart union is the necessary basis of a successful organic union, but an organic union without a heart union will be a source of discontent and contention....Our faith is that the churches should have been brought into hearty fellowship first and after that into organic union.[4]

Over the course of the twentieth century, the churches and leaders of the Annual Conferences of the Evangelical Congregational Church enjoyed "hearty fellowship." This fellowship has been much more frequent since the work of denominational long range planning began. A turning point in Annual Conference relations was the 1999 prayer summit where annual conference leaders repented of sinful and divisive attitudes. The repentance was followed by forgiveness and a commitment to build unity in the Church. These men and women and the dozens who labored to identify our mission, articulate our vision, and align our structures are the "new evangelical pioneers." They are leading us into new territory and we are exceedingly grateful.

While it is too early to properly evaluate the enduring influence of Vision 20/20 and the structures it spawned, current and emerging leaders would agree that the EC Church has "a hope and a future." The number of U.S. church plants is at a record high of fifteen, of which nine are ethnic ministries. Since 2000 dozens of men have entered our ministerial ranks as new candidates or seasoned pastors transferring from other denominations. A total of 154 congregations are organized into thirteen geographic districts under the direction of twenty-six lay and pastoral leaders. The congregations in these districts are learning the fine art of partnership. The number of churches with pastoral teams is increasing as the number of EC churches with more than two hundred people in morning worship increases. The National Conference is financially sound because her churches, with few exceptions, give as requested and beyond to fund a multitude of ministries. Global Ministries has enjoyed an average of $1.7 million in contributions from "mission-driven" ECers and their congregations. Global Ministries' indigenous church initiative will result in the formation of the first National Conference outside of the U.S., as the India Conference becomes National Conference India in 2005. And, perhaps most significant of all, a "heart union" has been effected from among the pastoral and lay leaders of the former Eastern, Western, and Latino Conferences. We are enjoying a refreshingly positive attitude even as we face the challenges of "doing denomination" in the 21st century. Christ Jesus our Lord is truly doing a great work in our midst!

The challenge for our future is to keep our eyes fixed firmly on Him while engaging the culture—every culture—with the truth of God's Word in the power of God's Spirit. That's what evangelicals did in the time of

Albright and Seybert, and that's what evangelicals must do in the future. And we must do so with the confidence that we are trusting "Him who is able to do immeasurably more than all we ask or imagine, according to His power that is work within us, to Him be glory in the Church and in Christ Jesus throughout all generations, for ever and ever! Amen" (Ephesians 3:20-21 NIV).

Notes

1. William Easum, "Where Is Jesus Going?," *NetResults* Nov/Dec 2001:27.

2. Jay Desko. *How to Cultivate Trust in Your Organization* (Langhorne, PA: PCB Graduate School, 2000).

3. Adapted from suggestions by Sigman and Desko.

4. W. F. Heil, "Episcopal Message," UEGenConfJ, 1926, 24.

Appendix 1

Timeline

1681   Pennsylvania founded by William Penn as a "holy experiment" in religious freedom

1759   Jacob Albright, founder of the Evangelical Association, born near Pottstown PA

1784   American Methodists hold Christmas Conference, officially organizing to "reform the nation and to spread scriptural holiness" in North America

1790   Several of Albright's children die, initiating a spiritual crisis in his life

1791   John Seybert born in Manheim PA

1796   Albright begins his preaching career

1800   Albright organizes three class meetings based on the Methodist model

1803   First Conference of the Evangelical Association held, with Albright being recognized as a "genuine evangelical preacher"

1808   Albright dies in Kleinfeltersville PA after a preaching tour in central Pennsylvania

1809   First *Discipline* of the Evangelical Association published

1810   Future Presiding Elder, John Dreisbach carries on impromptu merger negotiations with Methodist leaders Francis Asbury and Henry Boehm, but no merger results

1810   First Evangelical Association camp meeting held in New Berlin PA

1814   Social Conference held between Evangelical Association and United Brethren to discuss merger, but no merger results

1817   First Evangelical Association church building dedicated in New Berlin and first printing establishment also opened

1823   Orwigsburg PA revival moves power base of Evangelical Association from New Berlin to Schuylkill County

1826   Formation of the Western Conference

1832   First Evangelical Association Sunday School established in Lebanon PA

1832   First Evangelical Association *Discipline* in the English language printed

1832   First Charitable Society and Superannuation Fund established

1836   First issue of denominational newspaper, *Der Christliche Botschafter* (*The Christian Messenger*) published

1838   First Missionary Society organized

1839   John Seybert first bishop elected using procedure prescribed in *Discipline*

1848   First edition of English-language paper, *The Evangelical Messenger*, published

1850   Albright Memorial Chapel dedicated in Kleinfeltersville PA

1854   Printing operations moved to Cleveland, OH

1856   Sanctification controversy erupts

1858   W.W. Orwig publishes first denominational history

1859   Orwig and Solomon Neitz wage theological debate on East Pennsylvania Conference floor over the doctrine of sanctification

1863   J. J. Esher elected Bishop

1868   Many Evangelical Association members participate in the second annual Campmeeting for the Promotion of Holiness held in Manheim PA

1875   Thomas Bowman elected Bishop

1885   Bishop Esher reports on problems in Evangelical Association mission to Japan and submits report to editor of Church newspaper for publication, but editor prints it in edited form

1885   Publisher Harry Hartzler accused of editing out material critical of his brother, Jacob Hartzler, the Japan Mission Superintendent

1887   Harry Hartzler dismissed as editor

1891   Two General Conferences held, the majority ("Esherites") meeting in Indianapolis, IN; the minority ("Dubsites") meeting in Philadelphia PA

1894   Minority hold special session of General Conference in Naperville IL, removing themselves from the Evangelical Association and adopting the name, United Evangelical Church

1921   School of Methods founded at Waldheim Campmeeting in Allentown PA

1922   Evangelical Association and majority of United Evangelical Church reunite, but United Evangelical minority chooses to stay out of merger, and is renamed the Evangelical Congregational Church

1926   Burd and Rogers Home for the aged founded in Herndon PA

1931   Districts from Ohio and Western Pennsylvania, along with churches from Illinois, unite to form the Western Annual Conference

        Former campus of Albright College, Myerstown, PA purchased for $25,000

1947   Board of Missions created to assume direct oversight of the denomination's missionary activity

1953   Evangelical Congregational School of Theology founded in Myerstown PA

1958   Rock River Bible Camp, Dixon IL founded

1961   Evangelical Congregational Church Retirement Community opened in Myerstown

        Camp ECCO in Carrollton OH founded

1963   Twin Pine Ranch, near Stroudsburg PA purchased for use as a year-round camp and conference center

1965   *United Evangelical*, the denomination's newspaper, becomes a biweek
        ly publication

1973   Christian Service Fellowship contracted to assess denominational
        structures

1976   Church Center opens, consolidating the offices of the Bishop, the
        Western District Superintendent of the Eastern Conference, the Board
        of Missions, and the editorial staff of the *United Evangelical*

1978   CSF's recommendations implemented, creating the Divisions of
        Evangelism and Spiritual Care; Church Ministries; Church Services;
        and Missions

1986   Vision 21 outlined by Bishop John Moyer with major goals: the plant
        ing of 21 new churches (7 ethnic congregations); the recruiting of 21
        new pastors; and 21% growth in worship and Sunday School atten-
        dance and in the number of conversions, all by the dawn of the 21st
        century

1999   Vision 20/20 Task Force appointed by Bishop Michael Sigman, result
        ing in Basis of Union: a plan for uniting the Eastern, Western, and
        Latino Conferences into one National Conference

2002   Final General Conference of the E.C. Church held in Transfer PA in
        September

        Closing session of the Western Conference held in November

2003   Closing session of the Eastern Conference held in March

        First National Conference of the Evangelical Congregational Church
        held in Grantham PA

Appendix 2

Biographical Data for Bishops

Biographies of previous bishops can be found in *A History of the Evangelical Church* by Raymond W. Albright (Harrisburg: Evangelical Press, 1942).

William Franklin Heil

William F. Heil was born on May 1, 1857, in Berlinville, PA and was granted a license to preach by the East Pennsylvania Conference in 1880. He became a presiding elder in 1890 and in 1902 was chosen a bishop of the United Evangelical Church. After his second term as bishop he was chosen once again as a presiding elder in the East Pennsylvania Conference until 1918, when he was again elected a bishop of the UE Church. He was reelected in 1922 by the non-merging United Evangelicals and served one term. After his retirement in 1926 he served as editor of the *United Evangelical* until his death on November 6, 1930.

Heil had a sharp intellect and firm commitment to principle. Many found him inspiring; others found him exasperating.

Edwin Stephen Woodring

Edwin S. Woodring was born near Wescosville, Lehigh County, PA, on February 17, 1872, the son of John Joseph and Mary (Acker) Woodring. He attended Schuylkill Seminary, Muhlenberg College (Bachelor's and Master's degrees), and Moody Bible Institute. In 1930 Muhlenberg College conferred on him the honorary degree of Doctor of Divinity. Woodring was the first person licensed to preach by the United Evangelical Church at its first General Conference in 1894. He served the following churches: Chicago Adams Street, Genesco IL, Naperville

IL, Philadelphia Christ, Allentown PA Seibert, Tamaqua PA, and Allentown Trinity. Woodring served as a Presiding Elder from 1921 to 1926 and as Bishop from 1926-1935. Following his second term as Bishop he served as Presiding Elder from 1935-1943 and then as pastor of Trinity Church in Allentown until his retirement in 1946. Dr. Woodring died on February 25, 1957, in Harrisburg PA.

Bishop Woodring was primarily responsible for the founding of the School of Methods at Waldheim Park in Allentown, and he maintained an active interest in it throughout his life.

Charles Henry Mengel

Charles Henry Mengel was born at Summit Station PA on May 8, 1879. He was licensed to preach in 1899 and served the following churches in Pennsylvania: Herndon, Creswell, Lansdale, Adamstown, Shenandoah, Easton, and Allentown Bethany. He was elected Presiding Elder in 1922 and served for two terms. Following a pastorate at Lancaster Grace (1930-1934), Mengel was elected Bishop of the Evangelical Congregational Church and served from 1935 to 1943. He then served as pastor of Allentown Bethany until his retirement in 1949.

Mengel's principal interest was in the School of Theology. He worked doggedly for its inception and served as President of its Board of Trustees from 1946 to 1958. He also served as President of the Board of Trustees of the Burd and Rogers Memorial Home from 1923 to 1957. Mengel died on January 14, 1964.

Bishop Mengel was a man of firm convictions and exceptional organizational ability. He was able to see things in their proper perspective and commit himself wholly to well-defined objectives.

Albert W. Cooper

Albert W. Cooper was born on May 24, 1879, in Swan Village, Staffordshire, England, the son of the Rev. and Mrs. Samuel Cooper, who came to the United States in 1886 and settled in New Shenandoah PA. He attended Albright College and Providence University and received the Master of Arts degree from Temple University. Cooper was licensed to preach by the United Evangelical Church in 1900 and received into the East Pennsylvania Conference in 1903. He served as pastor of the following churches in Pennsylvania: White Haven, Frackville, Mauch Chunk, Allentown Grace, Reading Bethany, Reading First, Tamaqua, Allentown Bethany, Reading First (again), and Tamaqua (again). He was elected Bishop of the Evangelical Congregational Church in 1942 and served until his sudden death at Ocean Grove NJ on July 23, 1950.

Bishop Cooper was a preacher of unusual ability; his sermons were marked by clarity and backed by conviction. He had a vision for ecumenical cooperation.

John Adams Smith

John A. Smith was born on June 6, 1890, and graduated from Albright College in 1914. In 1954 his alma mater conferred on him the honorary degree of Doctor of Divinity. Smith was licensed by the East Pennsylvania Conference in 1909 and served the following churches in Pennsylvania: Lansford-White Haven, Pottstown, Allentown Grace, Bangor, Bethlehem Emmanuel (twice), and Shamokin. He served as Presiding Elder of the Western District of East Pennsylvania Conference (1938-1942) and Presiding Elder of the Eastern District (1943-1951) before his election as Bishop in 1951. After the end of his second term in 1959 he served as supply pastor at Bridgeville from 1961 to 1967. Bishop Smith died on February 14, 1983.

Dr. Smith took part in the actions of virtually every committee, society, agency, and organization of his Conference and the Evangelical Congregational Church. He served as President of the Board of Trustees of the Evangelical Congregational Church Retirement Village for twenty-six years, President of the Board of Missions for twenty-eight years, and President of the Preachers' Aid Society for a similar tenure. Through seventy years of active ministry he showed a firm faith, strong Christian convictions, and faithfulness to duty.

Harold Hallman Scanlin

Harold H. Scanlin was born in Philadelphia on December 21, 1906, the son of Robert and Jennie Hallman Scanlin. He attended Temple University and Elizabethtown College and received his theological education at Eastern Baptist Theological Seminary. Elizabethtown College conferred the honorary degree of Doctor of Divinity on him in 1951. Scanlin was licensed to preach in 1929 and served the following churches in Pennsylvania: Millersville, Pottsville, Lehighton, Mohnton, and Allentown Seibert. He served as Presiding Elder from 1951 to 1959 and as Bishop from 1959 to 1967. After his tenure as Bishop he served as the first President of Evangelical Congregational School of Theology from

1967 to 1975. Bishop Scanlin died on August 7, 1982, in Allentown PA.

Dr. Scanlin was a gifted administrator and served in every area of the church's ministry. For ten years he served as Superintendent of the School of Methods, but he also gave twenty-three years of service on the Board of the E.C.C. Retirement Village and twenty-seven years on the Board of Evangelical Congregational School of Theology. He was also active in interdenominational groups like the American Bible Society and the International Society of Christian Endeavor.

Paul Kreidler Cressman

Paul K. Cressman was born in 1905 and received his education at Lehigh University and the University of Illinois. He was teaching at Mt. Union College in Alliance OH when he was called to the ministry. Licensed by the East Pennsylvania Conference in 1931, he pastored the following EC churches in Pennsylvania: Herndon, Mahanoy City, Mauch Chunk, Bangor, and Tamaqua. He served two terms as a Presiding Elder (1958-1966) and one year as pastor at Reamstown before assuming the office of Bishop in 1967. Bishop Cressman died in office on December 18, 1972.

Cressman was noted for his friendly and warm spirit. He held many positions of leadership in the mission boards and societies of the church and also had an interest in educational activities, serving as Director of the East Pennsylvania Bible Conference from 1946 to 1957 and as a member of the Board of Trustees of Evangelical Congregational School of Theology for fifteen years.

Herbert Diemer Wittmaier

Herbert D. Wittmaier was born in 1909 and attended Bethel Church in Philadelphia before being licensed to preach in 1931. He was a graduate of Muhlenberg College and Moravian and Princeton Theological Seminaries and served the following churches in Pennsylvania: Reamstown, Williams Township, Allentown Zion, Allentown Boulevard, Reading Grace, Reading First, and Plymouth Meeting. Wittmaier was elected District Superintendent in 1966 and Bishop in 1973 following the death of Bishop Cressman. Re-elected in 1974, he served until 1979. Bishop Wittmaier died on August 1, 1992, at Lititz PA aged eighty-three years.

Wittmaier served on many agencies and boards of the church, most notably the Boards of Evangelical School of Theology and the

Evangelical Congregational Church Retirement Village. He was also an educator, serving on the faculties of Moravian Theological Seminary and Evangelical School of Theology. This kind, gentle, and witty man was a man of the Word and a man of prayer. He also loved to work with children.

John Edward Moyer

John E. Moyer was born in Allentown PA on May 1, 1932, the son of Howard E. and Esther (Waltz) Moyer. He attended Moravian College, Evangelical Congregational School of Theology, and Temple University. He was awarded the honorary degree of Doctor of Divinity by Moravian College in 1980 and the Doctor of Ministry degree with a major in church growth by Fuller Theological Seminary in 1995. Moyer was licensed to preach by the Eastern Conference of the Evangelical Congregational Church in April 1950, ordained Deacon in April 1956, and ordained Elder in April 1959. He served the following churches in Pennsylvania: Catasauqua, Columbia, Pottstown, and Emmaus. He served as Superintendent of the Western District of the Eastern Conference from 1973 to 1979 and as Bishop from 1979 to 1987. Following his tenure as Bishop he served as Professor of Pastoral Ministries at Evangelical School of Theology until 1998. His wife, the former Dorothy Berger, is a Registered Nurse.

Dr. Moyer displayed great pastoral skill in guiding the church through a time of transition and then went on to train and nurture a new generation of pastors, serving as a worthy model for them.

Richard Alvin Cattermole

Richard A. Cattermole was born on August 13, 1926, in Royersford PA, the son of John W. and Bessie Druckenmiller Cattermole. He received his education at Albright College and Evangelical School of Theology, Reading, PA, and received an honorary Doctor of Divinity degree from Albright College in 1982. Cattermole was licensed to preach in 1946 and ordained in 1952. He pastored churches in Temple and Schuylkill Haven PA before his election as denominational Director of Missions in 1970. As Director of Church Ministries from 1980 to 1988 he facilitated many changes in denominational structure and served as bishop from 1987 to 1991. He is married to the former Jane Reid, who was very active in the missionary work of the denomination, and has two children.

Bishop Cattermole was very active in Christian education, the church camping program, and also served as President of Christian Endeavor International.

Richard Woodland Kohl

Richard W. Kohl was born on June 17, 1934, in Coopersburg PA, the son of Claude and Edna Kohl. He was raised in Allentown PA and received degrees from Moravian College and Moravian Theological Seminary. He was licensed to preach in 1952, ordained deacon in 1957, and ordained elder in 1959. He served as pastor of EC charges at Clayton-Vera Cruz and East Greenville-Hosensack before entering the U.S. Army Chaplaincy in 1961. After his retirement as a Colonel in 1981, he began a church planting project that became the Wyndemere Heights Church in Lewisberry PA. Kohl served as Bishop of the Evangelical Congregational Church from 1991 to 1999. After his tenure as Bishop he pastored St. Paul's Church in Pine Grove PA and has served as interim pastor at Community Evangelical Church in Sinking Spring PA and at Hatfield PA. He is married to the former Mary Louise Kilpatrick and has three children.

Michael Wade Sigman

Michael W. Sigman was born on June 16, 1962, the son of Kenneth W. and Flo Geesey Sigman. He grew up in New Danville PA and attended the Bethel Evangelical Congregational Church in Conestoga PA. While attending Lebanon Valley College Sigman served as Youth Director at First Church in Palmya PA (1981-1983). Licensed to preach in 1983, he served as Youth Pastor at First Church in Reading PA (1984-1986) while attending Evangelical School of Theology. He was ordained in 1988 and assigned to establish Rosedale Community EC Church near Baltimore. Sigman served as pastor there until assuming the office of Bishop in 1999. He is married to the former Jennifer Freiday and has four daughters.

Appendix 3

The Officers of the E. C. Church

(Through 2006)

A. Bishops

William F. Heil   1922–1926
Edwin S. Woodring 1926–1935
Charles H. Mengel 1935–1942
Albert W. Cooper 1943–1950
John A. Smith 1951–1959
Harold H. Scanlin 1959–1967
Paul K. Cressman 1967–1972
Herbert D. Wittmaier 1973–1979
John E. Moyer 1979–1987
Richard A. Cattermole 1987–1991
Richard W. Kohl 1991–1999
Michael W. Sigman 1999–

B. Presiding Elders/Conference Superintendents and Conference Minister/Regional Elders

Eastern (Pennsylvania) Conference

Allentown District:
Charles H. Mengel 1922–1925
Edwin S. Woodring 1925–1928
George Wesley Marquardt 1928–1929

Harrisburg District
Edwin S. Woodring 1922–1925
Charles H. Mengel 1925–1930

Reading District, Allentown and Harrisburg
Presiding Elders shared 1922–1927
Jacob S. Heisler 1927–1929

Eastern District
Jacob S. Heisler 1929–1935
Edwin S. Woodring 1935–1943
John A. Smith 1943–1951
Harold H. Scanlin 1951–1959 *
Earl D. Ehrig 1959–1967
J. Karl Harper 1967–1975
David P. Heil 1975–1983
David R. Wolfe 1983–1986
Robert M. Daneker 1986–1994
Gerald E. Baum 1997–2006 ##
B. Bruce Wagner 2006–

Western District
Charles D. Huber 1930–1938
John A. Smith 1938–1942
Norman N. Lower 1942–1950
Harrison S. Heffner 1950–1958
Paul K. Cressman 1958–1966
Herbert D. Wittmaier 1966–1973
John E. Moyer 1973 -1987
David C. Greulich 1979–1987
David G. Roof 1987–1994
Ronald D. Miller 1994–1997
Frederick J. Moury 1997– ##

Western (Ohio) Conference

Ohio District
Henry D. Shultz 1923–1931

Illinois District
Charles G. Unangst 1923–1930 ++
William E. Seesholtz 1931–1939
Quillas A. Deck 1939–1941
Quillas A. Deck 1941–1947
Norman J. Broadway 1941–1945
Norman J. Broadway (asst.) 1945-1947
Norman J. Broadway 1947–1955
Robert S. Wilson (asst.) 1948–1951
Paul D. Dunn 1955–1963
Paul D. Gordon 1952–1960

George E. Ralph 1960–1962
George E. Ralph 1963–1968
Paul D. Gordon 1963–1971
Fred T. Fink 1968–1976
Alfred E. Anderson 1971–1975 ^
Paul D. Dunn 1976–1984
Robert W. Zetterberg 1984–1992
John C. Ward 1992–2000
Gary M. Brown 2000– ##

> * = Title change to District Superintendent in 1958
> ^ = Title change to Conference Superintendent in 1975
> " = Title change to Conference Minister in 1994
> : = Title change to Regional Elder in 1997
> ++ = 1923 to 1930 Illinois churches were part of Eastern PA Conference
> ## = Conference Minister in entire church

C. Editors of Denominational Magazine

William F. Heil 1922–1930
Staff 1930–1934
Jacob S. Heisler 1934–1943
Levi C. Hunt 1943
Harry E. Messersmith   1943–1955
Robert S. Wilson 1955–1971
William S. Sailer 1971–1973
Ronald B. Kuntz 1973–1981
H. Robert Samuels 1981–1985
David H. Reed 1985-1989
Dirk Pogue/Timothy Christman/Michael Sigman 1989–1991
Timothy Christman/Joel Copeland 1992–1995
Carol Kline/Timothy Christman 1996–2000
Church Center staff   2000–Connection

D. Publishers of Denominational Magazine

Harry E. Messersmith 1932–1943
Clarence J. Yoder 1943–1959
Lloyd R. Eshbach 1959–1963
Clarence C. Reeder 1963–1969
Edward J. H. Flexer, Donald E. Emig,. Clarence J. Yoder, H. Arlington Gerhart, and Stanley P. Heimbach served as managers of Church Center Press 1976

through 1981

E. Superintendent/Executive Director of Retirement Facility

Thomas Knecht 1924–1929
Samuel A. Heisey 1929–1937
Albert R. Kratzer 1937–1970
Russell A. Wise 1970–1976
Franklin H. Schock 1977–1994 ~
Bruce D. Hill 1994–2003
Steven Reiter 2003–

~ = Title change to Executive Director in 1989

Chaplains
Albert R. Kratzer 1970–1978
Clarence C. Reeder 1978–1982
David H. Reed 1982–2002
Dana M. Logan 2001–- Stone Ridge Campus
Timothy F. Christman 2002–-Albright Campus

F. Corresponding Secretary/General Secretary/ Director of Missions

Charles D. Huber 1930–1942
Thomas E. Paul 1942–1969
Marian Paul 1969
Richard A. Cattermole 1970–1980
Duane M. Ray 1980–1988
David M. Hornberger 1988–1994
John P. Ragsdale 1994–2004
James Ehrman 2004–

G. President of Branch WMS Societies/ Adult Missionary Fellowship

Eastern Conference

Mrs. Carrie Neitz 1923–1934
Mrs. Alice Schlappich 1934–1952
Mrs. Helen Manwiller 1952–1958
Mrs. Mary Elizabeth Detterline 1958–1974
Mrs. Mary Brandt 1974–1979
Mrs. Mary Good 1979–1991
Mrs. Betty Hughes 1991–2000

Norman Harner 2000–>

> = Title change to Commission on Missions

Western Conference

Mrs. Rebecca Shultz 1923–1927
Mrs. Jennie Wilson 1927–1942
Mrs. Stella Mineely 1942–1958
Mrs. Isabel Wilson 1958–1966
Mrs. Irma Taubenheim 1966–1974
Mrs. Norma Carr 1974–1982
Mrs. Helen Theobald 1982–1990
Mrs. Dorothy Bissenden 1990–1995
Mrs. Ann Brown 1995 -

H. Administrative Secretary/Director of Church Ministries

Richard A. Cattermole 1978–1988 +
Keith R. Miller 1989–2004

+ title change in 1982

I. Director of Christian Education

Raymond S. Wolfgang 1949–1951
Donald D. Metz 1988–1992

J. School of Methods/Camping

Eastern Conference

Edwin S. Woodring 1921–1926
Harrison H. Heffner 1927–1937
C. Preston Kichline 1938–1942
Harold H. Scanlin 1943–1952
Earl D. Ehrig 1953–1956
Luther R. Klinger 1957–1958
Milton E. Detterline, Sr. 1959–1963
Kenneth M. Weaver 1963–1970
James M. Shields 1970–

Western Conference

Lake Geneva, WI: Robert Wilson 1951
Beulah Beach, OH: Robert Wilson 1946–1951
Williams Bay, WI: Robert Wilson 1952–1957
Camp Otyokwah, OH: Paul Dunn 1951–1960

Rock River Bible Camp
George Ralph 1958–1963
Paul Gordon 1964–1968
Alfred Anderson 1969–1974
Robert Zetterberg 1975–1979
James Hansen 1980–1983
Gary Brown 1984–1987
Gary Brown/Glenn Hansen 1988
Glenn Hansen 1989
James Hansen 1990–1992
Gary Brown 1992–1998
David Carr 1999–2005

Camp ECCO
Paul Dunn, 1961 -
Richard Gordon
Fred Fink
Richard Reigle
Nelson Wilhelm
John Ward   1961–1989
R. Lester Bissenden
Gerald Davison
Dave Smith
Maurice Friedlund
James Hansen
Dirk Pogue 1989–1995
Paul Koelln 1995–1998
Thomas Griffin 1998–2003
Lewis Bennet 2003 -

K. Evangelical School of Theology

Presidents

Harold H. Scanlin 1967–1975
Leon O. Hynson 1975–1982
Ray A. Seilhamer 1982–1993
Kirby N. Keller 1993–2004
Dennis P. Hollinger 2004 -

Deans

Kenneth R. Maurer 1952–1970
J. Creighton Christman 1970–1980
J. Duane Beals 1980–1987
Kirby N. Keller 1987–1997

Rodney H. Shearer 1998–2002
Kenneth H. Miller 2002 – 2005
John V. Tornfelt 2005 –

Index

Watch night services 22, 69, 130, 243
Wesley, Charles 18-19, 62, 240
Wesley, John 18–26, 129, 144
Western Conference (E C) 174, 185-86, 188, 191, 193, 194-95, 197, 199-200, 202, 203-4, 206-8, 211, 221, 224-25, 234-36, 241, 248, 250-53, 255-58, 283-89, 292, 308-10, 313, 325, 327, 330-1, 333-34, 336-39
Western Union College 115, 116, 189
Wilson, Robert S. 9, 13, 191, 193, 223, 258, 364, 365
Wittmaier, Bishop Herbert D. 221, 258, 261, 272–73, 324, 360-1
WOMEN IN THE CHURCH* 72-74, 137-39, 207-8, 251-52, 323-34
Women's (Woman's) (Home and Foreign) Missionary Society (E A, U E, E C) 50, 72, 110, 137-39, 146, 186, 228, 251
Woodring, Bishop Edwin S. 102, 151–52, 174, 176, 178–80, 189, 193, 203, 206, 209, 238-39, 357–58
Worship *See* SUNDAY SERVICES

Y
Yeakel, Bishop Reuben 11, 12, 44-45
Yoder, Clarence J. 193, 204-5, 223–224, 232
YOUTH* (*See also* Camps, Christian Endeavor, School of Methods) 74-76, 140-42, 208, 252-53, 324-25

*Indicates recurring major themes that are treated in successive chapters of the book.